Decide Better

Lieven Raes • Susie Ruston McAleer
Ingrid Croket • Pavel Kogut
Martin Brynskov • Stefan Lefever
Editors

# Decide Better

## Open and Interoperable Local Digital Twins

Springer

*Editors*
Lieven Raes
Digital Vlaanderen
Brussels, Belgium

Susie Ruston McAleer
21c Consultancy
London, UK

Ingrid Croket
IMEC
Leuven, Belgium

Pavel Kogut
21c Consultancy
London, UK

Martin Brynskov
Open Agile Smart Cities (OASC)
Brussels, Belgium

Stefan Lefever
IMEC
Leuven, Belgium

ISBN 978-3-031-81453-2 ISBN 978-3-031-81451-8 (eBook)
https://doi.org/10.1007/978-3-031-81451-8

Digital Flanders Open & Agile Smart Cities This work was supported by Digital Flanders and Open & Agile Smart Cities.



This Springer imprint is published by the registered company Springer Nature Switzerland AG
The registered company address is: Gewerbestrasse 11, 6330 Cham, Switzerland

# Foreword

Local Digital Twins (LDTs) represent a novel frontier within today's digital landscape, extending the industry concept of digital twins, which focuses on building virtual replicas of specific systems to create innovative dynamic and predictive models for whole cities and regions. Going beyond the technical state-of-the-art, LDTs are a pivotal technology for interoperability, uniquely prioritising data integration, standardisation, and architecture federation whilst upholding European public values promoting ethical and socially responsible access, use, sharing, and management of data. Due to their core collaborative nature, LDTs excel at bringing data and people together to address policy decisions spanning mobility, land use, energy, environment, and health domains, among others.

In recent years, a number of innovative prototypes have showcased the decision-support potential of LDTs by integrating qualitative datasets, state-of-the-art simulation models, and interaction components to predict the impact of policies across various city systems. Successful real-world LDT pilots were implemented in Flanders, Pilsen, and Athens as a result of the EC-funded Digital Urban European Twins (DUET) project, and much of the knowledge and learning from these experiments are integrated throughout this book. Trailblazing examples such as the Helsinki digital twin underscore LDT governance-focused capabilities, showcasing their ability to facilitate interaction between city departments, citizens, and local businesses to enhance urban life through better decision-making and innovative societal services.

More than just a standalone technology, LDTs serve as powerful enablers in the broader context of digital transformation, aligning with governmental agendas worldwide. This transformation entails comprehensive changes in operational methodologies spanning technical, managerial, and legal dimensions, necessitating a holistic organisational overhaul. Their strength lies in the technology's integrative abilities, which centralise the data-to-knowledge process and support decision-making across operational, tactical, and strategic levels. Embraced by the European Commission in the form of a toolbox for empowering citizens and regions, organisations are now able to set up their own digital twins to address local use cases by integrating data, knowledge, legacy systems, and policy-making visions.

This book about LDTs explores a promising transformation concept for digital governance, wherein governments leverage new ICT advancements to create public value while upholding principles of openness, accessibility, re-usability, privacy, and informed political discourse. We commend the editors and authors on their excellent work and invite readers to delve into the insightful contents of this publication.

Enjoy reading!

Adminstrateur-generaal, Digital Flanders, Brussels, Belgium — Jan Smedts

Chair, Open & Agile Smart Cities and Communities, Brussels, Belgium — Karl-Filip Coenegrachts

August 2024

# Preface

## Towards an Open and Interoperable Local Digital Twin

Since its inception, the "digital twin" idea has evolved from an industry concept to having broader applicability in domains ranging from the human body to cities and regions. Nevertheless, the idea behind creating a digital and physical twin as one interconnected entity has remained the same. Although the term "digital twin" was recognised as early as 2002, it wasn't until 2017 that it emerged as a pivotal strategic technology trend, fuelled by the increased affordability of technologies like the Internet of Things (IoT), which resulted in their heightened appeal across diverse sectors. The idea of urban digital twins, or digital twins of a city (or part of a city), was also initially mentioned in the scientific literature in 2017. However, the majority of publications came after 2020. Initially focusing primarily on technical aspects, recent publications now encompass a diverse array of subjects spanning visualisation, operational management, governance, policy design, decision support, collaboration, user-centricity, citizen engagement, public involvement strategies, as well as legal, ethics, and transparency. The amalgamation of these contemporary areas of interest has given rise to the unified notion of Local Digital Twins (LDTs).

LDTs refer to the concept of digital replicas or simulations of a specific geographical area, such as a city, urban region, or local community. An LDT integrates various data sources, including real-time sensor data, geographical information, and socio-economic data, to provide a comprehensive virtual representation of the area. LDTs are designed to support evidence-informed decision-making by enabling stakeholders to visualise, analyse, and simulate different policy or operational scenarios, thereby enhancing understanding and management of complex urban systems and processes. They facilitate collaboration among multiple stakeholders, including policymakers, urban planners, citizens, and businesses, to address challenges and optimise the development and sustainability of local environments. LDTs consider values like privacy protection, FAIR (Findable, Accessible, Interoperable, and Reusable) data principles, and ethical use of AI. From a technical, implementation-oriented perspective, an LDT endorses openness, interoperability, and federated architectures.

Surprisingly, despite rising popularity, the concept of the LDT has yet to gain recognition in the scientific community. Due to the novelty of the challenges an LDT can address, minimal implementations have been documented and tested in scientific literature. This lack of acknowledgement may stem from the intricate nature of the LDT concept, which aims to address a myriad of policy issues spanning various city-related competencies, requiring expertise across multiple design disciplines such as ICT architecture, security, standardisation, geospatial, 3D and augmented visualisations, smart city knowledge, simulation modelling, data and information management, as well as policy design and formulation.

This situation should be set to change, as recent initiatives spearheaded by the European Commission have been instrumental in advancing state-of-the-art LDTs. Projects such as DUET, URBANAGE, URBREATH, the LDT Toolbox, and CitiVerse have brought together a diverse array of stakeholders, including universities, research institutions, and public sector organisations. These initiatives have not only extended the scope of LDTs but have also supported a wide range of policies, from local to European levels, encompassing high-performance computing, metaverse, common data spaces, and the Green Deal. This multitude of expertise, use case domains, implementation approaches, stakeholders, and their interconnectedness are all key aspects of this book.

## The Objective of the Book

This book seeks to offer fresh perspectives on digital replicas of cities, urban areas, and regions, aiming to articulate the significance of a digital twin approach for evidence-based decision-making at local and supralocal levels whilst at the same time upholding values such as interoperability, connectivity, accessibility, trust, privacy, and security. Introducing the novel concept of the LDT, it aims to disseminate insights to decision-makers, domain specialists, system designers, ICT architects, and governance experts. Beyond outlining foundational principles, the book explores the roles, requirements, features, architectural concepts, standards, interoperability, and the utilisation of IoT and simulation models. Finally, it also sheds light on the reusability of LDT concepts, encompassing benefit maximisation, legal and ethical considerations, as well as key lessons and recommendations.

## Organisation of the Book

The introductory chapter, "Defining Local Digital Twins," attempts to capture and explain the concept of LDTs, focusing on their distinct characteristics, essential capabilities, and implications for urban governance and management. The LDT concept is further explored in the three parts of this book.

## Part I: Local Digital Twins for Evidence-Driven Smarter Cities

The first section, "Local Digital Twins for Evidence-Driven Smarter Cities," delves into the digital twin concept's key players, applications, and prerequisites. It begins by examining digital twins from a demand-driven perspective, outlining trends and case studies, and defining the components that constitute LDTs. Chapters 1, 2 and 3 explore the potential of digital twins in bridging day-to-day operational decisions with evidence-informed policy-making for sustainable socio-economic outcomes. Key considerations include the extent to which LDTs can break down policy silos and enhance citizen-centric decision-making processes, as well as innovative approaches for addressing complex societal challenges and the essential requirements and features for embarking on a digital twin journey.

In the opening chapter, "Digital Twins for Urban Governance: General Desires, Expectations, Challenges," Pavel Kogut and Roland van der Heijden introduce readers to the evolution, drivers, use cases, reference frameworks, unresolved questions, and challenges associated with digital twins of cities. In the subsequent chapter, "Local Digital Twins for Smart Cities: Opportunities for Evidence-Informed Decision-Making," authors Lieven Raes, Grazia Concilio, Carolina Doran, Laura Temmerman, and Joep Crompvoets concentrate on LDT policy objectives, outlining the rationale for adopting LDTs and their potential to enhance urban intelligence for cities and citizens. The chapter scrutinises experimental possibilities and decision-making support afforded by LDTs. Lastly, the third chapter, "Local Digital Twins: A Central Urban Integrator to Break Down the Silos," penned by Tanguy Coenen, Maxim Chantillon, Ingrid Croket, and Lieven Raes, delves into the interdisciplinary capabilities of LDTs as urban integrators, proposing meta-requirements for LDTs and offering a feature set conducive to cross-domain evidence-based decision-making.

## Part II: Implementing a Reusable Local Digital Twin

Part II, "Implementing a Reusable Local Digital Twin," shifts focus towards the realisation of a reusable solution. This section, spanning Chaps. 4, 5, 6 and 7, adopts a more supply-oriented approach. It operates under the premise that since many urban challenges and data sources are similar across cities and regions, exploring how an open, reusable LDT architecture can make investments more attainable for all is prudent. By promoting interoperability through Minimal Interoperability Mechanisms (MIMs), alongside an open component-based architecture and adherence to international ICT standards on data, simulation models, and geospatial visualisations, a pathway forward is illuminated for cities at any stage of their digital transformation journey.

In the first chapter of part two, titled "Unlimited Potential: The Reusable Local Digital Twin," authors Ingrid Croket, Philippe Michiels, Stefan Lefever, and Gert Hilgers explore the design principles and reference architectures of LDTs, presenting a toolbox concept to facilitate a system-of-systems (SoS) approach. Moving on to Chap. 5, "Public Development: Towards Open Standards and Components for Local Digital Twins," by Lieven Raes, Bart De Lathouwer, Gert Hilgers, and Stefan Lefever, the focus shifts to LDT standards pertaining to core ICT concepts, data connectivity and integration, model integration, and visualisation, emphasising key aspects of interoperability and minimal interoperability mechanisms (MIMs) to ensure compatibility. In Chap. 6, "Connected Services: IoT Data to Fuel Your Local Digital Twin," authors Lieven Raes, Burcu Celikkol, Oliver Schreer, Jaap De Winter, Jéssica Baltazar, Susie Ruston McAleer, and Daniel Bertocci underscore the significance of IoT devices and networks in creating digital replicas of cities and regions, highlighting various levels of standardisation and interoperability as well as the sustainability aspect of different network types. Finally, in Chap. 7, "Future Ready Local Digital Twins and the Use of Predictive Simulations: The Case of Traffic and Traffic Impact Modelling," authors Chris Tampère, Paul Ortmann, Karel Jedlička, Walter Lohman, and Stijn Janssen delve into the simulation modelling and predictive capabilities offered by LDTs, drawing from their experiences in the EU DUET project to discuss the integration of models into LDTs to meet user needs through advanced scenario management, control, and interaction mechanisms.

## Part III: Maximising Impact of Local Digital Twins

Part III, spanning Chaps. 8, 9, 10 and 11, is about optimising the impact of LDTs. It focuses on maximising the value of LDTs by aligning the demand-oriented elements contained in part one of this book and the supply-oriented elements of Part II. This alignment creates new governance and adoption models to realise core benefits. Practical recommendations are provided to cities on how to get started on their own digital twin journey.

Chapter 8, titled "Local Digital Twins for Cities and Regions: The Way Forward," authored by Yannis Charalabidis, Gerasimos Kontos, and Dimitrios Zitianellis, delineates future research directions for LDTs, tracing their historical context and current status. Following this, in the subsequent chapter titled "Force Multiplier: Realising the Benefits of Open and Re-usable Local Digital Twins," Susie Ruston McAleer and Julia Glidden delve into the potential value LDTs offer. Through concrete implementation cases, they elucidate potential benefits and highlight scaling opportunities and challenges using an LDT maturity model, concluding with insights into scalability and governance strategies. Chapter 10, "Rights and Responsibilities: Legal and Ethical Considerations in Adopting Local Digital Twin Technology," authored by Francesco Mureddu, Alessandro Paciaroni, Tomáš Pavelka, Annabel Pemberton, and Luca Alessandro Remotti, addresses the legal and ethical dimensions of LDT technology. The authors discuss specific LDT implementation domains and cases, identifying legal and ethical challenges and proposing a stepwise approach and strategy to overcome these issues based on a gap analysis. Finally, Chap. 11, "Pioneering Practitioners: Key Lessons Learned from Local Digital Twin Implementations," by Lieven Raes, Jurgen Silence, and Karl-Filip Coenegrachts, draws on the experiences of early adopters of LDTs. This chapter offers concrete recommendations to future adopters based on the authors' experiences, with insights from field experts regarding evidence-informed policy-making and LDT implementation to help maximise impact.

## Conclusions

The 11 chapters collectively illustrate the potential of Local Digital Twins (LDTs) as an integrative solution for enhancing evidence-informed decision-making. Drawing on insights from administrative sciences, ICT technology, simulation modelling, and various domains such as transport, mobility, land-use planning, environment, and energy, they showcase the collaborative synergy offered by LDTs. This collaboration spans multiple domains, territories and stakeholder groups, with an adaptable and interoperable approach that can leverage cities' existing datasets and simulation models to foster more informed decision-making that transcends individual policy domains and geographical boundaries.

This book comprises a series of interconnected chapters synthesising the essential elements of LDTs. These elements are based on field experiments conducted by policymakers, smart city experts, modelling specialists, and ICT architects in the public, academic, and commercial sectors. Together, they provide a comprehensive overview of the fundamental components to develop a state-of-the-art, open, and reusable LDT framework conducive to evidence-informed decision-making.

Brussels, Belgium — Lieven Raes
London, UK — Susie Ruston McAleer
Leuven, Belgium — Ingrid Croket
London, UK — Pavel Kogut
Brussels, Belgium — Martin Brynskov
Leuven, Belgium — Stefan Lefever

# Acknowledgements

In the summer of 2019, the European Commission selected and financially supported the vision of 15 international partners, from government, research, and the private sector, to create a digital replica of cities and regions with the aim of improving policy impacts across different domains. This was the start of a three-year project called DUET (Digital Urban European Twins). Little did we know that a few months after the kick-off meeting in December, a lockdown would occur across most of the European Union. It was a challenging time for the consortium to realise a complex predictive digital twin solution in Athens, Pilsen, and Flanders without any face-to-face meetings. The foreseen co-creation workshops for project design purposes could not take place as planned. Instead, the usual whiteboards and sticky notes were replaced by electronic variants. As a result, the entire DUET project work occurred in 2D from behind computer screens.

The COVID-19 pandemic also created other unforeseen effects. Using predictive models in a digital twin context was reasonably new in 2020. Most digital twin examples focused on 3D rendering buildings and infrastructure, displaying sensors with measurement data. Suddenly, thanks to the need to track pandemic outbreaks, big data, time series, and predictive models have become common commodities in the tech and research world and are the subject of daily TV news. COVID coverage thus contributed to expediting and broadening data literacy among much of Europe's population. Predictive models detailing the likely number of new infections evolved based on knowledge and experience gained between outbreak waves and became frequent news items. Politicians engaged and involved scientists to help support policy-making with high societal impact, especially as the public and media insisted that decisions be grounded in scientific evidence.

Against this backdrop, digital twins, applied to societal challenges such as environment, health, mobility and spatial planning, gained prominence through conferences, project calls, research, implementation projects, and scientific publications. Initiatives such as the open, accessible Johns Hopkins COVID-19 dashboard contributed to evidence-based decision-making and made it possible to compare results between countries, states, and regions. This approach gave infection and mortality rates an international context on which policymakers could be judged. Today, there is little research regarding the impact of COVID-19 on data literacy and evidence-informed decision-making. Nevertheless, the pandemic has influenced the use of data-supported evidence as part of the decision process globally.

In late 2020, the DUET consortium succeeded in demonstrating the first digital twin prototype in our three pilot areas. When presenting the first results at the OASC (Open Agile Smart Cities) Cities to Cities Festival 2021, the idea of publishing a book highlighting the various elements of an open and reusable predictive digital twin first arose.

Since then, the DUET project concluded at the end of 2022. After three years of intense collaboration, with more than 200 presentations made across the world, and a memorable win in 2021 of the prestigious Smart Cities "Best-Enabling Technologies" Award during the World Smart City Conference and Expo in Barcelona, requests to learn more about our work continue to arrive steadily. As a Consortium, we therefore deem it essential to further share the visions, experiences, and knowledge we gained, both in DUET and in the many new initiatives that DUET partners are involved in, such as the European Local Digital Twin (LDT) Toolbox which is extending the DUET digital twin concept to 150 European cities. This book is the result. A result that was only possible with the support of a team of esteemed partners with whom it was a pleasure to work with.

Thanks go to my Digital Flanders colleagues Jurgen Silence, Gert Vervaet, and Tom Callens for their day-to-day involvement in coordinating and delivering DUET, and to Raf Buyle, Dwight Van Lancker, Bert Van Nuffelen, Martine Delannoy, Barbara Van Broeckhoven, Geert Mareels, and the Digital Flanders Smart Data team for their support. With the help of Jiri Bouchal and Hugo Kerschot from IS-Practice, the ideas, results, and outcomes of all partners were successfully managed against the overall project plan.

Further thanks go to our three DUET pilot sites in Athens, Pilsen, and Flanders (city of Gent) for their perseverance in continuing with the digital twin during challenging times. Special thanks to Ilia Christantoni and Dimitra Tsakanika from Dimos Athinaion Epicheirisi Michanografisis (DAEM) in Athens, Ludek Santora, Jana Jerabkova, Tomas Rehak, and Tomas Krblich from the city of Pilsen, and Begga Van Cauwenberge and Dries Meers from the city of Gent.

Without the expertise of partners AEGIS, ATC, GFoss, imec, KU Leuven, OASC, Plan4All/University of West Bohemia, TNO, and Virtual City Systems, it would have never been possible to realise the open digital twin architecture in practice. Special thanks to Marina Klitsi and Thanasis (Sakis) Dalianis from ATC for the thorough technical coordination. Thanks also go to the ICT architects, data specialists, and developers, Philippe Michiels, Stefan Lefever, and Konstantin Kostov from imec, Leonidas Kallipolitis from AEGIS, Lutz Ross, Thomas Adolphi, and Stefan Trometer from Virtual City Systems, Walter Lohman and Hans Cornelissen from TNO, Ricardo Pinho from OASC, Despina Mitropoulou from GFoss, and our simulation model experts, Karel Jedlička and Daniel Beran from Plan4All, Prof. Chris Tampère and Paul Ortmann from KU Leuven.

Tomáš Pavelka and Annabel Pemberton's legal expertise led to a Local Digital Twin (LDT) prototype compliant with EU legislation and ethics. Martin Brynskov,

Lea Hemetsberger, Cornelia Dinca, and Margarida Campolargo's knowledge helped the DUET consortium ensure minimal interoperability during the ICT standardisation.

With the help of Nils Walravens and Ruben D'Hauwers from imec VUB, all stakeholders were brought together, and new LDT business models were defined. A special thanks to 21C's Susie Ruston McAleer, Pavel Kogut, and Laura Gavrilut for DUET ideation, concept building and successful proposal writing and for managing the various dissemination activities, websites, and publications, as well as for this book's editing. At this point, a warm note of thanks must also go to Ingrid Croket from imec for also supporting the book editing process.

DUET was also supervised by external experts who formed a group of critical friends. Without the critical review of Andrew Stott, Prof. Yannis Charalabidis, Bart De Lathouwer, Michiel Van Peteghem, Christophe Stroobants, and Pieter Morlion, the DUET consortium would not have been challenged to continuously improve during the solution design, roll-out, and business modelling. We gratefully thank them for their steerage.

Last but not least from the DUET project, thanks for the cooperation and support of the air quality modelling specialists from VITO must go to Stijn Janssen, and Stijn Vranckx for implementing their state-of-the-art models as an external provider into the DUET LDT.

This book would never have been possible without the help of all chapter authors. Special thanks go to Prof. Joep Crompvoets, Prof. Chris Tampère, Paul Ortmann (KU Leuven), Prof. Gracia Concilio (Politecnico Di Milano), Roland van der Heijden (city of Rotterdam), Carolina Doran (European Citizen Science Association), Tanguy Coenen, Maxim Chantillon, Ingrid Croket, Stefan Lefever, Philippe Michiels (imec), Laura Temmerman (imec—Vrije Universiteit Brussel), Burcu Celikkol, Daniel Bertocci (imec—OnePlanet), Gert Hilgers, Karl-Filip Coenegrachts (OASC), Bart De Lathouwer (GeoNovum), Oliver Schreer (Fraunhofer—Heinrich Hertz Institute), Jaap De Winter, Jessica Baltazar, (SODAQ), Karel Jedlička (University of West-Bohemia), Walter Lohman (TNO), Stijn Janssen (VITO), Prof. Yannis Charalabidis (University of the Aegean), Gerasimos Kontos (Abu Dhabi University), Dimitrios Zitianellis (National Technical University of Athens), Julia Glidden (Pivotl), Susie Ruston McAleer, Pavel Kogut (21C), Francesco Mureddu, Alessandro Paciaroni (Lisbon Council), Annabel Pemberton (Sparring), Luca Alessandro Remotti (DataPower SRL), Jurgen Silence (Digital Flanders), and Tomáš Pavelka.

The book also greatly benefited from the enlightening ideas of external experts in academia, industry, and local administration, who either responded to our survey on LDTs or provided us with relevant case studies. Thanks are extended to Michael Batty (University College London), Patricia Molina (Tecnalia), Cornelia Dinca (Amsterdam Smart City), João Bastos (Porto Digital), Søren Lundsgård Jørgensen (Aarhus Futures Lab), Jarmo Suomisto (HELSINKI 3D+), and Sylvia Ilieva and Dessislava Petrova-Antonova (Big Data for Smart Society Institute—GATE Sofia).

In addition to the survey and case study respondents, additional experts contributed by reviewing chapters, providing examples, and recommending best practices.

Thank you, Roland van der Heijden (Rotterdam), Juan Echevarria Cuenca (Santander City Council), Juho-Pekka Virtanen and Timo Ruohomäki (Forum Virium Helsinki), Prof. Jantien Stoter (TU Delft), Prof. Vlado Cetl (North Varaždin University Croatia), Claire Ellul (University College London), Lachmi Khemlani (AECbytes), and Charalampos (Harris) Alexopoulos (University of the Aegean).

Thanks, of course, to the continuous support by the European Commission during and after the DUET project for promoting our achievements during conferences and through various EU communication channels. We are proud that the DUET approach contributed to the launch of the official LDT concept by Living-in.eu. Our achievements were only made possible by the driving force of Andrea Halmos and Eddy Hartog from DG Connect unit Technologies for Smart Communities, as well as our supportive project officer Wolfgang Bode. Thanks also to my PhD promotor, Prof. Joep Crompvoets from KU Leuven Public Governance Institute, for advising and supporting me during the entire writing process.

Finally, I want to give special thanks to the most important people in my life for their support and patience as I worked long hours to shape this book, my wife, Inge, and my son, Milan.

It has been an absolute pleasure to be surrounded by everyone mentioned here. I hope you will enjoy reading this book as much as I have enjoyed working on the DUET project, this volume, and the exciting but challenging theme of LDTs.

Consortium Coordinator of the EU Horizon programme DUET and COMPAIR projects,
Advisor at Digital Flanders, PhD candidate
Public Governance Institute KU Leuven
Brussels, Belgium

Lieven Raes

# Contents

# Contributors


**Jéssica Baltazar** SODAQ BV, Hilversum, The Netherlands

**Daniel Bertocci** Interuniversitair Micro-Elektronica Centrum – OnePlanet, Wageningen, The Netherlands

**Burcu Celikkol** Interuniversitair Micro-Elektronica Centrum – OnePlanet, Wageningen, The Netherlands

**Maxim Chantillon** Interuniversitair Micro-Elektronica Centrum, Leuven, Belgium

**Yannis Charalabidis** Department of Information and Communication Systems Engineering, University of Aegean, Samos, Greece

**Karl-Filip Coenegrachts** Open Agile Smart Cities, Brussels, Belgium

**Tanguy Coenen** Interuniversitair Micro-Elektronica Centrum, Leuven, Belgium

**Grazia Concilio** Department of Architecture and Urban Studies, Politecnico di Milano, Milan, Italy

**Joep Crompvoets** Public Governance Institute, Katholieke Universiteit Leuven, Leuven, Belgium

**Bart De Lathouwer** Geonovum, Amersfoort, The Netherlands

**Jaap De Winter** SODAQ BV, Hilversum, The Netherlands

**Carolina Doran** European Citizen Science Association, Berlin, Germany

**Julia Glidden** Pivotl, London, UK

**Gert Hilgers** Open Agile Smart Cities, Brussels, Belgium

**Stijn Janssen** Vlaamse Instelling voor Technologisch Onderzoek, Mol, Belgium

**Karel Jedlička** Department of Geomatics, University of West Bohemia, Pilsen, Czech Republic

**Gerasimos Kontos** Abu Dhabi University, Abu Dhabi, UAE

**Walter Lohman** Nederlandse Organisatie voor Toegepast-Natuurwetenschappelijk Onderzoek, Delft, The Netherlands

**Philippe Michiels** Interuniversitair Micro-Elektronica Centrum, Leuven, Belgium

**Francesco Mureddu** The Lisbon Council, Brussels, Belgium

**Paul Ortmann** Centre for Industrial Management, Traffic & Infrastructure Katholieke Universiteit Leuven, Leuven, Belgium

**Alessandro Paciaroni** The Lisbon Council, Brussels, Belgium

**Tomáš Pavelka** Dentons, Prague, Czech Republic

**Annabel Pemberton** Sparring, Prague, Czech Republic

**Luca Alessandro Remotti** DataPower Srl, Cagliari, Italy

**Oliver Schreer** Heinrich Hertz Institute, Fraunhofer, Berlin, Germany

**Jurgen Silence** Digitaal Flanders, Brussels, Belgium

**Chris Tampère** Centre for Industrial Management, Traffic & Infrastructure, Katholieke Universiteit Leuven, Leuven, Belgium

**Laura Temmerman** Interuniversitair Micro-Electronica Centrum-SMIT, Vrije Universiteit Brussel, Brussels, Belgium

**Roland van der Heijden** Digital City Rotterdam, Rotterdam, The Netherlands

**Dimitrios Zitianellis** University of the Aegean, Samos, Greece

# About the Editors

**Lieven Raes** is a distinguished professional holding master's degrees in Administrative Management and Land-Use Planning, showcasing a multifaceted expertise in public service innovation. Currently serving as a senior public servant at Digital Flanders within the Flemish government, Lieven has garnered extensive acclaim as a respected research and innovation consortium coordinator in the Smart City domain. Notably, Lieven spearheaded the EU (Horizon 2020) DUET project focused on Digital Urban European Twins, which received the prestigious Best Enabling Technologies award at the 2021 World Smart City Expo and Congress in Barcelona. Presently, Lieven assumes the role of coordinator for the EU COMPAIR Horizon 2020 consortium, facilitating the integration of Citizen Science with evidence-based decision-making through the utilisation of various domain-overarching IoT devices. Prior engagements include leading the (CIP) Open Transport Net consortium and the (Horizon 2020) POLIVISU consortium, all aimed at fostering data driven, evidence-informed decision-making. Alongside these achievements, Lieven played a pivotal role in driving the development of the Flanders e-government MAGDA platform, focusing on building permits and environmental permits. Continuously pushing the boundaries of research, Lieven is also engaged as a PhD candidate at the Public Governance Institute of the Katholieke Universiteit Leuven, further solidifying his commitment to advancing the realms of public administration and technological innovation.

**Susie Ruston McAleer** is an accomplished expert in research, innovation, and governance, dedicated to driving positive change and fostering inclusive digital innovation globally. For nearly two decades, she has empowered governments worldwide to leverage digital transformation for societal progress. As the founder of the digital innovation firm, 21C, Susie serves as a solution strategist, concept builder, and architect for award-winning digital research and innovation endeavours. Her exceptional track record includes securing over 20 multi-million Euro funding awards, notably Europe's inaugural Local Digital Twin project, recognised with a World Smart Cities Award. Currently, Susie contributes to research initiatives on AI trust (*THEMIS 5.0*), critical thinking elevation for combating disinformation

(*TITAN*), responsible data sharing (*DS2*), and leveraging digital twins for positive energy districts (*BIPED*). In pivotal consultancy roles, she has shaped Microsoft's public sector strategy, and informed IBM's perspectives on public sector technologies. Susie's contributions also extend to the scientific community, where she has authored and edited numerous specialist papers and journals, including a seminal book on eParticipation published by the United Nations and the Council of Europe. With a blend of practical experience and scholarly insight, Susie continues to help drive the discourse on digital governance, shaping a more inclusive, efficient, and responsive public sector for the digital age.

**Ingrid Croket** graduated as a Commercial Engineer at the University of Antwerp in 1997 and obtained a master's degree in Enterprise IT Architecture at the Antwerp Management School in 2022. She has broad experience in programme and IT project management in public and private companies. Ingrid has strong analytical skills and a good understanding of how to match digital technologies with business challenges, thus contributing to the strategic alignment between IT and business requirements. Ingrid has vast experience in managing complex digitalisation programmes, such as the replacement of mainframe IT infrastructure at the Province of Antwerp by a web-based document and process management system. As part of the Master in Enterprise IT Architecture programme she designed for her master project an enterprise architecture model identifying how smart services of a digital twin contribute to the achievement of the sustainability goals for a city. In her role as project lead and architect for the AI & Data team at imec, she was involved in the VLOCA project (Flemish Open City Architecture) and contributed to the design of the Local Digital Twin Toolbox project for the European Commission.

**Pavel Kogut** holds a Master's degree from the esteemed London School of Economics, underscoring his commitment to academic excellence and professional advancement. He is an experienced and meticulous researcher, data analyst, and project manager, boasting over a decade of comprehensive experience in the field of European research and innovation. Pavel's expertise extends across a diverse spectrum of European Smart City, Maritime, and Rural projects, encompassing notable endeavours such as DUET for digital twin supported decision-making, COMPAIR citizen science sensors for behaviour change, and PERMAGOV for enhancing marine governance. Pavel's contributions transcend mere participation; he is an active advocate for all his projects, undertaking speaking engagements at events and workshops across Europe, and he is a prolific author of scientific papers, showcasing his profound understanding and insights within the domain. Prior to his work at digital innovation firm, 21C, Pavel honed his skills as an assistant analyst at the Hague Centre for Strategic Studies, a prestigious think-tank. There, he contributed to projects commissioned by senior clients including the Ministry of Defence, the Ministry of Foreign Affairs, and the Dutch Safety Board. Preceding this, Pavel worked at the European Economic and Social Committee, collaborating closely with the EESC Labour Market Observatory on an impactful study concerning youth unemployment, demonstrating his early passion for fostering inclusive, positive change on a global scale.

**Martin Brynskov** , PhD, is a Danish academic and standardisation expert, serving as a Founding Board Member of Open & Agile Smart Cities & Communities (OASC). OASC is a global network of cities and communities, based in Brussels, that represents the needs of citizens and their communities towards Big Tech and regulators, advocating for Minimal Interoperability Mechanisms (MIMs). Related to the development of technical standards, Dr Brynskov is a contributor to ITU-T SG20 and related Focus Groups, co-leads the United Nations "United for Smart and Sustainable Cities and Communities" (U4SSC) new architecture for digital, sustainable development, leads the Living-in-EU Technical Subgroup overseeing the MIMs Plus specifications for Europe, and he chairs the Danish Standards Committee for smart and sustainable cities and communities. With research focused on place-based computing and interaction technologies, Dr Brynskov has coordinated and led European digital transformation initiatives. His work spans research, innovation, deployment and policy, with a focus on connected communities, interoperability, and ecosystems involving AI, IoT, data spaces, and Local Digital Twins. Notable projects he has led include CitCom.ai—the European Testing and Experimentation Facility (TEF) for AI and Robotics for Smart Cities and Communities, the European Data Space for Smart Communities and CommuniCity, which addresses the gaps in deploying emerging technologies, like AI and the metaverse, in marginalised communities. Dr Brynskov is a global expert, speaker, and advisor on digital transformation with a human-centric focus.

**Stefan Lefever** holds master's degrees in electronics and computer science and a postgraduate degree in business administration. He has 23 years of experience in the European telecom industry and has worked in different roles as an R&D engineer, system architect, enterprise architect, and program director, delivering critical telecom infrastructure towards telecom providers and operators in different markets and driving the innovation of the company technology towards SDN and NFV. His passion for innovation within connectivity, sensor, and data infrastructure within more societal domains embarked him in 2018 on a mission within imec to work on novel sensor devices, Open City Architecture and data ecosystems, early (Urban) Digital Twins, and IoT data platform architectures as Technical Director within the City Of Things Program. Within this program, Stefan participated in numerous European and Flemish research programs within the vertical domains of environment, mobility, logistics, and public health. Within these programs, his team focused mainly on the technology architecture of city sensors, IoT platforms, Local Digital Twins, and Data Spaces from an enterprise architecture viewpoint. His broad knowledge and experience of different technologies and ecosystems have been used to bridge the gap between research, innovation, and market uptake, and he fits very well with the Local Digital Twin as a system-of-systems concept.

# Chapter 1
# Introduction: Defining Local Digital Twins

**Lieven Raes and Susie Ruston McAleer**

## Contents



## 1.1 Introduction

The concept of Local Digital Twins (LDTs) has gained significant attention in recent years as a means to enhance urban management and governance. Initially mentioned by the European Commission (EC) in 2021 during a workshop called "Local Digital Twins, Forging the Cities of Tomorrow" held at the annual European Week of Regions and Cities conference, the first description referred to a *virtual representation* of a city's *physical assets*, using *data*, data *analytics* and *machine learning* to help feed *simulation models* that can be updated and *changed in real-time* as their physical equivalents change (European Commission, 2021). By creating a common view of real-time situations, LDTs aim to facilitate evidence-informed decision-making at operational, strategic, and tactical levels, thereby better meeting

L. Raes (✉)
Digital Flanders, Brussels, Belgium
e-mail: lieven.raes@vlaanderen.be

S. R. McAleer
21C Consultancy LTD, London, UK
e-mail: susie.mcaleer@21cconsultancy.com



L. Raes et al. (eds.), *Decide Better*,
https://doi.org/10.1007/978-3-031-81451-8_1

city governance and communities' needs. These effects, in turn, can lead to enhanced cost efficiencies, operational optimisation, better crisis management and more participatory governance.

## 1.2 Evolution of the Concept

The evolution of the LDT concept and its essential capabilities have significant implications for urban governance and management. Whilst the European Commission's initial description of an LDT focused on its role as a virtual representation of physical assets within a city, Arcaute et al. (2021), from University College London (UCL), emphasised the importance of modelling the city's physical structure in an increasingly *detailed and realistic manner.* The researchers highlighted the real-time operation of cities and the use of data analytics and machine learning, not just for short-term decision-making but also for medium to long-term design and management. This shift '*reduces the distance between (policy) design and implementation*' (Concilio, 2021), helping to create cities that can continuously and positively react and adapt to changing needs.

In 2022, Living-in.eu,[1] a European Commission initiative to help urban leaders collaborate and leverage the best from smart city technology, became a European champion for adopting LDTs. In this role, they formulated five capabilities they believe are essential to define the promising technology[2]:

- *Integration with other systems:* LDTs are *connected* to other systems, including other digital twins, dataspaces and simulation models, fitting into a system-of-systems (SoS) approach and federated architectural setups (Chaps. 4 and 5);
- *Service-oriented architecture:* LDTs are *integrated* with data, model, and visualisation services using service-oriented architecture, enabling seamless data exchange and broad interoperability (Chap. 5);
- *Visualisation capability:* LDTs provide *visualisation* capability, including the use of 3D maps, dashboards and story-telling tools, enhancing the understanding of data-informed decision-making (Chap. 2);
- *Data analysis and simulation:* LDTs allow for the *analysis* of data-based city processes, including *what-if* analysis capabilities, enabling the creation, exploration and analysis of future scenarios (Chap. 7);
- *Security:* LDTs ensure the overall system's security, including ICT security and access control, safeguarding user privacy and data integrity (Chap. 4).

[1] https://living-in.eu

[2] Together these capabilities define an LDT at stage 3 (*predictive*) of the 4 stage LDT Maturity Model (Chap. 9), but on a practical level it should be noted that potential adopters can start their digital twin journey with fewer data sets, a 2D visualisation and an unconnected prototype

Building upon the Living-in.eu definition, as part of the work to create a 'Local Digital Twin Toolbox[3]' which will support cities and regions that are less well-prepared for digital transformation, Robalo-Correia et al. (2023) expanded the concept of LDTs to include additional capabilities and dimensions. They defined an LDT as a:

> *…**virtual representation** of the **physical assets, processes,** and **people** within a **geographically located community**, which reflect and derive from **cross-sectorial, historical and (near) real-time data**. Its purpose is to enhance **evidence-based decision-making** at the **operational, strategic, and tactical levels** to better meet the needs of communities. LDTs combine multiple technologies, such as data analytics and artificial intelligence, enabling predictive and simulation models to be updated and changed as their physical equivalents change. It must be made clear that this definition is not static and shall encompass future technological and structural changes.*

This definition adds several elements to the original European Commission LDT description from 2021. Firstly, it moves away from defining LDTs as a strict implementation of physical assets to encompass both process and people elements in a socio-technical solution. The geospatial element, which refers to geographically located communities, also widens the scope of the LDT to cover more than just cities and urban areas (thus incorporating/superseding other market terms—urban digital twin and city digital twin).

Another significant aspect is the emphasis on cross-sectoral data encompassing historical and real-time information. As the primary goal of LDTs has been defined as enhancing decision-making for societal benefit, a crucial question arises regarding whether the integration of local knowledge and insights, often referred to as urban intelligence (Mattern, 2017), will contribute to better evidence-informed decision-making. Recent European research and innovation initiatives (DUET,[4] URBANAGE,[5] COMPAIR[6]) indicate that combining hard, measurable data with less measurable, more soft, qualitative, urban intelligence should deliver a more effective impact.

Additionally, Robalo-Correia's definition introduces a temporal element, defining a continuum that spans from real-time, daily operational management decisions to long-term policy-related (strategic) decisions. Thus, LDTs can help '*close the chasm between diverse policy domains between government and organisations…citizens'*, as described by Concilio et al. (2021).

The definition also stresses an LDT as a combination of technologies, including data analytics and AI, enabling simulation and prediction, referencing the future impact of simulated policies.

[3] https://oascities.org/european-local-digital-twin-toolbox-project

[4] Digital Urban European Twins (DUET), EU H2020 project, https://cordis.europa.eu/project/id/870697

[5] Enhanced URBAN planning for AGE-friendly cities through disruptive technologies (URBANAGE), EU H2020 project, https://cordis.europa.eu/project/id/101004590

[6] Community Observation Measurement & Participation in AIR Science (COMPAIR), EU H2020 project, https://cordis.europa.eu/project/id/101036563

Two other elements are also essential to be associated with LDTs. The first element is about ensuring users privacy and making sure the data complies with privacy regulations like the European General Data Project Regulations (GDPR) (European Parliament and Council, 2016) and ethical principles as outlined in, e.g., the EU Data Governance Act (European Parliament and Council, 2022) and Public Sector Information directive (PSI) (European Parliament and Council, 2019) as well as the FAIR-data (Findable, Accessible, Interoperable, and Reusable) principles (Wilkinson et al., 2016). Another differentiator is the focus on the openness and interoperability of LDTs. Openness and interoperability are essential to creating a network of interconnected digital twins, combining LDT components and existing legacy systems and allowing the exchange of information between systems to run, e.g. simulation models on, e.g., federated HPC systems.

## 1.3 Defining Local Digital Twins

Local Digital Twins (LDTs) represent a powerful tool for enhancing urban management and governance. By providing a virtual representation of physical assets, processes, and urban intelligence, LDTs enable evidence-informed decision-making and better meet the needs of communities. Moving forward, the interoperability, security, and analytical capabilities of LDTs will continue to evolve, further enhancing their utility in urban environments. Based on the considerations outlined in this paper, the following definition of an LDT is proposed:

An LDT is a **virtual representation** of the **physical assets**, **processes**, and **urban intelligence** within a **geographically located community**, which reflect and derive from **cross-sectorial**, **historical**, **and (near) real-time data**. It aims to enhance **evidence-informed decision-making** according to **ethical standards and principles** at the **operational, strategic, and tactical levels** to better meet communities' **needs**. LDTs support predictive simulation modelling, combining multiple technologies offering **open and interoperable components**, allowing **integration with legacy systems** and other components in a **federated architecture**.

## References

Arcaute, E., Barthelemy, M., & Batty, M. (2021). *Future cities: why digital twins need to take complexity science on board*. University College London—Bartlett School of Environment Energy and Resources.

Concilio, G., & Pucci, P. (2021). The data shake: An opportunity for experiment-driven policy making. In G. Concilio, P. Pucci, L. Raes, & G. Mareels (Eds.), *The data shake* (pp. 3–18). Springer International Publishing. https://doi.org/10.1007/978-3-030-63693-7_1

Directive (EU) 2019/1024 of the European Parliament and of the Council of 20 June 2019 on Open Data and the Re-Use of Public Sector Information (Recast), Pub L No. EU 2019/1024, EUR-Lex (2019). http://data.europa.eu/eli/dir/2019/1024/oj

European Commission. (2021). Local digital twin. https://living-in.eu/groups/solutions/local-digital-twin

Mattern, S. (2017). A city is not a computer. https://placesjournal.org/article/a-city-is-not-a-computer/

Regulation (EU) 2016/679 of the European Parliament and of the Council of 27 April 2016 on the Protection of Natural Persons with Regard to the Processing of Personal Data and on the Free Movement of Such Data, and Repealing Directive 95/46/EC (General Data Protection Regulation) (Text with EEA Relevance), Pub. L. No. EU 2016/679, EUR-Lex (2016). https://eur-lex.europa.eu/eli/reg/2016/679/oj

Regulation (EU) 2022/868 of the European Parliament and of the Council of 30 May 2022 on European Data Governance and Amending Regulation (EU) 2018/1724 (Data Governance Act) (Text with EEA Relevance), Pub. L. No. EU 2022/868, EUR-Lex (2022). http://data.europa.eu/eli/reg/2022/868/oj

Robalo-Correia, A., Sousa, M., Santos, F., Barroca, J., Niepceron, D., Mulquin, M., Campolargo, M., Pour S, M., Rasmussen, M., Branco, M., Ebrahimy, R., Ali, K., & Banaei, M. (2023). *D02.02 Mapping EU-based LDT providers and users (Deliverable D02.02; CNECT/2022/OP/0098—Procurement of the Technical Specifications for the Local Digital Twins (LDTs) Toolbox, p. 95)*. European Commission—DG CNECT. https://op.europa.eu/en/publication-detail/-/publication/7892c228-359f-11ee-800c-01aa75ed71a1

Wilkinson, M. D., Dumontier, M., Aalbersberg, I. J., Appleton, G., Axton, M., Baak, A., Blomberg, N., Boiten, J.-W., Da Silva Santos, L. B., Bourne, P. E., Bouwman, J., Brookes, A. J., Clark, T., Crosas, M., Dillo, I., Dumon, O., Edmunds, S., Evelo, C. T., Finkers, R., et al. (2016). The FAIR Guiding Principles for scientific data management and stewardship. *Science Data, 3*(1), 160018. https://doi.org/10.1038/sdata.2016.18

# Part I
# Local Digital Twins for Evidence-Driven Smarter Cities

# Chapter 2
# Digital Twins for Urban Governance: General Desires, Expectations, Challenges

**Pavel Kogut and Roland van der Heijden**

**Contents**



## 2.1 Introduction

Digital twins of cities as we know them today have their roots in virtual city models (VCMs) which gained prominence in the 1990s. Early VCMs were static virtual representations of cityscapes with some geometric properties. They showed terrain and urban structures but weren't particularly good at capturing urban dynamics. The reason is that the necessary technologies weren't advanced enough or simply didn't exist at the time. Consequently, data for representing processes and events 'between buildings' was in short supply.

P. Kogut (✉)
21C Consultancy LTD, London, UK
e-mail: pavel.kogut@21cconsultancy.com

R. van der Heijden
Digital City Rotterdam, Rotterdam, The Netherlands
e-mail: rjmm.vanderheijden@rotterdam.nl



L. Raes et al. (eds.), *Decide Better*,
https://doi.org/10.1007/978-3-031-81451-8_2

When Batty et al. (2001) did a review of VCMs, they found these proto-digital twins in 39 cities worldwide.[1] Fast forward to 2024, the digital twin landscape is bursting with activity (Caprari, 2022). In Europe alone, several dozen cities have digital twins at different scales and maturity levels, with increasing adoption rates observed in other world regions too. Places that boast a digital twin now (e.g. Amsterdam, London, Paris, Singapore, Vienna) had a VCM more than two decades ago, a sign that cities have come a long way since the days of primitive 3D models.

When the first cities started embracing digital twins in the mid-2010s (Ketzler et al., 2020), industrial applications of the technology had already been riding a wave of popularity. The idea that something can look and behave the same but be safer to use than its physical copy, made digital twins an appealing option for mechanical engineers and urban planners alike. From a historical perspective, where Apollo 13 is considered the first successful digital twin use case, the emergence of digital twins in cities was a long time coming but fully expected. And it is not just because of VCMs, which naturally had to evolve into more sophisticated models. Digital twins capitalise on several advanced technologies that have matured and gained traction over the past few decades.

## 2.2 Drivers of Digital Twin Adoption in Cities

**IoT Sensors**

Just as there is an app for everything, there is also a sensor for everything. Nowadays, cities are fitted with a myriad of sensing devices that, with time, have gotten cheaper, smaller and more versatile. We can now measure almost anything around us: motion, temperature, pollution, pressure, light, humidity, proximity, smoke, chemicals, seismic activity, and more. Not only that, Internet of Things (IoT) deployments in cities have evolved to acquire new properties. They are no longer about the passive collection of information but increasingly rely on actuators to turn control signals into physical outputs. Actuators can be programmed to manage almost any asset/action required, from bridge closure to traffic signalling. The surge in IoT deployments has paved the way for smart applications and services capable of analysing big data in real-time to provide actionable intelligence to human operators or make the necessary optimisation changes automatically. For digital twins, this meant more opportunities to influence and be influenced by changes in the real world to become more closely intertwined with the physical system they are designed to mirror.

**3D City Models**

New modelling approaches have transformed how cities are represented digitally. Alongside iconic models that are primarily concerned with visual appearance and geometry, more sophisticated, semantically enriched 3D models have gained prominence since the introduction of CityGML standard in 2008 (Heazel, 2021; Kolbe

[1] Only cities with a population of more than one million were included in the review

et al., 2021). CityGML provides a common semantic framework for sharing contextual information about urban infrastructures. In CityGML, typical objects contain, in addition to their geometric properties, information on traffic flows and speed limits (roads), on occupancy and energy consumption (buildings). As data from multiple domains overlaps at the level of spatial objects, CityGML users can run complex queries and simulations to inform planning. A user may select for inspection office buildings with a particular line of sight (e.g. overlooking a park) or find residential homes with low energy efficiency. CityGML has been used for a variety of purposes, including real-estate development, flooding simulation, traffic planning, noise and shadow mapping (Kolbe & Donaubauer, 2021; Virtual City Systems, 2021). These also happen to be areas where pioneering cities tested their first digital twin use cases (Sagar, 2020).

"All models are wrong, but some are useful", a famous statistician, George Box, once said, implying that models can never be true representations of reality, but they can still be good enough for some applications. Arguably, one of the key determinants of 'goodness' is the amount and quality of data available for modelling.

**Public Data Platforms**

Urban data platforms help cities manage data coming from different sources, sensor types, and infrastructures, normally through the use of open standards and interfaces, although proprietary examples also abound. The premise is that by enabling access to harmonised information, the platforms provide a common basis for developing data driven solutions for smart cities (Brandt et al., 2020).

The evolution and proliferation of urban data platforms has been an important determinant of digital twin adoption in cities worldwide. Case in point is the Helsinki Region Infoshare (HRI). A data catalogue offering open data from the Greater Helsinki region, HRI includes statistics, geospatial data and real-time APIs (Application Programming Interfaces) on topics ranging from living conditions to transport. HRI was set up in 2011, several years before Helsinki's digital twin and the accompanying city models were created. Both of these models are now available on HRI, along with more creative outputs like the Minecraft city model (City of Helsinki, 2021). Helsinki's entire 3D journey is older than HRI, though.

**A Decades-Long Journey of Helsinki 3D+**

In 1985, an international architectural competition for the development of Helsinki's city centre was announced. Reference materials were created with newly acquired graphic workstations to help with the evaluation of proposals. After seeing successful practical examples, city leaders decided to allocate resources for hardware purchases. New equipment acquired for map production was also suitable for experimental 3D modelling. This was the beginning of Helsinki's 3D journey. Today, Helsinki has two main 3D models: the Semantic CityGML and the Reality Mesh Model designed from aerial photography. The models are available to everyone as open data in several

(continued)

formats. Helsinki has made a strategic decision to maintain these models to support a variety of use cases. Minecraft and Unreal game engine are some of the recent, more creative exploitation pathways taken by the city to put the models to good use. Perhaps the best-known, oft-cited application is the Energy and Climate Atlas (Sect. 2.4.3).

**Mixed and Thematic Data Spaces**

Currently, only public data is shared through HRI. This is still the case with most data portals. For all the ambition to gather data from different providers (public and private), it is public authorities that usually contribute the most. It's easy to see why. Public authorities are mandated by law to share data in the interest of transparency and accountability, whereas private enterprises, if they think sharing data can undermine their competitive advantage, would naturally be inclined to keep their data private. Fortunately, the current narrative on data sharing is shifting towards interoperable, multi-source thematic data spaces. There, in addition to open government data, one can expect to find all kinds of restricted, licensed, private, and secure data from non-public actors.

Unlike traditional data portals where data is often passively distributed (e.g. as static tables), data spaces aim to publish data via standardised and, if necessary, anonymised dynamic data feeds. The idea paves the way for a living data ecosystem where information can be shared and reused across different vendors in an environment of trust (Bagheri et al., 2021). Those who think data spaces are a utopia only need to look at some recent implementations to see that progress may be slow but steady.

Back in 2015, Cityzenith made an announcement that ten leading smart cities adopted its next-generation IoT platform—the 5D Smart City—to unlock the value of collected data, much of which was unstructured and unused. The 5D Smart City was designed to handle all the available data for a city, both open and private. The data was normalised and aggregated to support use cases across key smart city areas like environment, infrastructure and security (Cityzenith, 2015).

The trend towards next-gen data spaces is observed in many other places, both geographic and contextual, as evidenced by the evolution of London Datastore (Greater London Authority, 2024) and the setup of lighthouse projects on mobility (mobility data space), agriculture (agdatahub) and manufacturing (EuProGigant). There are even plans to create common European data spaces,[2] a development which may eventually pave the way for the first digital twin on a continental scale.

**New Data Sharing Principles**

The relationship between data platforms and digital twins is not one-directional; the two share a mutual dependence. Digital twins are data-hungry systems; they need

[2] In nine areas: health, industrial and manufacturing, agriculture, finance, mobility, Green Deal, energy, public administration, skills

information—a lot of it and in good quality—to represent, visualise, analyse, influence and improve things in the real world. Data platforms, for their part, need digital twins to secure exploitation opportunities for the vast amount of information that is extensively collected but rarely utilised to the full extent. The mismatch between open data supply and demand is a known one. The open data movement that started in 2007 led many cities to launch data portals. Many datasets were published driven by the 'open by default' principle (opengovdata.org, 2007). However, these supply-side efforts did not immediately translate into widespread reuse, with inconsistent data quality only part of the problem (Romei, 2018). Data was often published in isolation for no particular purpose other than to meet regulatory requirements. Eventually, after seeing limited impact on innovation, a realisation came that, in order to have a transformative effect on governance, the rationale for data sharing must change; data must be 'published with a purpose' (Calderon, 2018).

Digital twins for urban governance, through local challenges they help address, can give meaning to this new principle. Parties are likely to share more if they see how their data translates into tangible changes on the ground. By demonstrating how data is used to design more inclusive public spaces, to proactively identify infrastructure failures, to optimise traffic flows, to select optimal energy efficiency measures, to build things better through first-time-right designs and to streamline emergency planning and response, digital twins can encourage all parties with a stake in urban development to contribute more.

**High-Performance Computing**

In principle, more data means more opportunities for digital twins to mirror cities in all their complexity. Better representation requires going beyond the built and natural environment to cover events and objects between buildings, above and below ground, at time scales ranging from hours to minutes or even seconds (which in emergencies can mean a difference between safety and tragedy). HPC (High Performance Computing) has been a game changer that allowed users to process large amounts of data at high speeds. Barcelona, Athens, Pilsen, Flanders and many other cities are using this technology in their digital twin. But can HPC really support an all-encompassing, city-wide twin at the spatio-temporal resolution described above? A twin aiming to represent a city in its entirety would need to deal with big data that is high variety, high velocity and high volume, a challenge for HPC, whose scalability can suffer at extreme scales (Wu et al., 2018).

But HPC has been evolving, including as a result of integration with other advanced technologies like Artificial Intelligence, or AI (MacAlpine, 2022). The answer to the raised question may lie in the new breed of supercomputers like EuroHPC or perhaps something considerably more powerful that is yet to come, such as quantum computing. What is certain, however, is that future digital twins that incorporate HPC will be able to run ever more complex tasks at higher speeds. It may or may not be enough for a perfect digital twin solution, but then again, what is perfect in this context? If perfection equates to a complete digital representation, such a requirement may be nice to have but not strictly necessary, especially for policymakers who treat quality of insight in several priority areas as more important than an eye-catching 3D model of the whole city. One could argue that local policy-makers value digital twins not so much for their visual attributes but fundamentally because they take guesswork out of day-to-day management and planning, making it easier to find optimal solutions in the age of rapid change.

## 2.3 Urban Governance: The New Reality

One manifestation of this change is constantly evolving preferences for making smart cities more inclusive. Cities that claim or aspire to be smart are challenged to cater to diverse needs in order to create an enjoyable environment for all. But meeting the needs of diverse groups is a tough balancing act. Some people would advocate for age-friendly measures to help older adults move around a city more easily. Others would say that investment should instead go towards youth-friendly policies and measures that support active lifestyles. For some, more lighting in parks is good as it makes people feel safe. Others might see it as light pollution that hurts wildlife, for example urban bats. Some might want a city to become a magnet for tourists and gig workers and would, therefore campaign for a higher share of the platform economy. Someone else, on the other hand, might find existing trends too disruptive and unsustainable and so would vehemently oppose more dark stores, AirBnBs, Ubers, and mass tourism.

Of course, these priorities are not necessarily mutually exclusive. In principle, there is no reason why progress cannot be made in several directions simultaneously. In practice, however, cities are constrained by resources, capabilities, and whatever else is driving the local agenda. Rapid urbanisation, climate change, geopolitical instability, irregular migration flows, ageing populations and the cost-of-living crisis are some of the major challenges facing today's cities. On top of the need to balance competing interests, these challenges overlap, adding another layer of complexity which forces decision-makers to seek cost-effective solutions that are optimal in some sense. A solution may not satisfy all stakeholders at once in equal measure, but it may pinpoint the lowest common denominator around which parties can coalesce.

Achieving that common ground requires a shared view of local reality. This won't happen if stakeholders continue working in silos, using isolated data to make a case for why their problem should get priority treatment. Overcoming the silo mentality is a step in the right direction. What is also needed is the realisation that problems in a digital age require data driven solutions. We live in a socio-physical world with a significant digital dimension. The new digital reality reframes our traditional way of living: how we study and work, commute and communicate, shop and look after our health, discover information and innovate. We can actually learn more from the digital world than the physical one about ourselves and others, about our immediate vicinity and places far away. Creating and testing data driven solutions to address problems in a socio-physical world is fast becoming a new normal, a process that has been accelerated by the adoption of digital twins.

Four primary functions of digital twins—to interconnect (all kinds of data sources, systems, applications, services, simulation models), to simulate (system behaviour and future states), to predict (changes in urban environment), to visualise (objects and events in different dimensions and levels of detail)—have spawned a number of use cases across the entire lifecycle of urban governance. The use cases are a mix of real-life examples, experimentations and highly speculative scenarios that target a specific domain within one or more stages (planning, construction, management).

## 2.4 Use Cases of Digital Twins for Urban Governance

### *2.4.1 Planning*

Cities have strict rules to regulate what can and cannot be built, demolished, changed, or used on land. The rules are in place to protect cultural and natural heritage, to ensure people's health and safety, to sustain good living conditions for humans and wildlife. Property developers looking to build something on a piece of land must produce optimal designs to meet planning regulations and wider policy objectives linked to climate neutrality, accessibility, energy efficiency, and so on. A digital twin with built-in AI and connections to data spaces would be handy in several ways. First, it would help to obtain all the necessary data about the site in question: its topography, vegetation, terrain, road network, other infrastructure objects, and climate. Second, by applying optimisation algorithms, a digital twin would aid parametric design to satisfy multiple compliance requirements. If the alignment from initial simulation is less than perfect, another round of iterations would help to identify areas for improvement, a process which can be repeated until an optimal design is achieved.

**Algorithmic Optimisation for Better Urban Designs in Sofia**
Rapid urbanisation is causing tensions between supply and demand for infrastructure and services. Many cities are ill-prepared to resolve them effectively, in part due to the lack of tools capable of integrating human and infrastructure factors. Sofiaplan, a municipal enterprise responsible for spatial and strategic planning at Sofia Municipality, is working with the GATE Institute to test the application of parametric design in a digital twin. The method provides data driven decision support for urban planning based on predefined neighbourhood indicators related to population density, access to social infrastructure, and transport connectivity, among others. Two possible solutions are tested. The first one deals with the allocation of a single building in a single empty lot. The new building can occupy between 25% and 65% of the lot while the

(continued)

angles of the footprint are constrained within the 60–120 degrees range. In the second approach, all empty lots are combined. A grid is then constructed on top of an entire free area with different possible land uses. The goal is to find optimal solutions that satisfy the gross floor area per person for each land use function e.g. residential, commercial, green space, educational, healthcare. The proposed solution is automated using a multi-objective optimisation algorithm called NSGA-II. A multi-objective problem is essentially a problem that should optimise at least two objectives while satisfying a lot of constraints. It deals with conflicting objectives, meaning that while one objective increases the other decreases. The output is not a unique global solution but several possible solutions within the Pareto-optimal set.

Post-design, a digital twin linking private and public administrative systems can be used to submit documents for a building permit. Traditionally, this process was laborious and time-consuming due to reliance on 2D plans. With a digital twin, the process is more than digitised; it becomes model-based, meaning that along with digital forms, a digital model of a site is submitted to a building authority for compliance checks (Ammar et al., 2022). Does the proposal align with the local building code? Does construction or expansion meet safety requirements? Does a planned building comply with energy efficiency standards? All this and more can be verified with a model-based compliance that is already a reality in cities the world over, from Vienna (City of Vienna, n.d.) to Victoria (Victoria State Government, n.d.).

Urban planners, architects, civil engineers, surveyors and property developers are the primary digital twin users at the planning stage. However, this pool is starting to expand as cities try to create more liveable urban environments that local communities want and need. Recently, cities have started experimenting with co-creation tactics at the pre-construction phase by giving citizens a chance to design public spaces through virtual prototyping. In Rotterdam, residents can play with 3D surroundings on their electronic devices. They can design an 'ideal' neighbourhood by adding benches, trees and other 'city furniture' all while keeping an eye on the available budget and planning permissions. Once satisfied with the output, people can go outside to view their creations in Augmented Reality (AR). Rotterdam's approach exemplifies a trend towards democratisation of urban governance. Here, digital twins are among the drivers of change that make urban planning more citizen-centric by transferring (some) power from experts to the people.

### 2.4.2 Construction

Construction projects are complex, with many moving parts, activities, and unexpected events. Construction is also dangerous. The International Labour Organisation estimated that at least 60 thousand fatal accidents occur each year on construction sites around the world (Lingard, 2013). If digital twins are meant to improve how cities are built, this improvement must include an improvement in safety during construction.

The industry is progressively adopting ICTs (Information and Communication Technologies) to turn building sites into rich data sources to guide decision-making during operations. Today, sensing technologies deployed on construction sites are wide-ranging. Drone footage, laser scans and cameras help to keep track of the construction progress. Microphones, cameras and LoRaWAN devices[3] help to monitor equipment performance and risks to occupational safety (Kaltiot, 2022). Sensors measuring pressure, temperature, wind, weight, vibration, humidity, and lighting help to assess environmental impact of the construction work (Salem & Dragomir, 2022).

However, despite these technological advances, industry stakeholders have a tendency to work in silos using their own preferred technologies (Sketchley, 2019). What is lacking is an integrated approach to connect different systems into one cooperating 'whole'. Sacks et al. (2020) propose a construction digital twin to address this fragmentation. The envisaged solution would act as a higher-level system facilitating interaction not just between assets, objects and processes on a construction site, but also with external systems. The twin would be capable of predicting unexpected events and, depending on the level of autonomy set, could act independently in some situations or let site managers decide how best to proceed based on supplied intelligence.

Consider a few safety scenarios to better understand construction digital twin's potential. Many crane accidents happen as a result of contact with power lines (Milazzo et al., 2016). The construction twin would obtain information on a city's energy infrastructure and communicate it to a tower crane operator in the form of alerts when contact is imminent. Another common cause of accidents is strong winds. To prevent them, the twin would run weather forecasts based on live measurements from on-site anemometers (wind speed sensors). Site managers could then use this information to decide whether a crane will have any difficulty working under wind pressure and, if so, should be taken out of service.

An interesting possible scenario involves the construction twin interacting with a manufacturing plant. After connecting to the plant's system and examining real-time information from a local transport network, the twin would predict an estimated time of arrival for expected deliveries. Such information can then be used to improve scheduling and minimise delays that are the bane of most construction projects.

Building things on land cannot happen without due consideration of things below ground. With an accurate, continuously updated sub-terrain digital twin, unwanted contact with a city's underground infrastructure can be avoided. Inadvertent damage to cables, pipes, tunnels and structures causes delays, health and safety risks, and additional financial expenditures. In Canada, the cost of underground damage

[3] Battery-powered devices that use long-range and remote area coverage to connect to the internet

during excavation work is estimated to be in excess of $1 billion dollars annually (GoGeomatics Canada, 2022). Besides human error, another reason why it happens is the lack of reliable information, as underground plans used during construction are often out of date or inaccurate. To prevent accidental strikes, manual inspections are being complemented with advanced radar technologies that help to create precise digital maps of buried infrastructure (IRMI, 2011; Zeiss, 2018). Canada, the US, the UK, the Netherlands, Belgium and Japan are some of the countries with projects underway to plug data gaps in this area, a necessary step towards a subterrain digital twin.

### 2.4.3 Management

Moving up the urban governance cycle, we can find more tried-and-tested applications of digital twins in energy, sewage management, and emergency planning. Let's take a quick look at one example from each category before turning our attention away from use cases towards technical implementation to understand how cities can go about building their own digital twin to reap the benefits.

The Helsinki Energy and Climate Atlas displays buildings as semantic objects in the CityGML environment (Helsinki Region Infoshare, 2018). Users can find out how much energy different buildings consume, how much solar energy can be received by different buildings, which materials were used in construction, when past renovations happened and what exactly was done. The Atlas can be used by anyone, and is of particular interest to housing companies, property developers and manufacturers of solar panels, who can use the tool even for commercial purposes as long as the the City of Helsinki is properly attributed.

Two Swedish cities Gothenburg and Helsingborg used a digital twin to reduce sewage spills resulting from heavy rainfall (Valverde-Pérez et al., 2021). The twin made flow predictions and proposed control strategies for human operators. In Helsingborg, spills were reduced by 32% when the operator acted on digital twin results.

In Australia, electricity company Endeavour Energy used a digital twin to simulate the impact of rising flood water to prioritise emergency response and recovery efforts (Ryan, 2022). Using open weather information from government sources, the twin was able to proactively alert emergency services about an impending flood activity days before it happened. What's more, digital twin-generated flood maps helped to prioritise inspections and understand potential hazards during rescue operations in affected areas.

All the different use cases from planning, construction and management should hopefully give readers some idea as to what's possible with the digital twin technology. While the benefits may be clear, it's important that readers also understand how digital twins work behind the scenes. Benefits will not come from an abstract twin. Cities need at least a working prototype to start generating value. Fortunately, reference architectures are aplenty to support cities in this endeavour.

## 2.5 Reference Architectures

A reference architecture is a template for building a fundamental system structure. Which one should cities use to build a digital twin? There is no right answer or a single solution as many frameworks have been proposed by different organisations to suit interested adopters.

**Digital Twin Consortium**

Creating a digital twin requires multiple capabilities, including in data services, system integration, user experience, security, and privacy. Capabilities for a chosen use case can be combined and then orchestrated through a platform to deliver digital twin applications. The US-based Digital Twin Consortium (DTC) provides recommended structures and integrations needed for the creation of a composable digital twin. DTC proposes a capabilities framework to support multidisciplinary teams in designing capability requirements at the level of specific use cases (Digital Twin Consortium, 2022).

**FIWARE**

Among DTC members is the Berlin-based FIWARE foundation, which developed its own reference architecture to support the creation of digital twins of "any kind in any domain" (Conde et al., 2022). The cornerstone of FIWARE's architecture is Context Broker (CB), a tool for managing context information. Context information describes what is currently happening in an urban environment, and so can be considered as metadata. We need metadata to understand raw data. On its own, a raw measurement of air quality, for example, will not mean much unless it includes information on time, location, pollutant description, and so on. In the FIWARE architecture, such representation is provided through entities and attributes, some of which can be very dynamic, with a propensity to change a lot over time, while others are mostly static, such as terrain, streets and buildings. CB allows context information to be updated and queried, and also notifies users when changes in context information take place.

**DUET**

Front and centre in the framework proposed by DUET[4] is another kind of broker—the data broker (DB). Through DB, different elements of the architecture are activated to perform functions such as managing and distributing multi-source data (message broker), making data sources findable (data catalogue), and providing metadata (knowledge graph). Supporting the work of DB are different gateways (Raes et al., 2022). The data gateway allows static and dynamic data sources to be connected to the system. The model gateway helps raw data obtain meaning by running algorithms on it. The API gateway, for its part, controls how different components interact. DUET's framework was tested in Athens, Flanders, and Pilsen.

---

[4] Digital Urban European Twins (DUET), EU H2020 project, https://cordis.europa.eu/project/id/870697

**CDBB**

Across the channel, the Centre for Digital Built Britain (CDBB), a partnership between government and academia, has been working on an ambitious national digital twin programme. It builds on previous efforts that saw many UK cities (Bradford, Leeds, York, Hull etc.) and industries[5] adopt digital twins. The added value of the national digital twin, as foreseen by CDBB, is a more integrated approach that allows isolated deployments to become part of a whole by forming an ecosystem of interconnected twins. Achieving this will require a high degree of interoperability, including a shared understanding of concepts like space and time, and a meaningful basis on which to interpret data from different owners. Furthermore, stakeholders must be able to securely connect new twins to the ecosystem and run authorised queries within it. The different ways in which interoperability can be achieved are described in CDBB's Information Management Framework (Walters, 2020).

Reference architectures proposed by DTC, FIWARE, DUET and CDBB are not the only ones available. Many more have been proposed by academics and international bodies like the World Economic Forum. It's beyond the scope of this chapter to review them all. The point is that these frameworks add to the vast body of knowledge on digital twins for urban governance. From it, people can learn about their drivers, adopters, use cases, benefits and design principles if building a digital twin is the goal.[6] This is also what has been covered so far in the chapter. Still, a few important questions remain unanswered. How should digital twins be governed? Is the idea of an all-encompassing twin feasible? What is the best way to represent social and other dimensions of modern cities? Are digital twins really unrivalled in the e-governance space? Time to address these critical questions one by one.

## 2.6 Outstanding Challenges

### *2.6.1 Platform Governance*

Schematically, a digital twin environment can be visualised as a three-layered cake with multi-source data at the bottom, different applications and use cases at the top, and a core city platform in the middle. At the two outer layers, the ownership lies with respective data owners and solution developers. When it comes to the middle layer, however, the answer to "Who should own the platform?" is less clear-cut. Traditionally, urban platforms have been owned and managed by local authorities. But some cities are pivoting towards a new governance model with the view to unlocking more value from a digital twin. Rotterdam is trying to develop a shared ownership structure for its core city platform. The aim is to facilitate balanced

[5] One example would be a digital twin of the water utility network used by Thames Water

[6] For a more in-depth discussion on design principles and building blocks, see Chap. 4 of this book

exploitation by creating incentives for private enterprises to offer commercial services with local needs in mind. Crucially, in this model the city would be one of several parties involved in platform management, not its sole driver and funder, as is widely the case today.

**Developing a New Governance Model for the Rotterdam Digital Twin**
Capabilities required to manage a digital twin are distributed across public and private sector organisations that bring different knowledge, skills and expertise to the table. Given its traditional role as a regulator, the public sector is best placed to set the 'rules of the game,' and should therefore be responsible for managing platform access, determining standards, overseeing privacy and ownership norms. The private sector is known for its agility and ability to bring innovative solutions to market, and is in the lead when it comes to spending on research and development. Thus, in a network-owned digital twin, the business community can take responsibility for co-financing and co-managing an urban platform while keeping a focus on innovation and commercialisation. For Rotterdam, this kind of public-private partnership provides an optimal governance model to manage a digital twin. The setup implies that the municipality shares risks and rewards with other local actors. Digital twin is seen as more than just technical infrastructure. Shared ownership of the platform is expected to create an environment of trust conducive to new business models and collaboration dynamics within the urban ecosystem. To balance commercial interests with public value, the city is working on a special structure to supervise business exploitation (through an ethics board) and to manage supply and demand in line with existing regulations (through a so-called 'market master').

### *2.6.2 Big Data Management*

While it may be desirable to have the whole city outfitted with sensors, the sheer volume of information to be generated in the process would pose considerable data challenges. In Barcelona, a smart city platform called Sentilo had 1800 sensors spread across the city, with deployments monitoring energy, noise, garbage collection, and parking spots (Sinaeepourfard et al., 2016). Sentilo produced 1.3 million records daily which required a relatively modest amount of storage space (5 GB). But this number is certain to skyrocket if Barcelona's 150 thousand lamp posts, 70 thousand buildings (some of which are probably fitted with hundreds if not thousands of in-door sensors),[7] 40 thousand garbage containers, and 80 thousand on-street public parking spots were plugged into the system. Even with these additions

[7] One building in Amsterdam called edge has approximately 28 thousand wireless sensors that measure everything from motion to temperature (Fruci, 2019)

the resulting IoT deployment would fall short of ubiquitous, for achieving that would require including other sources that measure the 'pulse of the city' like video cameras, magnetic loops, and air stations. Adding them would bring us closer to a fully connected smart city, but it would also exacerbate the integration challenge, not to mention privacy and security risks arising from the need to curate such a big eclectic dataset.

### 2.6.3 *Representation of Non-physical Equivalents*

Initial digital twin use cases aimed to provide a digital representation of a physical city that is accurate enough to guide urban planning. Before long, however, digital twins were challenged to go beyond the physical-digital duality (Batty, 2018). A city is more than its built environment; it's a space with multiple overlapping dynamics: social, economic, political, cultural. One could argue that the ultimate representation should strive to reflect these intangible equivalents in addition to physical forms and processes by which cities are characterised. Hudson-Smith et al. (2023) introduced the concept of digital multiples. If the goal is to eventually integrate extra dimensions, is it not better to talk about digital triplets (with social dimension included), or quadruplets (plus cultural), or quintuplets (plus political), instead of digital twins?

Although highly ambitious, the idea of representing a city through digital multiples has merit. If we are to develop it into a robust concept, a good starting point would be to try and understand how digital multiples can be created from a digital twin. Let's say we want to build a digital triplet by adding a social dimension to an existing twin. What measure would be enough to qualify a digital triplet as such? Would addressing social problems through a digital twin be enough? Or do we need a more substantial representation, one in which non-physical equivalents are adequately reflected through datasets, models, avatars, or mixed reality applications?

**Citizen Engagement**

Perhaps social dimension is achieved when digital twins are used by the broader public—what Batty et al. (2001) called 'forward visualisation'; the opposite of backward visualisation which is more expert-oriented. If this requirement is enough, then we already have digital triplets in many cities. We showed a use case from Rotterdam where citizens use a digital twin to co-create urban environments and view them in AR. We mentioned Helsinki's Minecraft model that allows users of all ages to really play with the city by virtually modifying its structures or removing them altogether (City of Helsinki, 2021). Another interesting example is the Herrenberg digital twin, which allows citizens to experience this German city in Virtual Reality (VR) to better understand how it performs economically, socially, and traffic-wise (Wray, 2020).

**Agent-Based Models**
Some might say that a social dimension is covered in digital twins through models representing traffic, noise and energy consumption, as these outcomes are a direct result of human activities. To an extent, they would be right. In agent-based traffic simulations, surveys are used to establish individuals' transport mode, trip purpose and departure/arrival time. Besides travel diaries, these models rely on census data to create a synthetic population with representative socio-demographic characteristics (GeoTwin, 2021).

**Serious Games**
Digital twins incorporating elements of a serious game can be seen as having a social dimension. Papyshev and Yarime (2021) propose a task-based approach for synthetic data collection whereby people are asked to conduct certain activities in a city based on how they would behave in a hypothetical situation, such as an emergency. The data collection exercise can be framed as a serious game in which citizens use phones and other GPS tracking devices to provide behavioural mobility data for use in event simulations.

**Digital Avatars**
Metaverse fans might say that a social triplet needs digital humans to be complete. With the advent of AI, questions about what constitutes a digital human have become more philosophical and therefore difficult to answer. Nevertheless, it didn't stop the concept from appearing, in 2021, on Gartner's hype cycle of emerging technologies (Panetta, 2021). There, digital humans were described as holographic avatars representing artists, patients, customer assistants, tour guides and many other personas exhibiting human-like behaviour.

**Emotional Mapping**
To urban planners, the notion of digital humans as pure volumetric simulations, however accurate and smart, may not be of immediate use. What would be more valuable is to know how people actually perceive their built environment: are they happy or distressed? Urban stressors like pavement defects, poor lighting or busy junctions without traffic lights can elicit physiological responses in the form of increased electrodermal activity (sweat), changes in a walking pattern, or faster heart rate. Understanding how people experience a city emotionally can inform more inclusive urban design practices that may have hitherto failed to adequately address special needs, such as those of the elderly or disabled. One study in the US captured data on environmental distress with a view to integrating it into a digital twin. Ahn et al. (2020) tapped into multimodal data sources, including wearables, to identify challenges to older adults as they moved about a city in Texas. In Europe, which has an ageing population, the EU-funded project URBANAGE[8] helped Helsinki, Santander and cities in Flanders to make age-friendly policies through digital twins.

[8] Enhanced URBAN planning for AGE-friendly cities through disruptive technologies (URBANAGE), EU H2020 project, https://cordis.europa.eu/project/id/101004590

Emotional mapping, if carried out at an aggregate level and over an extended period of time, can help track trends (positive or negative) in citizens' feelings toward a city, complementing other sources such as opinion surveys and social media feeds (Moreira de Oliveira & Painho, 2015). Areas where negative feelings are especially strong can be studied to understand what caused these hot spots to occur in the first place, and which issues are more important to different demographics, those related to walkability, safety, pollution, or deprivation?

To conclude this lengthy discussion, there is no easy answer to the question of social representation in a digital triplet. Presumably, similar difficulties will arise when we start tackling other dimensions. How to represent cultural life in a living digital form? What about economic activities and political processes—how to reflect them in a digital multiple? As we start moving away from twins to multiples, the problem of adequate representation may prompt further difficult questions, notably whether the digital twin concept is really best placed to capture all the different manifestations of the urban fabric. The extent to which a digital twin is able to incorporate various aspects of urban life and evolve into digital multiples will determine whether the concept will succeed or fail in the long run. Unless it evolves to become more robust, digital twins risk getting displaced by rival solutions with a better representational capacity. We already see how competing technologies are starting to claim many of the same benefits offered by digital twins.

### 2.6.4 Competitor Solutions

Proponents of digital twins point out that, unlike other smart city tools such as Geospatial Information Systems (GIS) and Building Information Models (BIM),[9] digital twins not only capture visual characteristics of a city, its terrain and built environment, they show how a city functions in terms of traffic, air quality, noise, wind, water level, and so on. When used as a sandbox for virtual policy prototyping, digital twins can manipulate mirrored processes and objects, allowing new solutions to be safe-tested without switching off critical infrastructures. By interconnecting cross-domain models, infrastructures, events and datasets, digital twins enhance the value of individual assets through horizontal reuse. So, something like a road intersection in a digital twin can be used for multiple simultaneous tasks: to manage traffic via a new signalling plan, to enforce car or pedestrian violations, to support navigation of autonomous vehicles. Finally, by making use of open interfaces, digital twins make urban policy more accessible to citizens, who generally lack specialised skills to use GIS, BIM or other advanced analytics tools.

Many of these benefits and differences are discussed extensively in academic and grey literature. One comparison that received less attention is the relationship with

[9] Geographic Information System (GIS) analyses and displays spatial data; Building Information Model (BIM) provides physical and functional features of a building

CIM (City Information Modelling). CIM emerged in the mid-2000s as an attempt to extend BIM to a city level (International Electrotechnical Commission, 2021). Cities that are currently developing digital twins see CIM as a necessary intermediary step. In Lancaster, CIM fuses GIS and BIM data for use in a digital twin (Cureton & Hartley, 2019). In Vienna, CIM is a key component of a geoTwin, which serves as a geometrical 3D base for a more sophisticated digital twin of the city (Lehner & Dorffner, 2020). What these examples show is CIM's seemingly subordinate position. It is akin to a younger sibling whose role is reduced to providing authoritative data to an older brother. However, the pecking order is starting to change.

CIM may have started with BIM and GIS, but over time it incorporated CityGML, IoT and cloud computing, then VR and AI (Xu et al., 2021). Some recent definitions describe CIM as "a fully integrated, semantically enabled super-BIM 3D city model that hyper-connects users to any contextual project data source or analysis tool—static or dynamic, spatial or nonspatial—from buildings, to roads and public spaces (open data), to streetlights (sensors/IoT), to people on the street (social media)" (Cityzenith, 2017).

Both technically and conceptually, CIM is evolving into a powerful enabling platform capable of supporting agile city planning, a far cry from the second-fiddle role it was assigned to originally. Some CIM advocates go even further (Future Cities Catapult, 2017). They envisage CIM developing into an ultimate planning system centred around a running 3D simulation of a city. This system would be open to citizens, allowing them to view and comment on infrastructure projects before they are built, and to understand exactly what such projects can deliver in terms of green areas, community spaces, walkability, and accessibility. This advanced CIM-based system would streamline the urban planning process through the use of e-compliance tools, making it easier to submit and approve planning applications. Besides architects, builders, urban planners and designers, CIM would provide monitoring information and predictive analysis to help policymakers drive better outcomes for cities. Impact measurement would be based not just on numbers but also qualitative/emotional experiences like health, wellbeing and happiness. Does any of it sound familiar?

## 2.7 Discussion

As demarcation lines become increasingly blurred between CIM and digital twins, cities that are planning their next stage of digital transformation might be wondering which of the two solutions should be their ultimate goal. Digital twins are all the rage these days, so should, in theory, win the hearts and minds of potential adopters more easily. However, the lingering hype is as much a blessing as it is a risk, something that can make the concept more confusing than appealing.

Digital twins appeared several times on the Gartner's hype cycle in recent years—as digital twins for business (2018), digital twins of government (2019), digital twins of a human (2021), and digital twin of a citizen (2022). Digital twins of government come closest to exemplifying digital twins for urban governance. Digital twins of government are meant to support "automated command-and-control operations" and the testing of "scenarios related to policy and legislation"—two important conditions for unlocking digital twin's true potential according to Gartner (Moore, 2019).

One problem with this view is the narrow focus on government, which gives the impression it should be the main creator, user, funder and champion of digital twins. As discussed earlier in the chapter, some cities are moving away from this role of prime custodian toward a decentralised, network-owned governance model. Another problem lies in the stated requirements. Automation and policy simulations are important capabilities that digital twins should have. However, they are not magic keys that unlock digital twin's full potential by a stroke of the wand. More important than these two conditions is digital twins' use by the ecosystem. Just as data obtains value when it's used, similarly digital twins unlock their potential when used by local stakeholders. It is at this moment that value is created, benefitting providers, users and digital twins themselves (as they can learn from new data to become better twins or multiples).

Digital twins of government is just one of many seemingly synonymous terms spawned by the hype. Other candidates include urban digital twins, digital city twins, and city-scale digital twins, to give just a few examples. In the absence of a commonly agreed definition, not only are the terms used interchangeably, they create unhealthy competition that leaves people none the wiser as to the basic tenets of digital twins. For instance, when we see square cuboids displayed on a 3D map in coloured gradients of green, yellow and red, is it appropriate to call it a digital twin or is it just a CityGML visualisation showing energy consumption in buildings? Is an application like the Helsinki Energy Atlas a digital twin? Or is digital twin application-, model- and use case-agnostic? In which case, digital twin is more about a 'neutral' technical platform, the middle layer between data and services.

Cities are often described as having digital twins, when in fact the scale of the solution is limited to a particular district, domain, or sector. International case studies abound with examples of digital twins being used to solve real-life problems, whether it's streamlining the planning approval process or preventing sewage overflows. Equally prevalent are experimental cases that—as yet—seem to have no bearing on how decisions are made in real life, with underlying solutions used mostly by people involved in the project to test new ideas, datasets, models or frameworks, but not necessarily by people who happen to be the project's target audience in policy, industry or civil society.

This is not to say that experimental cases are worthless. Quite the opposite. Proofs of concept are a necessary stepping stone to developing more complete solutions and—perhaps more importantly—to building acceptance and culture of change within organisations and communities known for their path dependence and reluctance to try new things. We need experimental and speculative cases to feed our ambitions and create images of the future where things work better than in the present or the past. One should be conscious, however, that describing benefits only or predominantly in the future tense will work for some time but not indefinitely.

Sooner or later people will want to see real results that justify the hype. Strange as it may sound but, when this happens, digital twins had better have something *tangible* to show for all the praise and investment they received.

## 2.8 Conclusion

Despite all the attention, it is not all plain sailing for digital twins going forward. The concept is facing many challenges which, if unresolved, can lessen its relevance in the future. These should be tackled urgently, starting with the definition problem.

Digital twins are not just government tools nor are they strictly about the city's physical environment. Digital twins for urban governance are local in so far as they reflect the multifunctional idea of space, a locale where many natural and human events take place. Everything that exists and happens in a given location is local in nature. All the physical, social, environmental, cultural, political and economic activities become potential targets for digital twins. Some of these local manifestations are already addressed in existing deployments (mostly as physical equivalents), some are just starting to get explored (social dimension), whilst the rest represent a long-term goal that will require new thinking and tools to be achieved (digital multiples). A cultural dimension, for example, may require the integration of ultra-realistic volumetric assets to create virtual cities where theatre buildings are not just 3D objects with semantic information (theatre name, address, schedule etc.), they are gateways to holographic performances that can be viewed in Virtual Reality (VR) without leaving one's home.

Digital twins for urban governance strive to become a virtual city that resembles a real one both in form and in substance, but not necessarily in every detail at the highest resolution possible. Parts of the twin can be activated on demand to achieve efficient performance and power savings.

Digital twins can be recognised by their use cases, models and technologies used, but fundamentally the concept is use case-, model- and technology-agnostic.

Current implementations barely scratch the surface of what is possible with digital twins, not least because they tend to be stand-alone examples in one area or a small number of related areas. Still, despite this unrealised potential, already today decision-makers can use digital twins to answer questions of medium complexity: how to ensure compliance with planning regulations? What features would residents like to see in a new public garden? How to minimise the impact of emergencies? What materials are used in the building stock? Where are the least energy efficient buildings in a city? When is a building due for renovation?

In the future, as technologies evolve, as better data becomes available, and as more twins and dimensions get interconnected, we will be in a better position to address more complex questions more effectively and impartially than today. Such as whose interests should be prioritised in the next development plan, those of older adults, young people, gig workers, or environmentalists? Where in a city do people feel happy or sad and how do social, economic and cultural factors explain the differences? When should roads be closed to traffic and open to pedestrians as part of a new dynamic space allocation (DSA) plan? How to minimise accidents and risk of delays during construction works?

Effectively addressing the above requires a top-level twin comprising multiple sub-twins across different dimensions, sectors, and industries. Building a twin with system-of-systems (SoS) characteristics will require combining existing digital twins with new ones that have yet to be created, in areas like welfare, social policy, culture, construction, mobility, and energy. A comprehensive SoS digital twin can become local in scale and in substance by uniting lower-level twins and digital multiples. A true Local Digital Twin (LDT) would unite digital twins of construction, a sub-terrain digital twin, digital twin of water treatment facilities, of traffic and built environment. An LDT would transcend physical boundaries of space to include non-tangible activities and experiences of people who live there. Multi-level interconnections in an advanced SoS style LDT will vary from basic to more advanced.

Some of the sub-twins will be simple digital models without real-time links to the physical context. An example would be volumetric avatars of dancers that can be activated on demand in virtual theatres or public spaces.

Some twins would be more sophisticated models capable of receiving data from the real-world and updating themselves based on changes in the corresponding physical object or environment. The one-directionality of these twins means that the ultimate decision-making power will rest with humans, who could use data driven insights to influence events on the ground—for example, where not to dig to avoid damaging underground utilities.

Also present in an SoS LDT would be bi-directional twins. These are more intelligent representations that can, using IoT sensors and actuators, influence their physical doppelganger or other twins with little or no human intervention. Imagine a scenario involving a DSA plan. The road twin would be able to define where, when, and how road space should be dynamically changed considering mobility, health and access needs at a certain point in time. In another scenario, where a large influx of electric vehicles is expected, the road twin would signal this prediction to the energy twin so that electricity can be channelled from quieter places to meet increased demand.

It is this bidirectional property and the fact that digital twins have the potential to evolve into digital multiples covering social, cultural, economic and other dimensions of a modern city, that set them apart from CIM (City Information Model), which even according to the latest definitions is concerned more with how to represent the physical-urban reality than how to change it.

After reading this chapter, cities looking to adopt digital twins should hopefully get a better sense of what the technology can do for urban governance, as well as its limitations. Future adopters are encouraged to provide case studies with demonstrable benefits in real-life sooner rather than later. A lot of experimental results have been reported by pioneering practitioners, thinkers and innovators to much fanfare. What this field now needs is more evidence of digital twin use by decision-makers to solve problems in the streets, not just in a simulation.

## References


Ahn, C., Ham, Y., Kim, J., Kim, J. (2020). *A digital twin city model for age-friendly communities: capturing environmental distress from multimodal sensory data*. http://hdl.handle.net/10125/63945

Ammar, A., Nassereddine, H., AbdulBaky, N., AbouKansour, A., Tannoury, J., Urban, H., & Schranz, C. (2022). Digital twins in the construction industry: A perspective of practitioners and building authority. *Frontiers in Built Environment, 8*.

Bagheri, S., Brandt, T., Sheombar, H., Van Oosterhout, M. (2021). *Value creation through urban data platforms: A conceptual framework*. http://hdl.handle.net/10125/70915

Batty, M. (2018). Digital twins. *Environment and Planning B, 45*(5), 817–820. https://doi.org/10.1177/2399808318796416

Batty, M., Chapman, D., Evans, S., Haklay, M., Kueppers, S., Shiode, N., Smith, A., & Torrens, P. M. (2001). *Visualizing the city: Communicating urban design to planners and decision-makers*. Esri Press. https://discovery.ucl.ac.uk/id/eprint/158113/

Brandt, T., Oosterhout, M., & Sheombar, H. (2020, April 17). *Digitally managed cities of the future—how close are we*? https://discovery.rsm.nl/articles/436-digitally-managed-cities-of-the-future-how-close-are-we/

Calderon, A. (2018, March 12). *Publishing with purpose. Introducing our 2018 strategy. Medium* https://opendatacharter.medium.com/publishing-with-purpose-introducing-our-2018-strategy-ddbf7ab46098

Caprari, G. (2022). Digital twin for urban planning in the green deal era: A state of the art and future perspectives. *Sustainability, 14*(10), 1–15. https://ideas.repec.org/a/gam/jsusta/v14y2022i10p6263-d820381.html

City of Helsinki. (2021). *A new Minecraft city model introduces Helsinki in more detail*. Helsingin Kaupunki. https://www.hel.fi/en/news/a-new-minecraft-city-model-introduces-helsinki-in-more-detail

City of Vienna. (n.d.). *Brise—the future of public administration*. DigitalesWien. https://digitales.wien.gv.at/en/projekt/brise-vienna/

Cityzenith. (2015). *Cityzenith Launches Next-Gen 5D IoT Platform in 10 Leading Smart Cities Around the World*. https://www.prnewswire.com/news-releases/cityzenith-launches-next-gen-5d-iot-platform-in-10-leading-smart-cities-around-the-world-300174540.html

Cityzenith. (2017, April 14*). From BIM to CIM: The rise of city information modeling and data-driven design*. Architect. https://www.architectmagazine.com/technology/from-bim-to-cim

Conde, J., Munoz-Arcentales, A., Alonso, Á., López-Pernas, S., & Salvachúa, J. (2022). Modeling digital twin data and architecture: A building guide with FIWARE as enabling technology. *IEEE Internet Computing, 26*(3), 7–14. https://doi.org/10.1109/MIC.2021.3056923

Cureton, P., & Hartley, E. (2019). *Lancaster city information model*. Imagination Lancaster. https://imagination.lancaster.ac.uk/project/lancaster-city-information-model-lcim/

Digital Twin Consortium. (2022). *Digital twin periodic table*. Digital Playbook https://www.digitalplaybook.org/index.php?title=Digital_Twin_Periodic_Table

Fruci, C. (2019, June 21). *Connecting smart cities with wireless sensors*. Radio Bridge. https://radiobridge.com/blog/connecting-smart-cities-with-wireless-sensors

Future Cities Catapult. (2017). *Future of planning—City Information Models (CIM)*. https://www.youtube.com/watch?v=uqRXNBTtYMA

GeoTwin. (2021). *Agent-based models as digital twins, the present and the futur*e. https://medium.com/agent-based-models-as-digital-twins-the-present

GoGeomatics Canada. (2022). *Developing a subsurface digital twin for Canada* | SUMSF 2022. https://www.youtube.com/watch?v=5hNtyhbK5Yo

Greater London Authority. (2024). *London datastore*. London Datastore https://data.london.gov.uk/

Heazel, C. (2021). *OGC City geography markup language (CityGML) part 2: GML encoding standard*. Open Geospatial Consortium. https://docs.ogc.org/is/21-006r2/21-006r2.html

Helsinki Region Infoshare. (2018). *Helsingin Energia- ja ilmastoatlas*. HRI. https://hri.fi/data/en_GB/showcase/helsingin-energia-ja-ilmastoatlas

Hudson-Smith, A., Signorelli, V., Dawkins, O., & Batty, M. (2023). More than one twin: An ecology of model applications in east London. In L. Wan, T. Nochta, J. Tang, & J. M. Schooling (Eds.), *Digital twins for smart cities: conceptualisation, challenges and practices*. ICE Publishing Ltd. https://www.icevirtuallibrary.com/isbn/9780727766007

International Electrotechnical Commission. (2021). *City information modelling and urban digital twins*. IEC. https://www.iec.ch/basecamp/city-information-modelling-and-urban-digital-twins

IRMI. (2011). *Underground construction risks—what's underground can kill*. https://www.irmi.com/articles/expert-commentary/underground-construction-risks

Kaltiot. (2022, October 10). *LoRaWAN devices and monitoring—Kaltiot*. https://kaltiot.com/en/iot-technology/lorawan-devices-and-monitoring/

Ketzler, B., Naserentin, V., Latino, F., Zangelidis, C., Thuvander, L., & Logg, A. (2020). Digital twins for cities: A state of the art review. *Built Environment, 46*(4), 547–573. https://doi.org/10.2148/benv.46.4.547

Kolbe, T. H., & Donaubauer, A. (2021). Semantic 3D city modeling and BIM. In W. Shi, M. F. Goodchild, M. Batty, M.-P. Kwan, & A. Zhang (Eds.), *Urban informatics* (pp. 609–636). Springer. https://doi.org/10.1007/978-981-15-8983-6_34

Kolbe, T. H., Kutzner, T., Smyth, C. S., Nagel, C., Roensdorf, C., & Heazel, C. (2021). *OGC city geography markup language (CityGML) part 1: Conceptual model standard (3.0)*. Open Geospatial Consortium. https://docs.ogc.org/is/20-010/20-010.html

Lehner, H., & Dorffner, L. (2020). Digital geoTwin Vienna: Towards a digital twin city as Geodata Hub. PFG. *Journal of Photogrammetry, Remote Sensing and Geoinformation Science, 88*(1), 63–75. https://doi.org/10.1007/s41064-020-00101-4

Lingard, H. (2013). Occupational health and safety in the construction industry. *Construction Management and Economics, 31*(6), 505–514. https://doi.org/10.1080/01446193.2013.816435

MacAlpine, J. (2022). *HPC closing the gap with quantum computing advantage*. Engineering.com. https://www.engineering.com/story/hpc-closing-the-gap-with-quantum-computing-advantage

Milazzo, M. F., Ancione, G., Spasojević-Brkić, V., & Valis, D. (2016). *Investigation of crane operation safety by analysing main accident causes (Proceedings Paper)*. ESREL 2016, Glasgow. https://kobson.nb.rs/nauka_u_srbiji.748.html?autor=Ancione%20G#.YzxTq3ZByUl

Moore, S. (2019). *Top trends from gartner hype cycle for digital government technology 2019*. Gartner. https://www.gartner.com/smarterwithgartner/top-trends-from-gartner-hype-cycle-for-digital-government-technology-2019

Moreira de Oliveira, T. H., & Painho, M. (2015). *Emotion & stress mapping: Assembling an ambient geographic information-based methodology in order to understand smart cities* (pp. 1–4). 2015 10th Iberian Conference on Information Systems and Technologies (CISTI). https://doi.org/10.1109/CISTI.2015.7170469

opengovdata.org. (2007). *The 8 principles of open government data*. https://opengovdata.org/

Panetta, K. (2021). *3 trends surface in the Gartner emerging technologies hype cycle for 2021*. Gartner. https://www.gartner.com/smarterwithgartner/3-themes-surface-in-the-2021-hype-cycle-for-emerging-technologies

Papyshev, G., & Yarime, M. (2021). Exploring city digital twins as policy tools: A task-based approach to generating synthetic data on urban mobility. *Data & Policy, 3*, e16. https://doi.org/10.1017/dap.2021.17

Raes, L., Michiels, P., Adolphi, T., Tampere, C., Dalianis, A., McAleer, S., & Kogut, P. (2022). DUET: A framework for building interoperable and trusted digital twins of smart cities. *IEEE Internet Computing, 26*(3), 43–50. https://doi.org/10.1109/MIC.2021.3060962

Romei, V. (2018, November 1). Governments fail to capitalise on swaths of open data. *Financial Times*. https://www.ft.com/content/f8e9c2ea-b29b-11e8-87e0-d84e0d934341

Ryan, S. (2022). *Mitigate flood risk with digital twin*. T&D World. https://www.tdworld.com/disaster-response/article/21243732/mitigate-flood-risk-with-digital-twin-technology

Sacks, R., Brilakis, I., Pikas, E., Xie, H. S., & Girolami, M. (2020). Construction with digital twin information systems. *Data-Centric Engineering, 1*, e14. https://doi.org/10.1017/dce.2020.16

Sagar, M. (2020, February 5). *The growing trend of city-scale digital twins around the world—OpenGov Asia*. https://opengovasia.com/the-growing-trend-of-city-scale-digital-twins-around-the-world/

Salem, T., & Dragomir, M. (2022). Options for and challenges of employing digital twins in construction management. *Applied Sciences, 12*(6), 2928. https://doi.org/10.3390/app12062928

Sinaeepourfard, A., García Almiñana, J., Masip Bruin, X., Marín Tordera, E., Cirera, J., Grau, G., & Casaus, F. (2016). *Estimating smart city sensors data generation: Current and future data in the city of Barcelona*. 2016 Mediterranean Ad Hoc Networking Workshop (Med-Hoc-Net): the 15th IFIP MEDHOCNET 2016: Vilanova i la Geltru´, Spain, June 20–21. https://doi.org/10.1109/MedHocNet.2016.7528424

Sketchley, E. (2019, February 28). *Breaking down the silos*. Planning, BIM & Construction Today. https://www.pbctoday.co.uk/news/digital-construction/bim-news/breaking-down-the-silos/53144/

Valverde-Pérez, B., Johnson, B., Wärff, C., Lumley, D., Torfs, E., Nopens, I., & Townley, L. (2021). *Digital water: Operational digital twins in the urban water sector*. International Water Association. https://iwa-network.org/publications/operational-digital-twins-in-the-urban-water-sector-case-studies/

Victoria State Government. (n.d.). *Digital Twin Victoria—discover how we're helping to set the digital foundations for a future-ready Victoria*. Victoria State Government—Department of Transport and Planning. https://www.land.vic.gov.au/maps-and-spatial/digital-twin-victoria

Virtual City Systems. (2021, December 2). *Explore CityGML* https://vc.systems/en/explore/technical-articles/citygml/

Walters, A. (2020, August 19). *Explaining the Information Management Framework (IMF) [Text]*. https://www.cdbb.cam.ac.uk/what-we-did/national-digital-twin-programme/explaining-information-management-framework-imf

Wray, S. (2020, May 21). How a small German town is using an advanced digital twin. *Cities Today*. https://cities-today.com/how-a-small-german-town-is-using-an-advanced-digital-twin/

Wu, Y., Xiang, Y., Ge, J., & Muller, P. (2018). High-performance computing for big data processing. *Future Generation Computer Systems, 88*, 693–695. https://doi.org/10.1016/j.future.2018.07.054

Xu, Z., Qi, M., Wu, Y., Hao, X., & Yang, Y. (2021). City information modeling: State of the art. *Applied Sciences, 11*(19), 9333. https://doi.org/10.3390/app11199333

Zeiss, G. (2018). Technical advances bring digital twin of underground infrastructure closer. *GIM International*. https://www.gim-international.com/content/article/technical-advances-bring-digital-twin-of-underground-infrastructure-closer

# Chapter 3
# Local Digital Twins for Smart Cities: Opportunities for Evidence-Informed Decision-Making

**Lieven Raes, Grazia Concilio, Carolina Doran, Laura Temmerman, and Joep Crompvoets**

## Contents




L. Raes (✉)
Digital Flanders, Brussels, Belgium
e-mail: lieven.raes@vlaanderen.be

G. Concilio
Department of Architecture and Urban Studies, Politecnico di Milano, Milan, Italy
e-mail: grazia.concilio@polimi.it

C. Doran
European Citizen Science Association, Berlin, Germany
e-mail: carolina.doran@ecsa.ngo

L. Temmerman
Interuniversitair Micro-Electronica Centrum-SMIT, Vrije Universiteit Brussel, Brussels, Belgium
e-mail: laura.temmerman@vub.be

J. Crompvoets
Public Governance Institute, Katholieke Universiteit Leuven, Leuven, Belgium
e-mail: joep.crompvoets@kuleuven.be




L. Raes et al. (eds.), *Decide Better*,
https://doi.org/10.1007/978-3-031-81451-8_3

## 3.1 Introduction

This chapter aims to map and assess opportunities a Local Digital Twin (LDT) can offer for more evidence-informed decision-making from different perspectives. Starting from policy-making, the chapter scrutinises why an LDT is needed for policy implementation and policy involvement purposes. From a stakeholder perspective, it asks how an LDT can help make all actors, including citizens, become better at co-creating smart cities. This question is combined with a more capabilities-related question about the kind of experiments an LDT can support. The dichotomy between the potential value for stakeholders and the capabilities required for policy support brings us to a conclusion about the opportunities, benefits, barriers and limitations of an LDT.

## 3.2 LDTs for Policy-Making Objectives

Urban digital twins or Digital City Twins (DCT) are conceptualised as next-generation urban modelling tools that use ubiquitous data produced through various digitalisation trends in the built environment and beyond. Nochta et al. (2019) conclude that urban digital twins and DCTs are mostly seen as realistic digital representations of physical city systems, assets and processes, providing digital simulation and management environments to aid decision-making. In contrast, the LDT concept focuses on elements such as urban intelligence, ethical standards, predictive modelling, openness, and interoperability that are not as prominent in the urban digital twins and DCT concepts (see the introduction chapter for the definition).

Policy decisions are an outcome of the policy-making process, and an LDT is a potential tool to provide evidence-based support for implementing policy-related decisions in various interacting smart city domains, as depicted in Fig. 8.1. In this context, three different perspectives are worth highlighting. The first one sees the digital twin as a high-potential policy-making tool for an entire city (van Heeswijk, 2021). The second one sees the digital twin in the context of smart city implementation. Miskinis (2019) states that "from urban planning to land-use optimisation, it [the digital twin] has the power to govern the city in an effective manner".

Across all perspectives, digital twins empower users by allowing them to simulate policy plans before they are implemented, "exposing problems before they become a reality." As such, the digital twin can be used as an inclusive instrument to involve citizens in urban governance, as illustrated in the Herrenberg and other digital twin case studies (Dembski et al., 2020). People's living environments are often directly affected by the result of a policy decision impacting the complex interactions between smart city domains; thus, aligning policy objectives and desired outcomes with citizens' expectations and (potential) impacts helps to foster collaboration and inclusiveness towards all (potentially) affected groups.

### 3.2.1 From a Policy-Making Perspective

The manifold experimentations conducted in the last years on the use of data—big, open data—have shown the great potential of these sources to support real-time monitoring of urban processes and operational actions, whether it is responding to emergencies, addressing mobility-related issues such as traffic jams and accidents, or scheduling adjustments in transport supply. However, big data's impact on the policy-making processes is still controversial and not fully understood (Concilio & Pucci, 2021). Critical ex-post evaluations on the potential and limits of data-informed policy-making have led several public bodies, such as the European Commission (EC) and the US Congress, to identify new possibilities and challenges related to the use of data in policy-making and analysis within specific areas of application (De Gennaro et al., 2016; Jarmin & O'Hara, 2016; Lim et al., 2018). LDTs, as the technology that builds upon this big-data, evidence-based policy-making tradition, must be seen in a similar light. Their complexity, dependency on data and simulation model variables, and place in the policy-making process still need further exploration. An important question is how the policy cycle model, with its traditional three-phase structure of policy design, implementation and evaluation (see Fig. 3.1), can best be applied to LDTs.

The *policy design stage* not only highlights a collective policy problem but also identifies goals and objectives for defining policy strategies, which can help develop actions to deal with the issue. The use of an LDT at this point depends on the formulated problems, goals and objectives and the type of data analysis needed. Exploratory analysis answers the "what is the data" question and focuses on gaining insight into data characteristics. This can be seen as a preparatory step as it does not directly result in policies. Reporting and monitoring focuses on data integration and aggregation. It contributes to the "what is happening" question. Descriptive analysis answers the question of "what happened", using standard statistical methods like a trend, relation and variation analysis in different scenarios, while diagnostic analysis centres around the "why did it happen" question as the first step toward a

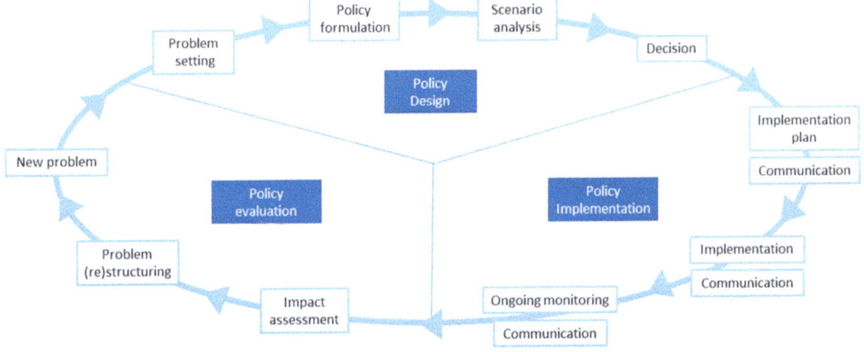


**Fig. 3.1** The policy lifecycle. (Verstraete et al., 2021)

decision. Predictive analysis, in turn, allows an understanding of "why something happened" and can help determine "what can be expected to happen next". Last but not least, prescriptive analysis helps to support decisions about "what to do to attain the desired outcome" (Verstraete et al., 2021). LDTs tested in Athens, Flanders and Pilsen during the DUET[1] project have demonstrated how a digital twin can contribute to exploratory analysis via data visualisation on a 2D/3D map and dashboards. Both contributed to a descriptive and diagnostic analysis by providing aggregated insights. The use of multiple (combined) simulation models made advanced predictive analysis possible. Using an LDT for prescriptive analyses to get the desired result is new to LDTs and demands high-quality data, models and analytical insights.

During the *policy implementation stage,* actions are planned according to an implementation plan. This plan usually provides a step-by-step approach covering different aspects (e.g. technical, financial, and societal). During the implementation, ongoing monitoring and communication are needed to monitor progress. A data collection and processing plan can be part of the implementation plan and strategy. The use of an LDT for policy implementation is currently state of the art. An interesting question to explore is whether an LDT can support or even replace parts of the on-paper implementation plan and make it more agile. The visualisation of Internet of Things (IoT) sensor data, whether or not combined with visualising on-terrain progress and simulation models incorporated in the LDT, can contribute to intermediate monitoring during the implementation phase and shorten the entire policy cycle design, implementation and evaluation feedback loop. The intermediate outcomes and results can provide feedback on communication and co-creation activities to citizens, communities and other stakeholders through LDT visualisations, dashboards and linked storytelling.

The *policy evaluation stage* scrutinises the desired and undesired outcomes and impacts achieved through implementing a policy. Policy evaluation can also be described as the systematic assessment of a government policy's design, implementation and outcomes (HM Treasury, 2020). Next to the classical design, implementation, and evaluation feedback cycle, the ROAMEF[2] development cycle framework, described in the HM Treasury green book, sees the evaluation as a process that runs before, during, and after implementation. It aims to improve the design of policies, identify strategic objectives, understand the mechanism of change, and support implementation management (HM Treasury, 2022).

Evaluation as a systematic assessment of an intervention's design, implementation and outcome involves three essential elements where an LDT can be an important part of the solution:

- *Understanding how an intervention is being or has been implemented, its effects, for whom, and why:* An LDT can visualise measures in the public domain, like road measures, new building developments or new infrastructure, to name a few.

[1] Digital Urban European Twins (DUET), EU H2020 project, https://cordis.europa.eu/project/id/870697

[2] ROAMEF stands for: Rationale, Objectives, Appraisal, Monitoring, Evaluation, Feedback

Simulation models can predict the effects, e.g. traffic intensities, noise and air quality or shadow and heat impact. Geospatial simulation, when used on its own or combined with spatial socio-demographic data, enables the discovery of who will be affected and how;

- *Comparing what happens with what was expected under the business-as-usual scenario (the appropriate counterfactual):* An LDT starts by visualising the business-as-usual scenario. This is usually done via geo-time series using, for example, sensor data from IoT measurements. It provides a geospatial basis for ex-ante measurements. Local implementations mostly require specific high-density ex-ante measurements before implementing new policy measures. Implementing a 'school streets' scheme (a temporary road closure when children arrive or leave the school) using local citizen science data shows the advantage of working with local ex-ante measurement data before implementing policy decisions. This approach provides added value through ex-ante and post-measurement comparison;
- *Identifying what can be improved, estimating overall impacts and cost-effectiveness:* An LDT allows the simulation of multiple policy scenarios to explore their effects on traffic volumes in the neighbourhood, including air quality and noise impact (see Chap. 7). A typical example is simulating the effect of street closure; the scenario can involve single or both directions where speed limits and/or road capacity are reduced.

Overall, an LDT may deliver many possibilities for policy evaluation as part of the classical policy-making cycle before, during and after the policy implementation. LDT usage can increase the policy-making process's flexibility and help turn data into evidence to support evidence-informed decision-making. The full potential LDTs can offer over existing policy-supporting tools is the combined, integrated use of predictive multi-domain simulation modelling and the support of YTT (Yesterday, Today, Tomorrow) IoT and model-based datasets.

### *3.2.2 From a Smart City Implementation Perspective*

Cocchia summarises that the reason for the birth of smart/digital cities is global citizens' demand for governments to improve their quality of life through innovative design and reconstruction of urban spaces (Cocchia, 2014). Deng et al. (2021) see the DCT as an inevitable digital transformation trend that helps cities unlock the benefits of real-time remote monitoring and enable more effective decision-making. The attention to smart cities has emphasised the use of ICT solutions to improve our lives in cities and regions. It has, in fact, added a direct social objective to ICT investments. A study by Mergel et al. (2019) based on interviews with multiple European, international, national, regional, and local governments, NGOs and private sector representatives in 2019 pointed out that the motivation for digital transformation, including high-value, real-time smart services, comes from the external environment instead of internal pressure.

In many regions and cities, themes like sustainable mobility, logistics, energy consumption, communication, urban planning, construction and disaster management are at the top of the policy agenda. Their effective implementation requires integrated ICT software solutions. Deng et al. (2021) see five types of new advanced technologies related to urban digital twins: (1) Surveying and mapping technologies to create and update 2D and 3D city maps. The technologies start from classical 2D and 3D mapping to automated Unmanned Aerial Vehicle (UAV) Lidar-based 3D mapping; (2) Building Information Models (BIM) making use of 2D and 3D mapping to add additional metadata about the building, its energy consumption, production, accessibility, to name a few; (3) IoT data in a smart city context involving the collection of dynamic data via sensor networks and transferring it to near real-time data and historical geo-time series; (4) Blockchain technologies related to a safe transfer of data messages; and (5) Advanced system resources handling vast amounts of data and computations. An additional element is the growing role of Artificial Intelligence (AI) in relation to smart cities. AI can potentially play an important role in auto-steering on-terrain equipment and devices, as well as in simulation modelling as part of an LDT. A bi-directional LDT is one where a digital twin can be used for (automatic) operational management on the ground through attenuator steering (e.g. sink poles, traffic lights, road signs, opening bridges), thus bridging the gap with (smart city) operation centres.

The potential of digital twins for policy-making is often scrutinised via a number of different use cases. With respect to urban logistics, Marcucci et al. (2020) suggest that digital twins can't be fully representative of the reality of urban freight transport. However, digital twin technology can play a significant role in supporting experimentation/piloting in urban logistics planning and policy-making. The authors emphasise the importance of the combined use of behavioural and simulation models to achieve the best results when it comes to data-informed decision-making.

The Amsterdam Urban Strategy platform (TNO, n.d.; Lohman et al., 2023) facilitates impact simulation in multiple smart city domains and use cases like urban planning, mobility, and the environment by combining a wide range of data, including social census data to integrate elements related to the social fabric of the city. An Inter Model Broker (IMB) connects multiple simulation models to predict impacts on air quality, noise pollution, costs, and health. Innovative is the use of a collection of key indicators to highlight areas where policy interventions are necessary, superfluous or underperforming. The platform adds a strategic decision component to the overall smart city policy and is used as a collaborative platform to bring various stakeholders together. The Amsterdam Urban Strategy tool enables a rapid assessment of policy scenarios' expected impacts. This flexibility makes the tool suitable for collaborative sessions where rapidly testing a wide range of solutions to finetune policy scenarios is preferred to a detailed calculation based on more advanced and time-consuming models.

### 3.2.3 From an Involvement Perspective

Developments in opening government data, advanced analytics, visualisation, simulation, gaming, and ubiquitous citizen access using mobile and personalised applications are shaping the interactions between policymakers and citizens (Janssen & Helbig, 2018). E-voting and online opinion polling, discussion fora of the late 1990s and early 2000s are moving towards the next generation of ICT policy-making tools where data, information, visualisations, analysis and scenario comparison play a more important role. Opening public-funded data as open data, as promoted by the EU PSI directive (European Parliament and Council, 2013) and EU Directive on open data and the re-use of public sector information, known as the 'Open Data Directive' (European Parliament and Council, 2019), has led to machine-readable data with fewer restrictions. EU Directives such as these will have a significant impact on suggestions for policy improvement as now data can be analysed and utilised by anybody. This result has led to a transfer of data and knowledge from the inside government to the outside (Janssen et al., 2012). These evolutions pave the way for advanced policy instruments like an LDT combining open data, turning it into knowledge and sharing it with citizens, community groups and local businesses. The LDT, as developed during the DUET project, goes beyond the traditional, often static, open data by integrating IoT sensor data and predictive models. This evolution to more complex data-oriented involvement and participation tools, as Janssen and Zuiderwijk (2014) mention, risks that those with more resources and expertise can use the results for lobbying and strengthening their own position. New citizen initiatives where citizens start to measure urban conditions themselves also create new ways of involvement, changing the traditional policy-making cycle where policymakers are usually in the lead. The self-organisation in the Groningen region in the Netherlands, where people started doing measurements themselves using IoT devices, is an example of agenda setting and evidence creation of the damage caused by earthquakes related to extracting natural gas. Another example is the Telraam (telraam.net) initiative, where people can install an IoT device to count traffic and collect evidence about traffic nuisance. An important question is whether citizen-collected data from a citizen science project can be used as local citizen knowledge in an LDT to integrate data about the living environment. A second question is whether and how this data can be processed to make it policy-ready for specific use in the evidence-informed decision-making process. One solution, described in Chap. 6, is to assess and process the data via professional calibration algorithms to check its validity and increase quality.

## 3.3 Importance of Collaboration for an LDT Policy Ecosystem

The LDT as an evolvable system is only successful if all stakeholders have an interest in the continuous usage and development of the capabilities of the system. In many cases, LDTs are still serving single-use cases, which does not create enough leverage for the sustainability of the system. Creating added value for the ecosystem of stakeholders is essential for the durability of the LDT solution. The LDT, the digital representation of the city's processes and assets, needs to interact with the physical reality in a trustful and accurate manner. Continuous integration between the digital and physical counterparts is essential to keep the system up-to-date and relevant for decision-makers. The LDT development and operations need to be integrated into city governance and connected with stakeholders.

Two important characteristics of city governance are the holistic view and co-creation, indicating that different actors are involved in addressing cross-domain city challenges. A strong enabler to proactively manage co-creation is inclusive urban planning that combines basic urban planning objectives such as land usage, infrastructure management and traffic management but also takes into account social and environmental impacts.

The objective of co-creation and co-production is to activate stakeholders beyond the government by engaging citizens and businesses and by building long-term relationships with knowledge experts to contribute to improving public service delivery. The engagement of different stakeholders is valuable for policy co-production, but this requires an institutional change within governmental institutions (Satorras et al., 2020). This is not only in the consultation and design stages but also at the implementation level, where common goals can be achieved and reinforced by working together. To organise and deliver smart city services, the city should think of itself as the orchestrator of an ecosystem, which implies taking up an integrator role to connect with all stakeholders involved (Del Río Castro et al., 2021). Creating visibility around sustainability projects encourages a positive attitude and incentivises private actors to get involved, which leads to increased capacity for sustainability projects. Research indicates that the main driver for businesses to join local sustainability partnerships is the opportunity to contribute to positive environmental changes and to the sustainability agenda of the local community, as companies are also forced to contribute to the Sustainable Development Goals (SDGs) (Ordonez-Ponce et al., 2021). There has been a growing interest among local decision-makers in developing a close relationship with scientific partners in a request to share knowledge and participate in the urban transformation and policy-making processes (Bansard et al., 2019). A multidisciplinary team bringing together researchers and practitioners from natural science, engineering and humanities domains enhances the transdisciplinary view on sustainability topics (X. M. Bai et al., 2017).

Collaborations with private sector actors that go beyond the customer-provider relationship are part of the LDT governance model. According to D'Hauwers and Walravens (D'Hauwers et al., 2021), a decentralised governance model with decentralised control (owned by the ecosystem or driven by the ecosystem) creates the best opportunity for private sector involvement, supporting decision-making and open innovation. A dedicated section about the different governance models and their potential impact on collaboration is discussed in Chap. 9.

## 3.4 Why an LDT?

Today, our physical living environment (PLE) consists of closely related systems that interact with a high degree of complexity. It contains elements like the built environment, spatial planning, traffic flows, public multimodal transport, infrastructures, pipelines, heat networks, water networks, data communication, green areas, and population (composition, demographic evolution). Mapping information, including information about PLE behaviour in the past, present, and future, can support decision-makers and future decision-making processes. Many of today's LDTs and Geospatial Information Systems (GIS) systems are oriented towards the 3D mapping of the PLE.

However, does using PLE data, IoT sensors, and simulation models differentiate LDTs from other existing Spatial Data Infrastructure (SDI) and GIS decision tools? The LDT definition suggests that elements like open architecture, interoperability, (domain overarching) simulations, privacy protection and ethics are needed (EU DG Connect, 2022).

Smart cities add the element of societal relevance and interconnectivity to the modernisation and digitalisation of the public domain. LDTs can do the same on the information and knowledge level for SDI, GIS and decision support tools. They also interconnect data, information, and knowledge to give it societal relevance.

Another angle from which to view an LDT is how it supports decision-making. The aforementioned tools often indirectly support decision-making by providing information and offering knowledge based on processed data for policy-making. The decision outcome can only be tested on the terrain after implementation. The potential to simulate complex what-if questions covering effects on multiple PLE domains creates new possibilities.

In addition, the ownership of an LDT matters and defines its use. It does not make sense for only one department to own and control an LDT, even if it is horizontal. Shared ownership, a shared information basis, and a common trust are key elements that make LDTs useful. Joint management can also help maintain societal principles like well-doing, openness, transparency, effectiveness, security, privacy, involvement, co-creation, open standards, and adaptability (see Chap. 9 for a discussion on an LDT governance model).

Another main differentiator is the system-of-systems (SoS) approach (see Chap. 4) of an LDT. More than any other IT system, an LDT is an integrator of data, information and knowledge accompanied by simulation models and visualisation clients to transform the input into useful output in terms of simulation results or visualisations offering new insights.

Other LDT related elements are also important in this context. The first element is ensuring users' privacy by guaranteeing that data complies with privacy regulations. Another element is the focus on LDTs'characteristics of openness and interoperability. Openness and interoperability are essential for creating a network of interconnected digital twins, combining LDT components and existing legacy systems, and allowing the exchange of information between systems. A more content-related element, introduced by the EC, is the LDTs ability to help achieve the European Green Deal goals and the EC's digital ambitions. The EC sees LDTs as a disruptive concept with untapped potential, allowing for greater co-creation with citizens (Ribeiro, 2021), which can potentially evolve into a tool for engaging local communities and businesses to increase local knowledge and awareness.

## 3.5 Does It Help to Make Our Cities and Citizens Smarter?

Smart cities and smart citizens go hand in hand. A smart city is not only a city with complex connected interactive systems but also a place where actors such as policy-makers, politicians, researchers, companies and citizens cooperate to achieve a sustainable living space and society. LDTs can potentially influence all actors' roles and involvement in the policy-making process. It is equally essential for all stakeholders to have open and transparent access to LDTs to support the creation of a level playing field amongst all actors to maximise insights and decision quality. A number of new and existing tools supporting the evidence-informed policy process can support achieving this goal.

### *3.5.1 Stakeholders Involved in LDT Driven Policy-Making*

To describe the actors' roles in an extended quadruple helix (Leydesdorff, 2011), a personas-based methodology has been used to give an overview of the added value that an LDT might offer. The (triple) helix model of innovation refers to a set of interactions between academia (the university), industry, and government to foster economic and social development. The fourth helix relates to culture and media-based public and civil society. At least two different personas are delineated for each actor based on typical roles encountered during LDT and evidence-based policy-making-related research projects.[3]

[3]Digital European Digital Twins project (DUET), Community Observation Measurement & Participation in AIR Science (COMPAIR), EU H2020 project, https://cordis.europa.eu/project/id/101036563, and Enhanced URBAN planning for AGE-friendly cities through disruptive technologies (URBANAGE), EU H2020 project, https://cordis.europa.eu/project/id/101004590

**The Policymakers (Government Helix)**
Policymakers can usually benefit from all the functionalities an LDT offers as a visualisation, simulation, planning, and communication tool. They are likely to be the group most affected by both the possibilities and limitations of an LDT caused by the available data, data quality and the combination of simulation models. Fully capitalising on the opportunity can only be achieved by leveraging the expertise of data scientists and simulation experts, combined with a high level of data literacy of everyone involved in the process. A substantial hurdle for policymakers in using LDTs is navigating the cultural norms of other departments, including a lack of trust in data, not understanding information outside their area of expertise, and limitations related to functionalities offered by domain-specific tools.

**Personas**
**Jana** is responsible for city planning and is involved in researching and redacting the Sustainable Urban Mobility Plan (SUMP). She wants to know the impact a new ring road will have on city traffic flows, air quality, and noise levels. Based on the LDT simulation results, she will propose adding accompanying measures to the SUMP to enhance city liveability.

**Bart** is looking for partners (commercial and academic) to co-design an integrative approach to develop and plan new data-based smart city services with local businesses, researchers and citizens. A view of the latest available IoT sensor services, Application Programming Interface (APIs) and the updated 3D model of the city and existing city dashboard will contribute to evidence-informed discussions and new insights into the local need and best location for new innovative city services.

**The Politicians (Government Helix)**
Politicians, as the final stage decision-makers, are individually or collectively responsible and accountable in a democracy. Evidence-based and evidence-informed decisions often prepared by policymakers need to be understood and elaborated by them. LDTs can visualise and explain the effects of a proposed decision or different decision scenarios in a more direct way and can help anticipate the decision-making process, discussions and arguments. Today, little is known about how LDTs affect the decision process, discussions and even relations amongst the involved politicians (and, by extension, policymakers) when multiple policy domains are affected.

**Personas**
**John**, a deputy mayor for citizen involvement and community work, wants to objectively determine citizen proposals to design public spaces and create green and shady resting spaces, using nature-based solutions in neighbourhoods that need to lower heat stress. The LDT helps him to communicate

(continued)

which areas of heat stress can be successfully reduced and made more accessible based on multiple parameters like the current heat stress, available greenery (e.g. trees, hedges, lawns, ponds) and street furniture (e.g. benches. Picnic tables).

**Marjane and Remi**, the mayor and deputy mayor for urban planning and mobility, must decide about the impact of a new SUMP. Both want to know the effect of street closures on traffic volumes, air quality, and noise produced by traffic. They will use the outcomes to define the potential urban impact and assess the need for mitigating measures in areas that will not be positively affected.

**The Companies (Industry Helix)**

LDTs offer a wide range of new market opportunities beyond LDT solution providers. An important and largely unexplored opportunity is in using the LDT to extend data spaces. Creating an open data and simulation model marketplace where highly specialised service providers, in simulation modelling and impact analysis, use an LDT to create added value for their customers by delivering new and better insights.

**Personas**

**Walter** works for a company which offers cities noise measuring models. Collecting and transforming data about a city's terrain, buildings, trees, surface material, and transport volumes, is a laborious and costly process. An LDT could deliver a more qualitative service by reducing the time spent on finding and making data interoperable and running simulation models. Walter can invest more time in refining the simulation model and analysing and interpreting the results.

**Thomas** is a developer of an LDT solution and needs to unlock and visualise complex data and simulation models in the map viewer. Using well-known IT standards, interoperable well-described data and metadata would reduce development time, increase overall reliability and broaden the market potential of his data- and modelling offering.

**The Researchers (Universities/Academics Helix)**

An LDT also offers added value to the research community by exposing new integrated datasets, including their metadata, and allowing researchers and policymakers to elaborate on the available data for their practical use. In analogy with private sector players, an LDT offers the opportunity to test new simulation models in a multi-policy-domain environment to study their broader impact and effects.

**Personas**

**Karel** investigates how traffic models can be extended beyond the mobility domain. He examines how ICT-technical and policy-related traffic models can steer and influence other simulation models. An LDT offers a flexible environment in which to implement multi-model cooperation practically.

**Daniella** is a specialist in low-cost (citizen science) air quality solutions and wants to improve the quality of the results of existing air quality sensors to make them more reliable and better usable for policy-making purposes. An LDT offers her an environment to integrate multiple types of sensors in a single environment. Thanks to the interoperable data from high-fidelity sensors available via the LDT, low-cost sensors can be calibrated and integrated into the digital twin.

**Communities and Citizens (Society/Public Helix)**

Traditionally, citizens in smart cities have been considered as having a passive role, for instance, as users or consumers of a service (Cowley et al., 2017). In this context, making communities and citizens 'smarter' has often revolved solely around developing their digital skills to enable them to access activities related to smart cities (Manchester & Cope, 2019). This techno-determinist vision adopts a simplistic top-down educational response where citizens are only seen as recipients of knowledge perceived as necessary to engage in an inevitable 'smart' future (ibid). However, the field of smart cities has recently witnessed a shift in mindset towards 'citizen-centricity', where 'smart' technologies are no longer seen as a service *for* citizens but *by* citizens (Castelnovo, 2018; Rodriguez Müller, 2021), working towards a more democratic city that would provide better and fairer public services, increasing welfare and wellbeing (Morozov & Bria, 2018; de Oliveira & Campolargo, 2015). By granting a more active role to citizens, LDTs can strive to overcome some shortcomings generally observed with smart cities and have the potential to go a step further and lead to citizen empowerment. In addition, by directly engaging with communities and citizens, cities have the opportunity to gain knowledge on those individuals who are normally not considered due to their distance to technology. This enables policymakers and politicians to discover hidden problems which might not have been previously considered without their perspective (from high pavements, silent traffic lights, and lack of parking spots that do not allow space for wheelchairs to more dramatic situations of neighbourhoods without easy access to primary services to detrimental levels of noise and air pollution). Further, the inclusion of citizens in LDT is crucial not only in its everyday use but in the entire policy process.

**Personas**

**Erika** lives on a busy two-way street. He is concerned about the health and safety of his children and would like to investigate the extent to which changing his street to a one-way street would impact immediate traffic and air pollution on his street and in his neighbourhood. Empowered by the results he retrieved from the LDT, he decided to start a petition and ask his local authorities to make the change.

**Cheng** just moved to a new area of town. She often comes home late for work and would like to choose the safest route on foot. However, she noticed that the LDT does not provide information that could help her. Fortunately, her local authorities have started a participatory process around the LDT, and she can propose the addition of new data and functionalities to the platform, such as adding data about street lighting, footpaths and cycle paths combined with points of interest like local grocery shops and pharmacies to find a safe and practical route.

### *3.5.2 LDT Tools for Stakeholder Engagement in Policy-Making*

Compared to classical 2D-oriented GIS, an LDT offers both 2D and advanced 3D data rendering and navigation possibilities. To allow all the actors to interact with the LDT and enable them to interpret the outcome of proposed policy measures or implementation scenarios themselves, an LDT can offer several valuable visualisation and interpretation tools. The LDT vision of openness and transparency means that visualisation tools are, in principle, open and accessible to all actors. Technical reasons (e.g. the cost of computer power), ethical reasons (e.g. protection of personal data), financial reasons (e.g. limited access to commercial services), or time reasons (e.g. scenario analysis and preparation) can limit the access to functionalities and use cases. The tools below focus on visualising LDTs. Other underlying LDT components (building blocks), like simulation tools or tools related to data gathering and processing, are discussed in Chap. 4.

**3D & 2D Map-Based Interfaces**

LDTs are, because of their visual attractiveness, often seen as a synonym for a 3D visualisation of the city. However, having a 3D map viewer isn't the only way to view your city. In several cases, having a 3D model isn't even necessary. A map viewer is, according to GIS market leader ESRI, an interactive web mapping and data visualisation application for creating, exploring, and saving web maps (Esri, 2022). An advanced map viewer in an LDT can offer a unique view of the city in 3D or 2D (elevated ground layer and 3D model LOD2 or higher), in combination with historical and near live IoT sensor data visualisation and the visual representation of interacting simulation model results.

**City Dashboards**

Mannaro et al. (2018) describe a city dashboard as a big data platform designed, on the one hand, to allow city users to get up-to-date information about a city and, on the other hand, as a way of providing access to a wide range of datasets about the city to help decision-makers. The city dashboard has become popular as a means to present big data effectively and to communicate important information (Suakanto et al., 2013). Mannaro et al. (2018) found out, based on the analysis of 20 publicly available dashboards, that the most common policy areas were environment, transportation, finance and safety. They and other authors distinguish four clusters related to the dashboard goals: (1) dashboards with data regarding the city administration; (2) dashboards presenting information of public interest; (3) dashboards focussing on data integration, analysis and decision-making (only detected as technical architecture concepts); (4) comparison between different cities (Mannaro et al., 2018). An LDT solution directed to policy-making and prediction supports data integration (interoperability), advanced analysis capabilities, and decision support by providing and even combining simulation models, bringing the ideas of cluster 3 into practice.

**Storytelling Tools**

Storytelling strategies are a successful way to convey information to diverse audiences whilst maintaining high engagement. This methodology is wildly untapped when it comes to including the voices of a wide range of participants in developing technology. This poses a unique opportunity in the development of LDTs. Many people are fearful of participating in projects with high technological content. Still, their views carry immense value. Storytelling is a successful way to make technology accessible and gain the necessary insight to make it inclusive and complete (MacLeod & Davidson, 2007). Some authors see storytelling as an important approach and instrument of (big) data literacy, which can be facilitated by data driven journalism, media or art projects (D'Ignazio & Bhargava, 2015).

**Citizen Participation Tools**

Citizen participation can take diverse forms, and LDTs should strive beyond their citizens' mere 'education' towards some levels of citizen power. As Arnstein (1969) pointed out, the redistribution of power allows citizens at risk of exclusion to be deliberately included in future political and economic processes. LDTs have the potential to offer some levels of citizen power, such as enabling citizens to negotiate and engage in trade-offs with traditional power holders such as municipality authorities or, at the highest level, allowing citizens to obtain the majority of the decision-making seats or even have a full managerial power in instances where it is relevant to do so.

Citizen participation can provide added value to LDTs themselves, and also during their development stage through the co-creation process. The term 'co-creation' was initially framed as a strategy in the late nineties. Kambil et al. (1996) present co-creation as a strategy to transform value propositions working with customers or complementary resources. A few years later, co-creation was presented as an important source of value enabled by the Internet (Kambil et al., 1999). Over the years, many tools have been created to support co-creation during the different phases. The

EU-funded iPRODUCE[4] project offers a comprehensive overview of useful tools during the research, team building, ideation, development, assessment/evaluation, and validation phases of the entire co-creation process. The co-creation tool integrated into the DUET (DUET, 2020a) LDT supports both the assessment/evaluation and validation phase by providing the ability to compare and comment on the effects of different policy scenarios.

## 3.6 What Kind of Experiments and Decisions Can an LDT Support?

Decisions affecting the local living environment touch multiple policy sectors, affecting different scales (regional, local, urban, and neighbourhood) at different time snapshots. All these elements affect the kind of policy experiments, supported decisions and demand for LDT solutions. A policy experiment in social science is any "policy intervention that offers innovative responses to social needs, implemented on a small scale and in conditions that enable their impact to be measured, prior to being repeated on a larger scale, if the results prove convincing" (European Commission, 2013). Concilio and Pucci (2021) see unprecedented opportunities in the wider availability of data and the growing technological advancements in data collection, management and analysis. These conditions question the very basics of the policy-making process toward new interpretative models. An LDT aims to deliver the framework and tools to support experimenting and decision-making in various (smart city) related policy areas.

### *3.6.1 Multi-sector Decision Support*

An LDT, as experimented with in Athens, Flanders and Pilsen during the DUET project, stands out in the way it simulates the effects of experiments in the mobility, environment and spatial planning domains (Cartas et al., 2022). The need for an overarching solution across policy domains became apparent during stakeholder meetings in the three pilot areas during the scenario specification phase, resulting in a list of user requirements (DUET, 2020b). More than 60% (8 out of 13) of the high-prioritised pilot cases (called epics) by city and regional stakeholders from different departments in these three pilot locations overarch a single policy domain. Five of the eight epics specifically mention citizen involvement, openness and reuse of the outcomes by the community. During the DUET project, it became apparent that an

[4] A Social Manufacturing Framework for Streamlined Multi-stakeholder Open Innovation Missions in Consumer Goods Sectors (iPRODUCE), EU H2020 project, https://cordis.europa.eu/project/id/870037

added value of an LDT is precisely how it connects data, tools, models, and multiple, often sector-specific, analysis frameworks to achieve new insights.

### 3.6.2 The 'Time Perspective': Supporting Strategic and Operational Decisions

The time and scale perspective influence the strategic perspective of policy experimentation and decision-making (Concilio et al., 2019). The authors differentiate a continuum between real-time, daily operational management decisions (connected to the shortest, real-time perspective) and long-term policy-related (strategic) decisions. Short-term management is embedded in the smart city sphere of operational decisions impacting cities, where decisions are less analytic and more routine that may depend on data driven learning mechanisms. Conversely, you have decisions with a long-term perspective using anticipatory reasoning. Various situations are possible between short-term and long-term decisions, characterised by their reversibility and level of experimentation (see Fig. 3.2). The operational versus strategic dimension is characterised by the differences between ICCC (Integrated Command and Control Centres) and LDTs solutions and reflects how ICCC is focused on supporting operational management and LDTs support long-term impact policy decisions.

Smart city operation centres, or ICCC, as installed in Rio de Janeiro, Chinese and Indian cities integrate multiple city functions in a single digital command-and-control system built further on the widespread traffic centres tradition. Typically, such operation centres bring operational real-time monitoring and management data

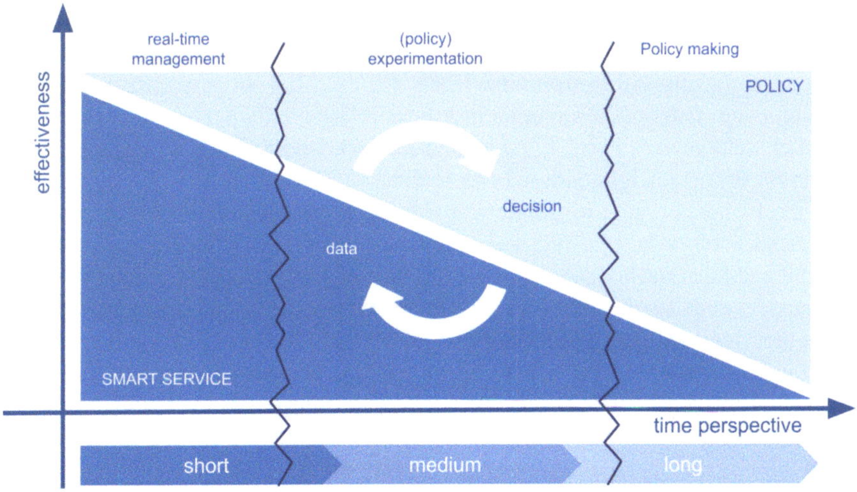


**Fig. 3.2** Real-time management versus policy-making. (Concilio et al. 2021)

together based on IoT devices, CCTV (Closed Circuit Television), intelligent cameras, and different types of linked attenuators. It is typically real-time and operational management-oriented and delivers smart on-terrain services. Praharaj (2019) concludes that ICCC projects in India based on the Rio de Janeiro centre are focused on real-time monitoring and management. The key trends, motivations and focus areas significantly emphasised surveillance of spaces and monitoring of transport and traffic through big data centres. The ICCC examples in Brazil and India focus on real-time management and smart services like disaster management in some cases. LDTs, as formulated by DG Connect (EU DG Connect, 2022), aim to predict strategic policy decisions based on simulation modelling and geo-time series data. The DUET project is one of the first ones to test an LDT approach in three locations simultaneously, addressing different policy dimensions (short-term, long-term, experimental) within one strategic framework.

### *3.6.3 Geospatial Differences (City, Countryside, Regional)*

The introduction of LDTs by EU DG Connect (2022) explicitly links the size and capacity of cities. In order to go beyond the current LDT examples, which involve large (and wealthy) cities and regions, it is especially important to consider the size and capacity of the urban area when applying the model to smaller cities or sparsely populated regions. The effects of size on implementing a digital twin for policy prediction using the same ICT platform were tested on a small-scale at three locations during the DUET project.

The city and metropolitan area of Athens (GR)—with more than three million inhabitants, implemented a digital twin prototype based on available open data, local sensor networks, and open source traffic models combined with commercial air quality models. The simulations in the centre of Athens (city of Athens) were only possible based on the available metropolitan area data. Alignment between local data at the city and metropolitan levels was essential but only sometimes present in practice. This spatial situation in Athens is potentially a model for other metropolitan areas such as Paris, London, and Madrid, where a digital twin appears to be only useful on a neighbourhood or a metropolitan scale.

In the Flanders region in Belgium (6.7 million inhabitants), an LDT prototype was tested using a mix of regional and local data sources, including combined regional and local traffic models, as well as advanced air quality and noise models. As Flanders consists of a network of interconnected cities that strongly influence each other, regional data is necessary to understand the local impact (e.g., traffic flows and air quality). This effect can be seen in Flanders's second largest city, Ghent, where a digital twin at the city level delivered added value but only worked well thanks to the use of regional data. A bonus of sharing the same data and simulation models is that the digital twins can be easily replicable in neighbouring cities.

Pilsen, with 160,000 inhabitants, is the biggest city in the West Bohemia region of the Czech Republic. Its digital twin solution combined excellent local traffic management data, a locally developed open traffic model, and a noise model, proving that a digital twin can deliver affordable added value for small to medium-sized cities. Pilsen fulfils a role as a small central city without large neighbouring cities and relies to a greater extent on its own data sets. This makes Pilsen's digital twin more independent of developments in neighbouring cities but limits its economy of scale.

Athens, Pilsen, and Flanders faced similar policy challenges despite the difference in scale and spatial situations. The demand for data, models, and visualisation capabilities in the evaluated domains of mobility, environment, and spatial planning appeared to be quite similar. Differences were mainly found in the spatial scale, the availability of qualitative data, and the complexity levels of data provision.

## 3.7 Opportunities, Benefits, Barriers and Limitations of LDTs

The recent focus on LDTs for policy-making to deliver services for and by citizens also takes societal effects and impacts into account. As previously mentioned, LDTs provide the *opportunity* to overcome the shortcomings and downsides of smart cities, helping them to move away from focusing exclusively on economic growth, techno-deterministic ideas, and eco-modernist mindset (Temmerman & Van den Broeck, 2021). To work toward a more 'just city'—a city that would be driven by the goals of democracy, diversity and equity—social justice should be a core consideration (Fainstein, 2014), and thus co-design and co-creation practices should become a core tenet of an LDT implementation methodology and process. Creating a 'just city' implies deep considerations for social justice not only on the outcome level but also on the process level of governance (Healey, 2003). In that respect, LDTs need to be open to allowing new public and private sector datasets combined with citizen science data to integrate all quadruple helix partners. Openness in terms of simulation models from different providers that can be combined is another LDT benefit that was tested during the DUET project and that showed the benefits of combining multiple sector-specific simulations to get new mutual insights. By considering these different elements when building and implementing an LDT solution, smart cities have the opportunity to create a more just city for all.

Recent studies have demonstrated that LDTs also have the *potential* to support wider involvement and participation with locally relevant issues and decision-making processes. More specifically, the reduction of complexity together with the spatial and visual representation provided by LDT platforms can include groups that are often disinterested in traditional formats like plans and planning concepts, such as youngsters, those with a low education background or migration background (Dembski et al., 2020). Participants who have interacted with an LDT platform through a virtual reality experience note that it is helpful to visualise different situations, their consequences and the associated planning process. Furthermore, the concreteness and transparency provided by the digital twin are seen as two main advantages of the virtual model identified as important in future interaction processes between citizens and local authorities (Deckert et al., 2020).

LDTs also have *limitations*. The validity of the LDT policy outcomes depends on the quality and accessibility of the available data and metadata, the accuracy and tuning of the simulation models on the terrain, the accumulated effects of modelling assumptions and the expertise of subject matter experts and data scientists. An uneven spread of data literacy amongst citizens and societal groups can lead to an uneven spread of information and knowledge. Translating LDT policy outcomes into evidence-based stories to enlighten different interpretations of results targeted to citizen groups can be part of more social equality and contribute to a 'just city'. Maybe the most important limitation of an LDT is that, as Shannon Mattern mentions, a lot of urban intelligence cannot be stored and processed in an information system: "Just as important as the data stored and accessed on city servers, in archival boxes, on library shelves and museum walls are the forms of urban intelligence that cannot be easily contained, framed, and catalogued". D'onofrio et al. (2019) describe urban intelligence as the cognitive intelligence of the city. A network based on individual intelligences (humans, electronic devices, etc.) creates unique and valuable insights from the city to foster its development.

We need to ask: what place-based 'information' doesn't fit on a shelf or in a database? What are the non-textual, unrecordable forms of cultural memory? These questions are especially relevant for marginalised populations, indigenous cultures, and developing nations. Performance studies urge to acknowledge ephemeral, performative forms of knowledge, such as dance, ritual, cooking, sports, and speech. These forms cannot be reduced to 'information,' nor can they be 'processed' (Mattern, 2017).

## 3.8 Conclusions

Local Digital Twins (LDTs) may be unique compared to other decision-making solutions in the way they support smart city-related and policy-related decisions by unlocking evidence-informed policy experimentation and decision support. They enable the testing of complex long-term decisions in a safe and collaborative environment.

Warren Buffet's phrase: "It's good to learn from your mistakes. It's better to learn from other people's mistakes", can be translated for the LDT into "It's good to learn from mistakes in the physical city, but it's better to learn from failures in the digital city". Failing in real life is often very impactful, but failing in the virtual world has less associated pain. Van Heeswijk (2021) sees a Digital City Twin (DCT) as a virtual proxy where you can test numerous decisions and run many scenarios to observe how their impacts unfold. The direct outcome of an LDT lies in its evidence-based outcomes leading to smart city-related and living environment-related policy decisions. From an analysis perspective, LDTs have shown to be useful for exploratory analysis via data visualisation on a 2D or 3D map and dashboard and can contribute to a descriptive and diagnostic analysis by providing aggregated insights. The use of multiple (combined) simulation models made advanced predictive analysis possible. Using an LDT for prescriptive analyses to get the desired result is new to LDTs and demands high-quality data, models and analytical insights.

An LDT contributes not only to the policy design phase but can also influence policy implementation and evaluation phase. It can be used for co-creation, citizen involvement, and the creation of citizen-oriented smart city solutions to achieve a more 'just city'. Compared to ICCC (Integrated Command and Control Centres), which focus on operational management, an LDT delivers a more long-term strategic and affordable instrument useful for policy domain and government-level decision-making.

Because of their complexity, LDTs also have some limitations related to the availability of information and knowledge, the lack of integrated urban intelligence, and limited experience with integrated co-design and co-decision approaches, among other things. The outcomes of an LDT are still dependent on the accuracy of available data; the simulation models used, local terrain, and expert knowledge. Governance strategies are needed to ensure that not only frontrunners are involved and take advantage of LDTs but also that a larger group of followers is supported and able to realise useful LDT use cases. The use of exploratory dashboards, easily accessible storytelling tools, and easy-to-interpret visuals are part of the solution that needs further exploration.

Last but not least, it is crucial to be aware that a lot of so-called 'urban intelligence' can't be stored in an LDT, processed by simulation models and considered in an LDT. The human interpretation of the evidence created by an LDT will always be crucial during policy experimentation and the entire policy-making process.

## References

Arnstein, S. R. (1969). A ladder of citizen participation. *Journal of the American Institute of Planners, 35*(4), 216–224. https://doi.org/10.1080/01944366908977225

Bai, X., McPhearson, T., Cleugh, H., Nagendra, H., Tong, X., & Zhu, T. (2017). Linking urbanization and the environment: conceptual and empirical advances. *Annual Review of Environment and Resources*. https://doi.org/10.1146/annurev-environ-102016-061128

Bansard, J. S., Hickmann, T., & Kern, K. (2019). Pathways to urban sustainability: How science can contribute to sustainable development in cities. *Gaia, 28*(2), 112–118. https://doi.org/10.14512/gaia.28.2.9

Cartas, C. F., Gavrilut, L., Koundouri, P., Markianidou, P., Mulquin, M., Munné, R., Mureddu, F., van Ooijen, C., Mc Alleer, S., Paic, A., Sanmartín, J. M., Sgouros, N., Silence, J., & Willems, M. (2022). *Data driven policy cluster—Policy prediction, the future of evidence-based policymaking? How data and converging technologies impact agenda setting and policy design*. Policy Cloud, DUET, AI4PublicPolicy, Intelcomp, Decido Project Consortia. https://www.decido-project.eu/wp-content/uploads/2022/04/POLICY_CLOUD_Policy_Prediction_WEB_Mar2022.pdf

Castelnovo, W. (2018). Coproduction and cocreation in smart city initiatives: An exploratory study. In M. P. Rodríguez Bolívar & L. Alcaide Muñoz (Eds.), *E-participation in smart cities: Technologies and models of governance for citizen engagement* (pp. 1–20). Springer International Publishing. https://doi.org/10.1007/978-3-319-89474-4_1

Castro, G. D. R., Fernandez, M. C. G., & Colsa, A. U. (2021). Unleashing the convergence amid digitalization and sustainability towards pursuing the sustainable development goals (SDGs): A holistic review. *Journal of Cleaner Production, 280*. https://doi.org/10.1016/j.jclepro.2020.122204

Cocchia, A. (2014). Smart and digital city: A systematic literature review. In *Smart city* (pp. 13–43). Springer International Publishing. https://doi.org/10.1007/978-3-319-06160-3_2

Concilio, G., & Pucci, P. (2021). The data shake: An opportunity for experiment-driven policy making. In *The data shake: Opportunities and obstacles for urban policy making*. Springer Nature. https://link.springer.com/chapter/10.1007/978-3-030-63693-7_1

Concilio, G., Pucci, P., Vecchio, G., & Lanza, G. (2019). Big data and policy making: Between real time management and the experimental dimension of policies. In *Computational science and its applications—ICCSA 2019* (pp. 191–202). Springer International Publishing. https://doi.org/10.1007/978-3-030-24296-1_17

Cowley, R., Joss, S., & Dayot, Y. (2017). The smart city and its publics: Insights from across six UK cities. *Urban Research and Practice, 11*(1), 53–77. https://doi.org/10.1080/17535069.2017.1293150

D'Hauwers, R., Walravens, N., & Ballon, P. (2021). *From an inside-in towards an outside-out urban digital twin: Business models and implementation challenges* (pp. 25–32). ISPRS Annals of the Photogrammetry Remote Sensing and Spatial Information Sciences, VIII-4/W1-2021. https://doi.org/10.5194/isprs-annals-VIII-4-W1-2021-25-2021

D'Ignazio, C., & Bhargava, R. (2015). *Approaches to building big data literacy*. MIT Media Lab. https://www.media.mit.edu/publications/approaches-to-building-big-data-literacy/

D'Onofrio, S., Habenstein, A., & Portmann, E. (2019). Ontological design for cognitive cities: The new principle for future urban management. In *Driving the development, management, and sustainability of cognitive cities* (pp. 183–211). IGI Global. https://www.igi-global.com/book/driving-development-management-sustainability-cognitive/214076

De Gennaro, M., Paffumi, E., & Martini, G. (2016). Big data for supporting low-carbon road transport policies in Europe: Applications, challenges and opportunities. *Big Data Research, 6*, 11–25. https://doi.org/10.1016/j.bdr.2016.04.003

de Oliveira, Á., Campolargo, M., & Martins, M. (2015). Constructing human smart cities. In *Communications in computer and information science* (pp. 32–49). Springer International Publishing. https://doi.org/10.1007/978-3-319-27753-0_3

Deckert, A., Dembski, F., Ulmer, F., Ruddat, M., & Wössner, U. (2020). Chapter 9—Digital tools in stakeholder participation for the German energy transition. Can digital tools improve participation and its outcome? The paper results of the authors' collaboration in the Reallabor Stadt:quartiere 4.0 ("Living Lab: City Districts 4.0"). In O. Renn, F. Ulmer, & A. Deckert (Eds.), *The role of public participation in energy transitions* (pp. 161–177). Academic. https://www.sciencedirect.com/science/article/pii/B978012819515400009X

Dembski, F., Wössner, U., Letzgus, M., Ruddat, M., & Yamu, C. (2020). Urban digital twins for smart cities and citizens: The case study of Herrenberg, Germany. *Sustainability, 12*(6), 2307. https://doi.org/10.3390/su12062307

Deng, T., Zhang, K., Shen, Z.-J., & (Max). (2021). A systematic review of a digital twin city: A new pattern of urban governance toward smart cities. *Journal of Management Science and Engineering, 6*(2), 125–134. https://doi.org/10.1016/j.jmse.2021.03.003

Directive (EU) 2013/37/EU of the European Parliament and of the Council of 26 June 2013 amending Directive 2003/98/EC on the re-use of public sector information text with EEA relevance, (2013). https://eur-lex.europa.eu/eli/dir/2013/37/oj

Directive (EU) 2019/1024 of the European Parliament and of the Council of 20 June 2019 on open data and the re-use of public sector information (recast), Pub. L. No. L 172/56, EUR-Lex (2019). https://eur-lex.europa.eu/legal-content/EN/TXT/?uri=celex%3A32019L1024

DUET. (2020a). D2.2 scenario specifications of the DUET solution. In *Corids EU research results*. DUET Consortium. https://cordis.europa.eu/project/id/870697/results

DUET. (2020b). D2.3 final list of user requirements for the DUET solution. In *Cordis EU research results*. DUET Consortium. https://cordis.europa.eu/project/id/870697/results

Esri. (2022). *Map viewer*. ArcGIS Developers. https://developers.arcgis.com/documentation/mapping-apis-and-services/tools/mapviewer/

EU DG Connect. (2022, March 31). Workshop—Local digital twins technology. Shaping Europe's Digital Future. https://digital-strategy.ec.europa.eu/en/events/workshop-local-digital-twins-technology

European Commission. (2013). Guide to social innovation. European Commission. https://ec.europa.eu/regional_policy/en/information/publications/guides/2013/guide-to-social-innovation

Fainstein, S. S. (2014). The just city. *International Journal of Urban Sciences, 18*(1), 1–18. https://doi.org/10.1080/12265934.2013.834643

Healey, P. (2003). Collaborative planning in perspective. *Planning Theory, 2*(2), 101–123. https://doi.org/10.1177/14730952030022002

HM Treasury. (2020). *Magenta book*. Central Government guidance on evaluation. https://assets.publishing.service.gov.uk/government/uploads/system/uploads/attachment_data/file/879438/HMT_Magenta_Book.pdf

HM Treasury. (2022). *The green book, central government guidance on appraisal and evaluation*. HM Treasury UK. https://assets.publishing.service.gov.uk/government/uploads/system/uploads/attachment_data/file/1063330/Green_Book_2022.pdf

Janssen, M., & Helbig, N. (2018). Innovating and changing the policy-cycle: Policy-makers be prepared! *Government Information Quarterly, 35*(4), S99–S105. https://doi.org/10.1016/j.giq.2015.11.009

Janssen, M., & Zuiderwijk, A. (2014). Infomediary business models for connecting open data providers and users. *Social Science Computer Review, 32*(5), 694–711. https://doi.org/10.1177/0894439314525902

Janssen, M., Charalabidis, Y., & Zuiderwijk, A. (2012). Benefits, adoption barriers and myths of open data and open government. *Information Systems Management, 29*(4), 258–268. https://doi.org/10.1080/10580530.2012.716740

Jarmin, R. S., & O'Hara, A. B. (2016). Big data and the transformation of public policy analysis. *Journal of Policy Analysis and Management, 35*(3), 715–721. https://doi.org/10.1002/pam.21925

Kambil, A., Ginsberg, A., & Bloch, M. (1996). Re-inventing value propositions. In *Stern working papers*. Stern University School of Business. http://kambil.com/wp-content/uploads/PDF/Value_paper.pdf

Kambil, A., Friesen, B. G., & Sundaram, A. (1999). *Co-creation: a new source of value*. Outlook, Number 2.

Leydesdorff, L. (2011). The triple helix, quadruple helix, ..., and an n-tuple of helices: Explanatory models for analyzing the knowledge-based economy? *Journal of the Knowledge Economy, 3*(1), 25–35. https://doi.org/10.1007/s13132-011-0049-4

Lim, C., Kim, K.-J., & Maglio, P. P. (2018). Smart cities with big data: Reference models, challenges, and considerations. *Cities, 82*, 86–99. https://doi.org/10.1016/j.cities.2018.04.011

Lohman, W., Cornelissen, H., Borst, J., Klerkx, R., Araghi, Y., & Walraven, E. (2023). Building digital twins of cities using the Inter Model Broker framework. *Future Generation Computer Systems, 148*, 501–513. https://doi.org/10.1016/j.future.2023.06.024

MacLeod, M., & Davidson, E. (2007). *Organizational storytelling and technology innovation*. 2007 40th Annual Hawaii International Conference on System Sciences (HICSS'07). https://doi.org/10.1109/hicss.2007.420

Manchester, H., & Cope, G. (2019). Learning to be a smart citizen. *Oxford Review of Education, 45*(2), 224–241. https://doi.org/10.1080/03054985.2018.1552582

Mannaro, K., Baralla, G., & Garau, C. (2018). A goal-oriented framework for analyzing and modeling city dashboards in smart cities. In *Smart and sustainable planning for cities and regions* (pp. 179–195). Springer International Publishing. https://doi.org/10.1007/978-3-319-75774-2_13

Marcucci, E., Gatta, V., Le Pira, M., Hansson, L., & Bråthen, S. (2020). Digital twins: A critical discussion on their potential for supporting policy-making and planning in urban logistics. *Sustainable Forestry, 12*(24), 10623. https://doi.org/10.3390/su122410623

Mattern, S. (2017). *A city is not a computer*. Places Journal, 2017. https://doi.org/10.22269/170207

Mergel, I., Edelmann, N., & Haug, N. (2019). Defining digital transformation: Results from expert interviews. *Government Information Quarterly, 36*(4), 101385. https://doi.org/10.1016/j.giq.2019.06.002

Miskinis, C. (2019, March 18). *Why digital twin is an essential tool for smart cities*. Challenge Advisory. https://www.challenge.org/insights/digital-twins-and-smart-cities/

Morozov, E., & Bria, F. (2018). *Rethinking the smart city: Democratizing Urban Technology*. Rosa Luxemburg Stiftung. https://onlineopen.org/media/article/583/open_essay_2018_morozov_rethinking.pdf

Nochta, T., Badstuber, N., & Wahby, N. (2019, June 1). *On the governance of city digital twins*. Insights from the Cambridge Case Study. https://www.repository.cam.ac.uk/handle/1810/293984

Ordonez-Ponce, E., Clarke, A., & MacDonald, A. (2021). Business contributions to the sustainable development goals through community sustainability partnerships. *Sustainability Accounting, Management and Policy Journal, 12*(6), 1239–1267. https://doi.org/10.1108/sampj-03-2020-0068

Praharaj, S. (2019). Development challenges for big data command and control centres for smart cities in India. In *Data-driven multivalence in the built environment* (pp. 75–90). Springer International Publishing. https://doi.org/10.1007/978-3-030-12180-8_4

Ribeiro, C. (2021, October 13). *Local digital twins: Forging the cities of tomorrow*. Eltis. https://digital-strategy.ec.europa.eu/en/library/local-digital-twins-forging-cities-tomorrow

Rodriguez Müller, A. P. (2021). Making smart cities "smarter" through ict-enabled citizen coproduction. In *Handbook of smart cities* (pp. 1–21). Springer International Publishing. https://doi.org/10.1007/978-3-030-15145-4_63-1

Satorras, M., Ruiz-Mallén, I., Monterde, A., & March, H. (2020). Co-production of urban climate planning: Insights from the Barcelona climate plan. *Cities, 106*, 102887. https://doi.org/10.1016/j.cities.2020.102887

Suakanto, S., Supangkat, S. H., Suhardi, & Saragih, R. (2013, June). Smart city dashboard for integrating various data of sensor networks. *International Conference on ICT for Smart Society*. https://doi.org/10.1109/ictss.2013.6588063

Temmerman, L., & Van den Broeck, W. (2021, September 7). *The decolonisation of the smart city through degrowth and serendipity*. 2021 IEEE International Smart Cities Conference (ISC2). https://doi.org/10.1109/isc253183.2021.9562902

TNO. (n.d.). *The healthy city: Accessible, safe and vibrant—Visualising information with urban strategy*. TNO Innovation for Life. Retrieved June 13, 2024. https://www.tno.nl/en/digital/smart-traffic-transport/societal-impact/healthy-city-accessible-safe-vital/

van Heeswijk, W. (2021, November 7). Need help making decisions? Ask your digital twin! Medium—Towards Data Science. https://towardsdatascience.com/need-help-making-decisions-ask-your-digital-twin-6e4cf328cb0

Verstraete, J., Acar, F., Concilio, G., & Pucci, P. (2021). Turning data into actionable policy insights. In *The data shake* (pp. 73–89). Springer International Publishing. https://doi.org/10.1007/978-3-030-63693-7_6

# Chapter 4
# Local Digital Twins: A Central Urban Integrator to Break Down the Silos

**Tanguy Coenen, Maxim Chantillon, Ingrid Croket, and Lieven Raes**

**Contents**



## 4.1 Introduction

This chapter approaches urban digital twins and Local Digital Twins (LDT) as data driven decision-support systems, as defined by Jones et al. in 2020. The main focus is on the role an LDT can play as a central urban integrator that allows public administrations to connect data from various policy fields by making use of different technologies, with the overall objective of strengthening data driven and evidence-based decision-making. Given the urban dimension, the LDT focuses on local (incl. Sub-local, e.g., districts) public administrations and the use of the LDT in its local application context. The integrator dimension refers to the so-called system-of-systems (SoS) view on LDTs: an LDT consists of "large-scale integrated systems which are heterogeneous and independently operable on their own, networked together for a common goal" (Altamiranda & Colina, 2019; Jamshidi, 2005, 2008). The LDT consists of various heterogeneous systems, delivering


T. Coenen (✉) · M. Chantillon · I. Croket
Interuniversitair Micro-Elektronica Centrum, Leuven, Belgium
e-mail: tanguy.coenen@imec.be; maxim.chantillon@imec.be; ingrid.croket@imec.be

L. Raes
Digital Flanders, Brussels, Belgium
e-mail: lieven.raes@vlaanderen.be





L. Raes et al. (eds.), *Decide Better*,
https://doi.org/10.1007/978-3-031-81451-8_4

domain-specific information to the local context. The specific value of an LDT lies thus in the connection that it makes between those different systems and related data to support domain-overarching and cross-silo policy-making. This chapter starts by understanding local data driven policy-making and how the concept of an LDT connects to policy-making, followed by the adopted methodological approach. After that, the policymakers' meta-requirements (MR) and meta-features (MF) of an LDT are detailed. The MF address the various MR conceptualised through the SoS paradigm.

## 4.2 Local Data Driven Policy-Making

Whether national, regional, or local, public administrations are responsible for policy and decision-making in conjunction with political decision-makers. This process is a policy cycle with several phases (Howlett & Ramesh, 2009, 2020). The following phases can be distinguished (Höchtl et al., 2016): agenda setting, policy discussion, policy simulation, policy acceptance, provision of means, implementation and evaluation. Figure 4.1 visualises how the LDT can interact with policy-making, whereby the LDT is more relevant to some phases than others. In the policy discussion, simulation and acceptance phases, the LDT can guide the discussion

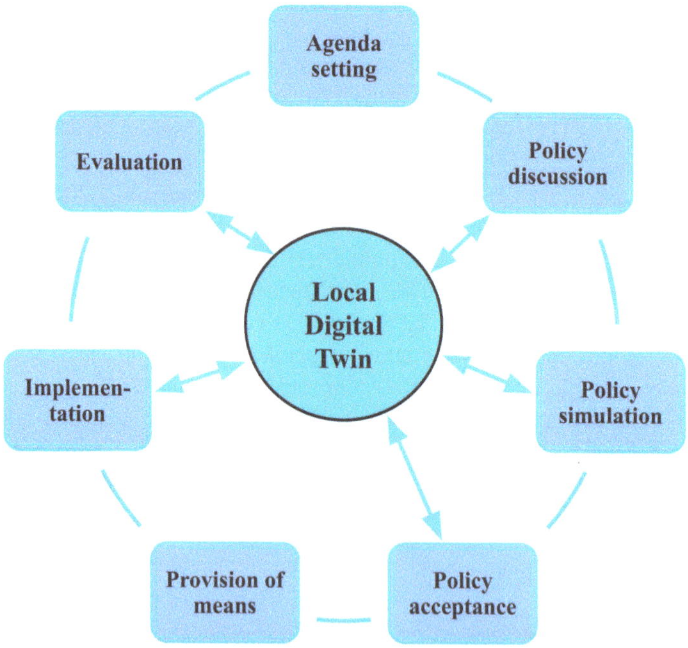


**Fig. 4.1** Connecting the policy cycle and the LDT

and provide a grounded basis for decision-making. In the evaluation phase, the LDT can provide the necessary analytical evaluation of the effects of the policy intervention.

When public administrations make policy decisions, they typically follow a policy cycle. This cycle should be considered when linking decision-making to the concepts of LDTs and the physical environment, which we will call the physical twin. The physical twin represents the 'real-world' physical environment affected by decisions based on the LDT. This physical environment is a complex mix of various interacting factors that span different public administration departments, such as mobility, climate, and urban planning. Because the physical twin involves these interconnected domains, the LDT must also represent this complexity. The LDT aims to be a digital replica of the physical environment, so it needs to integrate across the different domains managed by separate administrative departments. Only by doing so can the LDT accurately reflect the physical twin. Figure 4.2 illustrates how the physical twin, LDT, and policy-making processes interact.

Introducing an LDT in the policy cycle aims to ensure that data insights from different domains can underpin policy. Thus, LDTs support both administrative and political actors active in the policy cycle, creating public value for those impacted by policy actions and decisions. The support of an LDT in policy-making to create public value is based on the objective of public administration to strive towards evidence-based policy-making (Brindis & Macfarlane, 2019; Chantillon, 2023; Luthfi & Janssen, 2019).

Data is assumed to lead to evidence to be used in policy-making and that policy-making is a rational process. However, policy-making is not a purely rational process but one of 'bounded rationality'. Indeed, the intentions for rational policy-making might be present, but several factors create boundaries within which a decision is made, often decreasing the ability for rationality (Cairney, 2016; Honig & Coburn, 2008; van der Voort et al., 2019). LDTs interact with a complex ecosystem that does not follow rationality. However, an LDT, because of its focus on rational data and modelling, can provide evidence to feed into the policy cycle that local administrations follow. From this point of view, the LDT

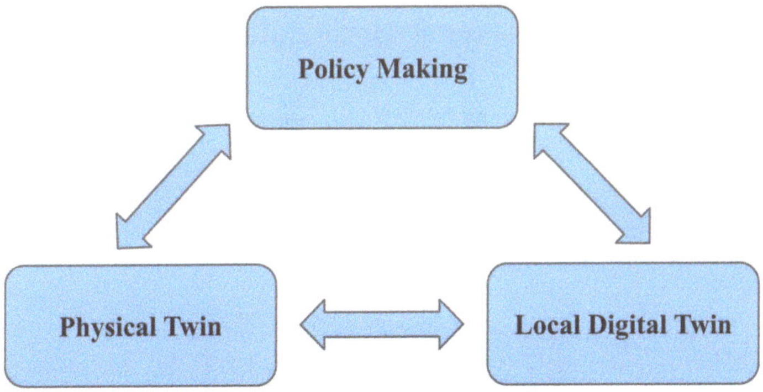


**Fig. 4.2** Interaction between policy-making, physical twin and LDT

can be conducive to experiments whereby policymakers will have requirements modelled in an LDT, potentially impacting policy-making and the state of the physical twin.

"An LDT is not a single technological concept; it is not a specific technology, but an idea that can be implemented with many advanced technologies." (Liu et al., 2021). Instead, an LDT can be viewed as a technological paradigm that many other technologies can fulfil. Compare LDTs to Enterprise Resource Planning (ERP) systems, for example. Implementing ERP systems in individual organisations, public or private, depends on the processes required when managing 'resources' that need to be 'planned'. Also, many different vendors of ERP systems exist that deliver ERP 'engines' that need to interact with each other. Taking ERP systems as an analogy, LDTs are being applied in many ways and via many different components to the policy-making challenges of local administrations, regions and countries. As a result, taking a high-level perspective of the requirements and features common to LDT implementations, as covered in this paper, can shed light on what LDTs offer.

## 4.3 Methodology

This chapter's structure is rooted in the field of Design Science Research. First, we will derive MR for LDTs. MR address a class of information systems, hence the term 'meta' (Walls et al., 1992). This approach is particularly appropriate for LDTs, as the concept of a digital twin does not generally point to a specific technological setup but rather an 'idea' or a loose coupling of an interacting SoS. Therefore, it is relevant and necessary to specify MR that apply to all possible implementations of the LDT concept. After discussing the MR, we will provide insights into the design of LDTs by proposing MF, which define the necessary components to deliver the MR, i.e., the functionalities expected from an LDT user.

## 4.4 Meta-Requirements for Experimental Policy-Making

In this section, we define MR representing the overarching needs of policymakers towards an LDT about policy-making and the physical twin. The MR can be considered user requirements derived from the role of a policymaker as the user of an LDT and as an actor in the process called policy-making, as described in Sect. 4.2. The MR we discuss in this section are the results of a 5-year LDT research and development work.

As part of this work, eight different research and innovation projects were executed in which requirements were gathered for an LDT. All the projects have a cross-domain basis that aligns with the conceptual meaning of an LDT. The list reflects the requirements gathered and bundled together at a higher level of abstraction. We did not perform an ex-post qualitative or quantitative analysis of the total requirements-gathering effort of each LDT project. As a result, we cannot claim that the presented list is an entirely accurate representation. However, we are confident that it represents the main requirements that end-users had about LDTs at the time of writing.

While an LDT can also be relevant for other actors or interaction among various actors, such as citizens, businesses, researchers and local policymakers, the focus here lies on policymakers. Indeed, an LDT is, in the first place, a tool that supports the policy cycle, which administrations can open to other actors such as citizens, businesses or researchers. The different MR are presented here and listed in Fig. 4.3. They follow the two main modes we see for LDTs: descriptive or predictive. In the explanatory mode, the LDT describes in real-time or historically what is happening in the physical twin. In predictive mode, the LDT provides insights into how the state of the physical twin will evolve in the future. The time interval over which the prediction takes place can be short (seconds, minutes, hours) or long (days, weeks, years).

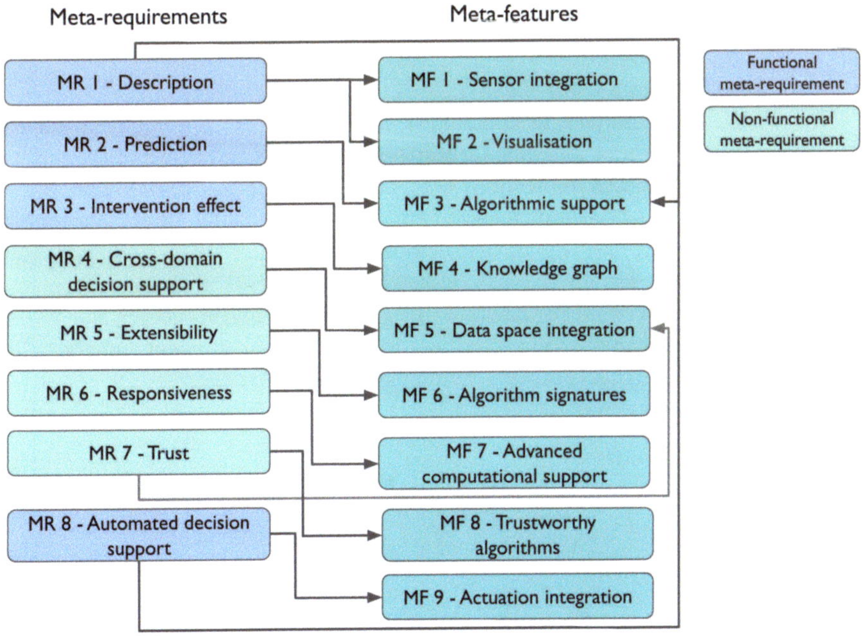


**Fig. 4.3** Overview of LDT meta-requirements and associated LDT features

To demonstrate the reason for the MR in real life, we have illustrated each with an implementation example from three LDT projects—the digital twin of Bruges,[1] PRECINCT[2] and URBANAGE.[3]

**Digital Twin of Bruges, Belgium (2020–2023)**
The objective of the digital twin of Bruges project was to enhance decision-making processes for the City of Bruges by creating and utilising a data driven LDT for policy impact exploration and experimentation. The LDT was designed with three main goals in mind. Firstly, it aimed to enable city managers, citizens, and businesses from different domains to explore and understand issues easily through a common visual platform. This approach would lead to more effective and trustworthy longer-term policy decisions. Secondly, the LDT provided real-time overviews of various city parameters to assess the impact of interventions. Lastly, the LDT aimed to aggregate cross-domain data to assist policy-making teams in planning and making decisions and hence demonstrate how an LDT helps to break down silo barriers, increase data quality, shorten the decision-making process, and enhance efficiency by bringing together data and people to tackle cross-domain issues. The digital twin of Bruges was implemented to demonstrate specific use cases for the City of Bruges.

**PRECINCT Project (2021–2023)**
The PRECINCT project (Preparedness and Resilience Enforcement for Critical Infrastructure Cascading Cyberphysical Threats and Effects focusing on district or regional protection) was developed for the Living Lab of Antwerp. It focused on implementing early warning systems to prevent the impact of flooding. The digital twin was used to evaluate flood predictions' impact and demonstrate the cascading effects on critical infrastructure. Different scenarios could be elaborated, describing possible mitigating actions for the local emergency services as input for the local government and emergency services to define a desired action plan.

[1] https://www.imec.be/nl/press/stad-brugge-ontwikkelt-digitale-tweeling

[2] Preparedness and Resilience Enforcement for Critical INfrastructure Cascading Cyberphysical Threats and effects with focus on district or regional protection (PRECINCT), EU H2020 project, https://cordis.europa.eu/project/id/101021668

[3] Enhanced URBAN planning for AGE-friendly cities through disruptive technologies (URBANAGE), H2020 project, https://cordis.europa.eu/project/id/101004590

**URBANAGE Project (2021–2024)**

The goal of the URBANAGE project was to create an ecosystem that made it easier for urban planners, decision-makers, and older adults to better co-design and develop more inclusive, healthier, and happier cities where people can retain their independence for longer. Powerful big data analytical models, citizen co-creation channels, and digital twin capabilities helped people understand the impact of existing and potential planning actions on older generations. As a result, cities can make better evidence-based planning choices to solve real citizen needs and address societal challenges to develop age-friendly cities.

### 4.4.1 MR 1: Description: As an End-User, I Want to Be Able to See the Real-Time/Descriptive State of the Physical Twin as Reflected by the LDT

A first MR is oriented to the possibility of having a digital understanding of the physical reality from a historical point of view and in real-time. Such a real-time understanding of the physical twin in the LDT requires constant data measurements within the physical twin and the continuous processing of data collected in physical reality for input into the LDT. Data must be collected across several policy domains to ensure that the physical twin and policy-making complexity—which encompasses effects in several domains—is supported in the LDT. Only by reflecting on this complexity will a policymaker be able to make sense of the real-time state of the physical twin as reflected by the LDT.

**Case: Digital Twin of Bruges, Belgium**

The digital twin of Bruges provides visual insights into real-time and historical data via a cartographic presentation (see Fig. 4.4) and graph view (see Fig. 4.5). The LDT allowed domain experts in traffic and environment to view historical and real-time data for specific regions in Bruges, enabling them to compare cross-domain data for certain streets. Domain experts in traffic and environment could use the LDT to gain an understanding of measurements from assets they had limited knowledge of, thus enabling them to use and trust the data from those assets.

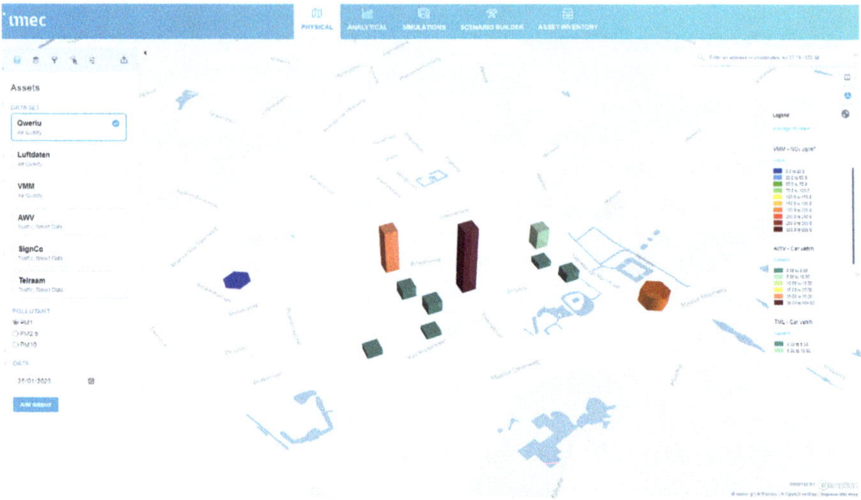


**Fig. 4.4** The Bruges LDT prototype allows the visualisation of three different air quality sources from Qweriu and Luftdaten sensors. The legend allows us to look for the concentrations, which are expressed in the BelAQI index

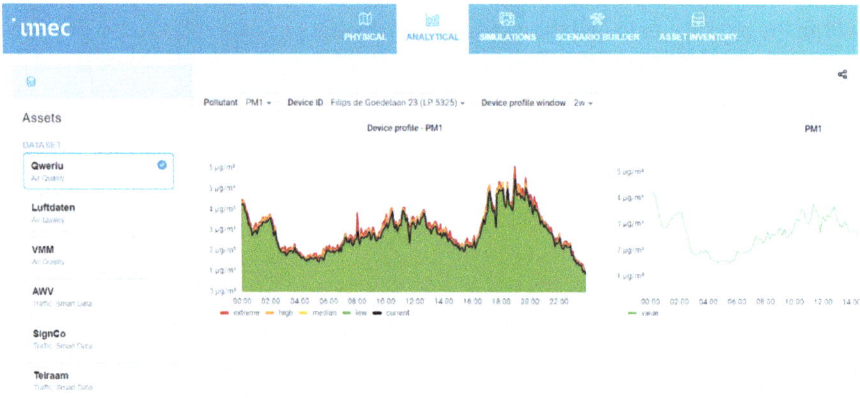


**Fig. 4.5** The Bruges LDT shows the minimum, maximum and mean values for a particular sensor in the selected past two weeks in graphs, allowing the user to put the actual measurement in context

### 4.4.2 *MR 2: Prediction: As an End-User, I Want to Be Able to See the Predicted State of the Physical Twin Within a Future Time Interval of My Choosing*

A second MR for policymakers is the need to understand the state of the physical twin, or physical reality, at a given moment when a current situation continues, without any further intervention from policymakers or other actors. This possibility allows policymakers to understand the consequences of not taking any further policy measures, consequently helping to bring forward arguments on why specific policy actions may be needed. Essential for this MR is the solid predictive ability of the LDT, underpinned by SMART data, algorithm management and data model transparency (Lefever et al., 2023).

**Case: PRECINCT Project**
The LDT environment connects to prediction models trained for a specific purpose. In the case of the PRECINCT project, a flood prediction model was used for the Antwerp region. The digital twin can visualise the nowcasting flood predictions for a specific period based on particular parameters from the model, such as probability and flood height, as visualised in Fig. 4.6. These predictions have a timespan of 2 h. The flood predictions are composed of multiple flood calculations, allowing the formulation of a predicted flood probability. Using the slider to change data variables, the probability of flood prediction can be explored, allowing the user to learn more about predicted flood height probabilities.

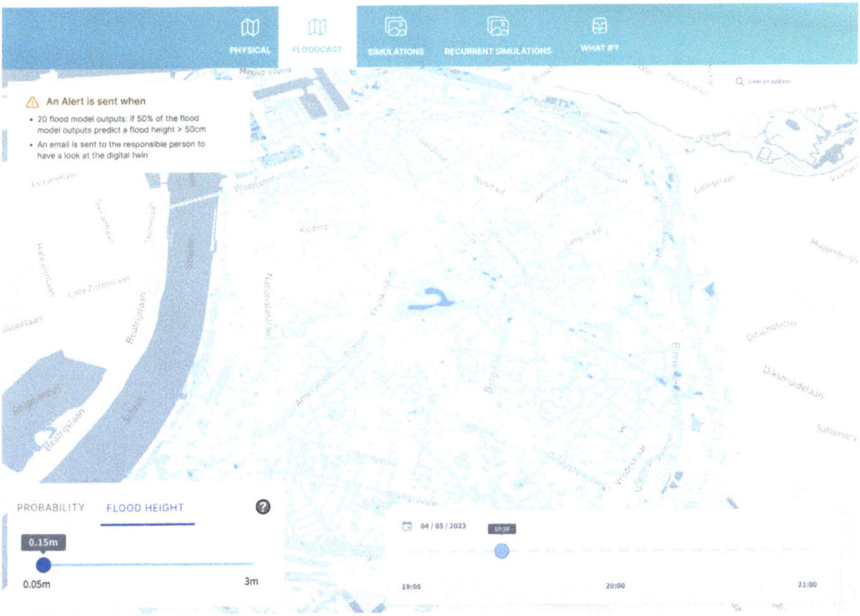


**Fig. 4.6** In the European LDT project PRECINCT, nowcasting flood predictions are shown

### 4.4.3 *MR 3: Intervention Effect: As an End-User, I Want to Be Able to Introduce Changes in the State of the LDT, to Be Able to Understand the Implications of This Change on the Physical Twin*

This third MR builds on MR2. To understand the effect of changes and different scenarios in the LDT on the physical twin, a policymaker will need the ability to make changes and simulate different scenarios in the LDT. Only by having the ability to make changes in the state of the LDT, a policymaker will benefit from the potential that a data driven decision support system like an LDT offers to the different phases of the policy cycle in which a policymaker finds themselves at various moments. This third MR is essential to policymakers in policy discussion and simulation phases.

**Case: Digital Twin of Bruges, Belgium**
The digital twin of Bruges provides scenario management features. The user can change the road infrastructure, such as altering a two-way street to a one-way street. The digital twin shows the traffic impact resulting from an intervention in the area (Fig. 4.7).

**Case: PRECINCT Project**
The PRECINCT digital twin has a feature that allows users to predict what could happen when a particular event occurs. This what-if scenario modelling allows, for example, firefighters or police to reflect on specific situations that may occur as a side-effect of a flood in the city of Antwerp (Fig. 4.8).

**Fig. 4.7** The digital twin of Bruges shows a split screen where you can see the changes in the road infrastructure in the left part and the related data impact on traffic in the right part of the screen

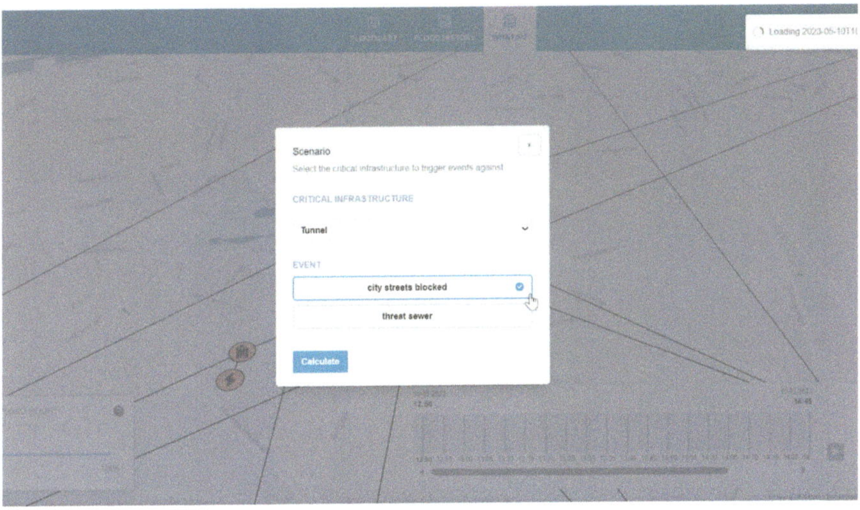


**Fig. 4.8** The what-if scenario tab allows the user to create a scenario. For example, what happens if the city streets around the tunnel are blocked because of the flood. Secondly, what happens to the tunnel if the sewer system is affected because of the flood

### *4.4.4 MR 4: Cross-domain Decision Support: As an End-User, I Want to Be Able to Make Cross-Domain Decisions Via the LDT*

This fourth MR is strongly associated with MR1, which underlines the need for constant data measurements within the physical twin, as well as the constant processing of the data and the input of the data into the LDT. Only by performing data gathering in a variety of policy domains can the complexity of the physical twin be captured in the LDT. This multi-pronged approach allows the policymaker to make policy decisions based on understanding the possible causes and consequences of impact in relation to other policy domains. The specific added value of an LDT is that it combines datasets from differing domains and brings new insights into the combined datasets and algorithms. For example, only an LDT can capture the physical twin reality of mobility regarding the many factors related to air quality, thus enabling a policymaker to improve air quality by utilising multiple data sources to create policy measures.

**Case: Digital Twin of Bruges, Belgium**
The scenario management implemented for the digital twin of Bruges does not only visualise traffic impact for a specific scenario but also the impact on air quality based on the traffic impact. The LDT enables model orchestration whereby the output of the traffic model is used as input for the air quality model (Fig. 4.9).

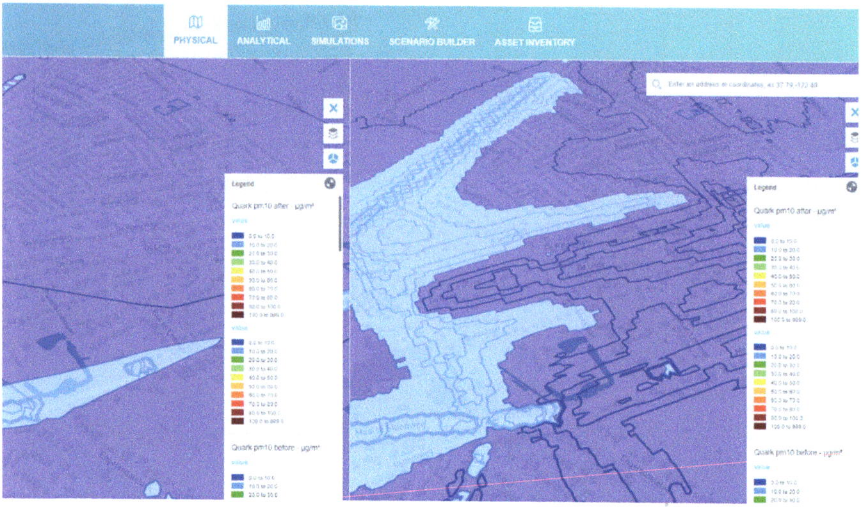


**Fig. 4.9** Presentation of the impact of traffic simulation and associated air quality for a specific scenario: On the left side, the air quality measurements before the intervention are shown, and on the right side, the predicted air quality measurements after the intervention

### *4.4.5 MR 5: Extensibility: As a User, I Want to Be Able to Include Extra Data and Models in the LDT to Extend the Reach of My Policy-Making*

At any point in time, given new developments that pertain to a changing reality, decision-makers may need to make decisions that are related to new domains or to new aspects of a domain that are already included in the LDT. Consequently, an LDT should allow policymakers to integrate new data sources that can be taken into account by the algorithms supporting a decision-making process.

**Case: URBANAGE Project**

In the URBANAGE digital twin, the Green Comfort model is one of the models used to calculate and simulate the perceived age-friendly comfort of the city's locations. Typically, the model uses relevant datasets such as city infrastructure (benches, public restrooms, vegetation, etc.) and health parameters (heat stress, air quality, etc.) as input to calculate a comfort score for the public. However, because comfort is subjective by nature and influenced by different circumstances, such a model must be designed with extensibility.

**Fig. 4.10** The GC model allows the addition of any number of indicators. In this case, the expert added a sub-index 'public_transport_indicator' to influence the Green Comfort (GC) index

The dynamicity of the Green Comfort model allows experts to adapt to changing contexts, for example, by adding new datasets (slipperiness in winter time), removing datasets (street light coverage in high summer), or even changing and combining calculation methods (combining vicinity and number of bus stops in the nearby area). Completely new indicators can also be added by experts based on citizen feedback (littering reports add a penalty to the comfort score). Because the output of any Green Comfort model run is a GeoJSON with features (namely hexagon surface units with scores attached to them), the result can be used as indicator input for another model run (GeoJSON, 2015). This method allows cities to create 'sub-indices' that aggregate and abstract away a logical group of data elements. For example, a new index could be created for 'sitting comfort', which is calculated by using the location of benches, citizen feedback on benches, the presence of shade, etc. These sitting comfort scores can be used as a new indicator in another model run to calculate age-friendliness or Green Comfort in turn (Fig. 4.10).

### 4.4.6 MR 6: Responsiveness: As an End-User, I Want to Get the Results of My Interactions with the LDT Within a Time Interval That Is Acceptable to Me

A sixth MR is focused on the time required for the LDT to deliver input for the policy-making process as a result of interaction by the end-user with the user interface. As an LDT is a data driven decision support system, not only is the data crucial, but also the algorithms that are transforming the data to increase the understanding of current situations (i.e., MR1—description) or for making statements about possible future scenarios (i.e., MR2—prediction and MR3—intervention effect). The acceptable time interval for a policymaker will depend on the policy domain to which an LDT applies, the specific context within one or multiple related policy domain(s), and the policy cycle stage that an LDT is supporting. For example, a longer time interval for an LDT to deliver results might be acceptable when the development policy is related to long-term urban planning in a policy discussion phase. On the contrary, a shorter time interval is required when making a decision on rerouting traffic in a city centre to counteract negative predictions about air quality the next day. However, it should also be noted that, given the longer-term and thus forward-looking perspective of the LDT in the case of urban planning, the trustworthiness of the prediction may decrease. Furthermore, this aspect of the responsiveness is also connected to the following MR focused on trust, and a differentiation can be made in the responsiveness of the LDT: One might want a quick (synchronised) answer from the LDT, which provides first results but in a rough and less detailed manner, thus being less trustful, and one might also prefer more detailed—and trustworthy—results, taking a longer (asynchronous) calculation time.

**Case: URBANAGE Project**

Experts (and citizens) can create comfort simulation scenarios using a scenario builder. With easy drag and drop, different elements can be added to the location of their choice, allowing them to create a scenario as detailed or superficial as they like. Once satisfied with the scenario, the scenario can be submitted, and the simulation can start. To the user, this is presented as a simple submission action, while the Green Comfort Solution Accelerator handles the full workflow behind the scenes. The scenario with the different parameters is stored, a simulation run is kicked off, and the workflow keeps track of the status. The user can check the simulation run status on screen, and

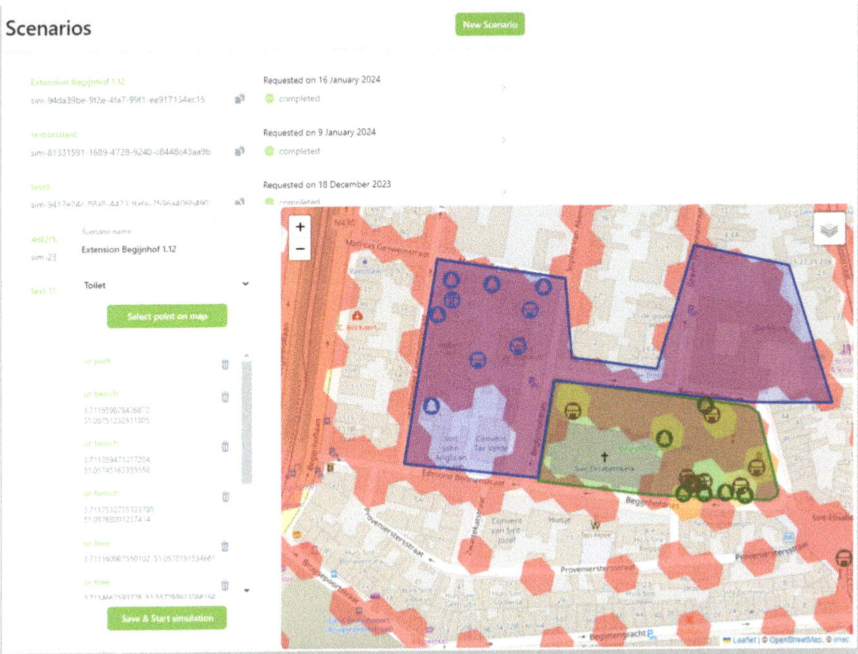


**Fig. 4.11** Users can keep track of simulation runs and their status in their list of scenarios

in a few seconds time (depending on the size and complexity of the scenario), the simulation is marked as complete, and can be reviewed in the URBANAGE digital twin (Fig. 4.11).

### 4.4.7 *MR 7: Trust: As an End-User, I Want to Receive Trustworthy Results from My Interactions with the LDT*

A policymaker needs to be able to trust the outcome of an LDT without necessarily needing a complete technical understanding of how the algorithms that transform the input data lead to descriptions or predictions. Without the necessary trust in the technology and the datasets, a policymaker will not be willing to use an LDT and the insights delivered by an LDT, leading to a lack of LDT uptake in the policy-making process. The differentiation in the meaning of the concept of 'policymaker' is highly relevant. Indeed, a policymaker within an administration can have various purposes, and the LDT can be used as a tool by multiple policymakers, so it should be trustworthy for all. The tool can, for example, be used by specific domain experts who can interpret the data and functioning of the models by relying on their personal expertise. On the other hand, policymakers with a horizontal view of the various policy domains may not have the necessary know-how to make a trustful interpretation of the data and suggestions of the LDT. Furthermore, as an LDT combines various stacked models, which all have a certain degree of uncertainty, it should not be surprising that this stacking leads to potentially lower levels of trustworthy outcomes of the LDT.

It is therefore considered necessary that those making use of the LDT as a tool in support of their work within the administration have a good knowledge of what they aim to use the LDT for. This knowledge will allow them to select relevant input variables, leading to more trustworthy results. Domain-overarching cooperation between experts to elaborate and refine multi-model-based modelling, leading to more tailored and trustful results, is necessary and contributes to organisational culture. Secondly, it might be worth further investigating how a verification or certification of the simulation model output in relation to the actual situation can be undertaken. This kind of verification, which needs to be done by experts within the administration, allows for a higher level of trust and could improve simulation models.

**Case: Digital Twin of Bruges, Belgium**

The LDT is required to register all data types and refer to the data values used in the LDT. This requirement is also relevant for all algorithms or models used, on a technical level to enable technical interoperability and on a user's level to support trustworthiness and explainability (Fig. 4.12).

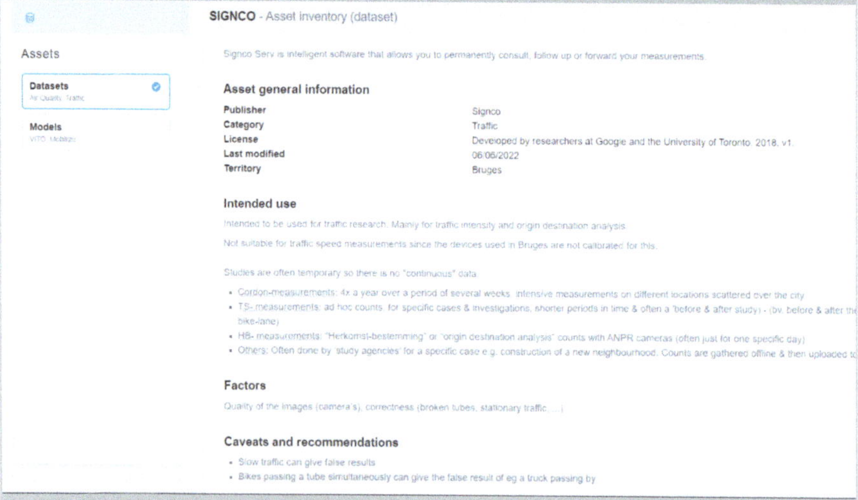


**Fig. 4.12** The asset inventory provides a user access to overall information on the datasets and the models that are used in the LDT

### 4.4.8 MR 8: Automated Decision Support: As an End-User, I Want to Be Able to Make Changes to the LDT That (Semi) Automatically Impact the Physical Twin

A final MR that strongly relies on (1) the trustworthiness of policymakers in an LDT and those being affected by policy-making decisions impacted by an LDT, (2) the degree of politicisation of a policy topic, and (3) the level of automation related to an LDT, is the willingness of policymakers to introduce changes in an LDT, which are then (semi)automatically introduced in the physical twin. Introducing those changes can keep a human in the loop or not. An example of this is related to decision-making on flooding. When, based on predicted rainfall data and water volume data, predictions can be made as to when a water basin will flood. With this predictive foresight the LDT can automatically decide to activate river/canal locks in the physical twin.

**Case: PRECINCT Project**

The PRECINCT project implemented a warning system based upon the outcome of the parameters of a flood model. The digital twin provides live flood predictions for the upcoming two hours, and in case the parameters exceed a predicted flood height and probability, an email alert is sent to the responsible person who can use the digital twin to visualise the predicted impact of high waters on critical infrastructure and run what-if scenarios to define mitigation actions (Fig. 4.13).

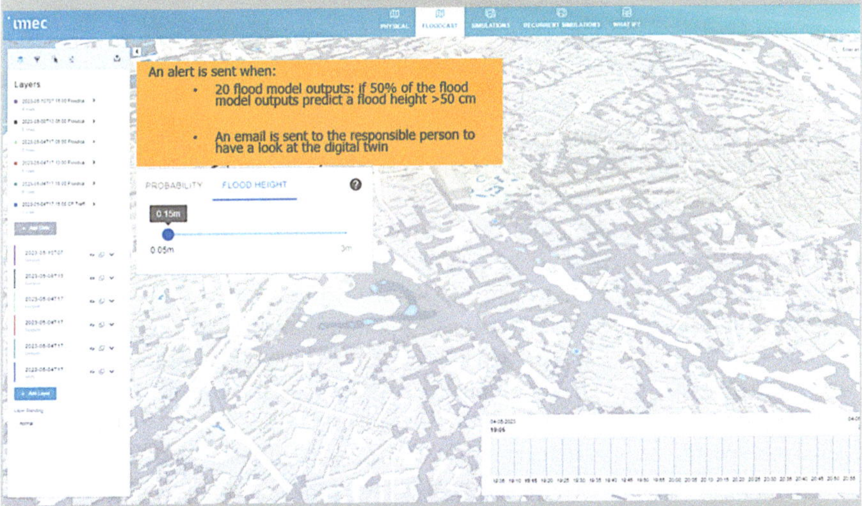


**Fig. 4.13** Based upon pre-defined parameters of predicted flood height and probability, the LDT sends an email to warn of the predicted flood so the LDT can be used to simulate mitigation actions

## 4.5 LDT Meta-Features

Now that we have discussed the MR discerned as relevant to LDTs, we can explore the relation between the MF addressing the MR as depicted in Fig. 4.3.

### 4.5.1 MF 1: Sensor Integration

MR 1 calls for a description of the state of the physical twin based on historical and real-time data. To understand the state of the physical twin, (Internet of Things) IoT sensor deployments are necessary, as they can measure various aspects of the physical twin. Examples of measurements relevant to local decision-making include water volumes, water quality, air quality, greenhouse gas emission, temperature or traffic flows. The type of sensor available determines, to a large extent, the type of data and quality which will be made available to the LDT, which in turn will impact the type of decision-making that can be supported. Storing real-time sensor data produces historical data, which can be used to describe certain aspects of the physical twin that can be insightful to the decision-maker. Still, storing, sending, and parsing historical sensor data can consume a lot of bandwidth and computational resources, which is why working with historical sensor data in the context of an LDT needs careful technical consideration. Not only will data and quality impact the type of decision-making that can be supported, but the overall metadata, particularly the provenance data and the calibration mechanisms, should also be considered.

### 4.5.2 MF 2: Visualisation

To describe the state of the physical twin (MR1), together with the need to measure the state of the physical twin through sensors (MF1) and to provide the policymaker with a trustworthy environment (MR7), a visualisation feature in the LDT is necessary. Among the visualisation sets, two main reference data visualisation sets can be distinguished, which can be brought to the tool user via dashboards, storytelling tools, gamification tools, augmented reality (AR) and virtual reality (VR). The first is Geospatial Information Systems (GIS) and Building Information Modelling (BIM). GIS can be defined as computer-based systems for the integration and analysis of geographic data (Kirby et al., 2017). The focus of GIS lies specifically on spatial data as a subfield of data. To an LDT, GIS is especially relevant, as policy-making is connected to a specific geospatial location (Esri, 2021; Kanani-Sadat et al., 2019).

Examples of policy domains in which location plays a key role are related to transport, the development and management of utility systems, the need to deal with environmental hazards and climate change, and public security (Masser & Crompvoets, 2015). This fact implies the necessity of geospatial data management as a basis for an LDT, and thus its integration with a GIS. Besides GIS, BIM can also be considered as an important reference data visualisation. A BIM refers to "a process by which a digital representation of the physical and functional characteristics of a facility is built, analysed, documented and assessed virtually, then revised iteratively until the optimal model is documented" (Yancinkaya & Adriti, 2013).

### 4.5.3 *MF 3: Algorithmic Support: AI and Non-AI Algorithm Integration*

Algorithms are key to ensuring that the data ingested by the LDT is 'fit-for-purpose' with regard to the type of decision to be supported. By this, we refer to the fact that raw data is almost never sufficient to allow the LDT end-user to make predictions (MR2), obtain the required descriptions (MR1), or make automated decisions (MR8). For example, in its raw form, sensor data (cf. MF1) only represents a single measurement at a single geospatial location and at a specific point in time, which is useless for most decisions. Indeed, policy-ready data is needed (Buongiorno Sottoriva et al., 2022). Such data becomes useful only by grouping multiple sensors and processing them over space and time intervals.

Algorithms must be developed to predict how certain phenomena will evolve and describe what the data looks like at full scale in the physical twin. These can either be based on Artificial Intelligence (AI) concepts (e.g., machine learning) or use approaches that are not typically classified as AI (e.g., support vector machines, decision trees). The field of AI has been making strong advances since 2012, especially in the field of neural networks, where different flavours (e.g. deep neural networks, convolutional neural networks, recurrent neural networks) and variants of these (e.g., long-short term memory, auto-encoders, transformers) can be used to make predictions of how a certain time series (the name given to the type of data produced by a sensor) will evolve in time and how to geospatially interpolate data. The latter is especially relevant to the description MR1, as a sensor reading (e.g., on air quality) at a specific geospatial location does not necessarily indicate how the situation will be at a specific distance from this sensor. However, algorithms that interpolate sensor data and create a reliable geospatial 'heat map', based on discrete sensor data, exist.

### 4.5.4 *MF 4: Knowledge Graph*

Another key feature is a knowledge graph, which is—when implemented—a multi-relational graph consisting of entities (nodes or vertices) and relations (edges). The LDT needs to bring together different data sources in an overall information model to support cross-domain decision-making (MR 4). A knowledge graph can then be used to gather and integrate data and information into a knowledge base (e.g., an ontology) where a 'semantic overlay' is used to map the relationships between different datasets (Privat, 2021). With the knowledge graph, the main advantages of an LDT are reflected by the ability to model and manage heterogeneity, complexity and enable interoperability between elements from different types of city-related data in a dynamic knowledge graph (Akroyd et al., 2021). In order to build a knowledge graph, it is essential that data sources can be mapped onto a unified ontology, preferably based on existing standards within the related domain, so that individual attributes of data sources are semantically described. This will allow the LDT user to find data sources using generic search terms, even if their native formats do not use such terms.

An LDT is an 'evolving' system that must be able to integrate new elements into the 'virtual' replica of the physical twin that are visualised in the knowledge graph. Based on the information from the knowledge graph, the LDT provides the capabilities to perform error detection (finding inconsistencies in the data) but also to contribute to knowledge completion by detecting missing information in the system (Sahlab et al., 2021). The knowledge graph will enable reasoning to derive new knowledge and perform machine learning on an LDT ecosystem, which supports active learning and reasoning, making an LDT Cognitive or Intelligent (Eirinakis et al., 2020).

### *4.5.5 MF 5: Data Space Integration*

MR4 is about the need for cross-domain decision support, pointing to the need to be able to make decisions that pertain to multiple domains at once. As an LDT is a data driven decision support system, this means that data should be available from a variety of domains. This is where data spaces become essential. A data space can be understood as a data ecosystem, defined by a sector or application, whereby decentralised infrastructure enables trustworthy data sharing with commonly agreed capabilities (Nagel, 2021). The essence of a data space are the pre-defined agreements that exist between the members of the organisational ecosystem that participate in the data space, and the aim to share data among each other. These agreements can pertain to the technical, business, or legal aspects of data sharing. The objective is to support 'data sovereignty', which refers to the ability of the data holder (the actor that produces the data) to keep control of the data, i.e., keep it within the location where the holder can control access to it, without transferring it to another location (e.g. another server), where the data holder loses control over the data. This requires a decentralised approach, in which a network of organisations share data along the agreements that have been made in the data space.

A data space is highly valuable in allowing cross-domain decision support in an LDT, as it will reduce the friction that can occur when trying to incorporate various data sets from a variety of organisations or organisational sub-units in the LDT. At the time of writing, two cross-domain efforts were underway to produce the necessary agreement to enable data spaces: the International Data Spaces Association

(IDSA) and Gaia-X. Both provide reference architectures for data spaces associated with open source components for the support of data space operations and data space governance processes. Finally, it must be underlined that data spaces require, on the one hand, data and governance, and on the other hand, SMART data, which can be understood as data that is trusted, contextual, relevant, cognitive, predictive and consumable (Lefever et al., 2023).

### 4.5.6 MF 6: Algorithm Signatures

MR5 is about the extensibility of an LDT to support a variety of physical twin domains as decision support needs to evolve over time. The main MRs that describe the functional needs of an LDT are MR1, MR2 and MR3. Both MR1 and MR2 rely on MF3 (algorithmic support). Being able to extend an LDT is mainly about being able to integrate new algorithms into it. To do this, these algorithms must be able to talk to each other and to the visualisation layer (MF4). This action requires the algorithms to have a 'signature', clearly describing what they need to operate correctly and what they produce. This approach means that model signatures should contain metadata on aspects such as the assumptions they make about the data they ingest, the format and semantics of the input data, the format and semantics of the output data and the quality of the data provided by the algorithm. In the last point, aspects like accuracy or the level of expected bias are essential to understand how well the algorithms can be expected to perform. The former parts, on inputs and outputs of the algorithms, are necessary to build algorithm chains that are needed to make algorithms work together in an LDT. An example would be a flood prediction algorithm that provides inputs to a traffic prediction algorithm on what traffic perturbations can be expected because of rainfall.

### 4.5.7 MF 7: Advanced Computational Support

To execute LDT algorithms in a way that provides the end-user with a response within a relatively brief delay (MR6), High-Performance Computing (HPC) infrastructure can be valuable. Such infrastructure is especially needed for the execution of algorithms that are not built on machine learning paradigms, such as neural networks. For neural network-based approaches, the computational resource required mainly resides in the algorithm's training phase. This activity is not commonly performed as the result of an end-user's request through the user interface but rather periodically and in batch mode. Such algorithm training is typically performed on specialised Graphic Processing Unit (GPU) computational infrastructure. Indeed, the inference tasks (tasks that activate the neural network to produce an output as a result of an input instead of changing its structure through learning) performed by a neural network-based algorithm typically return results within a brief interval, even on modest computational infrastructure. However, many algorithms relevant to LDTs do not use neural networks or other machine learning approaches. Instead, they build on the modelling of processes by human modellers (e.g. an LDT related to spatial planning will be fed by processes initially developed by policymakers, such as urban planning experts). Such models often require solving many mathematical equations before providing a result which fits the HPC infrastructure well. Therefore, especially when using such 'process-oriented' algorithms (which do not have the more energy-efficient inference phase of a neural network algorithm), HPC infrastructure can be necessary to provide the end user with an acceptable user experience, as waiting a long time for an algorithm to return a result can be frustrating and hinder the uptake of LDTs by policymakers. For neural network-based algorithms, HPC featuring GPU or other computational paradigms that accelerate the operations of neural networks (e.g., Google's Tensor Processing Units—TPU) can be very useful in supporting the online retraining of the algorithms.

### *4.5.8 MF 8: Trustworthy Algorithms*

Decision-makers must be able to trust the insights produced by the LDT (MR7) and the algorithms that produce them. According to the EU's 'High-level expert group on AI' (European Commission, 2019), this entails seven key dimensions: (1) Human agency and oversight, (2) Technical robustness and safety, (3) Privacy and data governance, (4) Transparency, (5) Diversity, non-discrimination, and fairness, (6) Societal and environmental well-being, and (7) Accountability.

We will briefly explain each of these dimensions in relation to LDTs. The *first* dimension, 'Human agency and oversight,' refers to ensuring humans retain a degree of oversight over the algorithm. It is not always easy to assess what algorithms learn, and examples exist of AI algorithms learning things that human society does not consider ethical. The *second* 'Technical robustness and safety' dimension requires algorithms to work well consistently. This statement means that they should be accurate and reliable. In case the algorithms should fail, it is necessary to have a fall-back plan. The concern to respect the privacy of datasets and to keep proper oversight over the data being used by the algorithms is the concern of the *third* 'Privacy and data governance' dimension. The *fourth* dimension of 'Transparency' requires the algorithms to provide insights into their operational logic in a way that a human can understand. In addition, it requires the systems built around the algorithm to be transparent towards the end user in indicating that the end user is interacting with an AI. The fact that some algorithms can learn to behave in a way biased towards certain societal groups is a primary concern of the *fifth* 'Diversity, non-discrimination, and fairness' dimension, which helps ensure that the algorithm is accessible by a great population diversity. To achieve trustworthy algorithms, it is necessary to include a large diversity of stakeholders in the algorithm's design and development. The overall societal impact of current and future generations is the concern of the *sixth* 'Societal and environmental well-being' dimension, especially its impact on the environment. Finally, the *seventh* 'Accountability' dimension points to the need, especially for critical applications, to be able to evaluate the performance, design and data of the algorithm and to be able to establish responsibility when things go wrong.

In sum, trustworthy algorithms must respect ethical, governance and technical principles (Floridi & Taddeo, 2016; European Commission, 2019; van Ooijen et al., 2019). Besides respecting these principles, the level of trust required in relation to the desired usage and outcome must be considered by users. For example, the degree of confidence related to the results of specific algorithms is also linked to the 'trust' of the data used for this algorithm. For example, when data is used to understand daily air quality in a specific location, the parameters for determining the reliability of the data will differ from those used when the data is analysed annually for a general overview of the city's air quality.

### *4.5.9 MF 9: Actuation Integration*

Automated decisions (MR8) are only useful if they can be executed automatically. An actuation mechanism is required to make the decision and thus change the state of the physical twin. Examples of actuation mechanisms in everyday life are streetlights, traffic lights and central heaters. In cities, such actuation mechanisms come in multiple forms. More and more actuators will likely be introduced in our cities in the coming years. These could, for example, be drones or automated delivery bots steered over certain routes in real-time that make different types of deliveries, like medical supplies or groceries. This can be done while respecting the state of the physical twin in terms of roadworks, ongoing mass events, etc. Another example could be valves in the sewer system that react in an automated way to flash floods. A traffic-related example are automated traffic lights based on a smart interpretation of the live traffic situation that already exists in some of our cities.

For each actuation example, it is essential to reflect on the fact that they should be 'trustworthy'. Meaning that the decision support and actuation process should be robust and that fall-back mechanisms kick in if the system fails. Human oversight will still be needed to ensure that the system works as intended and, for example, does not learn by itself to perform unintended behaviour. Finally, it must be underscored that these kinds of policy decisions strongly depend on the level of politicisation of the decisions: As the level of politicisation can quickly shift for specific policies, the automation of policy decisions can be considered potentially hazardous by policymakers (Chinn et al., 2020; de Brujin et al., 2022).

### 4.5.10 The System-of-Systems Paradigm

As demonstrated, policymakers will have several demands or needs regarding an LDT. These have been defined via the eight MR, and those MR can be addressed via MF. The different MF demonstrate that an LDT can be considered to consist of various systems. An LDT is where an integration of different systems has to take place, whereby the concept of an SoS comes into play. Indeed, an LDT can be considered to consist of "large-scale integrated systems which are heterogeneous and independently operable on their own, networked together for a common goal" (Altamiranda & Colina, 2019; Lin et al., 2023). This logic implies that the functionality in the overall system results from interactions between several operationally and managerially independent systems that cover specific domains or topics. Contributing to the purpose of an LDT addressing cross-domain systems and issues, every system follows its objectives (Klein & Van Vliet, 2013). Still, the sum of the entire system is more significant than that of the individual systems. The various systems composing an LDT can also be used for purposes other than serving the LDT and integration with other systems. The SoS paradigm allows us to define five systems that, when working together, produce the core added value of an LDT (see Fig. 4.13):

- *IoT system:* addresses MF1 and MF9
- *Visualisation systems:* Addresses MF2
- *Data space system:* Addresses MF5
- *Algorithm and data management system:* Addresses MF3, MF6, MF7, MF8
- *Scenario building system:* Addresses MF4

Figure 4.14 is a complex scheme containing many interrelationships between all the constituting parts of an LDT ecosystem, including MR, MF and systems. The figure reflects the complex nature of LDTs as a decision support system, including the interrelations between MR and MF an LDT toolset must support.

Figure 4.14 lies at the root of the reference architecture (described in Chaps. 5 and 6), which also explains the SoS principle for an LDT. The architecture covers various SoS elements as depicted above. Figure 4.14 and the reference architecture drawings are based on the findings of several research projects and studies, including DUET,[4] URBANAGE, PRECINCT, the digital twin of Bruges, and the LDT Toolbox (European Commission, 2023) and forms a fundament for the development of future LDTs.

[4] Digital Urban European Twins (DUET), EU H2020 project, https://cordis.europa.eu/project/id/870697

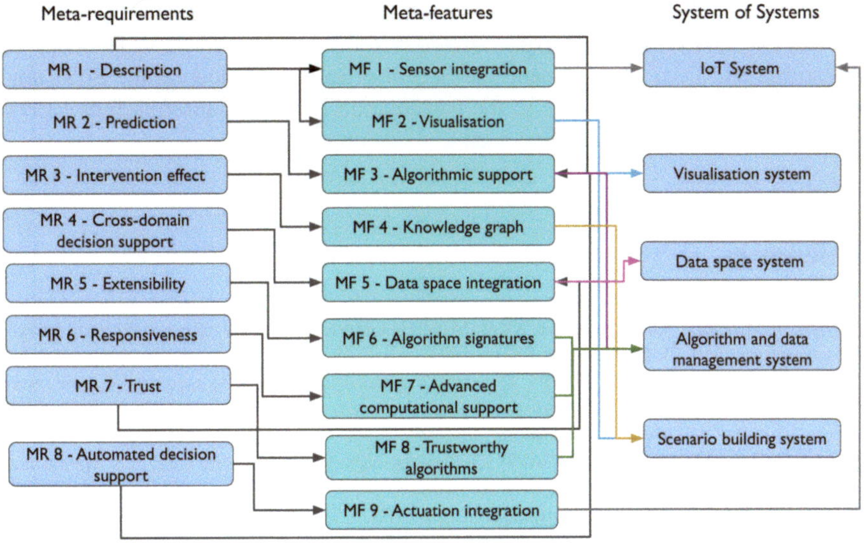


**Fig. 4.14** The LDT as a SoS

## 4.6 Conclusion

This chapter provided an understanding of a Local Digital Twin (LDT) as a system-of-systems (SoS), exploring its characteristics from the perspective of meta-requirements (MR) and meta-features (MF). The authors looked into the connection between an LDT, the physical twin, and policy-making in the context of local public administrations. The policy cycle is crucial in local administrations' policy-making process, often bringing together decision-makers from different policy domains. This policy cycle provides a structured logic for interaction with various stakeholders and the physical twin. The use of an LDT also needs to be connected to this policy cycle and the physical twin. Firstly, the complexity of the physical twin and, secondly, the policymakers' department requirements, their joint interaction with the physical twin, and their need to follow processes that build on the policy cycle. Eight MR and nine MF have been defined and described based on the author's experience with LDT research. Special attention was given to how these requirements contribute to LDTs supporting multiple domains, mainly in the field of smart cities, and their ability to predict policy outcomes. The outcomes can support a variety of interactions between a broad group of stakeholders and contributes to overcoming one-sided (policy) thinking silos and actions.

In conclusion, an LDT should not be seen as a standard software system serving a single objective type. An LDT is a technological concept that serves the evolving decision-support needs of the location to which it pertains, reflected in the policy cycle of local administrations. To frame the design and development of LDTs, we have applied the design science research concepts of MR and MF, describing aspects of LDT that will relate to many LDT instances. To deliver the MF, we propose approaching an LDT as the interplay of five systems: IoT, Visualisation, Data Space, Algorithm and Data Management and Scenario Building following the SoS paradigm. This chapter contributes to the narrative on LDTs and informs future LDT architects on the key aspects they need to focus on.

## References

Akroyd, J., Mosbach, S., Bhave, A., & Kraft, M. (2021). *Universal digital twin—A dynamic knowledge graph* (Vol. 2). Data-centric Engineering.

Altamiranda, E., & Colina, E. (2019). *A system of systems digital twin to support life time management and life extension of subsea production systems*. OCEANS 2019, IEEE. https://doi.org/10.1109/OCEANSE.2019.8867187

Brindis, C. D., & Macfarlane, S. B. (2019). Challenges in shaping policy with data. In S. Macfarlane & C. Abou Zahr (Eds.), *The Palgrave handbook of Global Health data methods for policy and practice*. Palgrave Macmillan. https://doi.org/10.1057/978-1-137-54984-6_3

Buongiorno Sottoriva, C., Nasi, G., Barker, L., Casiano Flores, C., Chantillon, M., Claps, M., Crompvoets, J., Franczak, D., Stevens, R., Vancauwenberghe, G., & Vandenbroucke, D. (2022). In C. Buongiorno Sottoriva & G. Nasi (Eds.), *Leveraging the power of location information and technologies to improve Public Services at Local Level*. Publications Office of the European Union. https://data.europa.eu/doi/10.2760/67126

Cairney, P. (2016). *The politics of evidence-based policy making*. Palgrave Pivot London.

Chantillon, M. (2023). *Data als brandstof voor slim lokaal beleid*. Imec. https://www.imec.be/nl/articles/data-als-brandstof-voor-slim-lokaal-beleid

Chinn, S., Sol Hart, P., & Soroka, S. (2020). Politicization and polarization in climate change news content, 1985–2017. *Science Communication, 42*(1), 112–119.

de Bruijn, H., Warnier, M., & Janssen, M. (2022). Thee perils and pitfalls of explainable AI: Strategies for explaining algorithmic decision-making. *Government Information Quarterly, 39*.

Eirinakis, P., Kalaboukas, K., Lounis, S., Mourtos, I., Rožanec, J., Stojanovis, N., & Zois, G. (2020). *Enhancing cognition for digital twins*. 2020 IEEE International Conference on Engineering, Technology and Innovation (ICE/ITMC).

Esri. (2021). *Esri sluit zich aan bij het Digital Twin Consortium*. https://www.esri.nl/nl-nl/nieuws/2021/esri-sluit-zich-aan-bij-het-digital-twin-consortium

European Commission, Directorate-General for Communications Networks, Content and Technology, Garcia Barron, M., Ramos, C., Birecki, E. et al., *Public report on the LDT toolbox detailed specifications requirements—D05.02*, European Commission, 2023. https://data.europa.eu/doi/10.2759/384198

European Commission, High-level expert group on AI. (2019). *Ethics guidelines for Trustworthy AI*. https://digital-strategy.ec.europa.eu/en/library/ethics-guidelines-trustworthy-ai

Floridi, L., & Taddeo, M. (2016). What is data ethics? *Philosophical Transactions of the Royal Society A—Mathematical Physical and Engineering Sciences, 374*, 20160360. https://doi.org/10.1098/rsta.2016.0360

GeoJSON. (2015). https://geojson.org/

Höchtl, J., Parycek, P., & Schöllhammer, R. (2016). Big data in the policy cycle: Policy decision making in the digital era. *Journal of Organizational Computing and Electronic Commerce, 26*(1–2), 147–169. https://doi.org/10.1080/10919392.2015.1125187

Honig, M. I., & Coburn, C. (2008). Evidence-based decision making in school district central offices toward a policy and research agenda. *Educational Policy, 22*, 578–608. https://doi.org/10.1177/0895904807307067

Howlett, M., Ramesh, M., & Perl, A. (2009). *Studying public policy: Policy cycles & policy subsystems*. Oxford University Press.
Howlett, M., Ramesh, M., & Perl, A. (2020). *Studying public policy: Principles & processes*. Oxford University Press.
Jamshidi, M. (2005). *System of systems engineering—A definition*. IEEE SMC.
Jamshidi, M. (2008). *Systems of systems engineering—Principles and applications*. Taylor Francis CRC Publishers.
Jones, D., Snider, C., Nassehi, A., Yon, J., & Hicks, B. (2020). Characterising the digital twin: A systematic literature review. *CIRP Journal of Manufacturing Science and Technology, 29*(36–52), 36–52. https://doi.org/10.1016/j.cirpj.2020.02.002
Kanani-Sadat, Y., Arabsheibani, R., Karimipour, F., & Nasseri, M. (2019). A new approach to flood susceptibility assessment in data-scarce and ungauged regions based on GIS-based hybrid multi-criteria decision-making method. *Journal of Hydrology, 572*, 17–31. https://doi.org/10.1016/j.jhydrol.2019.02.034
Kirby, R. S., Delmelle, E., & Eberth, J. M. (2017). Advances in spatial epidemiology and geographic information systems. *Annals of Epidemiology, 27*, 1–9.
Klein, J., & Vliet, H. V. (2013). *A systematic review of system-of-systems architecture research*. International ACM SIGSOFT Conference on Quality of Software Architectures.
Lefever, S., Michiels, P., Schuurman, D., Coenen, T., & Vintila, N. (2023). *White paper: Smart data operations for better data-informed decision-making*. imec. https://www.imec.be/sites/default/files/inline-files/White%20paper%20-%20smart%20data%20operations.pdf
Lin, M., Chen, T., Chen, H., Ren, B., & Zhang, M. (2023). When architecture meets AI: A deep reinforcement learning approach for system of systems design. *Advanced Engineering Informatics, 56*, 101965.
Liu, M., Fang, S., Dong, H., & Xu, C. (2021). Review of digital twin about concepts, technologies, and industrial applications. *Journal of Manufacturing Systems, 58*, 346–361.
Luthfi, A., & Janssen, M. (2019). Open data for evidence-based decision-making: Data driven government resulting in uncertainty and polarization. *International Journal on Advanced Science Engineering and Information Technology, 9*(3), 1071–1078.
Masser, I., & Crompvoets, J. (2015). *Building European spatial data infrastructures*. Esri Press.
Nagel, L., & Lycklama, D. (2021). *Design principles for data spaces*. Position Paper. Version 1.0. Berlin. https://doi.org/10.5281/zenodo.5105744
Privat, G. (2021). *Graph models for systems-of-systems digital twins*. https://doi.org/10.13140/RG.2.2.23047.93602
Sahlab, N., Kamm, S., Müller, T., Jazdi, N., & Weyrich, M. (2021). *Knowledge graphs as enhancers of intelligent digital twins*. 2021 4th IEEE International Conference on Industrial Cyber-Physical Systems (ICPS), IEEE. https://doi.org/10.1109/ICPS49255.2021.9468219
van der Voort, H. G., Klievink, A. J., Arnaboldi, M., & Meijer, A. J. (2019). Rationality and politics of algorithms. Will the promise of big data service the dynamics of public decision making? *Government Information Quarterly, 36*, 27–38.
van Ooijen, C., Ubaldi, B., & Welby, B. (2019). A data driven public sector: Enabling the strategic use of data for productive, inclusive and trustworthy governance. *OECD Working Papers on Public Governance, 33*. https://doi.org/10.1787/09ab162c-en
Walls, J. G., Widmeyer, G. R., & El Sawy, O. A. (1992). Building an information system design theory for vigilant EIS. *Information Systems Research, 3*(1), 36–59.
Yalcinkaya, M., & Ardit, D. (2013). *Building information modeling (BIM) and the construction management body of knowledge*. IFIP Advances in Information and Communication Technology.

# Part II
# Implementing a Reusable Local Digital Twin

# Chapter 5
# Unlimited Potential: The Reusable Local Digital Twin

**Ingrid Croket, Philippe Michiels, Stefan Lefever, and Gert Hilgers**

**Contents**



## 5.1 LDT as a City Service Aggregator

Since the late 1990s, cities have been transitioning to the digital era by developing digital services to improve interactions with their citizens and businesses. Many governments have introduced e-government projects to facilitate innovation, implementing websites and incorporating e-services into the city's processes. Specific e-processes, such as establishing e-tendering capabilities to support procurement, contributed to an increase in efficiency, transparency and speed of public administrations.

Improved process automation is a logical first part of the digitalisation journey of any organisation. However, many citizen processes still need to be digitised to their full extent. Some remaining challenges include the lack of two-way communication and service of transactions and inadequate protection concerning personal privacy (Torres et al., 2005). The e-government projects, later called 'smart governance' initiatives, aimed to evolve this approach by supporting the development of smarter

I. Croket (✉) · P. Michiels · S. Lefever
Interuniversitair Micro-Elektronica Centrum, Leuven, Belgium
e-mail: ingrid.croket@imec.be; philippe.michiels@imec.be; stefan.lefever@imec.be

G. Hilgers
Open Agile Smart Cities, Brussels, Belgium
e-mail: gert.hilgers@oascities.org

 
L. Raes et al. (eds.), *Decide Better*,
https://doi.org/10.1007/978-3-031-81451-8_5

cities with people, governance, and technology. In the 2014 EU study report 'Mapping Smart Cities in the EU', the following definition is used for a smart city: "A smart city is a city seeking to address public issues via ICT-based solutions based on a multi-stakeholder, municipally based partnership. The holistic view of the 'smart city' provides the foundation to integrate solutions and look for reusability and interoperability across different domain topics. A smart city addresses at least one initiative related to one or more of the following six characteristics: smart governance, smart people, smart living, smart mobility, smart economy and smart environment (Manville, 2014)."

Initially developed in 1994, the smart city concept became more present in practice and literature around 2010 when the EU introduced the Smart City Initiative to contribute to a low-carbon economy (Dameri & Cocchia, 2011). The concept of the smart city is broader than mainly automating processes, as was the main objective of e-government projects through increasing efficiency and process optimisation. The smart city embraces the fact that information technologies offer valuable tools to help the city provide new solutions for their challenges. The objective of the smart city is to use different data sources and advanced artificial intelligence to feed user-oriented decision tools to develop preventive strategies and govern human health and happiness in a city context (Sassen & Kourtit, 2021). The smart city requires a solid vision and approach to manage smart initiatives and link these to the cities' strategic objectives and policies. This approach changes how the city is managed, and the digital realm plays an increasingly important role along with the physical and social reality. The shift corresponds with the holistic approach adopted by the city of Rotterdam, which views the city as a combination of three aspects: the social, physical and digital environment. Digital reality is represented in the latter and considered a valuable asset (Bagheri, 2024).

According to the Smart City Guidance Package, a critical success factor in implementing digital tooling as an aid for a Smart Sustainable City is the implementation of a visualisation tool to map the different initiatives (Borsboom-van Beurden, 2019). A digital twin is a virtual representation of assets, processes and relationships that combines Smart Services for knowledge creation, decision support, and managerial learning to contribute to long-term business plans (Mirza, 2021). In this perspective, a 'strategic' Local Digital Twin (LDT) seems to be an effective solution not only to function as a visualisation tool but even more as a strategic decision-making tool to deal with a city's sustainability challenges, as described in Mirza's research. As such, the LDT is an aggregated method for reusing data, process knowledge, and domain expertise to deliver new insights to local stakeholders. This result is achieved by valorising digital assets and improving the city's policy-making and governance processes.

> The LDT is not a product but a reference framework that serves as a guide and aims to support anyone embarking on the journey to realise urban digital twins. A digital twin does not introduce a novel application as one product; instead, it capitalises on existing technologies, established concepts and methods and delivers multiple digital services.

### 5.1.1 Worldwide Endeavours for Reusability and Interoperability of LDTs

In recent years, a surge of worldwide initiatives has emerged to advance the principles of reusability and interoperability within digital twin technologies. These initiatives, driven by the imperative to enhance efficiency, sustainability, and innovation across various sectors, are reshaping the landscape of digital twin deployment and utilisation. Below, we provide a comprehensive overview of exemplary projects in the field.

Our starting point is the exploration of standardisation efforts, of which detailed examples are described in Chap. 6. International organisations, such as the International Organization for Standardization (ISO)[1] and the Institute of Electrical and Electronics Engineers (IEEE),[2] have been actively involved in developing standards for digital twins. These standards ensure compatibility, consistency, and interoperability among digital twin systems, facilitating seamless data exchange and integration. Initiatives focused on establishing common data exchange standards are crucial in ensuring interoperability among digital twin systems.

Efforts to define standardised data formats, ontologies, and communication protocols facilitate seamless integration and interaction between heterogeneous digital twin environments, enabling comprehensive data sharing and analysis. The Digital Twin Exchange is an online platform developed by the National Institute of Standards and Technology (NIST)[3] to foster the exchange of digital twin models and data. It aims to promote interoperability and facilitate collaboration among researchers and practitioners.

Open source initiatives have gained momentum, offering freely accessible software frameworks, tools, and libraries for developing and deploying digital twins. By leveraging open source solutions, organisations can reduce development costs, accelerate innovation, and promote interoperability through community driven development and contributions. Examples include Eclipse Ditto (Eclipse Foundation, n.d.), an open source framework for building digital twins, and FIWARE[4] (Panfilis, 2021), an open source platform for developing intelligent applications and services.

Numerous collaborative platforms and consortia have emerged, bringing together industry stakeholders, academia, and government bodies to foster collaboration and knowledge sharing in digital twins. Examples include the Digital Twin Consortium (Digital Twin Consortium, 2016), which promotes interoperability and best practices among industry, government and academia. Research institutions and innovation hubs worldwide are conducting projects to introduce new applications for the

[1] International Organisation for Standardization, https://www.iso.org/home.html

[2] Institute of Electrical and Electronics Engineers, https://www.ieee.org/

[3] National Institute of Standards and Technology, https://www.nist.gov/

[4] FIWARE, http://www.fiware.org/

LDT. The National Digital Twin program in the UK aims to develop a national framework for digital twins, while academic institutions like MIT[5] and Stanford research digital twin technologies. Big industry partners like Microsoft advocate for an integrated approach to digital twins, leveraging cloud computing, Internet of Things (IoT) devices, edge computing, and artificial intelligence (AI) technologies. Microsoft offers Azure digital twins, a platform that allows organisations to create comprehensive digital representations of their environments, enabling seamless integration with IoT data, spatial intelligence, and analytics capabilities (Microsoft, 2024). These environments include buildings, factories, farms, energy networks, railways, stadiums, and even entire cities. In the meantime, many smart cities worldwide are implementing digital twin technologies to improve urban planning, infrastructure management, and citizen services. Applied in many cities worldwide, from Boston and Amsterdam to Singapore and Dubai, CityGML is a crucial standard for representing 3D semantic city models.

These examples demonstrate the diverse initiatives and projects contributing to advancing reusability and interoperability in LDT technologies. Through collaborative endeavours and shared standards, stakeholders are poised to usher in a new era of interconnected digital ecosystems, revolutionising how we design, operate, and optimise complex systems in an increasingly interconnected world. Chapter 6 further explains the specific usage of different standards.

### *5.1.2 European Digital Ecosystem Initiatives*

The EU's strategic focus on advancing the digital transformation of smart cities and communities fosters the creation of a comprehensive ecosystem of initiatives, contributing to Europe's digital transition and the green transition (Green Deal). Since the start of the digital revolution, many EU projects have delivered new knowledge, guidance, and solutions to support cities and communities in their digital journey, and they are compliant with European legislation and EU values. Through the Living-in.eu Declaration (Living-in.EU Community, n.d.) representatives of public administrations at local, regional, national, or European levels have committed to principles linked to citizen-centricity, city-led approach, open innovation, ethical use of data, technology, and interoperability—the Living-in.EU movement envisions stimulating the uptake and scaling up of solutions equally for all cities across Europe, based upon solid multi-level governance cooperation. The Digital Ecosystem thus reveals a growing potential for digital solutions in cities.

To stimulate the 'open market philosophy', a Smart Cities Marketplace is created to engage cities, industries, researchers and other innovators to facilitate implementations of Smart Sustainable Cities and replication of successful implementations (Kaiser & Pejstrup, 2021). The Marketplace serves as a Digital Ecosystem that

[5] Massachusetts Institute of Technology, https://web.mit.edu/

brings together different parties, stakeholders and technologies as consumers and providers of digital Smart Services that contribute to Sustainable Development Goals (SDG) and promote reusable solutions. The release of many publications supports overall Smart City architectures and examples of use cases brought together by the UN initiative The United for Smart Sustainable Cities (U4SSC) (Publications – United for Smart Sustainable Cities (U4SSC), n.d.).

In 2018, the European Innovation Partnership on Smart Cities and Communities (EIP SCC) and the H2020 ESPRESSO[6] project developed a common approach for cities to develop new capabilities across different countries, identifying synergies to strengthen the dissemination of solutions across different geographical boundaries (Exner, 2016). From that perspective, the open urban data platform was introduced as a core enabler for developing new innovative services, which resulted in the publication of a standard on the reference architecture for an open urban platform (DIN SPEC 91357, 2017). This solution defines high-level specifications for cities to integrate cross-sector applications in a portable and interoperable manner, avoiding vendor lock-in and thus opening the market for different players to introduce innovative, interoperable solutions, building a large ecosystem of interoperable solutions.

A proposal was launched in 2021 to create a European Interoperability Framework for Smart Cities and Communities (EIFSSCC) building on the 2017 European Interoperability Framework (EIF) and EU-Tailored Minimum Interoperability Mechanisms Plus (MIM Plus) (EC DG-Connect, 2021). The framework inspires cities and communities, provides guidance with principles and recommendations and thus contributes to shaping the digital ecosystem. However, the actual implementation of a digital city is described and demonstrated within EU projects and translated into tangible solutions by developing reusable building blocks (BBs).

The Digital Europe Programme (DEP) (European Commission, n.d.-a) is a comprehensive EU funding programme to reinforce the EU's digital capacities in digital technology adoption and society-wide digital transformation. Within the context of this program, Digital BBs are defined as facilitating interoperability as a core enabler to deliver cross-country and cross-sector public services. BBs are open and reusable digital solutions endorsed by the European Commission. They come in frameworks, standards, or software as a service (SaaS). These BBs ensure compatibility with other market services and compliance with European legislation and standards. Six BBs on the EC Digital Europe portal (*Digital Homepage*, n.d.) cover generic functionalities like trusted authentication, secure data exchange, and electronic invoicing. The goal is to create an EU-wide digital service network that is interoperable, cost-effective, and secure, a network that speeds up the development of new solutions, as cities or service providers do not need to develop these generic functionalities from scratch. Easily integrated, they can connect with other solutions.

The GovStack publication has launched a similar initiative that resulted in an open source community and toolkit for Digital Government Services. Governments

[6] Systemic standardisation approach to empower smart cities and communities (ESPRESSO), EU H2020 project, https://cordis.europa.eu/project/id/691720

can find essential tools with use cases and guidance documents (GovStack Implementation Playbook, n.d.).

Considering the specific needs for cross-domain, holistic solutions that integrate different datasets and models, the Intelligent EU cities' mission has stated that "Cities are powerful brokers for the Twin Transition, as they are at the front line of social and economic challenges". Indeed, an LDT solution that can support local issues also has the potential on a global level to establish a European network of digital twins of the physical environment. Figure 5.1 shows how different initiatives support each other within the EU Smart and Sustainable City Ecosystem. The vision of the EU is that by 2030, many EU cities and communities should benefit from (AI-enabled) LDTs. Gradually, the network of LDTs could pave the way for their future integration into the digital twin of the Earth, managed by the Destination Earth (DestinE) (Destination Earth Initiative, 2023) project that aims to deliver solutions and insights helpful on a local and global level. In this context, the digital twin of the Earth is a digital replica of complex Earth systems based upon real-time observations combined with artificial intelligence that helps visualise, monitor and forecast natural and human behaviour to achieve the objectives of a green and digital transition.

Furthermore, the importance of Open Data Platforms and the European Data Strategy has resulted in the creation of European Data Spaces to create a market for data sharing that enables businesses and cities to make better use of data and make better decisions. Data Spaces feed the LDTs and fuel new intelligent data services for digital twins (Usländer et al., 2022). Testing and Experimentation Facilities (TEFs) (European Commission, 2023) are set up on the infrastructure and

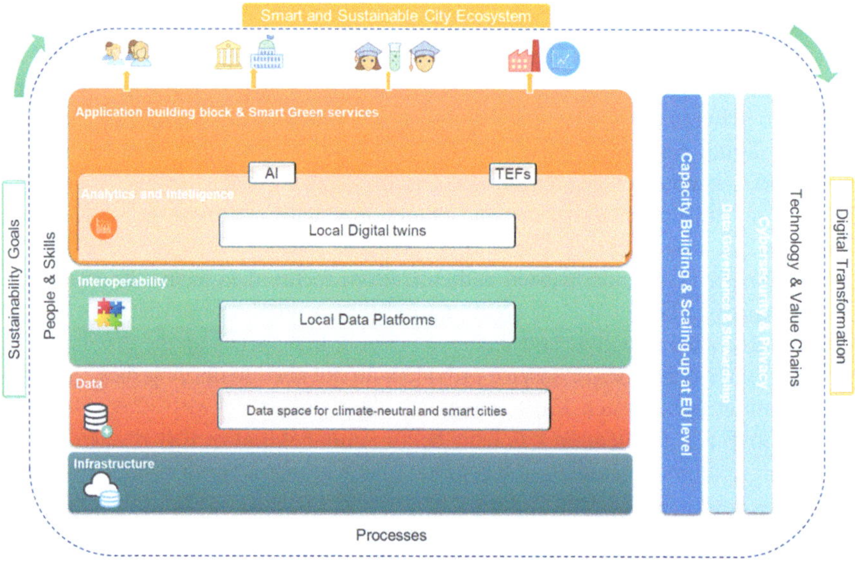


**Fig. 5.1** The EU smart and sustainable city ecosystem (European Commission, 2021)

application level to offer physical and virtual facilities where technology providers and stakeholders can test new AI-based soft-/hardware technologies in real-world environments.

Creating interoperable data spaces is a crucial enabler to making data easily accessible and usable for different applications, facilitating data reuse and services. The LDT Toolbox programme (Living-in.eu, 2022) launched by the EU aims to create an *LDT Toolbox* that provides reusable and interoperable BBs, accelerating the digitalisation of cities and enabling the implementation and rollout of LDT solutions. The LDT Toolbox development roadmap is aligned with other EU initiatives that are part of the EU Smart and Sustainable City Ecosystem, emphasising interoperability requirements and reusability of BBs developed in this programme (see Sect. 5.4).

### 5.1.3 The LDT View for the City

A literature study on city digital twin potentials identifies five critical themes and challenges in a city's digital twin: data management, visualisation, situational awareness, planning and prediction, integration and collaboration. These themes are essential to get a grip on and digitise the processes and their assets in the city, which are also crucial to unlocking value for citizens. Significant challenges to maximising the potential of LDTs lay within the need to enhance data efficiency, including cities' socioeconomic components and the possibility of integrating physical and digital counterparts in two directions (Shahat et al., 2021). In essence, LDTs connect data, and combined with visualisation techniques, they create situational awareness for the end users. The analytics and modelling capabilities enable users to plan, predict, and collaborate by integrating three essential elements: Data, visualisations, and analytics/models, as presented in the triangle model in Fig. 5.2.

Traditional applications constructed using predefined data sets, logic and user interfaces are often for a specific purpose. However, with the emergence of open data platforms, there is a shift in thinking towards considering data as a versatile and reusable asset, also often referred to as 'the new gold', crucial to providing data driven value creation (O'Halloran et al., 2020). The introduction of IoT has made real-time data accessible, which is extremely valuable in creating situational awareness for decision-makers. By combining this real-time data with models and analytics, new and additional insights are created by integrating data from various sources and domains. The user experience and visualisation solutions can vary based on a user's needs, and different interfaces may be designed based on the same data sources.

How an LDT is implemented varies depending on the purpose and capabilities set up in the digital twin. The system design facilitates the evolution from basic capabilities such as data visualisation to modelling and, ultimately, intelligent decision-making. Multi-sensor environment data fusion, virtual simulation modelling tools, and urban sensing technologies enable smart city analytics in a city

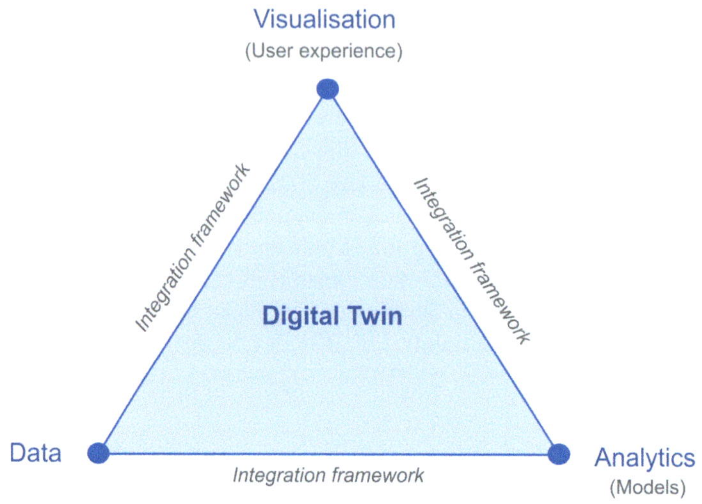


**Fig. 5.2** Digital twin data, models, visualisation, and integration (Barron et al., 2023)

context. For their part, predictive modelling algorithms, deep-learning-based sensing technologies, and significant urban data help to configure immersive hyperconnected virtual spaces in digital twin cities (Nica et al., 2023).

When focusing on *city data visualisations*, the LDT works with static and dynamic data sources and shows these data sources on a dashboard, using primary data modelling capabilities. This means that the data is presented descriptively in the digital twin dashboard, as it is available in domain-specific data sources measured by the sensors deployed in the city. New technologies for detailed geographical data visualisation provide accurate topographic map data. For instance, drone images made from 3D laser scans can provide relevant data visualisation of specific objects. 3D laser scanning is a method for accumulating dense point cloud data, including three-dimensional coordinates, reflectance, and texture on the measured object's surface. It can provide the basis for creating a 3D model of an object.

When a city wants to include *prediction, planning and modelling capabilities*, the LDT system design will be elaborated with extended functionalities like model management and model orchestration to enable prediction, simulation and scenario management and visualise the results in the digital twin solution. Models can be combined or chained where, for instance, the outcome of one model is the input for another model, thus offering the possibility to combine multi-domain simulations. In this context, the value of combining existing models from different domains requires input from various departments in the city and stimulates collaboration across departments. Urban planning, being a core responsibility of a city, brings together environmental, social and economic concerns and thus relies on cross-domain data and modelling capabilities, being an ideal area to engage different stakeholders.

At the ultimate intelligence level of an LDT, the concept of the 'cognitive digital twin' is introduced, where the system not only supports human decisions but also allows automated decision support and the creation of new intelligence based upon cognitive AI capabilities (Mandal, 2024). The evolution of AI technologies combined with the LDT as a rich and linked data environment is ideal for simulating the 'urban brain', connecting all urban-related concepts. Different data sources linked to the contextual reality of the LDT result in superior city performance in terms of operational efficiency, predictive abilities, autonomous decision-making, and citizen engagement, as the LDT allows the training of new algorithms and testing of their effectiveness. For instance, enhanced interactive experiences and visualisations facilitate improved citizen engagement as long as privacy concerns are considered. Overall, the cognitive LDT supports integrating and developing AI technologies to solve complex urban issues and create new insights for better decision-making.

## 5.2 LDT Design Principles

The Centre for Digital Built Britain released 2018 a paper proposing the Gemini Principles, structured under three key themes, as a basis to guide the national digital twin development and information management framework to enable this (Centre for Digital Built Britain, 2018). Under Purpose, digital twins should generate clear value, align with the public good, and benefit society. Trust emphasises the need for transparency, security, and accountability, ensuring that the digital twin is a reliable and ethical representation. Lastly, functionality focuses on the digital twin's ability to be adaptable, maintainable, and scalable, ensuring it can evolve with technological advancements and changing requirements. Collectively, these principles ensure that digital twins are technically sound and ethically and socially beneficial.

The Gemini principles are still relevant and referred to in several digital twin initiatives. In this section, we select related design principles and describe technical implementations that support these Gemini design principles.

### *5.2.1 Transparency and Trust*

Given that policy decisions may impact the lives of millions of people, in order to be able to use LDTs as decision support systems, the entire process, from the collection of data to the taking of the decision itself, should be transparent. This process requires the following principles to be adhered to:

- *Trust & accountability*: Decision-makers should be able to rely on data and algorithms provided by trusted publishers, and there should be a certain level of accountability for this;

- *Lineage*: Data versioning should be applied whenever data updates are needed. It should always be apparent where data comes from and what processing steps are applied before using data in an LDT;
- *Algorithm transparency*: Algorithms applied to the data should be sufficiently documented and transparent to understand their (i) limitations in terms of applicability and reliability, (ii) assumptions about the data inputs, (iii) vulnerability to produce unreliable data, e.g. in terms of training sets, configuration, and more.

These requirements imply a convergence of the semantics of different concepts across cases, scenarios, visualisations, reports, and more. In order to achieve this convergence, it is essential to apply governance to ensure transparency and clarity at all levels. A good example is the comparison of two traffic models for a city. Being able to compare two such models requires the use of common concepts and semantics so that, figuratively speaking, apples are compared to apples and not oranges.

### 5.2.2 Extensible, Robust, Adaptive and Open

As mentioned earlier, LDTs will benefit significantly from seamless interoperability. However, a certain level of pragmatism is required when approaching this integration challenge. LDTs should be open to accepting both existing and emerging technologies and standards. The domains of IoT, Big Data, Machine Learning (ML) and others are evolving rapidly, and digital twin design should accommodate the latest developments in these areas.

Secondly, these technologies should be integrated with scalability and robustness in mind. Scalability is essential because digital twins often require considerable computation power. Different architectural patterns are needed to deal with or avoid costs incurred from handling extensive data and heavy processing requirements.

Robustness is essential because, in a distributed system-of-systems reality, (data) connections are complex to guarantee. LDTs, including their components such as the simulation models, should thus be robust and only make a few assumptions about the operating environment, data inputs and outputs. The digital twins will rely on data and processing power provided by third parties and should assume that any kind of failure or loss of connectivity may occur. It should take measures to recover automatically from such events. This recovery is especially needed when data processing outcomes directly or indirectly control physical-world assets, but equally when decisions are made based on these outcomes, which may affect the well-being of citizens.

In IoT and big data, expecting an LDT to have all the necessary data locally is unrealistic. Large amounts of data may require more direct connections between the data provider and its consumers, even bringing the algorithm to the data, not the other way around. Situations where an LDT acts as an intermediary, can result in unacceptably high overhead and latency and may even cause concerns about data security. The idea behind this is that an LDT acts as a data and message broker and does not act as a data platform or platform running the models themselves. This setup fits into the 'separation of concerns' approach, whereby complex systems are broken down into smaller, more manageable parts to make them easier to understand, develop, secure, and maintain. Hence, the principles of federated data management, data discoverability and data processing are key in the context of LDTs.

### *5.2.3 Interoperability*

Since data, schemas, ontologies, algorithms and visualisation tools are provided by different parties, providing interoperability at various levels will benefit all. An LDT architecture should provide the proper abstractions to connect to and from interoperable systems.

When addressing LDTs, based upon system-of-systems (SoS) architecture, we are defining interoperability within and between large complex systems, which means we are looking at *the capability of systems or units to provide and receive services and information between each other and to use the services and information exchanged to operate effectively together in predictable ways without significant user intervention.*

Interoperability must be considered on many levels, commonly divided into three high-level drivers, as specified in the European Interoperability Framework and others.

- *Organisational interoperability:* Covers the relationships between organisations and individuals and their parts of the system, including business relationships (e.g. contracts, ownership, and market structures) and legal relationships (e.g. regulatory structures and requirements and protection of physical and intellectual property);
- *Informational interoperability:* Covers the content, semantics and format for data or instruction flows, such as the accepted meanings of human or computer languages and common symbols;
- *Technical interoperability:* Covers the physical and communication connections between devices or systems (e.g. power plugs and USB ports).

All three types of drivers must be addressed to achieve interoperability in any complex system. For a more detailed discussion of these levels, we refer to the Gridwise Interoperability Context Setting Framework (Widergren et al., 2008). This framework provides guidelines and standards designed to enhance interoperability, initially developed for the electric power grid to promote transforming the electric power system into a more efficient, reliable, and flexible infrastructure. However, the interoperability principles and drivers from this framework have been adopted across different domains and are very relevant for the SoS architecture of LDTs as described in Fig. 5.3.

Minimal Interoperability is needed to enable data ecosystems and the digital twins that they enable to work well, despite the different ways in which the agencies

**Fig. 5.3** Context setting framework – own interpretation derived from Gridwise interoperability (Widergren et al., 2008)

in the data ecosystem might collect and handle data, and how they design and manage the models. In the long term, it is vital to work towards an arrangement where all agencies providing data for an LDT follow the same set of detailed standards. However, that will only happen when agencies start seeing the value of sharing their data and analytics and converge their approaches towards deeper interoperability over time.

Therefore, pragmatic action is required to define a minimal level of interoperability within and between digital twins within a local community that can be implemented with relative ease by all participants and will facilitate the required interworking.

This minimal level of interoperability is *the capability of systems or units to provide and receive services and information between each other and to use the services and information exchanged to operate effectively in predictable ways with minimal user intervention.* It is essential to recognise that there are many intermediate levels of interoperability. The greater the interoperability, the lower the requirement for user intervention (Fig. 5.4).

[7] Open Agile Smart Cities, https://oascities.org/

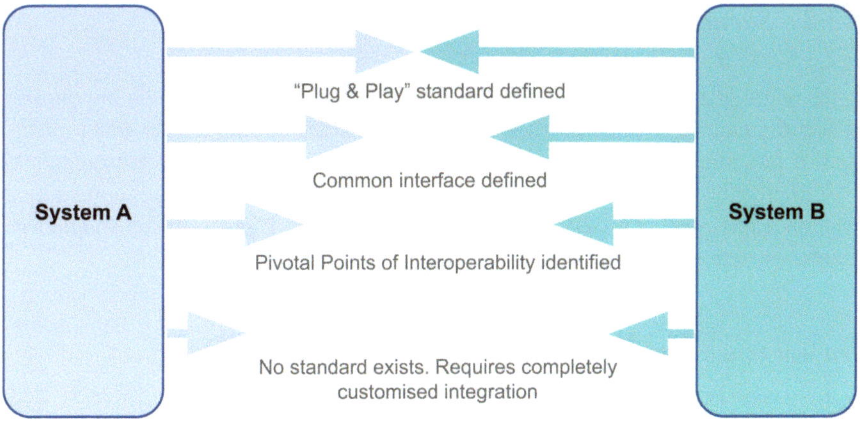


**Fig. 5.4** MIMs plus levels of interoperability (Living-in.EU, 2023)

**Table 5.1** Overview Minimum Interoperability Mechanisms (MIMs) (OASC, n.d.)

| MIM | Subject | Function |
|---|---|---|
| **MIM1** | **Context** | Data sets/streams are linked according to context |
| **MIM2** | **Data Models** | All data sets/streams use consistent data models |
| **MIM3** | **Contracts** | Appropriate data sets/streams are found, and agreement is easily reached for appropriate use |
| **MIM4** | **Trust** | Citizens are actively in charge of how data about them is used to benefit themselves and their community |
| **MIM5** | **Transparency** | Decision-making algorithms use data appropriately to make fair and transparent decisions |
| **MIM6** | **Security** | Data held and shared securely |
| **MIM7** | **Places** | Geospatial information is described consistently and accurately |
| **MIM8** | **Indicators** | KPIs rely on consistent data from across the ecosystem to enable reliable measurement of progress |
| **MIM9** | **Analytics** | Models and analytics used within the ecosystem work well with other models and analytics |
| **MIM10** | **Resources** | Information about city-related resources is appropriately shared |

Open & Agile Smart Cities and Communities (OASC)[7] is working with its community of cities and regions and in partnership with Living-in.EU on developing a set of Minimal Interoperability Mechanisms (MIMs) (OASC, n.d.). The MIMs address critical issues in a local data space by considering different methodologies used by the various agencies participating in that data space. Ultimately, MIMs ensure that those issues are managed effectively overall. As of early 2024, a list of ten MIMs at various stages of development is available, as presented in Table 5.1.

The list in Table 5.1 will likely grow with additional MIMs addressing other key issues necessary to support *minimal but good enough.* MIM-based specifications within data spaces, digital twins, and metaverses is essential to enabling the reusability of data and systems.

### 5.2.4 Security by Design

In the realm of LDTs, which amalgamate data from diverse sources, the importance of security cannot be stressed enough. Crafting a security architecture that protects against potential data breaches and ensures that data owners maintain command over their information is essential. This guidance aims to share three foundational principles to foster secure data management within LDTs and to establish an environment where safety and control are paramount.

#### Prudent Data Sharing

- *Considerate data sharing:* Adopting a sane approach to data sharing is wise. Sharing only what is strictly necessary for a task significantly reduces the risk of exposing sensitive information. This outcome is of major importance when dealing with privacy-sensitive data sources;
- *Bringing algorithms to data:* Whenever feasible, bringing algorithms and models directly to where the data resides is advisable. This practice limits unnecessary data movement, decreasing the risk of compromising data during transfer or storage. This requirement requires algorithm portability and reusability to be a design principle;
- *Sharing insights over raw data:* Instead of distributing raw data, it might be more prudent to share the insights and results derived from the data. This method safeguards the original data while providing stakeholders with the necessary information.

#### Embracing Secure Technologies

- *Adopting open identity management:* Utilising open frameworks for identity management and governance can significantly enhance the security of user authentication and authorisation processes, ensuring that only the right eyes have access to sensitive data;
- *Setting clear data space agreements:* It is crucial to articulate the terms and conditions regarding data usage through comprehensive data space agreements and policies. These should delineate ownership, access rights, and the responsibilities of all parties involved, creating a transparent and secure data-sharing environment;
- *Secure data transmission:* Opting for secure and encrypted protocols for data transfer is paramount. This requirement ensures the confidentiality and integrity of data as it moves from one point to another, safeguarding against unauthorised access.

### Ensuring Robust Data Control

- *Implementing data space frameworks:* Leveraging established data space frameworks can be instrumental in managing data access and enforcing data usage policies, thereby providing a secure framework for data sharing and collaboration;
- *Adopting on demand data loading:* Where possible, consider on-demand data loading, which fetches data only as needed for specific operations. This approach reduces the volume of data stored locally, diminishing the potential fallout from a security incident;
- *Developing data retention strategies:* Securing data includes determining how long it needs to be kept and securing methods for its disposal once it is no longer needed. These strategies should be integral to the data space agreements, ensuring clarity and security throughout the data lifecycle.

By embracing these guiding principles, LDTs can achieve a high level of security, effectively minimising the risks associated with data breaches and allowing data owners to maintain control over their information confidently.

Data Spaces, in general, and Gaia-X (Gaia-X Association, 2022), in particular, offer tools and frameworks that form the bedrock of governance within a data-sharing ecosystem. These tools and frameworks cultivate trustful data sharing in several ways. Firstly, they establish a clear governance model that outlines data ownership, access rights, and responsibilities of participating entities. Secondly, they promote common standards, ensuring interoperability and seamless data exchange regardless of the origin. Lastly, Gaia-X emphasises shared principles such as transparency, data sovereignty, and security. These principles foster consensus amongst stakeholders, creating a predictable and trustworthy environment where sensitive data can be confidently shared.

## *5.2.5 Separation of Concerns*

### Separating Control from Data

Separating control from data is a fundamental design principle critical to ensure the scalability and flexibility of LDTs. This principle distinguishes between the mechanisms that govern the behaviour and operation of systems (control) and the information these systems process and manage (data). Given the inherently distributed nature of LDTs, adhering to this principle ensures enhanced modularity and flexibility. For instance, in storing and managing historical IoT data, the systems designed for data storage should focus solely on the efficiency and integrity of data handling. In contrast, data publication and transfer mechanisms should operate independently, prioritising security and bandwidth considerations. Similarly, within the algorithmic components of LDTs, maintaining a separation between the data and the control flow allows algorithms to be adaptable and reusable across different contexts and applications. By decoupling the data, which is subject to change and variation, from the control logic, which dictates the operational rules and procedures, LDT systems gain the ability to evolve and scale without compromising on robustness and reliability.

### Separating Type from Data

Separating type from data is a nuanced approach to separating concerns, where the schema and semantics of the data are maintained independently from the format in which the data is stored or transferred. This distinction is particularly vital in environments where data needs to be versatile and adaptable to components' specific requirements. For example, smart city applications' user interface (UI) data often necessitates verbose formats like JSON (JavaScript Object Notation). These formats are human-readable and easily manipulated but may not be the most efficient processing speed and resource utilisation. JSON's structure represents the hierarchical relationships within the data, which is crucial for dynamic UIs that respond to complex data states. On the other hand, high-performance algorithms, such as those processing large volumes of IoT data in real-time, require more efficient, compact data representations. By separating the type and semantics of the data from its storage or transfer format, data is provided in a machine-readable way (e.g. Resource Description Framework – RDF), and systems can choose the most appropriate representation for each use case, enhancing performance and scalability while preserving the integrity and utility of the data across diverse applications.

### Decoupling of Components

Limiting the coupling between components is paramount to ensure an open and flexible architecture within the framework of LDTs for smart cities. This approach minimises dependencies among various system components, allowing each to operate and evolve independently. For instance, decoupling historical data storage from contextual information management in an IoT stack enhances system robustness by allowing changes or upgrades to one component without necessitating modifications to others. This segregation also facilitates the integration of diverse data sources and types, enabling a more comprehensive and dynamic data landscape.

Moreover, the commitment to using open protocols and interfaces plays an important role in the LDT architecture. By standardising how components communicate and interact, LDTs can leverage common data processing and transformation tools, bridging the gap between disparate standards and formats. This approach promotes interoperability among different components and systems and ensures that the architecture remains adaptable to new technologies and standards. Open protocols and interfaces underline the ecosystem's capacity to support a wide array of applications and services, thereby enhancing the overall utility and scalability of LDTs in the smart city infrastructure.

**Fit-for-Purpose Standards and Technologies**

Embracing fit-for-purpose standards and technologies is a key principle in developing LDTs, acknowledging the diverse landscape of existing, often overlapping standards and tools. This principle underlines the importance of flexibility and inclusivity in the architectural design of LDTs, steering away from rigid commitments to specific standards or technologies. LDTs should be engineered to support a wide spectrum of standards and technologies, accommodating the varied needs of different components, applications and stakeholders within the smart city ecosystem. This approach ensures interoperability and seamless integration among disparate systems and future-proofs the LDT infrastructure by allowing it to adapt to new technologies and standards as they emerge. By serving as a versatile platform that can bridge the gaps between different standards and technologies, LDTs can harness the strengths of each, leading to more robust, efficient, and scalable smart city solutions. This inclusivity and adaptability are crucial for fostering innovation and collaboration, ultimately enhancing the functionality and resilience of smart city infrastructures.

## 5.3 LDT Reference Architectures

### *5.3.1 The LDT Systems*

The LDT serves as a data driven tool for decision support, impacting decision-making across operational, tactical, and strategic levels by integrating data and models from various domains. Consequently, the architecture of the LDT prioritises interoperability and scalability, forming an open framework capable of accommodating diverse technologies and solutions. This framework enhances the potential for evidence-based decision-making without constraints. To deep dive into the potential of an LDT based on its architectural setup, we address four different domains to explain the way of working:

- Data Systems and services;
- Connecting data and model via case scenario management;
- User Interaction (UI) and visualisation;
- LDT Management components.

### Data Systems and Services

LDTs often depend on components delivered by external providers. The technical design of the digital twin needs to consider that data sources are published using different transport protocols in varying formats and, in many cases, do not conform to any (semantic) standards. Such diversity is difficult to handle in an integration setting. It is important to understand that the digital twin cannot be a middleman in transferring data. This action would slow down data throughput, especially in cases concerning high data volumes, resulting in unacceptable performance. The LDT must use the expertise and best practices handled by data systems and focus on data integration and management to process the data in an LDT context.

Data Systems refer to various technologies and platforms for capturing, managing and processing data. The new approach in terms of data architecture applies the 'data mesh' concept that consists of four principles: domain driven data ownership, data as a product, a self-service data platform, and federated computational governance. Data is stored in the source system responsible for the data governance processes and is made available through data services for different authorised data consumers. In that sense, the data is proposed as a 'product' and made available via federated indexes (Geonovum, 2022).

At the basis of all data management, data needs to apply to the *FAIR data principles*: Findable, Accessible, Interoperable, and Reusable. Converting data into useful insights requires process transformations from raw data to 'smart data', performing data operations steps executed within interoperable and standardised data (Lefever S et al., 2023) (Fig. 5.5).

Having the data functionalities and principles established in the relevant data systems, the LDT components will almost always connect directly to the data source via one of the supported technical interfaces. Below are some examples to clarify this:

- A visualisation component that needs to update the location of public transport vehicles on a map will subscribe directly to the update feed of the vehicles;
- A model calculating air quality using live sensor data will subscribe directly to the sensor feed and publish the results elsewhere;

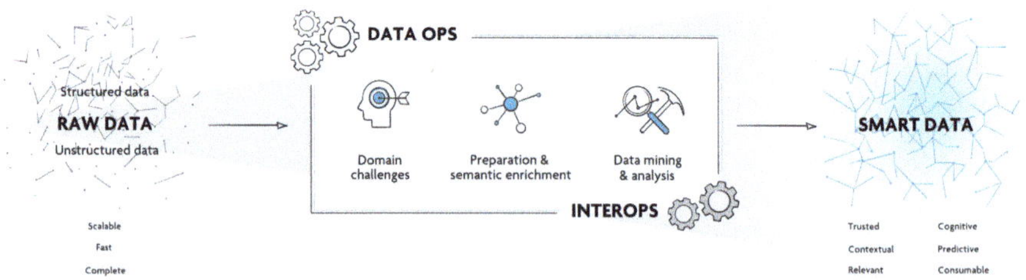


**Fig. 5.5** Smart data transformation process (Lefever et al., 2023)

- A visualisation client visualising air quality will connect to a Web Feature Service (WFS) service fed by an algorithm/model that connects to the air quality results and maintains the WFS service.

Deployment of data sources should strategically ensure the best performance. Transferring large volumes of data is in direct conflict with a responsive interface. When a responsive environment is required, this need must be considered.

Because the LDT addresses multi-domain topics, it has to deal with different data schemes and models. Data standards, such as vocabularies and code sets, are critical for the interoperability of data and data systems. Data standards support semantic interoperability, meaning the ability of systems to exchange the data to interpret the data correctly. However, data standards are not always easy to define and implement. This fact is exactly why *Data Spaces* try to converge at a different level: they do not try to enforce the use of standards to data publishers. Instead, they try to encourage it by aligning on how to publish data regardless of their format, schema or semantics. A Data Space is a decentralised infrastructure for trustworthy data sharing and exchange in data ecosystems based on commonly agreed principles. A Data space is an essential enabler of the data economy. Shared digital tools, infrastructure components, and common rules facilitate data sharing and enhance basic data principles, such as FAIR Principles and data interoperability. The evolution and potential of digital twins must be considered in parallel with the evolution and deployment strategy of the Data Spaces (Bastidas et al., 2018). LDTs will benefit from the realisation of Data Spaces as all key components (data, algorithms, tools, schemes, etc.) are discoverable and interoperable.

Michael Grieves, acknowledged to be the first scientist to introduce the digital twin concept, has recently updated the initial definition of a digital twin, which consists of three elements: physical and virtual space and connectivity, with two additional dimensions: data and services. This results in a five-dimensional digital twin model initially applied to smart manufacturing, where the data space is the centre and serves the other dimensions. The proposed setup is not only relevant for the manufacturing industry but can serve different domains addressed by the LDT architecture (Fig. 5.6).

LDTs are the consumers and producers of data products which require various data services. The LDT system delivers these services for all types of data products, and the data services are interoperable with other functionalities of the LDT. To demonstrate that these services are delivered by interoperable services/tools, we refer to the relevant BBs defined in the LDT Toolbox project and explained in more detail in Sect. 5.4.3.

- *Data ingestion:* Different technologies like geo web services, Application Programming Interface (APIs), and event streaming services will be required to ensure data publishing and (near) real-time data processing capabilities. A message broker handles these types of data services (BB.11 Message Broker);
- *Data querying:* A data query service needs to be able to connect to different data systems or components to manage data publishing functionalities (BB.04 Data query service);

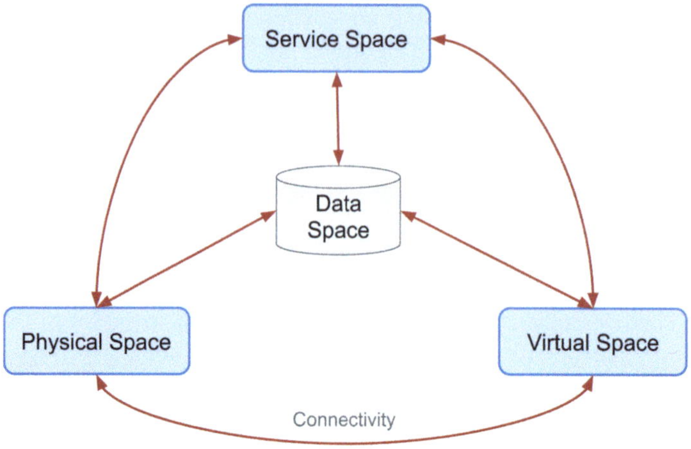


**Fig. 5.6** Five-dimensional DT model for smart manufacturing (Turcanu et al., 2024)

- *Data management:* Semantic data model, data ontology and ensuring data transparency and explainability is enabled by an asset registry (BB.16 Asset Registry);
- *Data storage:* Data generated by the LDT model must be stored efficiently. Data transformations must be managed; in some instances, data replication will be needed for a particular use case (delivered by BB.05 Data Replication Client). These datasets will need to be managed within the LDT data environment, thus requiring also its data storage capabilities (BB.18 Data Storage);
- *Synthetic data generation:* These tools are based upon statistical models and algorithms designed to generate simulated, synthetic data to increase data volumes or comply with data privacy issues (BB.17 Synthetic Data Generation Tools);
- All data services require *transparent workflows* enabled by a data workflow orchestration component (BB.06 Data workflow and component orchestration).

## Connecting Data and Models Via Case & Scenario Management

A key strength of an LDT is its ability to enable users to combine data and conduct analysis using prediction or forecasting models. The user needs to be able to create new insights by tweaking the model's parameters and compare the different results to make data driven decisions. The main BB to enable these capabilities is the Case & Scenario Manager (BB.02) which plays a crucial role in defining scenarios, connecting the models to the data assets, and delivering contextual information for the users.

An *LDT case* groups all data around a specific smart city topic. For example, a smart city case could be a comparative study of circulation plans in a city that helps city planners choose the most desirable plan. Typically, a case will have multiple scenarios attached to it to compare, e.g. several alternative circulation plans, and assess their performance in specific KPIs. The scenario concept allows experimentation with data and settings in isolation from the other scenarios. Within a scenario, it is possible to run experiments that correspond to the individual results of experiments, which can be stored individually. This approach allows users to tweak scenario and model settings and keep the separate results for comparison.

A case is often worked on and prepared by a team of people until it is ready to be shared with a broader audience. As such, it can initially be seen as a kind of project that people are working on together, and in a later phase, it can be shared as a common view amongst decision-makers and the general public to ensure everybody has the same perspective.

Currently, there is no semantic description of cases and scenarios, nor is there a schema or standard API for its management. Such a standard may foster further interoperability between digital twin BBs as digital twin technology matures.

**Case: DUET[8] project LDT Scenario Description and Stepwise Approach**
To clarify how cases and scenarios workww, we briefly discuss an example. The specific end-to-end scenario we are looking to support is the following: *Given a specific street network configuration in a city, we want to provide insight to city planners and other experts on the effects of making changes in the street network configuration such as closing down one or more streets or changing traffic flow directions in several streets. Effects on traffic intensity and air quality due to changes to traffic flows are measured and visualised.*

**Setting up such an experiment requires several steps:**

- Creating a new case and documenting it comprehensively;
- Setting up the scenarios and adding the necessary data sources*, in this case:
  - Model of the street network of the city;
  - Traffic intensity data source;
  - Air quality data source.
- Adding a reference to the traffic model and specifying that it needs to use the street network data source as input and a traffic intensity data source as output;
- Providing the necessary configuration for the traffic model;
- Adding a reference to the air quality model and specifying that it needs to use the traffic intensity data source as input and the air quality data source as output;
- Providing the necessary configuration for the air quality model.* *The above data sources will also be used for visualisation purposes*

[8] Digital Urban European Twins (DUET), EU H2020 project, https://cordis.europa.eu/project/id/870697

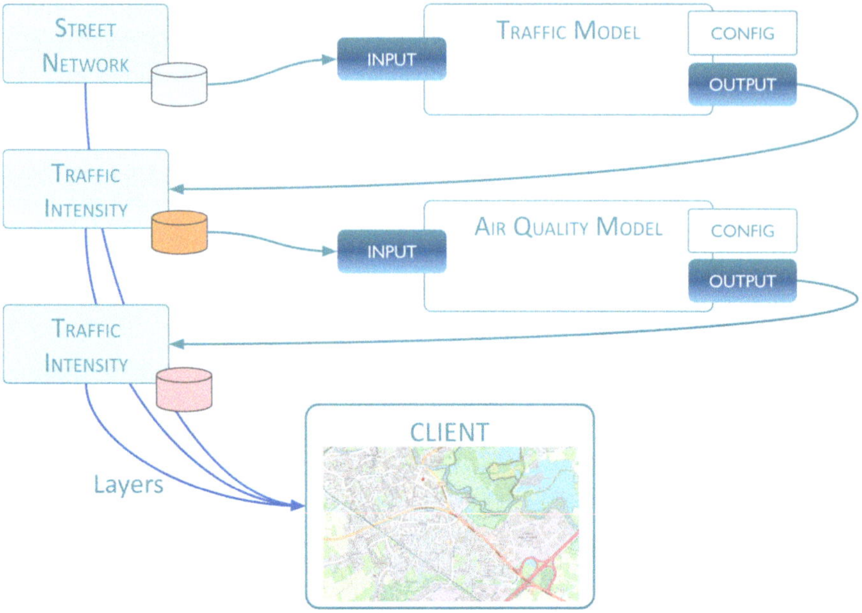


**Fig. 5.7** How a scenario wires up data sources and models (DUET, 2021)

This scenario has been implemented for the cities of Pilsen (Czech Republic) and Ghent (Belgium) (Fig. 5.7).

Figure 5.8 sketches how cases and scenarios are structured and how they refer to data sources and algorithms (or models) in the federated asset catalogue.

Understanding the difference between a model signature and a model call is essential. A *model/algorithm signature* describes a model in terms of what kind of input data it expects (data schema) and how it expects it to be delivered (technical interface). The same goes for the output data it produces. It does *not* point to specific data sources. A *model/algorithm call* is an application of a model in a specific context (a scenario in the case of digital twins). A model call refers to actual data sources for specifying input and output parameters.

### User Interaction and Visualisation

An LDT has a dedicated user environment that includes analysis and visualisation tools. User interaction (UI) is enabled by deploying an Integrated environment (BB.09 Integrated environment) to deliver a seamless user experience that takes care of performance optimisation, personalisation, multi-platform support and

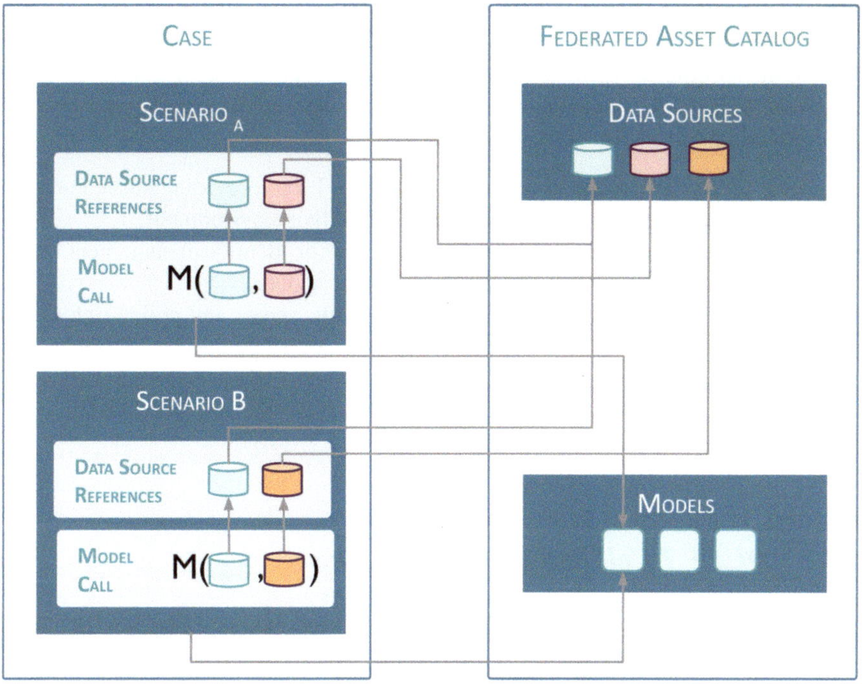


**Fig. 5.8** Case and scenario management addressing data and model sources (DUET, 2021)

smooth interaction workflows. This user-centric design ensures that the user's needs are at the forefront of the LDT's development. Different visualisation applications can be developed based on the user's needs to provide an appropriate user experience tailored to the specific users' needs. A city administrator may have access to sophisticated 2D/3D maps to define and run scenarios.

In contrast, citizens may use a simplified map in an app to encourage them to deliver feedback, for instance, to report a dangerous traffic situation. The added value of incorporating real-life data from citizens is that it encourages citizen engagement and enables the establishment of interaction and communication lines with citizens; these two functionalities are provided through integration with Collaboration & Community management systems (BB.03 Collaboration & community management system). Engaging citizens or other stakeholders in design processes for city planning, can be done by extended reality features (BB.07 Extended Reality) to foster UI and user experience feedback. All visualisation and UI applications use the same standard LDT architectural foundations, such as the interaction service that will deliver the exact context information (BB.10 Interaction service). Visualisation clients can implement the interaction APIs interface and use the many existing Geospatial Information Systems (GIS) and IoT standards for visualisation. This approach will benefit reusability and interoperability.

**LDT Management Components**

Next to the specific capabilities regarding data, models and visualisations, the LDT also requires generic management components to handle the scoping, integration concerns and non-functional requirements:

- Setting up the geographical boundary of the LDT and providing sufficient context information on the objectives for the digital twin environment;
- Configuring trusted federated service providers for identity management, asset catalogue management and perhaps app store providers;
- Onboarding users and configuring security groups, access and policy rights;
- Data encryption, trust party certification, private and public key (security and privacy policy);
- Infrastructural management, including performance management, monitoring, security auditing, etc.

### *5.3.2 DUET T-Cell Reference Architecture*

A reference architecture is a generalised blueprint and a set of principles applied to different components to deliver solutions in a common domain. The reference architecture facilitates the design of concrete architectures and the communication between domain professionals, allowing them to incorporate the continuous evolution of technology. The need for a reference architecture applies to the city domain because of its complexity, where different stakeholders and heterogeneous systems and technologies must coexist and interact (Bastidas et al., 2018). An LDT Reference architecture intends to have a reference framework that different cities and regions can use. Above all, it should allow applications to be deployed quickly and sustainably. Systems must be able to connect to platforms and communicate with each other while complying with LDT design and construction principles.

The DUET project perceives the urban digital twin as an SoS that embraces many of the design principles outlined in Sect. 5.2. Using the T-Cell as an analogy, it envisions a digital twin as a set of locally deployed tools capable of connecting to different remotely deployed data sources and services, much like the T-Cell uses its receptors to connect to other organisms and cells (Fig. 5.9).

The T-cell architecture thus distinguishes between centrally deployed components within the red boundary and connections to outside components using one or more gateways. Such gateways can come in many forms, including data space connectors to connect to static and dynamic data. Although the DUET architecture does not assume data space connections, their concept can be beneficial for digital twin deployment at the technical, organisational and legal levels.

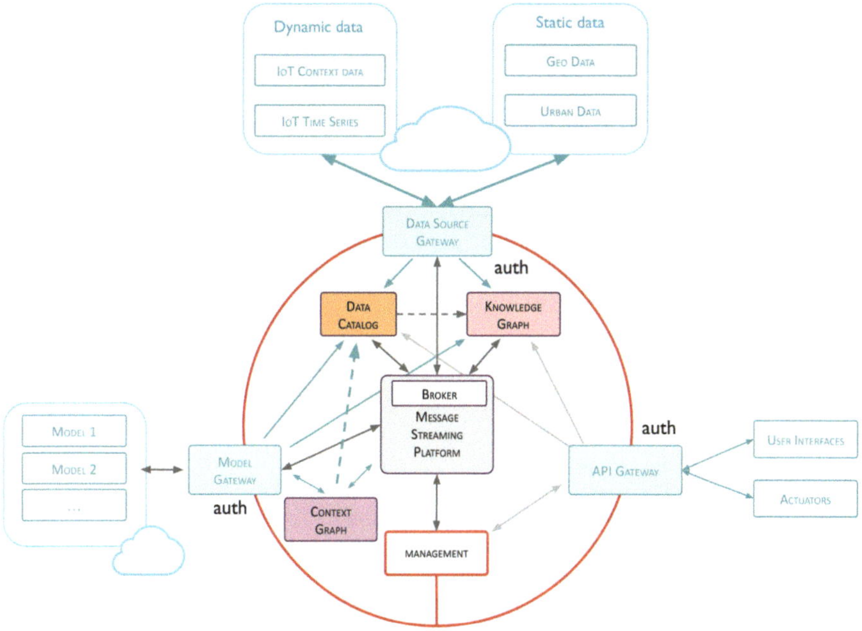


**Fig. 5.9** Open urban digital twin architecture, based on the DUET project architectural design (DUET, 2020)

## *5.3.3 Reference to Other Architectural Frameworks*

### Data Spaces & Federated Design

Data space architecture, while not a digital twin reference architecture per se, plays a pivotal role in enhancing the deployment and robustness of digital twins at various levels. Data space architectures, which rely on the principle of federation, are fundamentally designed to manage a wide array of data types and sources, providing a cohesive environment where data can be accessed and shared without necessitating uniformity in data formats or schemas. This architecture is particularly beneficial in the context of digital twins, which rely heavily on integrating and analysing diverse data streams to create accurate and dynamic representations of physical entities or systems. Data spaces are conducive at the following levels:

- *Uniformity of identity access control:* Data spaces propose a uniform approach to identity and access management, thus promoting the sovereignty and portability of identities and credentials. This feature avoids the need for new identities and credentials to access the various distributed services of a digital twin;

- *Discoverability:* Data spaces use federated catalogues where data and service publishers can make their services discoverable. This approach includes metadata on the kind of data, its applicability, the formats and protocols in which they are made available, and last but not least – their terms of use;
- *Policies and agreements:* Data spaces also provide a framework for managing data and service access policies that stipulate the conditions for potential data users to make use of data or a service. Some of these limitations can also be enforced by technical components deployed in a data space, such as allowing data users to comply with applicable regulations effortlessly. Additionally, any agreements between data publishers and data users are managed and used at the level of access control;
- *Governance and standards:* Data spaces are typically created by communities of common interest. They govern participants in an environment of trust. Additionally, they can promote the use of standards and technologies to achieve higher levels of interoperability.

Different initiatives such as SIMPL (European Commission, n.d.-c), IDSA (International Data Spaces Association, n.d.), iShare (iShare Foundation, n.d.) and Fiware (Panfilis, 2021) all promote their architecture from a particular vantage point. Regardless of the specific architecture or approach, it is key that they pursue maximal interoperability at every one of the above levels to realise the potential of data spaces. That said, the whole point of data spaces is to break out of the platform silos. Therefore, a data space that is not interoperable with other data spaces limits the potential for innovative data services.

**EIRA: European Interoperability Reference Architecture**

The European Interoperability Reference Architecture (EIRA) (European Commission, n.d.-b) is an architecture content metamodel defining the most salient Architectural Building Blocks (ABBs) needed to build interoperable e-government systems. The EIRA is maintained under the DEP and provides a common terminology that can be used by people working for public administrations. The EIRA uses (and extends) the ArchiMate language as a modelling notation and uses service orientation as an architectural style. EIRA provides many architectural ingredients that can help to set up successful LDT initiatives. It is a comprehensive arsenal that allows the reuse of standards, technologies, and solutions and helps avoid the reinvention of the proverbial wheel.

## 5.4 LDT Toolbox: Architecting Reusable Systems for the Digital Twin

The transformation journey of EU cities and communities towards LDT adoption is a gradual and cumulative process. The objective of the LDT Toolbox as part of the Digital European Programme (DEP) is to serve cities and communities across Europe and to support the development and expansion of their LDTs based upon reusable systems. The Toolbox includes a set of BBs, each of which can be recognised as an independent accelerator for implementing and operationalising LDTs. In this section, we will elaborate on the LDT Toolbox design and present the underlying concepts described as a result of the LDT Toolbox design project.

### 5.4.1 LDT as a System-of-Systems

The purpose of an LDT is to enhance evidence-based decision-making at the operational, tactical and strategic levels for the city or community, addressing cross-domain topics. The LDT builds upon the knowledge, experience and solutions available in the digital ecosystem market and can adopt new capabilities, as interoperability principles support its design. Therefore, the LDT combines multiple technologies such as data analytics, AI modelling and visualisation of the physical environment's current, historical, and forecasted state. The LDT, being the master system that interacts with other subsystems, uses data and services from existing sources that can exist outside the LDT system. A system, regardless of its complexity or geographic distribution (i.e. its scale), can be called a system-of-systems (SoS) when and as long as its constituents are operationally and managerially independent. An SoS delivers a (new) capability based on the capabilities provided and combined by its subsystems (Maier, 1998). The SoS architectural approach is not new within the scope of IoT platforms and smart cities. Hence, it also focuses on the reusability of systems to serve more complex issues (Cadavid et al., 2020).

In the design of the LDT Toolbox, the concept of an LDT as an SoS is key. It, therefore, is constructed as an open architecture that supports easy access for connecting solutions and data based on interoperability and modularity principles.

### 5.4.2 Capabilities and Subsystems

The overall design of the Toolbox is based upon the definition of the capabilities which are derived from a consultation round with all stakeholders to identify the capabilities needed that contribute to the digital journey of implementing an LDT. This design includes strategic, technical, and legal capabilities that are linked to different ambition levels and result in the identification of technical and non-technical BBs that are by design technology and vendor-agnostic, reusable and interoperable.

A common reference for the definition of the LDT capabilities is provided by the Digital Twin Consortium[9] in the description of the digital twin Capabilities Periodic Table, describing 6 major categories: Data Services, Integration, Intelligence, User

[9] Digital Twin Consortium, https://www.digitaltwinconsortium.org/

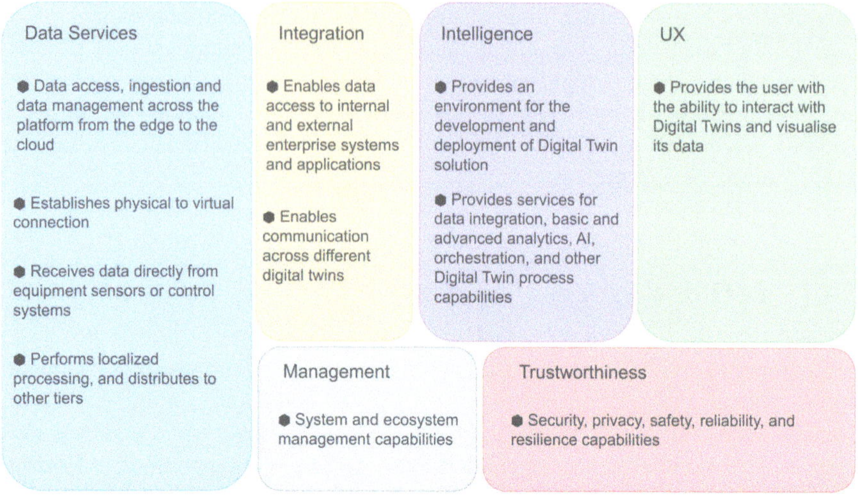


**Fig. 5.10** Digital Twin Capabilities Periodic Table, own interpretation (Digital Twin Consortium, 2016)

Experience, Management and Trustworthiness. These categories are also reused in the LDT Toolbox capabilities mapping (Fig. 5.10).

The descriptions used often refer to enabling services and capabilities, such as data services, rather than actual data management processes. This supports the SoS approach, where the actual data management is offered by separate systems, and the main focus of the LDT is to connect the subsystems in an interoperable way. This enlarges the scope of a digital twin solution as it is an aggregated framework that builds upon other systems, and its strengths lie in the integration capacity and the ability to support the creation of new digital services by combining different systems.

### *5.4.3 Building Blocks*

The ultimate goal of the LDT Toolbox is to deliver interoperable solutions that are grouped by the identification of different BBs. A BB provides a level of abstraction to translate the LDT capabilities into functional and technical requirements that can be addressed by one of several digital tools. Based upon the desired capabilities and required functionalities to respond to a certain use case, a city can select the most suitable tool, knowing that the tool will be interoperable with other existing or future requirements to achieve higher ambition levels. To illustrate how these BB are defined and how they interact, a reference architecture for an LDT (see Fig. 5.11) is described, which is an important tool to help cities and communities plan their LDT roadmap and procurement. Relationships between BBs are explained at a high level to support different functionalities across different use case implementations (Barron et al., 2023).

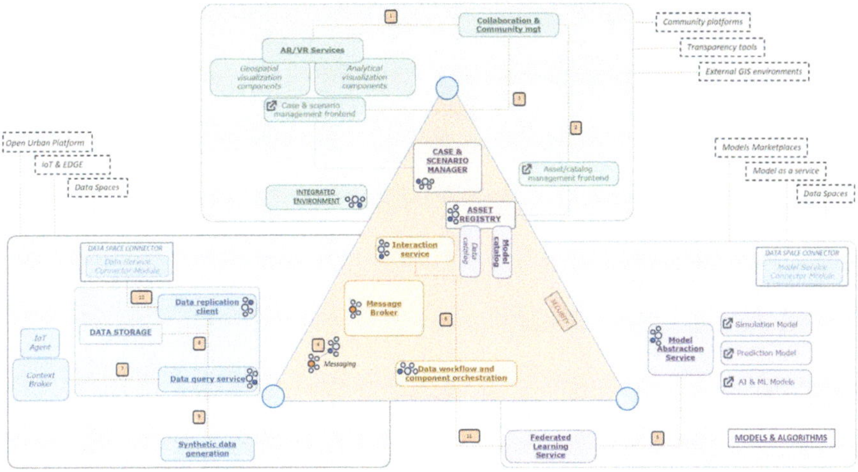


**Fig. 5.11** LDT Reference architecture: SoS vision on the BB interactions (Barron et al., 2023)

In the scope of the LDT Toolbox design, a prioritised list was established for the BBs for which a first set of tools will be developed in the following years (2024–2027). The combination of tools that fulfil the requirements for these BBs in terms of functionality and interoperability will demonstrate that BBs can be 'reused' to serve different use cases in various cities.

The BBs are linked to capabilities linked to differing ambition levels. This modular approach emphasises the evolution path of LDTs driven by particular use cases for a city. However, in the end, the adoption of the BBs will grow as new capabilities are added to an LDT implementation.

Each BB is linked to at least one of the four LDT ambition levels of the DUET LDT maturity model (see Chap. 10). The ambition level column of Table 5.2. depicts the level where a BB can deliver the most added value.

**Digital Twin Maturity Levels (DUET, 2022)**

*Awareness level 1* focuses on research and skill development for cities new to digital twin technology, identifying urban domains for application, defining test cases, and planning pilot projects with necessary data, technology, and stakeholder involvement.

*Exploratory level 2* involves training city officials and implementing the first pilot to test simulations, with evaluations guiding potential expansion while ensuring data privacy and security.

In *Insightful Level 3,* cities evaluate the exploratory outcomes to set expansion goals, update simulation models, invest resources, and establish governance structures to support scaling.

*Future-ready level 4* integrates the expanded digital twin with existing city systems, evaluates integration with other cities' twins, leverages AI for optimisation, and promotes continuous improvement and public engagement.

**Table 5.2** List of selected BBs for the LDT Toolbox (Barron et al., 2023)

| # | Building Block (BB) | BB Category | Capability | Ambition Level |
|---|---|---|---|---|
| **BB.01** | **Reference Architecture** | Strategy | Public ProcurementLDT Roadmap Management | 1 – Awareness of twins |
| **BB.02** | **Case & Scenario Manager** | Integration Components | Usage Context Information Provisioning | 4 – Intelligent twins |
| | | | Case, Scenario & Experiments Management | 2 – Experimental twins |
| **BB.03** | **Collaboration & Community Management System** | Visualisation and UX | Citizen Engagement and Case & Scenario Feedback Gathering Collaboration and Community Management | 2 – Experimental twins |
| **BB.04** | **Data Query Service** | Data Services | Data Publishing | 2 – Experimental twins |
| **BB.05** | **Data Replication Client** | Data Services | Data Replication | 2 – Experimental twins |
| **BB.06** | **Data Workflow and Component Orchestration** | Integration components | Data Processing, Data Flows & Component Orchestration | 2 – Experimental twins |
| | | | Data Transformation | 3 – Predictive twins |
| | | | Technical Transparency & Explainability | 4 – Intelligent twins |
| **BB.07** | **Extended Reality (AR/ VR Services, etc.)** | Visualisation and UX | Augmented Reality (AR)Virtual Reality (VR) | 4 – Intelligent twins |
| | | | Advanced Visualisation & Geo Dashboarding | 2 – Experimental twins |
| **BB.08** | **Federated Learning Service** | Algorithms & Models | Federated Learning & Training | 3 – Predictive twins |
| **BB.09** | **Integrated Environment** | Visualisation and UX | Integrated User Experience | 2 – Experimental twins |
| **BB.10** | **Interaction Service** | Integration Components | Interaction Support | 2 – Experimental twins |
| **BB.11** | **Message Broker** | Integration Components | (Near) Real-time Data Processing,Data Publishing and Subscribing,Data Ingesting, Data Streaming,Urban Measuring, Sensing & ControlAlerts and Notification | 3 – Predictive twins |
| | | | Data Flows & Component Orchestration, Interaction Support | 2 – Experimental twins |
| | | | Supervised or Unsupervised Actuation, Command & Control | 4 – Intelligent twins |

| | | | | |
|---|---|---|---|---|
| **BB.12** | **Model Abstraction SDK/ Service** | Algorithms &, Models | Model Abstraction & Model Hosting | 2 – Experimental twins |
| **BB.13** | **Model Catalog** | Algorithms & Models | Algorithm & Model Management | 2 – Experimental twins |
| | | | Accountability Information Provisioning | 4 – Intelligent twins |
| **BB.14** | **Model Usage Guidelines** | Governance & Conformance | Model Governance & Compliance | 2 – Experimental twins |
| **BB.15** | **Algorithms & Models** | Algorithms & Models | Prediction,Machine Learning & AI | 3 – Predictive twins |
| | | | Simulation | 2 – Experimental twins |
| **BB.16** | **Asset Registry** | Data Services | (Meta) Data Schema Management, Data Source Management & Ontology Management | 1 – Awareness of twins |
| | | | Semantic Governance & Compliance | 2 – Experimental twins |
| | | | Procedural Transparency,Technical Transparency & Explainability | 4 – Intelligent twins |
| **BB.17** | **Synthetic Data Generation Tools** | Data components | Semantic Governance & Compliance | 2 – Experimental twins |
| | | | Procedural Transparency,Technical Transparency & Explainability | 4 – Intelligent twins |
| **BB.18** | **Data Storage: Data Lake, Data Warehouse, Data Lakehouse** | Data Components | Data Processing, Data Replication, Data Storage & Data Time Travel | 2 – Experimental twins |
| | | | Data Transformation | 3 – Predictive twin |
| | | | Technical Transparency & Explainability | 4 – Intelligent twins |

As described in the SoS concept, the LDT can benefit from existing systems and tools. Therefore, the selected list of BBs focuses on the BBs necessary to fulfil specific needs to operate an LDT environment, reusing functionalities and tools for different use cases.

Each BB is designed to comply with industry standards and interoperability requirements, ensuring their quality and reliability. The objective of an LDT Toolbox is to develop BBs that can interoperate 'horizontally' across different use cases relevant to cities and communities and 'vertically' within the broader scope of digital solutions created in the overall EU ecosystem, where we can find DS4SSCC and other data space initiatives as depicted in Fig. 5.12.

Horizontal scalability means that a BB from an LDT Toolbox, like a case and scenario manager and the associated assets, like case and scenario descriptions, can be used uniformly by different cities to support their specific use cases. Vertical interoperability means this LDT BB can interoperate with a BB like Identity Management from the DS4SSCC inventory (DS4SSCC-DEP, n.d.). Specifically, the city can use this Identity Manager BB for specific internal applications like e-government processes. It is thus beneficial that the same BB can also be used for the LDT and interoperate with the case and scenario manager.

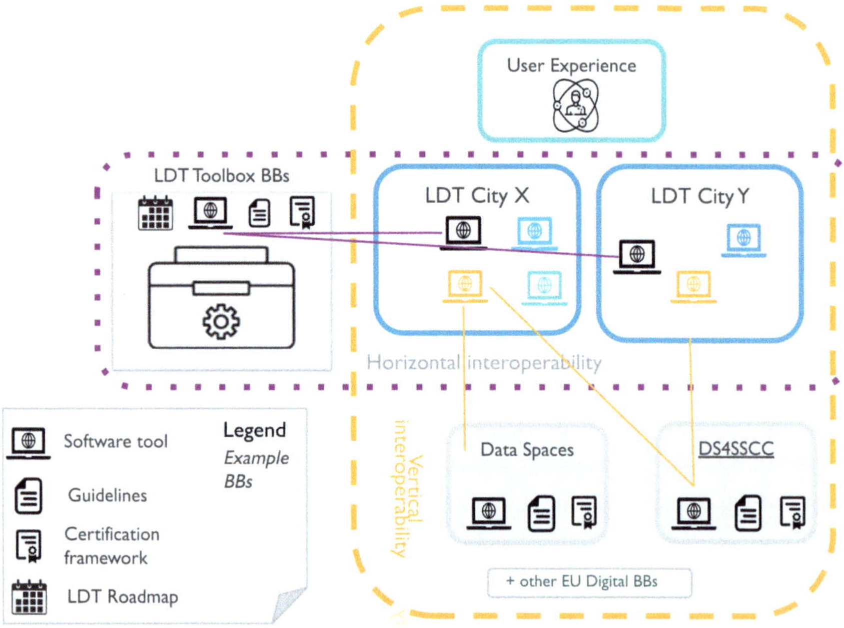


**Fig. 5.12** LDT Toolbox: Interoperability of building blocks (Barron et al., 2023)

## 5.5 Conclusion

A Local Digital Twin (LDT) effectively integrates city services across various domains by combining data from multiple sources. The LDT reference architecture and design principles underpin a dynamic system capable of providing new data insights, modelling, and visualisation capabilities. This system-of-systems (SoS) approach emphasises the reusability of building blocks (BBs), allowing for continuous development and integration of new data sources and technologies. It unlocks the unlimited potential of subsystems in specialised areas, whether at the technical level, such as data spaces, or in domain-specific applications, ensuring these components can be reused and adapted as needed.

Moreover, the reusability of these BBs facilitates faster deployment of new services and solutions, as existing components can be repurposed and recombined in innovative ways. This modular approach saves time and resources and fosters innovation, as developers and city planners can experiment with different configurations. Additionally, reusable components can be shared across various cities and regions, promoting a collaborative environment where best practices and proven solutions can be disseminated and implemented more widely.

By prioritising reusability, the LDT ensures that the city's digital infrastructure remains adaptable and future-proof, capable of evolving in response to new challenges and opportunities. This approach supports a sustainable and scalable urban development model, where continuous improvement is driven by the efficient reuse of existing assets, ultimately leading to more innovative, responsive, and resilient cities.

## References

Bagheri, S. (2024). *Digital city Rotterdam: Open urban platform*. Rotterdam School of Management, Erasmus University. https://doi.org/10.4135/9781071937853

Barron, M. G., Ramos, C., Birecki, E., & Carvalho, F. (2023). *Public report on the LDT toolbox detailed specifications requirements D05.02*. European Commission. https://data.europa.eu/doi/10.2759/384198

Bastidas, V., Helfert, M., & Bezbradica, M. (2018). A requirements framework for the design of smart city reference architectures. In *Proceedings of the 51st Hawaii International Conference on System Sciences*. https://doi.org/10.24251/hicss.2018.317

Borsboom-van Beurden, J. (2019). *Smart city guidance package full document* (J. Kallaos, Ed.). Smart Cities Marketplace. https://smart-cities-marketplace.ec.europa.eu/insights/solutions/smart-city-guidance-package-full-document

Cadavid, H., Andrikopoulos, V., & Avgeriou, P. (2020). Architecting systems of systems: A tertiary study. *Information and Software Technology, 118*, 106202. https://doi.org/10.1016/j.infsof.2019.106202

Dameri, R., & Cocchia, A. (2011). *Smart city and digital city: Twenty years of terminology evolution*. ITAIS.

Destination Earth initiative. (2023, March 13). *About Destination earth - A highly accurate digital model of our planet*. Destination Earth. https://destination-earth.eu/

Digital homepage. (n.d.). Retrieved June 25, 2024. https://ec.europa.eu/digital-building-blocks/sites/display/DIGITAL/Digital+Homepage

Digital Twin Consortium. (2016, September 30). Digital Twin Consortium. https://www.digitaltwinconsortium.org/

DIN SPEC 91357. (2017). https://www.dinmedia.de/de/technische-regel/din-spec-91357/281077528

DS4SSCC-DEP. (n.d.). *Interactive portal for building data spaces in Smart Communities*. DS4SSCC. Retrieved June 25, 2024, from https://inventory.ds4sscc.eu/

DUET. (2020). *D3.8 Digital Twin data broker specification and tools v1*. In Cordis EU research results. DUET Consortium. https://cordis.europa.eu/project/id/870697/results

DUET. (2021). D3.9 Digital Twin data broker specification and tools v2. DUET. https://www.digitalurbantwins.com/deliverables

DUET. (2022, October 31). *DUET's digital twin maturity model supports cities in their digital transformation*. DUET. https://www.digitalurbantwins.com/post/duet-s-digital-twin-maturity-model-supports-cities-in-their-digital-transformation

Eclipse Foundation. (n.d.). *Eclipse DittoTM • open source framework for digital twins in the IoT*. Eclipse Ditto. Retrieved June 25, 2024. https://eclipse.dev/ditto/

European Commission. (2023, June). *Testing and Experimentation Facilities (TEFs): Questions and answers*. Shaping Europe's Digital Future. https://digital-strategy.ec.europa.eu/en/faqs/testing-and-experimentation-facilities-tefs-questions-and-answers

European Commission. (n.d.-a). *Digital Europe programme*. European Commission. Retrieved July 26, 2024. https://commission.europa.eu/funding-tenders/find-funding/eu-funding-programmes/digital-europe-programme_en

European Commission. (n.d.-b). *European interoperability reference architecture (EIRA)*. Interoperable Europe - Joinup; interoperable Europe. Retrieved June 25, 2024. https://joinup.ec.europa.eu/collection/european-interoperability-reference-architecture-eira

European Commission. (n.d.-c). *Simpl: Cloud-to-edge federations empowering EU data spaces*. Shaping Europe's Digital Future. Retrieved June 25, 2024. https://digital-strategy.ec.europa.eu/en/policies/simpl#1712822729753-3

European Commission - Directorate-general for communications networks, content and technology. (2021, March). *Workshop report Digital Twins Technology Workshop*. https://ec.europa.eu/newsroom/horizon2020/redirection/document/75837

Exner, J.-P. (2016). The ESPRESSO - Project – A european approach for smart city standards. In *Computational science and its applications -- ICCSA 2016* (pp. 483–490). Springer International Publishing. https://doi.org/10.1007/978-3-319-42111-7_38

Gaia-X Association. (2022, March 25). *Gaia-X: A federated secure data infrastructure*. Gaia-X. https://gaia-x.eu/

Geonovum. (2022). *Consultatie Referentiearchitectuur Stelsel Digitale tweeling fysieke leefomgeving*. Geonovum. https://www.geonovum.nl/over-geonovum/actueel/consultatie-referentiearchitectuur-stelsel-digitale-tweeling-fysieke

GovStack implementation playbook. (n.d.). Implementation-Playbook. Retrieved April 22, 2024. https://govstack.gitbook.io/implementation-playbook

International Data Spaces Association. (n.d.). *The future of the data economy is here*. International Data Spaces. Retrieved June 25, 2024 from https://internationaldataspaces.org/

iShare Foundation. (n.d.). *Trust Framework for Data Spaces*. iSHARE. Retrieved June 25, 2024. https://ishare.eu/

Kaiser, G., & Pejstrup, E. (2021). Smart cities and communities. Joinup; Smart Cities Marketplace. https://smart-cities-marketplace-brochure.eu/.2023/#page=1

Lefever, S., Michiels, P., Schuurman, D., Coenen, T., & Vintila, N. (2023). *Smart data operations for better data-informed decision-making*. IMEC. https://www.imec.be/sites/default/files/inline-files/White%20paper%20-%20smart%20data%20operations.pdf

Living-in.eu. (2022, November). *Funding* Opportunity - Digital Europe Program, co-design of the Local Digital Twins (LDT) toolbox technical specifications for advancing the transformation of smart communities. *Living in EU*. https://living-in.eu/news/funding-opportunity-digital-europe-program-co-design-local-digital-twins-ldt-toolbox-technical

Living-in.EU. (2023). MIMs Plus version 6.0 Approved by the Living-in.EU Steering Board. *Living-in EU*. https://living-in.eu/sites/default/files/files/approved-mims-plus_li.eu_v6.0.docx_1.pdf

Living-in.EU Community. (n.d.). Declaration on joining forces to boost sustainable digital transformation in cities and communities in the EU. *Living in EU*. Retrieved June 25, 2024. https://living-in.eu/declaration

Maier, M. W. (1998). Architecting principles for systems-of-systems. *Systems Engineering, 1*(4), 267–284. https://doi.org/10.1002/(SICI)1520-6858(1998)1:4<267::AID-SYS3>3.0.CO;2-D

Mandal, S. (2024). A privacy preserving federated learning (PPFL) based cognitive digital twin (CDT) framework for smart cities. *Proceedings of the AAAI Conference on Artificial Intelligence, 38*(21), 23399–23400. https://doi.org/10.1609/aaai.v38i21.30400

Manville, C. (2014). *Mapping smart cities in the EU*. European Parliament. https://www.europarl.europa.eu/thinktank/en/document/IPOL-ITRE_ET(2014)507480

Microsoft. (2024). *Digital twins—Modeling and simulations*. Microsoft Azure; Microsoft. https://azure.microsoft.com/en-us/products/digital-twins

Mirza, J. (2021). Supporting strategic management decisions. *Strategic Direction, 37*(11), 7–9. https://doi.org/10.1108/sd-10-2021-0119

Nica, E., Popescu, G. H., Poliak, M., Kliestik, T., & Sabie, O.-M. (2023). Digital twin simulation tools, spatial cognition algorithms, and multi-sensor fusion technology in sustainable urban governance networks. *Mathematics, 11*(9), 1981. https://doi.org/10.3390/math11091981

O'Halloran, D., D'Souza, F., & Forum, W. E. (2020, July 29). How data can benefit everyone and harm no one: A new model. *World Economic Forum*. https://www.weforum.org/agenda/2020/07/new-paradigm-business-data-digital-economy-benefits-privacy-digitalization/

OASC. (n.d.). *Minimal Interoperability Mechanisms – MIMs*. Open Agile Smart Cities. Retrieved April 24, 2024. https://oascities.org/minimal-interoperability-mechanisms/

Panfilis, G. D. (2021, February 2). *FIWARE - Open apis for open minds*. FIWARE. https://www.fiware.org/

Publications – United for Smart Sustainable Cities (U4SSC). (n.d.). Retrieved June 25, 2024. https://u4ssc.itu.int/publications/

Sassen, S., & Kourtit, K. (2021). A post-corona perspective for smart cities: 'Should I stay or should I go?'. *Sustainability, 13*(17), 9988. https://doi.org/10.3390/su13179988

Shahat, E., Hyun, C. T., & Yeom, C. (2021). City digital twin potentials: A review and research agenda. *Sustainability, 13*(6), 3386. https://doi.org/10.3390/su13063386

Torres, L., Pina, V., & Acerete, B. (2005). E-government developments on delivering public services among EU cities. *Government Information Quarterly, 22*(2), 217–238. https://doi.org/10.1016/j.giq.2005.02.004

Turcanu, I., Castignani, G., & Faye, S. (2024, January 6). On the integration of digital twin networks into city digital twins: Benefits and challenges. *2024 IEEE 21st Consumer Communications & Networking Conference (CCNC)*. https://doi.org/10.1109/ccnc51664.2024.10454704

Usländer, T., Baumann, M., Boschert, S., Rosen, R., Sauer, O., Stojanovic, L., & Wehrstedt, J. C. (2022). Symbiotic evolution of digital twin systems and dataspaces. *Automation, 3*(3), 378–399. https://doi.org/10.3390/automation3030020

Widergren, S. E., Hardin, D., Ambrosio, R., & Cohen, D. (2008, January 1). *GridWise interoperability context-setting framework*. Unknown. https://www.researchgate.net/publication/239883349_GridWise_Interoperability_Context-Setting_Framework

# Chapter 6
# Public Development: Towards Open Standards and Components for Local Digital Twins

**Lieven Raes, Bart De Lathouwer, Gert Hilgers, and Stefan Lefever**

**Contents**



## 6.1 Introduction

Standards are not the first concern when a new concept or technology like Local Digital Twins (LDTs) emerges. Standards are considered premature when the focus lies on implementing new functionality-oriented implementations, often starting with a proof of concept. Standards, especially open standards, potentially conflict with creators' and commercial companies' visions to enter the market first and can conflict (entirely or partially) with patents and intellectual property. On the other

L. Raes (✉)
Digital Flanders, Brussels, Belgium
e-mail: lieven.raes@vlaanderen.be

B. De Lathouwer
Geonovum, Amersfoort, The Netherlands
e-mail: b.delathouwer@geonovum.nl

G. Hilgers
Open Agile Smart Cities, Brussels, Belgium
e-mail: gert.hilgers@oascities.org

S. Lefever
Interuniversitair Micro-Elektronica Centrum, Leuven, Belgium
e-mail: stefan.lefever@imec.be



L. Raes et al. (eds.), *Decide Better*,
https://doi.org/10.1007/978-3-031-81451-8_6

hand, a complex multi-layered system like an LDT, combining legacy ICT components, can only function in a sustainable way when these components can communicate and interact. Both viewpoints create friction that a set of minimal standards and interoperability concepts can bridge. The Minimal Interoperability Mechanisms (MIMs) (OASC, 2024) by OASC[1] and international standards from ISO,[2] W3C,[3] and OGC,[4] as well as domain-specific standards in each smart city domain, provide a good starting point to realise a complex system-of-systems (SoS) LDT. This chapter will provide insights into the standards landscape by pinpointing relevant standards related to Chap. 5, "Unlimited Potential: The Reusable Digital Twin", which focuses on LDT Architecture and Components, and Chap. 4 "Digital Twins: A central urban integrator to break down the silos", which focuses on LDT meta-requirements and features. This chapter also aims to pinpoint essential areas for implementing standards to assure interoperability and the importance of domain-related standards when realising use cases in these areas.

## 6.2 LDT Standards: A Wide Area – Introduction

A review of the digital twin standards landscape by Kung et al. (2022) listed over 250 relevant documents and papers. The amount and wide variety sketch a complex web of information covering horizontal/cross-domain related and geospatial standards and a diverse landscape of theme-specific standards related to construction, buildings, energy, industrial design, and robotics, amongst many others.

The central element in the LDT architecture is the management of theme-specific cases. Cases are detailed instances of a specific problem, such as planning a sustainable urban mobility measure or evaluating the impact of a new urban development. Cases are the basis for the main interactions between users and the LDT and are managed by Case Management Services (CMS). A typical task of a CMS is running what-if scenarios. A scenario operates inside a case and contains a configuration that can be used to evaluate different potential solutions to the policy issue as defined in the case. Experiments in an LDT context are specific model/data source configurations within a scenario, representing a distinct set of inputs, parameters or conditions applied to models. This creates a multi-level structure where a case defines the overall problem, a scenario outlines a solution or approach, and an experiment represents a specific configuration of models and data used to evaluate the scenario (Barron et al., 2023). The integration framework components in Fig. 6.1 are essential to realise the case-to-scenario LDT approach seamlessly to the end users of the LDT.

[1] Open Agile Smart Cities, https://oascities.org/

[2] International Organization for Standardization, https://www.iso.org/home.html

[3] World Wide Web Consortium, https://www.w3.org/

[4] Open Geospatial Consortium, https://www.ogc.org/

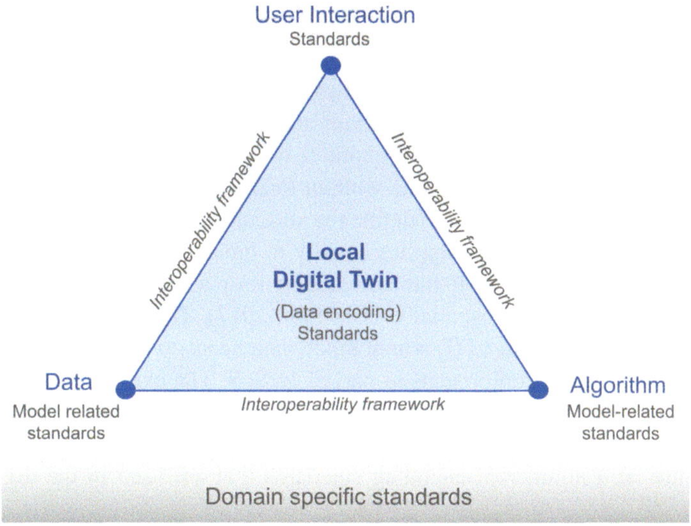


**Fig. 6.1** Based on Digital Twin; data, models, visualisation & integration – LDT interoperability framework (Barron et al., 2023)

In this chapter, we focus on standards directly related to the LDT case management and standards that are part of the LDT integration and interoperability triangle, integrating data, analytics and User eXperience (UX) subsystems and domain specific standards as depicted in Fig. 6.1.

## 6.3 LDT Standards and Capabilities

An LDT as an SoS integrates the data, analytics and UX subsystems as depicted. The central LDT component combines at least an asset registry assisted by a data and message broker and a case and scenario manager. Data sources (and products), whether integrated into data spaces (see Chap. 5) or a visualisation component with associated user experience, are two other essential components to realise an LDT case. The analytics/models component is used in impact modelling and policy prediction. Each of the elements of the LDT triangle (Fig. 6.1) stands for specific requirements and capabilities supported by standards and specialised tools. Starting from generic encoding standards supporting the cooperation between the data, model-related standards, visualisation-related standards and user-interaction standards. Apart from the generic IT standards, domain-specific standards used in specific LDT use case domains like transport and environment need to be considered.

### 6.3.1 LDT Data Encoding-Related Standards

The datasets exchanged by geospatial software products like LDTs have to be structured in a way that allows other applications and products to read the data and interpret the information it contains. Without a well-defined structure, enabling an application to read and interpret data without losing or missing information would be almost impossible. The need to define the structure and organisation of data formats and messaging protocols applies equally to binary formats such as GeoTIFF (Devys et al., 2019) as it does to human-readable formats such as XML (Bray et al., 2006; W3C, n.d.; Open Geospatial Consortium, 2017). The choice of an encoding standard is essential for an LDT, where much data needs to be exchanged between different, often legacy, components as part of an SoS. The use and focus on encoding standards to design an LDT as an SoS also points to the fact that little standardisation work has been done on open LDT integration frameworks. Table 6.1 Provides an overview of a number of encoding standards that are used in the digital twin context.

### 6.3.2 Data Model-Related Standards

Data fuels LDTs and data models are necessary to create a representation of the static environment (e.g. landscape, buildings, and transport infrastructure) in the public and private domain. To create a static environment, slow-moving data is needed. In an LDT context, fast-moving data provides the changing conditions of external parameters found in the living environment. Data from various external services like weather, traffic, and sensor networks provide information that can be monitored directly or become part of a geo-time series, i.e., feed into simulation models. Another form of data is user data, which provides insights that can't be measured directly on the terrain. Metadata, or data about data, links the various data types and is often used to create a catalogue of data for specific LDT cases and scenarios.

#### Slow-Moving Data

Slow-moving data is considered as data that doesn't change often, and doesn't need to change (update, modify or delete) regularly. In the context of LDTs, data about the physical living environment (e.g. buildings, roads, and public infrastructure ranging from bridges to benches) provides good examples of 'slow-moving' datasets. Most LDTs start from a dataset representing city assets.

CityGML, CityJSON and IFC (Industry Foundation Classes) are all open standards aiming to represent city-scale information. They are semantically rich and able to define a city with much detail. IFC, CityGML and its alternative encoding

**Table 6.1** Useful and well-used relevant encoding standards for LDTs

| Name | Description |
|---|---|
| CSV (Comma Separated Value) | A simple format is used to store tabular data, such as spreadsheets or databases, where each line of the file is a data record. |
| JSON (JavaScript Object Notation) and JSON-LD | JSON (Crockford, n.d.) is a lightweight data interchange format. It is easy for humans to read and write. It is easy for machines to parse and generate based on a subset of the JavaScript Programming Language Standard. JSON is a text format that is entirely language-independent but uses conventions familiar to programmers of the C family of languages, including C, C++, C#, Java, JavaScript, Perl, Python, and others. These properties make JSON an ideal data-interchange language. JSON became an ISO/IEC standard in 2017 (ISO/IEC, 2017). |
| YAML | YAML (Ben-Kiki et al., 2021) shares characteristics similar to JSON but uses Python-styled indentation to indicate nesting. Yaml also represents data as key-value pairs, supports more data types and is closer in its use of natural language to support developer use (Amazon Web Services, n.d.). |
| XML | XML (Bray et al., 2006; W3C, n.d.) is a more heavy-weight format (compared to JSON) and serves a similar purpose: a data-interchange format. Bindings for the most commonly used programming languages are available. The XML format is verbose and tends to bloat to very large sizes. XML is no longer considered as "the standard" for new data-interchange models. |
| PROTOBUF (Protocol Buffers) | Protobuf ("protocol buffers documentation", n.d.) is Google's language-neutral, platform-neutral, extensible mechanism for serialising structured data. Contrary to JSON, protobufs are not humanly readable and are faster (smaller) to transmit. (The idea behind protobuf is that human readability is not a primary feature, but performance is). |
| MPEG-V | MPEG-V outlines an architecture and specifies associated information representations to enable interoperability between virtual worlds (e.g. the digital content provider of a virtual world, gaming, simulation) and between real and virtual worlds (e.g. sensors, actuators, vision and rendering, robotics). MPEG-V is also known as ISO/IEC 23005 and has seven parts: (1) Architecture, (2) Control Information about syntax and semantics, (3) Sensory Information, (4) Virtual World Object Characteristics focussing on metadata, (5) Data Formats for Interaction Devices, (6) Common Types and Tools semantics and data types, (7) Performance and Reference Software ("MPEG-V", n.d.). |

CityJSON all promote vendor-neutral or agnostic and usable capabilities across various hardware devices, software platforms, and interfaces. IndoorGML provides a standard for indoor navigation in complex buildings and can also be considered as an example of slow-moving data.

### CityGML

CityGML (ISO 19136) defines an open conceptual model and exchange format for representing, storing, and exchanging virtual 3D city models. It facilitates the integration of urban geodata for a variety of applications for smart cities and urban digital twins, including urban and landscape planning; Building Information Modelling (BIM); mobile telecommunication, disaster management; 3D cadastre; tourism; vehicle and pedestrian navigation; autonomous driving and driving assistance; facility management, and; energy, traffic and environmental simulations (Haezel, 2021; Kolbe et al., 2021).

CityGML 3.0 is an evolution of the previous CityGML versions. While the previous versions standardised a GML exchange format, CityGML 3.0 standardises the underlying information model and can be implemented in various technologies, including GML and JSON (ibid). CityGML 3.0 contains important evolutions that support the creation of digital twins like Dynamizer, Versioning and Point Clouds. The Dynamiser feature allows for the integration of time-dependent data into the static city model, enabling simulations and analyses that can reflect changes over time. Dynamizers can be linked to any attribute of a city model element, providing a robust mechanism for incorporating real-time data feeds into the digital twin environment. The Versioning feature supports the management of the lifecycle of urban objects, allowing users to store, retrieve, and query different versions of objects as they change over time. This property makes CityGML 3.0 a powerful tool for long-term urban planning and historical analysis. The Point Cloud feature, for its part, supports detailed and accurate representations of the physical characteristics of urban environments, which are derived from real-world data. This is particularly useful for the precise modelling of terrain, buildings, and other infrastructure components in a digital twin setup.

City-JSON

CityJSON (Ledoux & Dukai, 2023) is an OGC Community Standard and data exchange format for digital 3D models of cities and landscapes. It aims to be easy to use (for reading, processing, and creating datasets), and it was designed with programmers in mind so that tools and application programming interfaces (APIs) supporting it can be quickly built. The JSON-based encoding of CityJSON implements a subset of the OGC CityGML data model (version 3.0) and includes a JSON-specific extension mechanism. Using JSON instead of GML allows us to compress files by a factor of 6 and simultaneously simplify the structure of the files. In addition to CityGML 3.0, work is being done on semantic compatibility by implementing semantic web technologies and by moving multidimensional urban data into linked-data models using Web Ontology Language (OWL) technology (Vinasco-Alvarez, 2020). OWL is a Semantic Web language designed to represent rich and complex knowledge about things, groups of things, and relations between things. OWL is a computational logic-based language that allows knowledge expressed in OWL to be exploited by computer programs to verify the consistency of that knowledge or to make implicit knowledge explicit (W3C OWL Working Group, 2012).

IFC (Industry Foundation Classes)

IFC is a standardised, digital description of the built environment, including buildings and civil infrastructure. The IFC schema specification can describe how a facility or installation is used, how it is constructed, and how it is operated. Today, IFC is typically used to exchange information from one party to another for a specific business transaction (Building Smart International, n.d.). IFC is an open, international standard (ISO 16739-1:2018) and can also be encoded in XML (Bray et al., 2006; W3C, n.d.) and JSON (ISO, n.d.).

IDS (Information Delivery Specification)

The IDS specification is a candidate standard being developed by buildingSMART International to support the definition of information requirements in a way that is easily read by humans and interpreted by computers. The main goal is to help people in the built asset industry define their exchange requirements better and add clarity among various stakeholders. It ensures asset owners can specify accurately what they want and gives project participants a better insight into what they need to deliver. It adds certainty and clarity when combined with other standards and services. IDS aims to be used to specify any data in the built asset industry but works best on data that is structured according to the IFC standard (van Berlo et al., n.d.).

IndoorGML

IndoorGML is an OGC® standard for representing and exchanging indoor navigation network models. IndoorGML aims to establish a common schema for indoor navigation applications. It models the topology and semantics of indoor spaces, which are needed for the components of navigation networks. Nevertheless, IndoorGML contains only a minimum set of geometric and semantic modelling of construction components to avoid duplication with other standards, such as CityGML and IFC.

IndoorGML defines the following information about the indoor space: (1) navigation context and constraints, (2) space subdivisions and types of connectivity between spaces, (3) geometric and semantic properties of spaces and connectivity, and (4) navigation networks (logical and metric) and their relationships. The standard is implemented as a Geography Markup Language version 3.2.1 application schema (Lee et al., 2022).

### Fast-Moving Data (IoT)

Fast-moving (or dynamic) data in an LDT context typically represents features that move geographically or generate a frequent stream of observations based on sensor information.

### Moving Features Standard

The OGC Moving Features standard ISO 19141 (ISO, 2008) specifies standard encoding representations of the movement of geographic features. Moving feature data, typically representing vehicles or pedestrians, become relevant in urban planning and mobility models that can be part of an LDT. Innovative LDT use cases are expected to require an overlay and integration of moving feature data from different sources to create greater social and business value. Examples of applications that require integrated simulation are disaster risk management, traffic information services, security services, navigation for robots, aviation or maritime traffic monitoring, and wildlife tracking and conservation. The OGC Moving Features standard supports encodings in XML (Bray et al., 2006; W3C, n.d.), JSON (Crockford, n.d.; ISO, 2017) and CSV (Asahara et al., 2019).

### IoT Standards

Internet of Things (IoT) devices were developed following the development and popularity of mobile devices like smartphones, GPS modules, and (mobile) data networks. To connect IoT devices to networks and allow data usage, numerous standards and protocols have been developed by telecom organisations like the ITU[5] and the ETSI.[6] On the level of data exchange and semantics, the ISO-IEC (International Electrotechnical Commission), IEEE,[7] W3C (World Wide Web Consortium) and OGC (Open Geospatial Consortium) have implemented multiple standards described in Sect 7.3.

### Metadata

Metadata is often described as “data about data”. ISO also speaks about information about a resource. “Resource” is a purposely general term to emphasise the generality of the ISO metadata standards and models. A resource can be a service, a collection site, software, a repository, or many other things. Metadata in an LDT context,

---

[5] International Telecom Union, https://www.itu.int/en/

[6] European Telecom and Standardisation Institute, https://www.etsi.org/

[7] Institute of Electrical and Electronics Engineers, https://www.ieee.org/

where multiple datasets, usually from different sources, become available, is important to allow sensible data selection and provide the necessary insights into the visualised results of an LDT. Metadata, a form of a metadata registry (MDR), is needed to maintain a database of metadata. MDR may contain the semantics of data and, ideally, will support geospatial metadata standards that can be easily transformed into multiple metadata publication formats, as depicted in Fig. 6.2. According to ISO, an understanding of data is fundamental to their design, harmonisation, standardisation, use, reuse and interchange (ISO/IEC, 2023a). The metadata element is part of the Federated Asset Catalog component in Chap. 5's architecture.

The asset catalogue has to cover two main metadata-related requirements. First, to standardise metadata of datasets, algorithms and simulation models, data processing components, schemas, vocabularies, ontologies, and applications in a human-readable way. Second, to allow machine-to-machine communication. A shift from the Dublin Core towards ISO or Geospatial Data Catalogue Vocabulary – GEO-DCAT (European Commission, n.d.-a) application formats supporting the ISO 19115 Geographic Information – Metadata standard (ISO, 2014), Geographic Information Services standard ISO 19119 standard (ISO, 2016), Geographic Information – XML schema implementation ISO 19139 standard (ISO, 2019) and the EU Inspire data specification in Europe (European Commission, n.d.-b), is advisable to cover additional metadata elements. These additional elements include

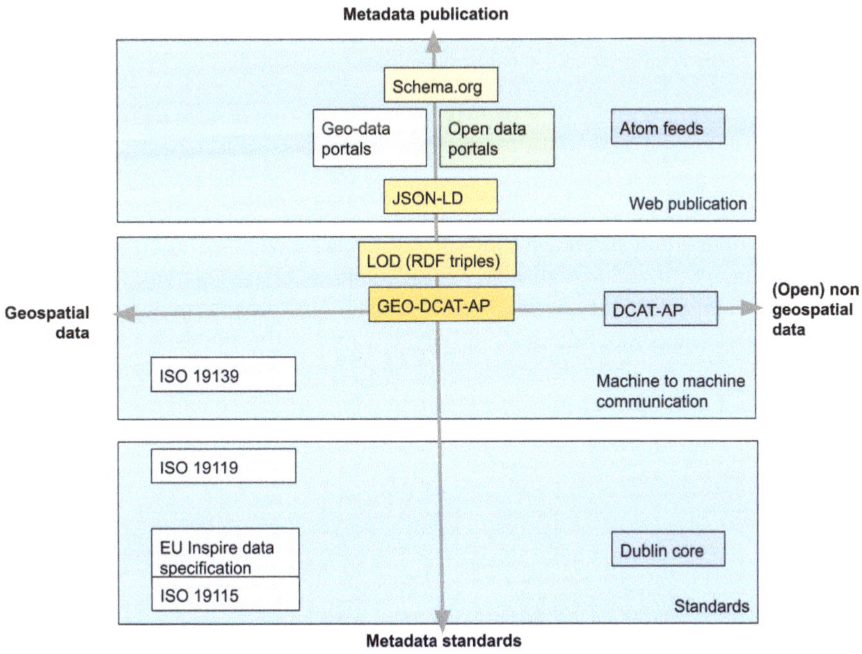


**Fig. 6.2** Overview of MetaData standards (Raes et al., 2019)

the difference between datasets and dataset series, as well as spatial data elements, including coordinate reference systems, spatial extents, maintenance frequency, spatial resolution, and distribution formats.

### *6.3.3 Algorithm and Model-Related Standards*

Harpham et al. (2019) conclude that the (urban) environment is made up of a complex set of interconnected processes. Therefore, understanding the environment requires not only understanding the processes in isolation but also the interactions between these processes. Traditional methods of simulating such environmental interactions have included passing the outputs of one numerical model into another or creating a single 'super-model' covering a variety of processes, according to the authors. However, in a complex LDT context where multiple models pass information towards each other, depending on the situation as input or output data, the simulation model (components) should be able to exchange data without changes to the core of the simulation model itself. Until today, only a few initiatives have been taken in the standardisation field to cope with this requirement. Domain overarching (agnostic) semantics play an important role, too. A common understanding of geospatial concepts is needed to allow models to work together in a useful way. This goes beyond geospatial reference systems to include shared data ontologies, e.g. a joint understanding of useful concepts like a road segment used by traffic models extended to air quality models.

#### Model Interaction Standard (OpenMI)

The purpose of the OGC OpenMI Interface Standard is to define an Open Modelling Interface. The purpose is to enable a runtime exchange of data between process simulation models and also between models and other modelling tools such as databases and analytical and visualisation applications. A key design aim has been to bring about interoperability between independently developed modelling components, where those components may originate from any discipline or supplier. The ultimate aim is to transform integrated modelling into an operational tool accessible to all, and so doing, open up opportunities created by integrated modelling for innovation and wealth creation (Vanecek & Moore, 2014).

**Algorithm Transparency Standard (ATS)**

The (ATS is an initiative by Eurocities[8] to set shared categories of information that cities can use to help people understand how the algorithms used in local administrations work and what their purpose is. It also allows people to compare different algorithms within and across cities. This standard supports documenting decisions and assumptions for both management of artificial intelligence (AI) governance and providing meaningful transparency in a standardised way (Groenen & Eurocities, 2022). The algorithm standards are ideally part of the data and model catalogue, where specific metadata about datasets using the described metadata formats is available. The ATS is very useful as part of the simulation model metadata, which contains one or more algorithms by default.

With the rise of AI, specifically machine learning models, specific MLOps (Machine Learning Operations) methods are being developed. These methods could be catalysts for more de facto standardisation in the field of managing algorithms and pipelines.

### *6.3.4 Visualisation-Related Standards*

An LDT front-end is usually associated with a 3D city view on a Personal Computer. New extended reality solutions (XR) provide a more immersive city view. The visualisation standards below comprise Geospatial, 3D Visualisation, and XR initiatives, including Augmented Reality (AR) domains.

**Geospatial-Related Standards**

Amongst the many GIS-related standards like the Open Geospatial Consortium (OGC) WMS (de la beaujardiere, 2006), WFS (Vretanos, 2010), KML (Burggraf et al., 2015) and CAD-related standards from ISO, ANSI,[9] ASME,[10] and IEEE,[11] the open CityGML (Heazel, 2021; Kolbe et al., 2021) and IndoorGML (Lee et al., 2022) standards are strongly related to visualising public domain and building information, frequently used in urban digital twins.

---

[8] Eurocities, https://eurocities.eu/

[9] American National Standards Institute, https://www.ansi.org/

[10] American Society of Mechanical Engineers, https://www.asme.org/

[11] Institute of Electrical and Electronics Engineers, https://www.ieee.org/

OpenGL

OpenGL® is a widely adopted 2D and 3D graphics API in the industry, applied in a wide variety of applications on different computer platforms. OpenGL is window- and operating system-independent as well as network-transparent. OpenGL enables developers of software for PCs, workstations, and supercomputing hardware to create high-performance, visually compelling graphics software applications in markets such as CAD, content creation, energy, entertainment, game development, manufacturing, medical, and virtual reality (Khronos Group, n.d.-a). An alternative to OpenGL is Microsoft DirectX (Microsoft, n.d-a).

CDB (Common Database)

OGC CDB defines a standardised model and structure for a single, "versionable" virtual representation of the earth. A CDB structured data store provides a geospatial content and model definition repository that is plug-and-play interoperable between database authoring workstations. CDB originates in the (military) flight simulation world, combines fast and slow-moving features, and ensures that all representations are based on the same updated information (Reed, 2021).

## 3D Data Visualisation Standards

3D Object Visualisation glTF, glB and USD

glTF™ (GL Transmission Format) is a royalty-free specification for efficiently transmitting and loading 3D scenes and models by applications. glTF is suited to present elements from the built environment in an LDT 3D visualisation context to visualise complex objects like vehicles and street furniture. The standard focuses on visual fidelity and less on data semantics compared to more verbose formats like CityGML. glTF minimises the size of 3D assets and the runtime processing needed to unpack and use those assets. glTF defines an extensible, common publishing format for 3D content tools and services that streamlines authoring workflows and enables interoperable use of content across the industry. glTF 2.0 has been released as the ISO/IEC 12113:2022 (ISO/IEC, 2022a) International Standard (Khronos Group, 2024).

A glB file (.glb), which stands for "GL Transmission Format Binary file", is a standardised file format used to share 3D data. It can contain information about 3D models, scenes, models, lighting, materials, node hierarchy, and animations. A glB file is more compact and has faster loading times than glTF but has more limited editing possibilities.

Also, Universal Scene Description (USD), often referred to as open USD, serves as a framework designed for the exchange of 3D computer graphics data. Emphasising collaboration, non-destructive editing, and facilitating various perspectives on graphics data, the framework provides a robust platform for seamless interaction (Pixar Animation Studios, 2021). OpenUSD offers more than a file format. It's an open source 3D scene description used for 3D content creation and interchange among different tools (NVIDIA Corporation, n.d.).

#### Extensible 3D (X3D)

X3D is a set of royalty-free ISO/IEC ("X3D Specifications – ISO/IEC-19775-1", n.d.) standards for declaratively representing 3D computer graphics. X3D includes multiple graphics file formats, programming-language API definitions, and runtime specifications for delivering and integrating interactive network-capable 3D data.

### Extended Reality (XR)

XR (Extended Reality) is an umbrella term covering immersive technologies, including VR (Virtual Reality), AR (Augmented Reality) and MR (Mixed Reality). At a minimum, all these technologies allow the user to interact with a semi-virtual environment and even with real elements simultaneously. XR can play a complementary role in visualising data driven representations of real-world environments. The XR-related commonly used APIs below are worth studying when implementing immersive elements into your LDT solution.

#### OpenXR

OpenXR is a royalty-free, open standard that provides direct access to XR runtimes across diverse platforms and devices. The OpenXR Adopter's Program enables consistent cross-vendor testing and reliable operation of OpenXR across multiple platforms and devices with OpenXR-conformant products (Khronos group, n.d.-b). OpenXR supports multi-vendor VR headsets. Another technology offering similar features is steamVR (Valve Corporation Authors, n.d.).

#### OpenVR/SteamVR

OpenVR, usually referred to as SteamVR, is another commonly used software platform tailored for VR applications. It furnishes developers with a suite of tools and APIs (Application Programming Interfaces) to facilitate the creation and dissemination of VR content across diverse VR headsets. Versatile in its support, SteamVR accommodates an array of devices and encompasses functionalities such as tracking, rendering, and input management (Steamworks, 2024).

### XR Content Creation Platforms

Beneath the mesmerising XR encounters lies an intricate ecosystem of tools and platforms that empower the crafting of such content. However, these are not standards; the platforms below are being used increasingly to create immersive digital twins.

Unity is one of the foremost platforms for XR content development. Its engine facilitates crafting immersive experiences across various platforms, spanning VR headsets, AR devices, and beyond. It has an extensive array of tools, asset libraries, and a wide community.

Unreal Engine is another example of a popular content creation platform and comprises a series of 3D computer graphics engines. Originally tailored for PC first-person shooters, it has since found application across diverse gaming genres and has garnered significant adoption in other sectors, like the media and movie industry (Okoro, 2023).

More recently, so-called game engines like Unity and Unreal have been used in Chicago (Huitzilihuitl, 2019), Paris (John, 2021), Shanghai (Weir-McCall, 2020) and Utrecht (Gemeente Utrecht, n.d.) to visualise the city's digital twin.

### ARML (OGC)

The scope of the ARML 2.0 standard is to provide an interchange format for AR applications to describe an AR scene, focusing on vision-based AR. The format describes the virtual objects that are placed into an AR environment, as well as their registration in the real world. ARML 2.0 is specified as an XML grammar (Bray et al., 2006; W3C, n.d.). The goal of ARML 2.0 is to provide an extensible standard and framework for AR applications to serve the AR use cases that are currently being used or developed. Many different standards and computational areas developed in different working groups come together with AR. ARML 2.0 needs to be flexible enough to tie into other standards without actually having to adopt them, thus creating an AR-specific standard with connecting points to other widely used and AR-relevant standards (Lechner, 2015).

### AR Content Creation Platforms for Mobile Devices

Apple's ARKIT and Google ARCore platforms both deliver a wide range of Augmented Reality possibilities for the iOS and Android mobile operating systems. Supported features include motion tracking, scene/environmental understanding, and light and scale estimation (Katchin Tech, 2023).

### *6.3.5 User-Interaction Standards*

The user-machine interaction of complex systems directed to a broad group of users, including people with limited knowledge and even persons with disabilities, is challenging. An LDT is a complex integrated environment, including collaboration and community elements related to complex visualisations, that can profit from a wide range of consistent specifications, best practices and design languages to avoid complicated systems and negative user experience.

#### LDT Integrated Environment

Creating a unified and consistent user experience for an LDT is needed to enhance understandability, usability, efficiency, and accessibility. Key elements are (I) Consistency: user interfaces and interaction pattern; (II) Workflows: well-defined and logically connected; (III) Sharing and synchronisation: seamless sharing and synchronised data sharing across different components and tools; (IV) Multi-platform: Integrated environment extendable across various platforms like desktops, mobile devices and XR devices; (V) Personalisation: options to define personal requirements and preferences (Barron et al., 2023).

WAI-ARIA is a W3C-recommended technical specification for accessibility best practices. It offers guidelines for web pages, dynamic content and User Interaction (UI) components. It especially helps with dynamic content and advanced user interface controls developed with HTML, JavaScript, and related technologies. Without WAI-ARIA, certain functionality used in Web sites is not available to some users with disabilities, especially people who rely on screen readers and people who cannot use a mouse (W3C, 2023). WAI-ARIA specification helps developers to create content that conforms with the Web Content Accessibility Guidelines, WCAG2.0. WCAG2.0 covers a wide range of recommendations for making Web content more accessible. Following these guidelines will make content accessible to a broader range of people with disabilities, including blindness and low vision, deafness and hearing loss, learning disabilities, cognitive limitations, limited movement, speech disabilities, photosensitivity and combinations of these. The WCAG 2.0 are written as testable statements that are not technology-specific (Caldwell et al., 2008).

Google Material Design is an open, well-used WAI-ARIA-compatible design language and system for creating consistent user interfaces across different platforms and devices (Google, n.d.). However, WAI-ARIA and the Google Material Design toolset can not unlock the full LDT 2D and 3D visualisation and navigation potential for people with disabilities. However, some descriptive LDT parts, like case and scenario descriptions and community discussions, can be made accessible following accessibility guidelines and practices. On the API level, Swagger offers a popular framework that enables developers to describe, document and visualise REST APIs (IBM, n.d.) through the open API standard (Smartbear software, n.d.).

**Collaboration and Community Management**

Collaboration and community management comprise a combination of tools and processes aimed at involving the public in service improvement, policy development, and decision-making. The toolset typically includes interviews and surveys, observation and community management, co-design and co-creation, and feedback analysis. Next to the standards mentioned above, like WAI-ARIA, WCAG2.0, and Material Design, the following initiatives are specifically crucial in collaboration and community management.

In Europe, community management and collaboration involving personal data are affected by the GDPR regulation to protect personal data (European Parliament and Council, 2016).

A promising way to store personal data shared with the community, supported by W3C, is Solid. Solid aims to improve privacy and data ownership on the Web through a proposed set of conventions and tools for building decentralised social applications (W3C Community Development Team, n.d.). One of the developed technology tools is encrypted data vaults. Also relevant are authentication and authorisation standards (see Sect. 6.5.5).

### *6.3.6 Domain-Specific Standards*

The previous standards can be considered domain-agnostic standards that help realise LDT solutions. Nevertheless, an LDT can also profit from domain-specific standards used in each smart city domain, e.g. transport and mobility, environment, and spatial planning. These standards can relate to defining domain-specific vocabularies and ontologies but can also comprise the standardisation of IoT measurements and the standardisation of impact and visualisation. The examples below introduce the different types of smart city domain-specific standardisation initiatives and examples in three popular smart city domains.

**Smart city Domain-Related Standards**

SAREF (Daniele et al., 2020) stands for Smart Applications REFerence and provides a suite of ontologies, forming a shared consensus model intended to enable semantic interoperability between solutions from different providers and among various activity sectors in the IoT. SAREF is ideal to contribute to the development of data spaces. SAREF is a suite of individually versioned ontologies containing a core ontology, a set of reference ontology patterns that provide guidelines on using and extending SAREF, and different extensions for vertical domains. Examples of smart city-related domain-specific extensions are the smart city domain extension itself and the energy, environment, building, smart agriculture, water and e-health domains.

The Smart Data Models initiative (Abid, n.d.) is another initiative aiming to support the adoption of a reference architecture and compatible common data models underpinning a digital market of interoperable and replicable smart solutions. The initiative tries to define harmonised representation formats and semantics usable in a wide variety of applications that both consume and publish data. The proposed models are located in several domains relevant to LDTs, such as smart cities, smart water, smart energy, smart health, smart environment, and smart logistics.

#### Spatial Design and Planning

An essential standard in the broad domain of spatial design and planning, and one of the cornerstones of every LDT 3D visualisation, is BIM. The definition of a BIM standard states that building information modelling is: "a digital representation of physical and functional characteristics of a facility. A BIM is a shared knowledge resource for information about a facility forming a reliable basis for decisions during its life cycle; defined as existing from earliest conception to demolition" (LetsBuild, 2023).

The first global BIM standard is ISO 19560 (ISO, 2018), referring to the digitisation and organisation of data about civil engineering works and buildings and includes the BIM concepts and principles and the delivery phase of the assets. The ISO 19560 forms the basis for local BIM implementations.

#### Mobility-Related

The mobility domain has a long tradition of standardisation initiatives in the fields of Intelligent Transport Systems and traffic information. DATEX II is a good example of a real-time traffic data exchange standard, while General Transit Feed Specification (GTFS) is a well-used standard related to (real-time) public transport data exchange.

DATEX II is the European electronic language to exchange traffic information and data. It has grown from a standard for exchanging traffic-related data between road-traffic control centres to a coherent set of standards supporting the digitalisation and automation of the entire road transport ecosystem that contributes to the safe, green and efficient travelling of persons and goods. DATEX II supports two closely related use cases: providing information from data sources to data consumers on the one hand and supporting joint traffic management operations of collaborative competent authorities on the other ("Datex II organisation", 2021).

In the public transport domain, the GTFS is a worldwide open standard for distributing relevant information on transit systems. It allows public transit agencies to publish their transit data in a format that can be consumed by a wide variety of software applications. Today, the GTFS data format is used by thousands of public transport providers. GTFS consists of two main parts: GTFS Schedule and GTFS Real-time. GTFS Schedule contains information about routes, schedules, fares, and geographic transit details. GTFS Realtime contains trip updates, vehicle positions, and service alerts. It is based on Protocol Buffers for serialising structured data (GTFS.org, n.d.).

#### Open LR, an Example of a Domain Overarching Semantic Standard

OpenLR™ describes a method and a format for encoding, transmitting and decoding (map-independent) references of locations. Locations are objects in a digital map, like points, paths and areas. The method makes it possible to encode a location in a map, send it to a system with another (possibly different) map, and find the location back in this receiving map. Provided that both the encoder map and decoder map meet 'navigable map' standards (in terms of accuracy and content), the encoder does not need to know about the decoder map, and the decoder also does not have to care about the map used for encoding the location. The format to transmit such location reference is compact so that it can be used in systems having bandwidth restrictions. The OpenLR™ standard can handle line locations (e.g. paths), point locations (e.g. POIs) and area locations (e.g. regions) in a digital map (TomTom International B.V., 2012).

#### Air Quality

Also, in the environmental field, numerous standards exist. The ISO/TC146 Committee on Air Quality has published over 200 standards, including more than 25 related to the ambient atmosphere, including the description of detailed pollutant measurement methods applied, e.g. PM, NO2 and black-carbon sensors. On an ontology level, multiple (science) initiatives proposed semantic air quality models, but until now, they have not led to a joint, well-used standard (Calbimonte et al., 2015; Vámos et al., 2024). Also, in terms of defining Air Quality Indexes (AQI), including meaningful colour codes, different initiatives are leading to other scales. China, Europe, India, and the US have their own AQI indexes. One of the most impactful global initiatives to define a worldwide AQI is done by the Breezometer initiative (Breezometer, 2018).

## 6.4 Towards an Interoperable LDT

Complex systems like LDTs demand an interoperability strategy that allows us to move forward in the design of LDT solutions and to guarantee interoperability using standards and (open) future-proof software components. The Pivotal Points of Interoperability (PPI) concept allows ICT architects to define areas where interoperability has the highest priority and impact. The Minimal Interoperability Mechanisms concepts (see Chap. 5) help to define the level of interoperability needed to ensure strategic interoperability, making it possible for the current state of play of the technological (standardisation) landscape to move forward.

### 6.4.1 The Importance of Pivotal Points of Interoperability (PPIs)

One of the key challenges in the smart city space, and thus also LDTs, is the abundance of standards and technologies available for smart cities and IoT. These standards and technologies are usually documented in large volumes of descriptions and processes, which makes their application integration difficult.

Yet, there are some concepts and component standards that independent teams arrived at in common. For example, no one would be surprised that most smart city applications use existing internet standards as the technology choice for exchanging information.

These well-known and used concepts and components have been conceptualised as 'Pivotal Points of Interoperability – PPIs' (NIST, 2021). If these PPIs are known, integrating a new component into an existing deployment will be simplified. For example, knowing that the syntax of data exchanged is either eXtensible Markup Language – XML (Bray et al., 2006; W3C, n.d.) or JavaScript Object Notation – JSON (Crockford, n.d.) yields a small set of boundaries for integration if technology A (the incumbent) and technology B (the next great idea) were chosen differently.

The PPI concept was developed by the US (NIST).[12] It was initially focused on Cyber-Physical Systems (or IoT) in general. Still, a group of standardisation agencies, facilitated by NIST, developed the Internet Enabled Smart City framework (NIST, n.d.-a) to identify how it could be used to support interoperability in smart cities.

The PPI concept is extendable and helpful in defining complex SoS solutions like LDTs. In complex integrative systems, it is not possible or desirable to be fully comprehensive on standards. Standardising all possible solution elements will limit the opportunity for discovery and innovation. The concept of PPIs is that through the analysis of prominent technologies, feasible strategic standardisations are made to guarantee a high level of interoperability and leave flexibility to realise the necessary solutions. One potential approach is defining PIP to standardise interfaces between software layers like infrastructure, data, aggregation, business, and visualisation-oriented layers in the case of an LDT.

[12] National Institute of Science and Technology, https://www.nist.gov/

On an infrastructure level, IPv6 and TLS 1.2 related to cybersecurity are good examples of PPIs in a (federated) LDT architecture with multiple cooperating servers connected via the internet.

Data service standards are related to the data and aggregation layer. PPI standards are related to data syntax and semantics, including content-related data ontologies describing slow- and fast-moving data. Catalogue and metadata standards, offering insights into data and simulation models, can use existing metadata standards, and can eventually be extended to cover simulation model-related metadata.

The interaction-related PPI is primarily linked to the aggregation and business layer. However, there is a lack of standards that allow for the meaningful context-related exchange of messages and data between specific domain-oriented simulation models, encoding standards, and open data and message broker tools. PPIs related to visualisation are relevant at two levels: using standardised geospatial dataset models like CityGML, IFC, and 3D object rendering standards. Next to that, there are multiple software platforms to visualise data in different types of XR environments (Fig. 6.3).

The NIST partnership developed a framework to help identify potential PPIs through objective analysis. Therefore, the framework identifies a set of 'aspects/concerns' covering the key areas against which any IoT-related system can be analysed. Aspects can be related to functionalities, business elements, human interaction, trustworthiness, timing, data, boundaries and lifecycle elements. For each aspect, potential domains of concern can be formulated (NIST, n.d.-b).

### *6.4.2 Minimal Interoperability Mechanisms (MIM) for LDTs*

The GridWise Architecture Council formulated three levels of interoperability in their ContextSetting Framework of 2008: The technical base level (A) concentrates on syntaxis comprising physical/logical connectivity, network interoperability and syntactic interoperability. The Information level (B) focuses on semantics comprising the semantic understanding and business context, and the organisational level (C) is described as a pragmatic level containing business procedures and objectives and economic/regulatory politics (GridWise Architecture Council, 2008). An analysis of the LDT related standards clarifies that, despite the organisational and business-oriented nature of LDTs, the relevant existing standards are mainly oriented to the technical and information levels (A and B).

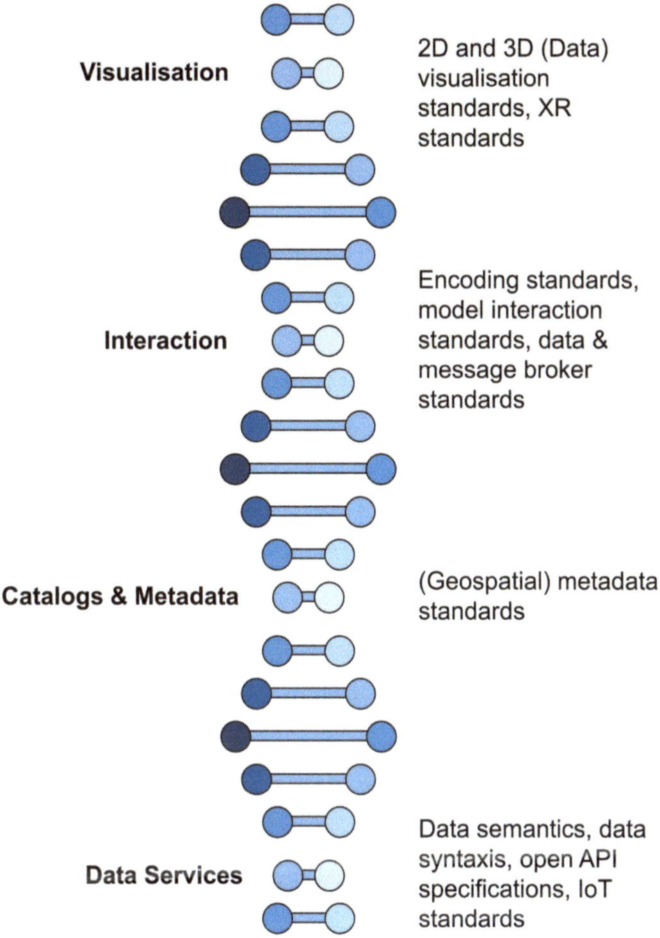


**Fig. 6.3** LDT Pivotal Points of Interoperability Domains

An in-depth analysis by Barron et al. (2023) defines the concept of Building Blocks (BB), providing a level of abstraction that translates LDT capabilities into specifications for possible tools and standards in a vendor-agnostic way and links them to the OASC MIMs (OASC, 2024). A total of 18 LDT BBs have been defined, covering elements like strategy, integration, visualisation and UX, algorithms and models, data services and data components (Table 6.2).[13]

The study is based on the MIM methodological concept and concludes that Minimal Interoperability is minimally good enough[14] for LDT core integration

[13] For an in-depth review of the LDT building blocks and MIMs check Chap. 5 of this book.

[14] Good enough meaning existing standards are applicable; however, there will be a need for extra effort to support integration with other BBs

**Table 6.2** LDT building blocks (BB) – Minimal Interoperability Mechanisms (MIM) relation and maturity levels (Barron et al., 2023)

| BB | Building Block (BB) | BB Category | Relevant MIMs | Maturity Level |
|---|---|---|---|---|
| **BB.01** | **Reference Architecture** | Strategy | All | N/A |
| **BB.02** | **Case & Scenario Manager** | Integration Components | MIM4[a], MIM 5[b], MIM6[c] | Good enough |
| **BB.03** | **Collaboration & Community Management System** | Visualisation and UX | MIM4, MIM 5, MIM6 | Good enough |
| **BB.04** | **Data Query Service** | Data Services | MIM6 | Good enough |
| **BB.05** | **Data Replication Client** | Data Services | MIM5 | Good enough |
| **BB.06** | **Data Workflow and Component Orchestration** | Integration Components | MIM5 | Plug and Play[d] |
| **BB.07** | **Extended Reality (AR/VR Services, etc.)** | Visualisation and UX | MIM4, MIM5, MIM6, MIM7[e] | No existing standard[f] |
| **BB.08** | **Federated Learning Service** | Algorithms & Models | MIM4, MIM5, MIM6 | No existing standard |
| **BB.09** | **Integrated Environment** | Visualisation and UX | MIM6 | No existing standard |
| **BB.10** | **Interaction Service** | Integration Components | MIM6 | No existing standard |
| **BB.11** | **Message Broker** | Integration Components | MIM5, MIM6 | Good enough |
| **BB.12** | **Model Abstraction SDK/ Service** | Algorithms & Models | MIM9[g] | No existing standard |
| **BB.13** | **Model Catalogue** | Algorithms & Models | MIM5 | Good enough |
| **BB.14** | **Model Usage Guidelines** | Governance & Conformance | MIM5, MIM9 | No existing standard |
| **BB.15** | **Algorithms & Models** | Algorithms & Models | MIM1[h], MIM4, MIM5, MIM6 | Good enough |
| **BB.16** | **Asset Registry** | Data Services | MIM2[i], MIM5 | Plug and Play |
| **BB.17** | **Synthetic Data Generation Tools** | Data Components | MIM1 | Good enough |
| **BB.18** | **Data Storage: Data Lake, Data Warehouse, Data Lakehouse** | Data Components | MIM2 | Good enough |

[a]OASC MIM 4: Trust – Personal Data Management
[b]OASC MIM 5: Transparency – Fair Artificial Intelligence
[c]OASC MIM 6: Security – Security Management
[d]Plug and Play meaning: Standards exist and facilitate interoperability and integration
[e]OASC MIM 7: Places – Geospatial Information Management
[f]No existing standard meaning: Needed standards and policies for this BB and associated tools are not defined yet
[g]OASC MIM 9: Analytics – Data Analytics Management
[h]OASC MIM 1: Context – Context Information Management
[i]OASC MIM 2: Data Modules – Shared Data Models

components (e.g. BB.02 Case & Scenario Manager, BB.06 Data Workflow and Component Orchestration, BB.11 Message Broker), but there is room for improvement on the level of Interaction Services (BB10). Data-related BBs such as BB.04 Data Query Service, BB.05 Data Replication Client, BB.17 Synthetic Data Generation Tools, and BB.18 Data Storage (Data Lake, Data Warehouse, Data Lakehouse) can guarantee sufficient levels of maturity, although much remains to be done on semantics and business-procedures level. Minimal Interoperability on the Algorithm and Model level can ensure that multiple domain-related simulation models can interact in a reasonably new domain where standards are not yet available. At the level of model catalogues (BB.13) and domain-specific algorithms and models (BB.15), minimal Interoperability can be guaranteed. However, no standards are available for model abstraction, such as specific software development kits (BB.12) or model usage guidelines (BB.14). The domain of Visualisation and UX, which has several BBs relevant for LDTs, can be seen as different compared to the other BB categories since many solutions and technologies are available.

## 6.5 LDT Components and Standards

Based on the first LDT BB concept by Barron et al. (2023), the above requirement and capability-related standards based on Fig. 6.1 are related to the LDT BB-based reference architecture described in Chap. 5. Together with visualisation and UX-related components and standards, as well as more horizontal-oriented visualisation standards, the section provides an overview of the LDT standardisation landscape. The focus is on central LDT integration components; data service-related and algorithm and model-related components that form the LDT core and allow evidence-informed policy prediction.

### *6.5.1 LDT Integration Components*

The LDT Integration BBs deliver the following LDT capabilities dependent on the supported LDT cases and ambition levels: context information provisioning, case/scenario/experiments management, data processing, data flow and component orchestration, data transformation, technical transparency and explainability, interaction support, (near) real-time data processing, publishing, subscribing, ingesting, actuation command and control.

### BB.02 Case and Scenario Management

The Case and Scenario Management BBs trigger the execution of algorithms on data and are, therefore, the key element that can link certain outputs of algorithms to the functional context in which it was used. Applying model and data assets can only be made accountable if it is linked to the functional usage.

No specific standards or solutions for case and scenario management have been found. However, it should be possible to envision an open API specification along with some business rules for creating such a service. Ideally, the solution is accompanied by an ontology and supports JSON-LD (Kellog et al., 2020). This will help maintain interoperability and extensibility overall.

The Case and Scenario manager is the primary interface for the digital twin user and has important links to other core BBs (BB.03, BB.04, BB.06, BB.10, BB.11, BB.13 and BB.16).

### BB.06 Data Workflow and Component Orchestration

The Data Flow and Component Orchestration building block controls flow orchestrations and facilitates the ability to execute multiple separate but interrelated steps in a data and control flow in the right order. This BB takes the raw data and facilitates the data processing into valuable insights or actionable information. Data workflows are commonly needed to support data (processing) pipelines, data integration, data analysis and data visualisation applications and are thus relevant for all types of LDTs.

Relevant data processing and transformation standards are JSON (Crockford, n.d.), XML (Bray et al., 2006; W3C, n.d.), SQL (ISO/IEC, 2023b) while Protobuf ("Protocol Buffers Documentation", n.d.) also assist data processing. Relevant open tools are Apache airflow (Apache Software Foundation, n.d.-a), Flyte (Flyte Project Authors, 2024), Apache NiFi (Apache Software Foundation, n.d.-b) and Apache Beam (Apache Software Foundation, n.d.-c).

The Data Workflow and Component Orchestration BB is part of the core LDT and plays an essential role in ensuring the support between data, models and visualisation and has links to other core BBs (BB.04, BB.10, BB.11 and BB.12).

### BB.10 Interaction Service

The Interaction Service supports the interaction of data, models and visualisation through a client interface. The service keeps track of changes made in an LDT in the hypothetical context of a scenario. Scenarios are executed in steps and trigger changes – made by a user or via an LDT client – leading to interactions with other BBs. Adding sound barriers, closing down roads, or updating the virtual state of a city after a computation are examples of changes that need to be tracked so that the digital twin becomes interactive and changes can be replayed.

Relevant standards to encode changes are JSON (Crockford, n.d.), XML (Bray et al., 2006; W3C, n.d.) and Protobuf ("Protocol Buffers Documentation", n.d.). Also, communication protocols to facilitate asynchronous communication, providing reliable message delivery, including AMQP (ISO/IEC, 2014), MQTT (ISO/IEC, 2016), Websockets (Rice, 2024; PubNub Inc., n.d.), REST (IBM, n.d.), SOAP (Gillis, n.d.) and Protobuf are essential to ensure that message not get lost in transit.

The Interaction Service BB has a strong link with the following BBs (BB.05, BB.06 and BB.11).

**BB.11 Message Broker**

The Message Broker is a critical component at the heart of an LDT architecture linked with almost all LDT BBs. It abstracts over the message streaming algorithm that provides streaming and buffering capabilities of high-velocity data. It serves as an intermediary layer to manage the distribution of messages, ensuring that they are correctly delivered to the correct recipients and, if necessary, ensuring that they are adequately transformed to meet the recipient's needs. The Message Broker (1) enables communication between LDT components, (2) maintains message channels, e.g. topics and queues, (3) provides a unified API, (4) ensures reliable message delivery, (5) provides features for message filtering, and (6) scales to manage high message volumes. Operation mechanisms are publish-subscribe and message queueing.

Useful standards for data processing, publishing, describing, and streaming are LDES (Colpaert, 2023), Kafka (Apache Software Foundation, 2023d), MQTT (ISO/IEC, 2016), and Websockets (Rice, 2024; PubNub Inc., n.d.). Standards related to IoT, including measuring, sensing, control and actuation (command and control), are NGSI-LD (Kellog et al., 2020), LDES and OGC IoT standards (see Chap. 7). Protobuf ("Protocol Buffers Documentation", n.d.) can be a standard for scalable publish-subscribe and low-latency message management. Message Queuing, including communication with (un)available subscribers of uncoupled components, can be standardised using Apache Kafka and RabbitMQ (Broadcom, n.d.). The two aforementioned components and MQTT can ensure a reliable delivery, preventing message loss.

In addition to open software tools like RabbitMQ, Apache Kafka offers solutions for message servicing and data transport through Apache ActiveMQ (Apache Software Foundation, n.d.-d) and ZeroMQ (ZeroMQ authors, n.d.).

## *6.5.2 LDT Data Service-Related Components*

The data service-related LDT BBs combine data storage, data publishing, data replication, data transformation, data time travel, (meta) data schema management, data source management, semantic governance and compliance, and procedural and technical transparency capabilities related to the LDT supported cases and ambition levels.

## BB.04 Data Query Service

Data Query Services provide a secure interface to access, explore, and understand the data within the digital twin. They allow users to ask questions and perform analyses on the data using a standard query language, typically SQL (ISO/IEC, 2023b), GraphQL (The GraphQL Foundation, n.d.) or SPARQL. However, other interfaces can also be used, especially when scalability is essential and running arbitrary queries is not desirable (e.g. using Linked Data and Linked Data Event Streams). An LDT typically calls on different data sources and models. Thus, it is vital that the necessary data can be queried or requested, which can be managed and modified to conduct the desired scenarios and experiments.

Relevant querying standards are SQL (ISO/IEC, 2023b), GraphQL (The GraphQL Foundation, n.d.), SPARQL (Garlik & Seaborne, 2013), REST (IBM, n.d.), LDES (Colpaert, 2023), and NoSQL (MongoDB, Inc., n.d.-a). In terms of SQL syntax, the versions starting from SQL-92 (version 3) to the more recent versions SQL2019 (version 8) and SQL2023 (version 9) are important to consider (ISO/IEC, 2023b). As output formats, JSON (Crockford, n.d.), CSV, and XML (Bray et al., 2006; W3C, n.d.) are essential standards that need to be supported.

Relevant open tools are Apache Druid (Apache Software Foundation, 2023a), Presto (The Presto Foundation, n.d.), Apache Spark (Apache Software Foundation, n.d.-e), Apache Hive (Apache Software Foundation, 2023b), Apache HBase (Apache Software Foundation, n.d.-f), Apache Drill (Apache Software Foundation, 2022b), Apache Impala (Apache Software Foundation, 2023c); ElasticSearch (Elasticsearch B.V., n.d.) and LDES (Colpaert, 2023).

The used tools must be able to interact with the LDT's data storage tools and depend on the following BBs: BB.05, BB.06, BB.09, BB.16 and BB.17.

## BB.05 Data Replication Client

Maintaining an accurate and up-to-date representation of a city in an LDT is a complex task due to the dynamic nature of urban environments. Capturing the evolving changes from different asynchronous sources can be a complex problem since digital twins continuously produce results based on these changing data resources. These can be the output of models, IoT platforms, and physical environment changes. A data replication strategy and the client bringing the strategy into practice are instrumental for the success of an LDT. Hence, this BB is to interface with such a system from the context of an LDT. There can be different strategies to deploy data replication in streaming and batch mode. A crucial aspect is to maintain versions of key data objects, as it is crucial for data lineage and data archiving.

In the federated approach, data source systems keep track of versions and offer access to previous versions that can be replicated within the LDT. An alternative way is event sourcing, where the data sources publish their data changes as events that are stored in a strictly ordered, immutable manner.

Relevant standards for data replication that enable subscription to, and receipt of event streams are MQTT (ISO/IEC, 2016), AMQP (ISO/IEC, 2014), Kafka (Apache Software Foundation, 2023d), and LDES (Colpaert, 2023). Formats relevant for the support of data serialisation are JSON (Crockford, n.d.), LDES, Protobuf ("protocol buffers documentation", n.d.), and Avro (Apache Software Foundation, 2022a). Prometheus (The Linux Foundation, n.d.) and Grafana (Grafana Labs, n.d.) can be used to monitor and alert data streams.

The Data Replication Client relates to all data production and consumption interface BBs, as well as the data storage and archiving BBs like BB.04, BB.16, BB.17 and BB.18.

## BB.16 Asset Registry

An LDT relies on external assets like data, simulation models, environment models, and more. Because these assets are dynamic, an asset governance system is needed.

*Asset governance* is defined as the capability to manage data schemas, data vocabularies, business glossaries, and their interrelations. An essential component of this governance is managing asset metadata and providing lineage and provenance records for utilising these assets, tracing back to the decisions made based on them. The role of the Asset Registry is to serve as an index cataloguing the assets involved in the digital twin. While the asset documentation can exist external to an LDT instance, the registry is integral for traceability and discoverability.

Relevant standards are ontology management from the W3C and OGC and data source management (metadata) standards like DCAT-AP (Raes et al., 2019) or geospatial-oriented ones like ISO 19115 (ISO, 2014). Standards for data source and algorithm discovery and management are RDF ("Resource Description Framework (RDF)", 2014), DCAT-AP, ISO19115, OpenAPI (The Linux Foundation®, 2022) and GraphQL (The GraphQL Foundation, n.d.). In contrast, SPARQL (Garlik & Seaborne, 2013) and GraphQL are tailored for data source, model, and algorithm interrogation.

Relevant open tools to consider are the comprehensive knowledge archive network, CKAN (Open Knowledge Foundation, n.d.), Apache Atlas (Apache Software Foundation, 2018), Amundsen-Lyft (Grover, 2019), and the DataHub project (DataHub Project Authors, n.d.).

The Asset Registry, a core LDT component, has strong links to BBs BB.02, BB.06, and BB.13.

**BB.17 Synthetic Data Generation Tools**

Synthetic Data Generation Tools are software tools or frameworks designed to create artificial or simulated data that closely resemble real-world data. These tools use algorithms and statistical models to generate data with similar statistical properties, distributions, and relationships as the original data. Synthetic data generation tools can provide significant high-level insights with datasets that resemble actual data without compromising privacy or security.

Relevant standards are NGSI-LD (Kellog et al., 2020), JSON (Crockford, n.d.) and XML (Bray et al., 2006; W3C, n.d.). Open software tools are Synth (OpenQuery inc., 2021) and the more popular OpenSynthetics (OpenSynthesis, n.d.).

**BB.18 Data Storage: Data Lake, Warehouse, Lakehouse**

Data Storage refers to the retention of data provided and recorded through various recording devices or provided by users. Databases are designed to store and manage vast amounts of data systematically, allowing users and applications to access, query, and manipulate information. Three data storage management architectures apply to LDTs. A Data Warehouse collects raw data and centralises it in a repository organised in a relational database format. A Data Lake stores vast amounts of data in its natural format, such as raw, unstructured and structured data where no predefined schemes are required. A Data Lakehouse combines both former aspects. Data Lakehouses utilise similar data structures from data warehouses and combine them with data lakes' low-cost storage and flexibility.

Relevant standards are SQL (ISO/IEC, 2023b), GraphQL (The GraphQL Foundation, n.d.), SPARQL (Garlik & Seaborne, 2013), REST (IBM, n.d.), LDES (Colpaert, 2023) and NoSQL (MongoDB Inc., n.d.-a). Relevant open software components are the Microsoft Entity Framework (Microsoft, n.d.-b) and Hibernate object-relational mapper – ORM ("Hibernate ORM", n.d.), the PostgreSQL (The PostgreSQL Global Development Grouprence, n.d.), MySQL (Oracle, n.d.), MongoDB (MongoDB Inc., n.d.-a), Apache Cassandra (Apache Software Foundation, n.d.-g) database systems and the Redis (Redis Ltd., n.d.) in memory storage key-value database.

The Data Storage LDT component is strongly related to BB.04 and BB.16.

### *6.5.3 Algorithm and Model-Related Components*

The algorithm and model-related BBs deliver a wide range of capabilities, such as federated learning and training services, model abstraction and hosting services, algorithm and model management, accountability information provisioning, prediction, and machine learning AI. The use of these capabilities is independent of LDT cases and ambitions.

### BB.08 Federated Learning Service

Federated Learning is an advanced machine learning paradigm where a shared global model is trained across multiple decentralised edge devices or servers holding local data samples without explicit data exchange, i.e. the model is brought to the data. In the context of LDTs, this method can be particularly beneficial as it allows for training on a vast array of locally gathered data, which might pertain to various parts of the urban environment, without the need to transfer this data to a central location. This can enhance privacy and security while maintaining the benefits of collaborative learning.

To ensure interoperability, JSON (Crockford, n.d.), XML (Bray et al., 2006; W3C, n.d.), and Binary serialisation techniques are suitable for handling various data formats and schemes. To guarantee API versioning, standards formats and schemes, event driven synchronisation, distribution and storage standards are needed. Websockets (Rice, 2024; PubNub Inc., n.d.) and AMQP (ISO/IEC, 2014). Model exchange formats and standardised communication protocols such as ONNX (The Linux Foundation, 2019) and TensorFlow SavedModel (TensorFlow Developers, 2024) can be used to allow Federated Learning to be scalable towards an increasing group of participants and data sources. Popular open source tools supporting Federated Learning elements are TensorFlow Federated (TFF) (TensorFlow Developers, 2024) and Flower (Flower Labs GMBH, n.d.).

### BB.12 Model/Abstraction SDK/Service

The Model Abstraction Service can be an API or Software development kit that serves as a vital conduit in a digital twin setup, facilitating the control, orchestration, execution and composition of diverse models. Its purpose includes supporting different execution modes, enabling interoperability and managing model data. Additionally, it ensures secure access, offers scalability, supports error handling, and provides logging for performance tracking. This component acts as the backbone of any predictive LDT, bridging the gap between complex models and the user interface. There have been previous attempts to standardise model interactions, like OpenMI (Vanecek & Moore, 2014), by defining abstractions, but they have yet to lead to a standardised abstraction or open interface that can be used as a reference point in the state-of-the-art.

Several standards are available, starting from the API/SDK design principles, including language-agnostic APIs like gRPC (gRPC Authors, n.d.) and Rest (IBM, n.d.). LDES (Colpaert, 2023), MQTT (ISO/IEC, 2016), Apache Kafka (Apache Software Foundation, 2023d), and RabbitMQ (Broadcom, n.d.) are standardised output and data subscription formats. SCXML (Barnett et al., 2015) can be used as a standard for tracking the execution of the model states. Popular Open Software tools supporting model abstraction are TensorFlow Extended (TFX) (TensorFlow Developers, n.d.), Kubeflow (The Kubeflow Authors, n.d.) and MLFlow (MLflow Project, n.d.).

The Model/Abstraction component is strongly related to BB.08, BB.13 and BB.15.

## BB.13 Model Catalogue

In a multi-domain predictive LDT, attention is needed to track which models are being used and their purpose to align with the outward-facing MIM5 capabilities of fairness, transparency, explainability, and even accountability. A Model Catalogue plays a vital role in the management of machine learning models (and others) in a digital twin environment. It is responsible for machine learning models' storage, versioning, and metadata tracking. Where an Asset Registry focuses more on the internal and technical aspects of asset management and governance, the model catalogue exposes the algorithm assets more elaborately towards external usability. Critical elements of a catalogue are versioning, metadata tracking, discoverability, provenance and transparency.

Applicable standards are related to metadata. The relevant ones are DCAT (Raes et al., 2019), ISO 19115 (ISO, 2014), schema.org ("Schema.org", 2024), DAML (Digital Asset (Switzerland) GmbH, 2023) and Google Model Cards (Fang & Miao, 2020). TFX (TensorFlow Developers, n.d.), PMML (Grossman et al., 1999), ONNX (The Linux Foundation, 2019), Seldon (Seldon Technologies Limited, n.d.) and MLFlow (MLflow Project, n.d.) are worth considering to track the model's state. Equally relevant are BB.12 Model/Abstraction SDK/Service output and data subscription formats, such as LDES (Colpaert, 2023), MQTT (ISO/IEC, 2016), Apache Kafka (Apache Software Foundation, 2023a) and RabbitMQ (Broadcom, n.d.). Language-agnostic API/SDK Design Principles like gRPC (gRPC Authors, n.d.) and REST (IBM, n.d.) can provide a uniform interface to interact with different models irrespective of their underlying implementation.

The Model Catalogue component is strongly related to BB.12, BB.15 and BB.16.

## BB.15 Algorithms and Models

An LDT should facilitate the evolution towards incorporating diverse algorithms and models pertinent to the complexities of smart cities and communities. Although various models already exist for individual domains, providing stakeholders with insights into each domain's present condition and hypothetical scenarios, the LDT's advantage lies in its capacity to standardise the accessibility of these algorithms and models for all stakeholders. This fosters evidence-informed decision-making across multiple domains. Thus, within an LDT framework, the emphasis is on fostering interactions between different fields and disciplines. The pivotal role of algorithms and models thus becomes a critical driver of the LDT's efficacy. Michiels et al. (2021) see the following roles for algorithms and models: (1) spatial interpolation where no direct measurement data is available, (2) integration, presentation and analysis of complementary data sets, (3) cross-correlation of data from different domains, (4) inference of properties/attributes that are not directly measured, (5) conversion of measurements and state information into KPIs, (6) extrapolation (prediction) of business as usual (BAU) and what-if scenarios.

Standard formats necessary for model interoperability and orchestration are JSON (Crockford, n.d.), XML (Bray et al., 2006; W3C, n.d.), RESTful HTTP (IBM, n.d.), Kafka (Apache Software Foundation, 2023d), RabbitMQ (Broadcom, n.d.) and Kubernetes (The Kubernetes Authors, n.d.). The following open generic popular software tools can be used: TensorFlow (TensorFlow Developers, 2024), Eclipse MOSAIC (Eclipse Foundation, 2024), Eclipse SUMO (Eclipse Foundation, n.d.), and Apache BEAM (The Apache Software Foundation, n.d.-c).

Popular tools in the field of transport are the proprietary traffic models of PTV Visum (PTV Planung Transport Verkehr GmbH, n.d.) and Omnitrans (Goudappel BV, n.d.). The MATsim (MATSim Community, n.d.) and TraMod (Traffic Modeller authors, n.d.) are open alternatives. In the air quality field, the SRM1 and SRM2 models (Kenniscentrum InfoMil, n.d.), the OPS model (RIVM Authors, n.d.), the LOTOS-EUROS model (TNO, n.d.) and the IFDM model (VITO NV, n.d.).

Examples of noise simulation models are open NoiseModelling and NoisePlanet solutions (CNRS & Université Gustave Eiffel, n.d.).

The Algorithms and Models building block is closely related to BB.12, BB.13, BB.14 and BB.16.

**BB.14 Model Usage Guidelines**

Model Usage Guidelines establish a framework enabling users to select suitable modelling techniques pertinent to the specific problem, encompassing data-level considerations. This encompasses directives on model implementation, encompassing algorithm/technique selection, appropriate space/time resolutions for data processing, streaming requisites, data quality considerations, and other relevant factors.

The guidelines relate to all model and algorithm building blocks, including BB.08, BB.12, BB.13, BB.14, and BB.15.

### *6.5.4 Visualisation and UX-Related Components*

The visualisation and UX-related components act as a mirror where all the LDT outcomes come alive. Supported capabilities vary depending on the case and ambition context, offering an integrated user experience that includes advanced 2D and 3D visualisation and (geo) dashboarding, augmented reality visualisation, virtual reality visualisation, citizen engagement in cases and scenarios, scenario feedback gathering, collaboration, and community management.

### BB.03 Collaboration and Community Management System

This BB combines tools and processes needed to involve the public in decision-making, policy development, and service improvement. These practices are particularly important for governments, organisations, and institutions seeking to gather insights, opinions, and feedback from citizens or users to enhance their operations and address their needs effectively. Key elements of this BB focus on delivering effective communication channels, delivering participation methods to enable citizens to participate in decision-making processes, ensuring accessibility to all citizens, and offering transparency and feedback incorporation into the policy-making process.

There are no specific ICT standards related to collaboration and community management. Examples of open participation platforms are Shareabouts (OpenPlans authors, n.d.), MySociety (SocietyWorks Ltd., n.d.), Decidim (Associació de Software Lliure Decidim, n.d.), YourPriorities (Citizens Foundation, n.d.) and CitizenLab (Citizen Lab authors, 2023). Covise (HLRS Authors, n.d.) is an example of a collaborative visualisation platform. Sociocracy 3.0 (Bockelbrink et al., n.d.) and OpenGov platform (OpenGov Authors, n.d.) are two open examples of policy simulation and process engagement tools, while Polis (Polis Authors, n.d.) is more focused on collaborative decision-making. Consul (Consul Democracy, 2023) and Helios Voting (Helios Authors, n.d.) support e-petitions and e-voting.

The Collaboration and community management building block is closely related to BB.02, BB.07, and BB.09.

### BB.07 Extended Reality

XR is a comprehensive term that encompasses various immersive technologies, including virtual reality (VR), augmented reality (AR), and mixed reality (MR). In each instance, XR facilitates an immersive user experience, allowing interaction with virtual elements within a (semi-)virtual environment, sometimes concurrently with real-world elements. The interplay between LDTs and XR lies in their complementary functions when immersed in data driven depictions of real-world settings.

The integration of XR technologies into LDTs holds potential advantages in fostering interactivity and engagement among diverse stakeholders, such as urban planners, decision-makers, citizens, and communities. This integration can yield a more profound comprehension of urban environments, enhancing engagement and fostering collaboration and inclusivity by enabling active participation in prospective developments. Interactive exploration through data layers, real-time modifications to virtual city elements, and simulation of diverse scenarios can optimise the way in which cities are designed.

Relevant standards are WebXR (W3C Immersive Web Working and Community Groups, n.d.), OpenXR (Khronos group, n.d.-b), OpenVR (Steamworks, 2024), glTF (Khronos Group, 2024), MPEG-V ("MPEG-V", n.d.), ARML (Lechner, 2015) and ARCore (Katchin Tech, 2023).

The Extended Reality building block is closely related to BB.03 and BB.09.

## BB.09 Integrated Environment

The principal aim of an Integrated Environment is to establish a cohesive and uniform user experience, thereby augmenting usability, efficiency, and accessibility. This objective is realised through software integration, semantic interoperability, and adherence to design best practices.

An Integrated Environment needs to offer a cohesive user experience characterised by several key elements:

- *Consistency*: Interfaces and interaction patterns remain uniform across different tools, aiding user familiarity and reducing the learning curve;
- *Smooth workflows*: Well-defined and logically connected workflows enable users to perform tasks seamlessly, minimising interruptions;
- *Data sharing and synchronisation*: Seamless sharing and real-time data updating across various tools maintain integrity and coherence;
- *Multi-platform support*: The environment extends across different platforms, ensuring consistency and usability;
- *Personalisation*: Customisation options cater to individual user preferences without compromising consistency;
- *Accessibility*: Designed to be inclusive, the environment accommodates users with disabilities or impairments;
- *Collaboration and communication*: Facilitates smooth communication and collaboration among multiple users;
- *Error handling*: Implements mechanisms to manage errors gracefully and guide users toward resolution without disruption;
- *Performance*: Optimised performance ensures responsive interactions and minimises delays for an enhanced user experience.

Relevant standards are the WAI-ARIA (W3C, 2023) and WCAG 2.0 (Caldwell et al., 2008) for accessibility of web pages, dynamic content and UI components; REST APIs (IBM, n.d.) and LDES (Colpaert, 2023) for data synchronisation; Websockets (Rice, 2024; PubNub Inc., n.d.) for collaboration support; I18n and L10n (Unabel Inc. Authors, 2022) for internationalisation and location; OpenMetrics for feedback gathering and user testing; and OpenAPI (The Linux Foundation, 2022) for documenting API specifications.

Prometheus (The Linux Foundation, n.d.) offers a well-supported toolkit for monitoring and alerting on time-series data. Jaeger (The Jaeger Authors, n.d.) offers a distributed tracing system for monitoring and troubleshooting, while the Swagger framework (Smartbear software, n.d.) offers a solution for describing, documenting and visualising REST APIs through the OpenAPI standard.

The Integrated Environment building block is closely related to BB.11.

### 6.5.5 Security Standards

An LDT solution should follow several security guidelines. During the design, defensive measures should be integrated for all LDT solution elements. An LDT also needs to be a resilient system that is able to repel, e.g. denial-of-service attacks, withstand usage spikes, avoid penetration, and spot suspicious activities. Regarding high-value or critical LDT BBs, it is essential to ensure that security technology is always available. The security design needs to be considered on the level of the overall LDT solution and a single use case level (Barron et al., 2023). The first level of security is on the LDT network requirements and architecture level, as the ITU recommends (ITU-T, 2022). The following LDT BBs specify security-related standards.

#### BB.01 Reference Architecture

The LDT reference architecture (Barron et al., 2023) mentions four security-related components to be applied: (1) user identification and management, (2) access management, (3) encryption, and (4) failover.

#### BB.03 Collaboration and Community Management

The collaboration and community management BB focuses on interacting with citizens to build a trustful, sustainable relationship. This requires collaboration and a community management system that includes user self-registration, community management, and login functionality. Useful standards are the Oauth 2.0 standard protocol for authorisation ("OAuth 2.0", n.d.) and the OpenID interoperable authentication protocol (OpenID Foundation, n.d.).

#### BB.04 Data Querying

A versatile LDT solution contains a data and model catalogue, allowing data querying and simulation modelling. If data and services aren't open and require a fee for their licence or usage (e.g. HPC processing costs), users can only access them when they are authorised to ensure security and confidentiality. Authentication of users/applications and implementing mechanisms such as Role-Based Access Control (RBAC) might be in place. The ISO/IEC information security management requirements for data integrity, confidentiality, and availability provide important guidelines that are key to ensuring a safe and resilient LDT (ISO/IEC, 2022b).

### BB.05 Data Replication Client

Maintaining an accurate and up-to-date representation of a city in an LDT is a complex task due to the dynamic nature of urban environments. Data replication can be done in different ways. It can be done in a federated way, replicated in the LDT itself or via event sourcing, where the data sources publish their data changes as events. The transmission can be secured using OAuth 2.0 ("OAuth 2.0", n.d.), HTTPS or the cryptographic protocols Secure Socket Layers (SSL) and Transport Level Security (TLS).

### BB.08 Federated Learning

Federated Learning (FL) is an advanced machine learning paradigm where a shared global model is trained across multiple decentralised edge devices or servers holding local data samples without explicit data exchange (i.e., the model is brought to the data). To implement FL, next to an appropriate networking and security infrastructure, certain data encryption algorithms (e.g. Triple DES, AES, RSA, Blowfish, Twofish (Arcserve, 2023)) and data anonymisation techniques (e.g. data masking, pseudonymisation, generalisation, perturbation, swapping (Devane, 2023)), must be considered.

### BB.17 Synthetic Data Generation Tool

Synthetic Data Generation offers the technology to create artificial or simulated data and can be used to protect and offer GDPR-compliant privacy.

## 6.6 Conclusions

The new LDT concept combines openness, transparency, stakeholder involvement, advanced analytics, predictive modelling and advanced data visualisation, including 3D and Extended Reality (XR). Realising a system that combines this vast list of requirements, legacy systems, new ICT components, and building blocks (BB) is challenging. It demands a sensible combination of standards and well-supported software tools to allow agile future development.

Because of its system-of-systems (SoS) nature, LDTs combine multiple IT domains and specialisations, ranging from data management and simulation modelling to advanced visualisation and complex scenario management. In all these areas, a wide variety of standards is involved.

Despite the vast number of applicable standards, especially in the data and visualisation domain, the core LDT components responsible for managing the processing of data and events have to fall back on quite generic syntactic standards, often encoding-related standards. There is a clear lack of standards in the semantic and business domains to realise semantic interoperability and the exchange of meaningful messages between simulation models to realise model cooperation. As a consequence, much effort still goes into labour-intensive, complex, and specific links between datasets and data and simulation models.

A wide range of useful open software components, partially based on the mentioned underlying standards, are available in many of the LDT domains, including simulation modelling, visualisation in XR, artificial intelligence (e.g. federated learning), data and model cataloguing, and collaboration and community management. Further development of semantic and business-oriented standards is needed as a framework for future component cooperation.

Pivotal Point of Interoperability (PIP) and Minimal Interoperability Mechanisms (MIMs) are the two frameworks that give direction as to which standards should be followed and which tools should be used to ensure interoperability in key (pivotal)-points of the LDT. These pivotal points are located in the data services domain to guarantee data interoperability, covering at least syntax and semantic levels. Integrating all datasets, simulation models, and interaction tools in an asset-registry and metadata system is another pivotal point. A third PIP is located at the level of a standardised message broker tool, including the well-known encoding and data and message broker standards. This PIP is crucial to streamlining cooperation between the core LDT BBs. The need for cross-domain semantic standards and model interaction standards is mainly located here. The interaction with visualisation clients is another PIP, where 3D data visualisation standards and XR standards and tools are available. Security and privacy standards can be considered a fifth horizontal PIP overarching the other relevant LDT PIP domains.

Recent initiatives such as the EU LDT Toolbox contribute to the formulation of MIMs that support BBs mentioned in Chaps. 4 and 5. Such initiatives lay the groundwork for a standards-based procurement of LDTs that handle overarching digital twin cases across multiple domains.

To conclude, with the current technology, architectural concepts, and interoperability frameworks, it is possible to realise an advanced LDT solution as a SoS, integrating legacy systems with new LDT components. However, on a use case level, no optimal solutions are available yet that would allow to avoid tailor-made, specific connectors between mutual data sets, simulation models, or a combination of both. Further research into and development of semantic ontologies and standards within the broad smart city domain is needed to enhance the development of more efficient LDT solutions in the future.

## References


Abid, A. (n.d.). *Smart Data Models*. Github – Smart Data Models. https://github.com/smart-data-models

Amazon Web Services. (n.d.). *What's the Difference Between YAML and JSON*. AWS. https://aws.amazon.com/compare/the-difference-between-yaml-and-json/

Apache Software Foundation. (2018). Apache Atlas. https://atlas.apache.org/#/

Apache Software Foundation. (2022a). *Apache Avro™—A data serialization system*. Apache Avro. https://avro.apache.org/

Apache Software Foundation. (2022b). *Apache Drill—Schema-free SQL Query Engine for Hadoop, NoSQL and Cloud Storage*. Apache Drill. https://drill.apache.org/

Apache Software Foundation. (2023a). *Apache® Druid—Druid is a high performance, real-time analytics database that delivers sub-second queries on streaming and batch data at scale and under load*. Druid. https://druid.apache.org/

Apache Software Foundation. (2023b). *Apache Hive—The Apache Hive ™ is a distributed, fault-tolerant data warehouse system that enables analytics at a massive scale and facilitates reading, writing, and managing petabytes of data residing in distributed storage using SQL*. Apache Hive. https://hive.apache.org/

Apache Software Foundation. (2023c). *Apache Impala—Apache Impala is the open source, native analytic database for open data and table formats*. Apache Impala. https://impala.apache.org/

Apache Software Foundation. (2023d). *Apache Kafka—Apache Kafka is an open-source distributed event streaming platform used by thousands of companies for high-performance data pipelines, streaming analytics, data integration, and mission-critical applications*. Kafka. https://kafka.apache.org/

Apache Software Foundation. (n.d.-a). Apache Airflow™—Airflow™ is a platform created by the community to programmatically author, schedule and monitor workflows. *Apache Airflow*. https://airflow.apache.org/

Apache Software Foundation. (n.d.-b). *An easy to use, powerful, and reliable system to process and distribute data—NiFi automates cybersecurity, observability, event streams, and generative AI data pipelines and distribution for thousands of companies worldwide across every industry*. https://nifi.apache.org/

Apache Software Foundation. (n.d.-c). The Unified Apache Beam Model—The easiest way to do batch and streaming data processing. Write once, run anywhere data processing for mission-critical production workloads. *Beam*. https://beam.apache.org/

Apache Software Foundation. (n.d.-d). *ApacheMQ – Flexible & Powerful Open Source Multi-Protocol Messaging*. https://activemq.apache.org/

Apache Software Foundation. (n.d.-e). Apache Spark—Unified engine for large-scale data analytics. *Apache Spark*. https://spark.apache.org/

Apache Software Foundation. (n.d.-f). *Apache HBASE*. https://hbase.apache.org/

Apache Software Foundation. (n.d.-g). Apache Cassandra—Open Source NoSQL Database—Manage massive amounts of data, fast, without losing sleep. *Apache Cassandra*. https://cassandra.apache.org/_/index.html

Arcserve. (2023, September). *Cybersecurity—5 Common encryption algorithms and the unbreakables of the future*. Arcserve. https://www.arcserve.com/blog/5-common-encryption-algorithms-and-unbreakables-future

Asahara, A., Shibasaki, R., Ishimaru, N., & Burggraf, D. (2019). *OGC® moving features encoding part I: XML core* (Version 1.0.2.). Open Geospatial Consortium. https://docs.ogc.org/is/18-075/18-075.html

Associació de Software Lliure Decidim. (n.d.). *Decidim is a digital platform for citizen participation*. Decidim Free Open-Source Democracy. https://decidim.org/

Barnett, J., Akolkar, R., Bodell, M., Burnett, D. C., Carter, J., McGlashan, S., Torbjörn, L., Helbing, M., Hosn, R., Raman, T. V., Reifenrath, K., Rosenthal, N., & Roxendal, J. (2015). *W3C – State Chart XML (SCXML): State Machine Notation for Control Abstraction* (Version 1.0). W3C. https://www.w3.org/TR/scxml/

Barron, M. G., Cristiana, R., Carvalho, F., Regêncio, N., Correia, A., Birecki, E., et al. (2023). *D05.02 Public report on the LDT Toolbox detailed specifications requirements*. European Commission. https://data.europa.eu/doi/10.2759/384198

Ben-Kiki, O., Evans, C., & döt Net, I. (2021, October 1). *YAML Ain't Markup Language (YAML™) version 1.2*. https://yaml.org/spec/1.2.2/

Bockelbrink, B., Priest, J., & David, L. (n.d.). *Evolve Effective Collaboration At Any Scale—Sociocracy 3.0 free social technology for growing agile and resilient organizations*. S3. https://sociocracy30.org/

Bray, T., Hollander, D., Layman, A., & Tobin, R. (2006). *Extensible Markup Language (XML)* (1.1 (Second Edition)). W3C. https://www.w3.org/XML/

Breezometer. (2018). *How we built a Global Air Quality Index for all*. Medium. https://breezometer.medium.com/breezometers-global-air-quality-index-real-time-street-level-data-e4474746ad5a

Broadcom. (n.d.). *RabbitMQ – One broker to queue them all*. RabbitMQ. https://www.rabbitmq.com/

Building Smart International. (n.d.). *Industry Foundation Classes (IFC) – An Introduction*. https://technical.buildingsmart.org/standards/ifc/

Burggraf, D., McClendon, B., Weiss-Malik, M., Askay, S., Colaiacomo, L., & Martell, R. (2015). *OGC KML Version 2.3* (Version 2.3). Open Geospatial Consortium. https://www.ogc.org/standard/kml/

Calbimonte, J.-P., Eberle, J., & Aberer, K. (2015). Semantic data layers in air quality monitoring for smarter cities. In *Proceedings of the Sixth Workshop on Semantics for Smarter Cities, CONF*, pp. 3–19.

Caldwell, B., Cooper, M., Reid, L. G., & Vanderheiden, G. (2008). *Web Content Accessibility Guidelines (WCAG) 2.0* (2.0). W3C. https://www.w3.org/TR/WCAG20/

Citizen Lab authors. (2023). *CitizenLab—Your dedicated community engagement platform, backed by a team of experts*. CitizenLab. https://www.citizenlab.co/

Citizens Foundation. (n.d.). Your Priorities—Citizen Engagement Platform. *CITIZENS.IS – Citizens Foundation*. https://citizens.is/

CNRS & Université Gustave Eiffel. (n.d.). *NoiseModelling is a free and open-source tool designed to produce environmental noise maps on very large urban areas. It can be used as a Java library or be controlled through a user friendly web interface*. NoiseModelling. https://noise--planet.org/noisemodelling.html

Colpaert, P. (2023, September). *Linked Data Event Streams (LDES)*. https://semiceu.github.io/LinkedDataEventStreams/

Consul Democracy. (2023). *CONSUL Democracy—The most complete citizen participation tool for an open, transparent and democratic government*. CONSUL – Democracy. https://consuldemocracy.org/

Crockford, D. (n.d.). *Introducing JSON*. https://www.json.org/json-en.html

Daniele, L., Garcia-Castro, R., Lefrançois, M., & Poveda-Villalon, M. (2020). *SAREF: The Smart Applications REFerence ontology*. ETSI.. https://saref.etsi.org/core/v3.1.1/

DataHub Project Authors. (n.d.). *Datahub—The #1 Open Source Metadata Platform*. Datahub. https://datahubproject.io/

Datex II organisation. (2021). *Basics of DATEX II* (Version 3.4). https://docs.datex2.eu/basics/index.html

de la Beaujardiere, J. (2006). *OGC Web Map Service (WMS) Version 1.3* (Version 1.3). Open Geospatial Consortium. https://www.ogc.org/standard/wms/

Devane, H. (2023, April). *What are the top data anonymization techniques?* Immuta Blog. https://www.immuta.com/blog/data-anonymization-techniques/

Devys, E., Habermann, T., Heazel, C., Lott, R., & Rouault, E. (2019). *OGC GeoTIFF Standard* (Version 1.1). Open Geospatial Consortium. https://www.ogc.org/standard/geotiff/

Digital Asset (Switzerland) GmbH. (2023). *Daml*. Daml. https://docs.daml.com/daml/intro/0_Intro.html

Eclipse Foundation. (2024). *Eclipse Mosaic—A multi-domain and multi-scale simulation framework for connected and automated mobility*. Eclipse Mosaic. https://eclipse.dev/mosaic/

Eclipse Foundation. (n.d.). *Simulation of urban mobility*. SUMO. https://eclipse.dev/sumo/

Elasticsearch B.V. (n.d.). Elastic—Accelerate time to insight with Elasticsearch and AI. *Elastic*. https://www.elastic.co/

European Commission. (n.d.-a). *GeoDCAT Application Profile for data portals in Europe*. Joinup. https://joinup.ec.europa.eu/collection/semantic-interoperability-community-semic/solution/geodcat-application-profile-data-portals-europe

European Commission. (n.d.-b). *INSPIRE Knowledge Base—Infrastructure for Spatial Information in Europe*. https://knowledge-base.inspire.ec.europa.eu/index_en

Fang, H., & Miao, H. (2020, July). *Introducing the model card toolkit for easier model transparency reporting*. Google Research Blog. https://blog.research.google/2020/07/introducing-model-card-toolkit-for.html?m=1

Flower Labs GMBH. (n.d.). *Flower—A Friendly Federated Learning Framework*. Flower: The Friendly Federated Learning Network. https://flower.ai/

Flyte Project Authors. (2024). *Build & deploy data & ML pipelines, hassle-free—The infinitely scalable and flexible workflow orchestration platform that seamlessly unifies data, ML and analytics stacks*. Flyte. https://flyte.org/

Garlik, S. H., & Seaborne, A. (2013). *SPARQL 1.1 Query Language* (Version 1.1). W3C. https://www.w3.org/TR/sparql11-query/

Gemeente Utrecht. (n.d.). *Utrecht in 3D*. Gemeente Utrecht. https://www.utrecht.nl/bestuur-en-organisatie/publicaties/utrecht-in-3d/

Google. (n.d.). *Material Design version 3—Get started*. Material Design. https://m3.material.io/

Goudappel BV. (n.d.). *Traffic modelling software OmniTRANS Expert*. https://www.goudappel.nl/en/expertise/data-and-it-solutions/traffic-modelling-software-OmniTRANS-Expert

Grafana Labs. (n.d.). *Grafana—Get there much faster. From dashboards to centralized observability*. Grafana Labs. https://grafana.com/

Gridwise Interoperability Framework Team. (2008). *Interoperability Context-Setting Framework*. Version 1.1, 52.

Groenen, J. & Eurocities. (2022). *Algorithmic Transparency Standard (version* (Version 0.3.1 (beta)). https://www.algorithmregister.org/standard

Grossman, R., Bailey, S., Ramu, A., Malhi, B., Hallstrom, P., Pulleyn, I., & Qin, X. (1999). The management and mining of multiple predictive models using the predictive modeling markup language. *Information and Software Technology, 41*(9), 589–595. https://doi.org/10.1016/S0950-5849(99)00022-1

Grover, M. (2019, April). *Amundsen—Lyft's data discovery & metadata engine*. Medium. https://eng.lyft.com/amundsen-lyfts-data-discovery-metadata-engine-62d27254fbb9

gRPC Authors. (n.d.). *gRPC – A high performance, open source universal RPC framework*. gRPC. https://grpc.io/

GTFS.org. (n.d.). *GTFS: Making Public Transit Data Universally Accessible*. https://gtfs.org/

Harpham, Q. K., Hughes, A., & Moore, R. V. (2019). Introductory overview: The OpenMI 2.0 standard for integrating numerical models. *Environmental Modelling & Software, 122*, 104549. https://doi.org/10.1016/j.envsoft.2019.104549

Heazel, C. (2021). *OGC City Geography Markup Language (CityGML) Part 2: GML Encoding Standard*. Open Geospatial Consortium. https://docs.ogc.org/is/21-006r2/21-006r2.html

Helios Authors. (n.d.). *Helios—Trust the vote*. Helios Voting. https://vote.heliosvoting.org/

Hibernate ORM – Your relational data. Objectively. (n.d.). *Hibernate*. https://hibernate.org/orm/

HLRS Authors. (n.d.). *COVISE (Collaborative Visualization and Simulation Environment)*. HLRS – High-Performance Computing Center Stuttgart. https://www.hlrs.de/solutions/types-of-computing/visualization/covise

Huitzilihuitl. (2019). *A digital twin of the city of Chicago along with automated sensors* [Computer software]. https://github.com/enricolu/digital-twin
IBM. (n.d.). *What is a REST API?* https://www.ibm.com/topics/rest-apis
ISO. (2008). *ISO 19141:2008 Geographic information Schema for moving features* (1.0). ISO. https://www.iso.org/standard/41445.html
ISO. (2014). *ISO 19115-1:2014(en) Geographic information—Metadata.* https://www.iso.org/obp/ui/en/#iso:std:iso:19115:-1:ed-1:v1:en
ISO. (2016). *ISO 19119:2016(en) Geographic information—Services.* https://www.iso.org/obp/ui/en/#iso:std:iso:19119:ed-2:v1:en
ISO. (2018). *ISO 19650–1:2018 Organization and digitization of information about buildings and civil engineering works, including building information modelling (BIM)—Information management using building information modelling* (Version 1). ISO. https://www.iso.org/standard/68078.html
ISO. (2019). *ISO/TS 19139–1:2019(en) Geographic information—XML schema implementation.* https://www.iso.org/obp/ui/en/#iso:std:iso:ts:19139:-1:ed-1:v1:en
ISO. (n.d.). *ISO 16739-1 Industry Foundation Classes (IFC) for data sharing in the construction and facility management industries* (Edition 2). ISO. https://www.iso.org/standard/84123.html
ISO/IEC. (2014). *ISO/IEC 19464:2014 Information Technology Advanced Message Queuing Protocol (AMQP) v1.0 specification* (Version 1.0). https://www.iso.org/standard/64955.html
ISO/IEC. (2016). *ISO/IEC 20922:2016 Information technology Message Queuing Telemetry Transport (MQTT) v3.1.1* (Version 3.1.1). https://www.iso.org/standard/69466.html
ISO/IEC. (2017). *ISO/IEC 21778:2017 Information technology—The JSON data interchange syntax* (1.0). ISO. https://www.iso.org/standard/71616.html
ISO/IEC. (2022a). *ISO/IEC 12113:2022 Information technology Runtime 3D asset delivery format Khronos glTF™* (2.0). https://www.iso.org/standard/83990.html
ISO/IEC. (2022b). *ISO/IEC 27001:2022 Information security, cybersecurity and privacy protection/ Information security management systems Requirements* (Version 3). https://www.iso.org/standard/iso-iec-27001-2022-v2
ISO/IEC. (2023a). *ISO/IEC 11179-1:2023(en) Information technology—Metadata registries (MDR)—Part 1: Framework.* ISO. https://www.iso.org/obp/ui/#iso:std:iso-iec:11179:-1:ed-4:v1:en
ISO/IEC. (2023b). *ISO/IEC 9075-1:2023 Information technology Database languages SQL* (6). ISO. https://www.iso.org/standard/76583.html
ITU-T. (2022). *Digital twin network—Requirements and architecture—Recommendation ITU-T Y.3090.* International Telecommunication Union. https://www.itu.int/rec/T-REC-Y.3090-202202-I/en
John, L. (2021, November 12). *Reimagining Paris with the help of an urban digital twin.* Unity Blog. https://blog.unity.com/industry/reimagining-paris-with-the-help-of-an-urban-digital-twin
Katchin Tech. (2023, October 25). *ARKit vs. ARCore: Comparison for augmented reality app development.* Medium. https://katchintech.medium.com/arkit-vs-arcore-comparison-for-augmented-reality-app-development-8eacbf7ba267
Kellog, G., Champin, P.-A., & Longley, D. (2020). *JSON-LD 1.1—A JSON-based Serialization for Linked Data* (Version 1.1). W3C. https://www.w3.org/TR/json-ld11/
Kenniscentrum InfoMil. (n.d.). *Kenniscentrum InfoMil—SRM-1 en SRM-2.* https://www.infomil.nl/onderwerpen/lucht-water/luchtkwaliteit/slag/aerius-lucht-rekentool-nsl-rekentool/handleiding/algemeen/srm-1-srm-2/
Khronos Group. (2024). *What is glTF?* giTF. https://www.khronos.org/gltf/
Khronos Group. (n.d.-a). *OpenGL Overview.* https://www.khronos.org/opengl/
Khronos Group. (n.d.-b). *OpenXR Unifying Reality.* https://www.khronos.org/api/index_2017/openxr#openxr_news
Kolbe, T. H., Kutzner, T., Smyth, C. S., Nagel, C., Roensdorf, C., & Heazel, C. (2021). *OGC City Geography Markup Language (CityGML) Part 1: Conceptual Model Standard* (3.0). Open Geospatial Consortium. https://docs.ogc.org/is/20-010/20-010.html

Kung, A., Baudoin, C., & Tobich, K. (2022). *Report of TWG Digital Twins: Landscape of Digital Twins* (1.0). Zenodo. https://doi.org/10.5281/ZENODO.6556917

Lechner, M. (2015, February 22). *Augmented Reality Markup Language 2.0 (ARML 2.0)* (1.0). Open Geospatial Consortium. https://www.ogc.org/standard/arml/

Ledoux, H., & Dukai, B. (2023). *OGC CityJSON 2.0.0. Standard* (Community Standard 20-072r5; 2.0.0). Open Geospatial Consortium. http://www.opengis.net/doc/CS/covjson/2.0

Lee, J., Li, K.-J., Kolbe, T. H., Zlatanova, S., Morley, J., Nagel, C., & Becker, T. (2022). *OGC® IndoorGML* (1.1). Open Geospatial Consortium. https://docs.ogc.org/is/19-011r4/19-011r4.html

LetsBuild. (2023). *An overview of BIM standards*. LETSBUILD. https://www.letsbuild.com/blog/bim-standards

MATSim Community. (n.d.). *MATSim is an open-source framework for implementing large-scale agent-based transport simulations*. MATSim Multi-Agent Transport Solution. https://www.matsim.org/

Michiels, P., Cornelissen, H., Ortmann, P., Tampère, C., Notelaars, L., & Finck, J. (2021). *DUET Deliverable 3.4 Smart City domains, models and interaction frameworks v2*. DUET Consortium. https://cordis.europa.eu/project/id/870697/results

Microsoft. (n.d.-a). *DirectX 12 Ultimate Getting Started Guide*. https://devblogs.microsoft.com/directx/directx-12-ultimate-getting-started-guide/

Microsoft. (n.d.-b). *Microsoft.net Entity Framework documentation hub*. Learn .Net. https://learn.microsoft.com/en-us/ef/

MLflow Project. (n.d.). *mlFlow—ML and GenAI made simple—Build better models and generative AI apps on a unified, end-to-end, open source MLOps platform*. mlFlow. https://mlflow.org/

MongoDB, Inc. (n.d.-a). *MongoDB Atlas—The multi-cloud developer data platform*. MongoDB. https://www.mongodb.com/atlas

MPEG-V. (n.d.). MPEG. https://www.mpeg.org/standards/MPEG-V/

NIST. (2021, November). *NIST's Pivotal Points of Interoperability Enable Smart City Standardization*. https://www.nist.gov/news-events/news/2021/11/nists-pivotal-points-interoperability-enable-smart-city-standardization

NIST. (n.d.-a). *Developing a consensus Framework for Smart City Architectures*. International Technical Working Group on IoT-Enabled Smart City Framework. https://pages.nist.gov/smartcitiesarchitecture/

NIST. (n.d.-b). *Consensus PPI – Working group files, aspects/concerns*. Smart City Framework. https://pages.nist.gov/smartcitiesarchitecture/community/consensusppi/

NVIDIA Corporation. (n.d.). *What is Universal Scene Description?* NVIDIA Developer. https://developer.nvidia.com/usd

OASC. (2024). *Minimal Interoperability Mechanisms – MIMs*. Open Agile Smart Cities. https://oascities.org/minimal-interoperability-mechanisms/

OAuth 2.0 Industry-standard protocol for authorization. (n.d.). https://oauth.net/2/

Okoro, I. (2023, October 27). *Tools and Platforms for XR Content Creation*. Medium. https://medium.com/imisi3d/tools-and-platforms-for-xr-content-creation-debd35235b06

Open Geospatial Consortium. (2017). *Data Encoding Standards*. OGC E-Learning. https://opengeospatial.github.io/e-learning/data-encoding-standards/basic-index.html

Open Knowledge Foundation. (n.d.). *CKAN – The world's leading open source data management system*. CKAN. https://ckan.org/

OpenGov Authors. (n.d.). *OpenGov—Software for Modern Government—Software purpose-built to power more effective and accountable government*. OpenGov. https://opengov.com/

OpenID Foundation. (n.d.). *What is OpenID Connect*. https://openid.net/developers/how-connect-works/

OpenPlans authors. (n.d.). *Shareabouts—A mapping application for crowdsourced info gathering*. Github. https://github.com/openplans/shareabouts

OpenQuery Inc. (2021). *Synth—The Open Source Data Generator*. Synth. https://www.getsynth.com/

OpenSynthesis. (n.d.). *The Open Community for the Creation and Use of Synthetic Data in AI*. https://opensynthetics.com/
Oracle. (n.d.). *MySQL*. MySQL. https://www.mysql.com/
Pixar Animation Studios. (2021). Universal Scene Description. https://openusd.org/release/index.html
Polis Authors. (n.d.). *Polis—Input Crowd, Output Meaning*. Polis. https://pol.is/home
Protocol Buffers Documentation. (n.d.). https://protobuf.dev/
PTV Planung Transport Verkehr GmbH. (n.d.). *PTV VISUM – The world's leading transport planning software*. PTV Group. https://www.ptvgroup.com/en/products/ptv-visum
PubNub Inc. (n.d.). *PubNub Guide, What are WebSockets?* PubNub. https://www.pubnub.com/guides/websockets/
Raes, L., Vandenbroucke, D., & Reznik, T. (2019). *OGC® GeoDCAT-AP*. Open Geospatial Consortium. https://portal.ogc.org/files/?artifact_id=82475
Redis Ltd. (n.d.). *Redis—The open-source, in-memory data store used by millions of developers as a cache, vector database, document database, streaming engine, and message broker*. Redis. https://redis.io/
Reed, C. (2021). *OGC CDB (Common Database)* (Release 1.2). Open Geospatial Consortium. https://www.ogc.org/standard/cdb/
Regulation (EU) 2016/679 of the European Parliament and of the Council of 27 April 2016 on the Protection of Natural Persons with Regard to the Processing of Personal Data and on the Free Movement of Such Data, and Repealing Directive 95/46/EC (General Data Protection Regulation) (Text with EEA Relevance), Pub. L. No. Regulation (EU) 2016/679, EUR-Lex (2016). https://eur-lex.europa.eu/eli/reg/2016/679/oj
Resource Description Framework (RDF) (Version 1.1). (2014). https://www.w3.org/RDF/
Rice, A. (2024). WebSockets Living Standard. https://websockets.spec.whatwg.org/
RIVM Authors. (n.d.). OPS – Operationele Prioritaire Stoffen Model. *RIVM De zorg voor morgen begint vandaag*. https://www.rivm.nl/operationele-prioritaire-stoffen-model/documentatie
S. Gillis, A. (n.d.). *SOAP (Simple Object Access Protocol)*. TechTarget. https://www.techtarget.com/searchapparchitecture/definition/SOAP-Simple-Object-Access-Protocol
Schema.org. (2024, February). *Schema.Org*. https://schema.org/
Seldon Technologies Limited. (n.d.). *Deploy machine learning models at scale 85% Faster*. SELDON. https://www.seldon.io/
Smartbear software. (n.d.). *API development for everyone*. Swagger. https://swagger.io/tools/
SocietyWorks Ltd. (n.d.). mySociety—Technology, research and data used by individual citizens, journalists, and civil society in over 40 countries around the world. *mySociety*. https://www.mysociety.org/
Steamworks. (2024, February 12). *Steamworks documentation—OpenVR*. https://partner.steamgames.com/doc/features/steamvr/openvrdecision
TensorFlow Developers. (2024). *TensorFlow* (v2.15.1) [Computer software]. [object Object]. https://doi.org/10.5281/ZENODO.4724125
TensorFlow Developers. (n.d.). *TFX end-to-end platform for deploying production ML pipelines*. TensorFlow. https://www.tensorflow.org/tfx
The GraphQL Foundation. (n.d.). *GraphQL – Describe your data—Ask for what you want—Get predictable results*. GraphQL. https://graphql.org/
The Jaeger Authors. (n.d.). *Jaeger: Open source, distributed tracing platform—Monitor and troubleshoot workflows in complex distributed systems*. JAEGER. https://www.jaegertracing.io/
The Kubeflow Authors. (n.d.). *Kubeflow—The Machine Learning Toolkit for Kubernetes*. https://www.kubeflow.org/
The Kubernetes Authors. (n.d.). *Kubernetes, also known as K8s, is an open-source system for automating deployment, scaling, and management of containerized applications*. Kubernetes. https://kubernetes.io/
The Linux Foundation. (n.d.). *Prometheus—From metrics to insight—Power your metrics and alerting with the leading open-source monitoring solution*. Prometheus. https://prometheus.io/

The Linux Foundation®. (2019). *ONNX – Open Neural Network Exchange The open standard for machine learning interoperability*. ONNX. https://onnx.ai/

The Linux Foundation®. (2022). *OpenAPI – The world's most widely used API description standard*. OpenAPI Initiative. https://www.openapis.org/

The PostgreSQL Global Development Group. (n.d.). *PostgreSQL: The World's Most Advanced Open Source Relational Database*. https://www.postgresql.org/

The Presto Foundation. (n.d.). presto—Fast and Reliable SQL Engine for Data Analytics and the Open Lakehouse. *Presto*. https://prestodb.io/

TNO. (n.d.). LOTOS-EUROS – An open-source chemical transport model (CTM) that is used for a wide range of applications supporting scientific research, regulatory programmes and air quality forecasts. *TNO Air Quality Modelling*. https://airqualitymodeling.tno.nl/lotos-euros/

TomTom International B.V. (2012). *OpenLR™ White Paper, Version: 1.5 revision 2*. TomTom International B.V. https://www.openlr.org/location-referencing/

Traffic Modeller authors. (n.d.). TraMod Traffic Modeller—Traffic is dynamic; your decision-making should be too! *Traffic Modeller*. https://trafficmodeller.com/

Unabel Inc. Authors. (2022, October). *I18n vs. L10n: Internationalization and Localization Decoded*. Unabel Inc. https://unbabel.com/i18n-vs-l10n-internationalization-and-localization-decoded/

Valve Corportation Authors. (n.d.). Steam VR. *Steam*. https://www.steamvr.com/en/

Vámos, C., Scheider, S., Sonnenschein, T., & Vermeulen, R. (2024). Ontology of active and passive environmental exposure.

van Berlo, L., Drogemuller, R., & Omrani, S. (n.d.). *What is Information Delivery Specification (IDS)*. BuildingSmart International. https://www.buildingsmart.org/what-is-information-delivery-specification-ids/

Vanecek, S., & Moore, R. (2014). *OGC® Open Modelling Interface Interface Standard* (OGC 11--014r3; p. 122). Open Geospatial Consortium.

Vinasco-Alvarez, D., Samuel, J. S., Servigne, S., & Gesquière, G. (2020). *From citygml to owl* [PhD Thesis]. LIRIS UMR 5205.

VITO NV. (n.d.). IFDM – High Resolution Air Quality Modelling. *VITO*. https://vito.be/en/product/ifdm-high-resolution-air-quality-modelling

Vretanos, A. P. (2010). *Web Feature Service (WFS) Version 2.0* (Version 2.0.(2)). Open Geospatial Consortium. https://www.ogc.org/standard/wfs/

W3C. (2023). *Web Accessibility Initiative -ARIA Overview* (Version 1.2). https://www.w3.org/WAI/standards-guidelines/aria/

W3C. (n.d.). *Extensible Markup Language (XML)*. Retrieved 4 August 2024, from https://www.w3.org/XML/

W3C Community Development Team. (n.d.). Solid Community Group. W3C Community and Business Groups. https://www.w3.org/community/solid/

W3C Immersive Web Working and Community Groups. (n.d.). *The WebXR Device API provides access to input and output capabilities commonly associated with Virtual Reality (VR) and Augmented Reality (AR) devices. It allows you develop and host VR and AR experiences on the web*. WebXR. https://immersiveweb.dev/

W3C OWL Working Group. (2012, December 11). *Web Ontology Language (OWL)* [W3C Semantic Web Standards]. https://www.w3.org/2001/sw/wiki/OWL

Weir-McCall, D. (2020, September 15). *51World creates digital twin of the entire city of Shanghai*. Unreal Engine. https://www.unrealengine.com/en-US/spotlights/51world-creates-digital-twin-of-the-entire-city-of-shanghai

X3D Specifications—ISO/IEC-19775-1. (n.d.). *Web3D Consortium*. https://www.web3d.org/standards/number/19775-1

ZeroMQ authors. (n.d.). ZeroMQ – An open-source universal messaging library. *0MQ*. https://zeromq.org/

# Chapter 7
# Connected Services: IoT Data to Fuel Your Local Digital Twin

**Lieven Raes, Burcu Celikkol, Oliver Schreer, Jaap De Winter, Jéssica Baltazar, Susie Ruston McAleer, and Daniel Bertocci**

**Contents**



## 7.1 Introduction

An important ambition of Local Digital Twins (LDT) lies in the seamless integration of data and knowledge from yesterday, today and tomorrow. Connected sensor devices, mostly internet-based IoT devices, are crucial in feeding LDTs with up-to-date and reliable information on the different aspects of urban dynamics. IoT

L. Raes (✉)
Digital Flanders, Brussels, Belgium
e-mail: lieven.raes@vlaanderen.be

B. Celikkol · D. Bertocci
Interuniversitair Micro-Elektronica Centrum – OnePlanet, Wageningen, The Netherlands
e-mail: burcu.celikkol@imec.nl; daniel.bertocci@imec.nl

O. Schreer
Heinrich Hertz Institute, Fraunhofer, Berlin, Germany
e-mail: oliver.schreer@hhi.fraunhofer.de

J. De Winter · J. Baltazar
SODAQ BV, Hilversum, The Netherlands

S. R. McAleer
21C Consultancy LTD, London, UK
e-mail: susie.mcaleer@21cconsultancy.com



L. Raes et al. (eds.), *Decide Better*,
https://doi.org/10.1007/978-3-031-81451-8_7

networks and devices play a crucial role as providers of urban dynamic data monitoring elements. Fueled by IoT, (geo)time-series data (Carfantan et al., 2020) is essential to feed different simulation models like weather and climate models, traffic models (especially dynamic traffic models), air quality and noise models. IoT data also plays an essential role in operational management, like live traffic or water management. This chapter focuses on the types and characteristics of IoT, from IoT standards to connect with various sensor networks and IoT devices, the sustainability element of IoT to maintain dataflows through to several interesting IoT use cases related to LDTs.

The concept and use of IoT devices go back to the mid-1990s when sensor nodes were developed to sense data from uniquely identified embedded devices and seamlessly exchange information. This concept can be seen as the basic idea of IoT (Khan et al., 2012; Pal et al., 2016; Akyildiz et al., 2002). Device-to-device communication was introduced in 1999 by Bill Joy as part of an internet taxonomy. The term Internet of Things was first coined by Kevin Auston, executive director of Auto-ID Centre, in 1999. The term and concept became more popular in 2003 (Madakam et al., 2015). Madakam et al. (2015) define IoT as "An open and comprehensive network of intelligent objects that can auto-organise, share information, data and resources, reacting and acting in the face of situations and changes in the environment."

Despite no overall accepted definition of IoT, some other well-referred definitions related to LDTs are relevant. Atzori et al. (2010) define the Internet of Things as three key ideas: middleware, which is internet-oriented; sensors, which are things-oriented; and knowledge, which is semantics-oriented. From a definition point of view, these three types are different from each other and are individual entities. However, they intersect with each other to derive the potential benefits of IoT. The three definition elements are also part of the LDT system-of-systems (SoS) concept, where the internet is used as the ultimate cooperation instrument, using live city information and knowledge creation to support policy-making.

Bélissent et al. (2010) focuses on the multi-domain perspective and perceives IoT as a smart environment to offer services to various domains like education, administration, healthcare, transportation, etc., with the help of information and communications technology (ICT).

ISO/IEC (2018) states that IoT involves connecting physical entities ('things') with IT systems through networks. They conclude that it is foundational to IoT that electronic devices interact with the physical world. Sensors collect information about the physical world, while actuators can act upon physical entities. Sensors and actuators come in many forms, such as thermometers, accelerometers, video cameras, microphones, relays, heaters, and industrial manufacturing or process control equipment. Mobile technology, cloud computing, big data and deep analytics (predictive, cognitive, real-time and contextual) all play an important role in gathering and processing data to achieve the final result of controlling physical entities by providing contextual, real-time and predictive information that impacts physical and virtual entities.

IoT is part of the smart concept evolution where the world is becoming more connected. IoT is seen as part of the so-called 'hyper-connected' world (Choi, 2014). IoT influences many elements such as network communication, data communication and semantics, data management and new sensor technologies.

The use of IoT in an LDT context is related to its use in the various smart city domains: smart agriculture, city services, energy, health, home, industry, infrastructure and transport. IoT is an enabler in that it permanently translates information from the physical to the digital world. This information can be further processed to knowledge relevant in one or more domains above to support decision-support and policy-making. This is why IoT is an indispensable enabling technology for LDTs.

When it comes to the ICT architecture, IoT has much in common with the LDT multi-layered architecture. Syed et al. (2021) describe a five-layer architecture model, distinguishing between a sensing layer of domain-specific sensors, actuators and mobile elements passed to a middleware layer over a network layer that exists through different network technologies and topologies (Fig. 7.1). The middleware provides a generic open application interface (APIs) and performs data management to offer a wide-ranging palette of services for use in LDTs.

The availability of more affordable IoT sensor technology and accessible network technology enables denser IoT sensor networks that can provide more localised city data, which in turn provides opportunities for policy support. Additionally, IoT- and LDT driven decision-making can benefit from new possibilities offered by citizen science. In Europe, citizen science initiatives are pushing the boundaries of the state of the art. The COMPAIR project, for example, blends science, technology, and co-innovation to increase the role of community-based IoT networks in local policy-making. For this purpose, several different sensors and apps are developed to

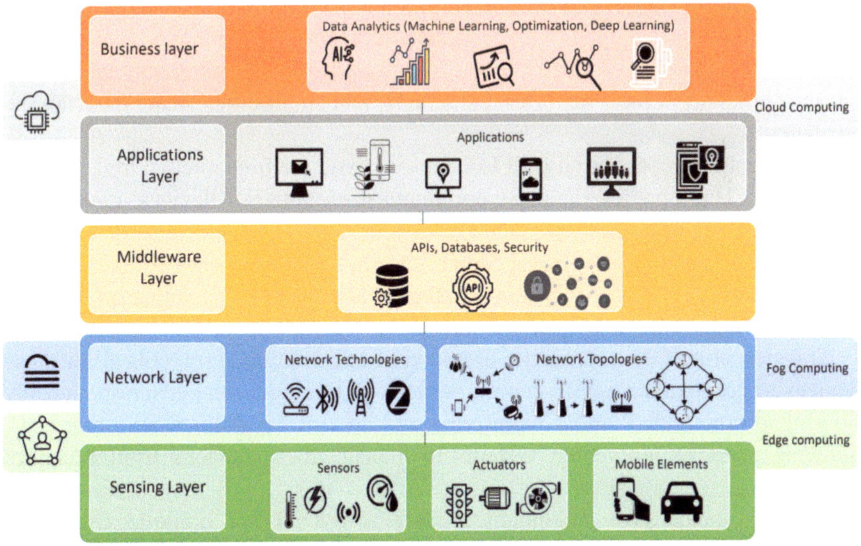


**Fig. 7.1** IoT architecture (Syed et al., 2021)

empower urban stakeholders to act on climate change and air pollution (COMPAIR consortium, 2024).

Beyond citizen science, IoT contributes to geospatial and time-bound measurements that can be stored as geo-time series (Carfantan et al., 2020). The spatiotemporal element of IoT provides an important context for combining data coming from different kinds of sensors and data streams into an LDT. The use of spatial and temporal reasoning based on an ontology of space was described by Stock in the late nineties (Stock, 1997). Today, the spatio-temporal element is an integral part of almost all useful IoT standards in the smart city context. Real-time sensor data appears less critical for long-term policy decision support but is necessary for operational management and forms an essential input for ICCCs (Integrated Command and Control Centers).

In this chapter, we discuss the types and characteristics of IoT sources, data standards and semantics, IoT sensor networks as part of an LDT and practical IoT sensor-based use cases to explain the important role IoT devices play as part of LDTs. This chapter also sketches the standards landscape to support a successful IoT implementation.

## 7.2 Types and Characteristics of IoT Devices

In the context of smart cities and LDTs, IoT devices play a crucial role in collecting and exchanging data to enable intelligent and efficient urban management. These devices can be categorised into various types based on their functions and applications (Janani et al., 2021). The list below provides a non-exhaustive overview of IoT domains related to smart cities and public space monitoring (Table 7.1).

IoT devices are deployed in a wide range of diverse environments, each tailored to meet specific needs. While common IoT characteristics bind them together, the nuances of smart homes, factories, containers, and smart cities shape their unique attributes.

In the realm of connectivity, all IoT devices share the fundamental trait of being networked. This enables seamless communication between devices, creating an interconnected ecosystem. The backbone of these devices lies in their ability to collect and process data through embedded sensors. Whether it's environmental data, machine status, or user behaviour, these devices are designed to capture information relevant to their context (Lynn et al., 2020).

Transmission of data forms the lifeblood of IoT systems. Protocols allow these devices to communicate with central systems or other devices, ensuring a steady flow of information. Remote monitoring and control capabilities are ubiquitous, allowing users or automated systems to manage these devices from a central location.

Security stands as a paramount concern across all IoT domains (Radoglou Grammatikis et al., 2019). Robust measures are essential to secure data transmission, authenticate devices, and guard against unauthorised access. This

**Table 7.1** IoT device types and characteristics

| Sensor Functions | Sensor Type* | Network Type** |
|---|---|---|
| **Sensors for Monitoring Physical Conditions and Chemical Substances** | | |
| Environmental sensors: measure parameters such as air quality, temperature, humidity, and pollution levels | Mono-directional | Both |
| Noise sensors: monitor noise pollution levels in different areas of the city | Mono-directional | Both |
| Light sensors: control street lighting based on ambient light conditions | Bi-directional | Both |
| Water quality sensors: monitor the quality of water sources and detect contaminants | Bi-directional | Both |
| **Infrastructure Monitoring Devices** | | |
| Structural health monitoring sensors: monitor the condition of bridges, buildings, and other infrastructure | Mono-directional | Both |
| Smart grid sensors: monitor and manage the electrical grid to optimise energy distribution | Bi-directional | Wired |
| Traffic monitoring sensors: collect data on traffic flow, congestion, and vehicle movements | Bi-directional | Both |
| **Public Safety and Security Devices** | | |
| Surveillance cameras: monitor public spaces for safety and security | Mono-directional | Wired |
| Explosion detection systems: detect and locate explosions to improve emergency response | Mono-directional | Both |
| Smart streetlights with cameras: combine lighting with video surveillance for enhanced security | Mono-directional | Both |
| **Transportation and Mobility Devices** | | |
| Smart parking sensors: help drivers find available parking spaces and optimise parking management | Mono-directional | Both |
| Connected vehicles: vehicles equipped with IoT technology for real-time communication with each other and infrastructure | Bi-directional | Wireless |
| Public transportation trackers: provide real-time information on the location and status of public transport | Mono-directional | Wireless |
| **Waste Management Devices** | | |
| Smart bins: monitor waste levels and optimise waste collection routes | Mono-directional | Both |
| Environmental sensors for landfills: monitor the environmental impact of landfills | Mono-directional | Both |
| **Information and Display Devices** | | |
| Smart kiosks: provide information on local services, events, and wayfinding | Mono-directional | Both |
| Digital signage: display real-time information and advertisements in public spaces | Mono-directional | Both |
| **Communication Devices** | | |
| IoT Gateways: Facilitate communication between various IoT devices and the central network | – | – |
| Communication Nodes: Enable device-to-device communication in a mesh network | – | – |

** Sensor type: Mono-directional or Bi-directional; ** Network type: Wired, Wireless or Both* commitment to security is integral to the trustworthiness of these interconnected systems.

Zooming into specific contexts reveals the distinctive characteristics of IoT devices. In smart homes, the focus pivots towards user comfort, convenience, and energy efficiency. Devices like smart thermostats, lighting, and security cameras integrate seamlessly with voice assistants and mobile applications, offering users unprecedented control over their environments (Sharma, 2023).

In smart factories, the emphasis shifts to industrial automation, process optimisation, and efficiency. Industrial sensors, programmable logic controllers, and robotic systems orchestrate a symphony of precision. These devices integrate with manufacturing execution systems, forming the backbone of modern manufacturing (Phuyal et al., 2020).

Containers and logistics present a unique challenge, demanding devices that can track and monitor the location, condition, and security of goods during transportation. GPS trackers, temperature sensors, and security systems work in tandem to ensure the integrity of shipments. Integration with logistics management systems enables real-time tracking and route optimisation (Xchange, 2020).

Smart cities, with their focus on urban planning, sustainability, and public services, deploy a diverse array of devices. Environmental sensors, traffic monitoring systems, and public safety devices contribute to a networked urban infrastructure. Integration with city management platforms and data analytics drives informed decision-making, paving the way for intelligent urban development (Raes et al., 2022).

### *7.2.1 Strengths and Weaknesses of Wired and Wireless IoT Devices*

The mode of internet connectivity, whether wired or wireless, introduces a spectrum of differences that extend beyond the mere method of linking to the internet. For devices tethered to wired networks, such as Ethernet connections, a notable characteristic is their inherent limitation in mobility. These devices find their home in stationary settings, reliant on physical connections to the network infrastructure. The installation process involves the intricacies of routing physical cables, a time-consuming endeavour that may demand modifications to existing infrastructure. Yet, once in place, the stability and high-bandwidth connectivity offered by wired connections are often noteworthy.

On the other end of the spectrum, wireless IoT devices, whether connected via Wi-Fi, SIM cards, or narrowband technologies, present a paradigm shift towards flexibility and mobility. Unfettered by physical cables, these devices boast the ability to operate in varied locations. Installation becomes a more agile process, unencumbered by the complexities of physical cables, though the performance of wireless connections can be influenced by factors such as signal strength, interference, and network availability.

The discrepancy in data transfer speed and bandwidth further delineates the distinction between these connectivity modes. Wired connections, by nature, tend to deliver higher data transfer speeds and more consistent bandwidth, a boon for applications requiring substantial throughput like industrial automation or video streaming. Conversely, current wireless connections including the current 4G and low power and bandwidth IoT networks may grapple with comparatively lower speeds, with bandwidth affected by variables such as signal strength and network congestion.

Considerations of power consumption add another layer to this dichotomy. Devices with a limited need for power linked through Ethernet can, on many occasions, draw power directly from the network infrastructure, offering an advantage for devices with stringent power constraints. Conversely, wireless devices, especially those reliant on battery power, must navigate the delicate balance of energy consumption. Transmitting data wirelessly often proves to be more power-intensive, impacting the overall battery life of these devices.

Security considerations also tilt the scale. Wired connections are generally deemed more secure due to their resistance against certain types of wireless attacks. The need for physical access to the network infrastructure acts as an additional layer of protection. Meanwhile, wireless connections, susceptible to eavesdropping and unauthorised access, necessitate robust security protocols, such as WPA3 (Wi-Fi Alliance authors, 2024) for Wi-Fi, to safeguard IoT devices against potential threats.

In the realm of costs, the balance tips between installation and maintenance expenses. Wired infrastructure often incurs higher costs due to the complexities of physical cabling and potential alterations to existing structures. In contrast, wireless solutions present lower installation costs and enhanced scalability, particularly in scenarios where the deployment of physical cables proves impractical or economically prohibitive.

Ultimately, the selection between wired and wireless IoT connectivity is a nuanced decision, dependent on the specific demands of the application. Many IoT implementations strategically blend both wired and wireless connections to achieve an optimal balance between performance and flexibility, showcasing the adaptability inherent in the ever-evolving landscape of interconnected devices.

However, in terms of innovation, the advent of new types of mobile sensors has reshaped possibilities within the IoT ecosystem. Mobile sensors, characterised by their portability and adaptability, usher in a new era of data collection methodologies. The ability to involve new IoT data sources, such as those emanating from citizen science initiatives, becomes a pivotal aspect of this paradigm shift.

### 7.2.2 *Principles and Standards of IoT Connectivity in a Hyper-Connected LDT Context*

Within the framework of a smart city digital twin, the significance of device-to-device communication becomes paramount. It enables real-time collaboration, where the diverse array of IoT devices harmoniously exchange information, contributing to the dynamic responsiveness of the city simulation. This real-time exchange of information isn't merely a technicality; it's the core of a system that responds to the ebb and flow of a city's live conditions, which demands a high level of interconnectivity directly affecting the sensing layer, network layer, and middleware layer of the LDT multi-layered (classic) architecture, as depicted in Fig. 7.1. IoT devices, in an LDT context, communicate with the different architectural building blocks, as discussed in Chaps. 5 and 6. The most important building blocks are related to data storage, including data lakes and data warehousing,[1] which covers data storage, data transformation, data replication, and data processing capabilities. The data connection itself is established and processed through the various communication protocols and technologies below.

### Cloud Communication

- *MQTT (Message Queuing Telemetry Transport):* A lightweight and efficient publish-subscribe messaging protocol commonly used for IoT. It enables devices to publish messages to a central server (broker) and subscribe to receive messages from other devices or the server (MQTT.org, 2022);
- *CoAP (Constrained Application Protocol):* Is designed for resource-constrained devices. CoAP is a lightweight protocol that allows devices to communicate with the cloud using HTTP-like methods such as GET, POST, PUT, and DELETE (Bormann, 2016);
- *HTTP/HTTPS (Hypertext Transfer Protocol/Secure):* IoT devices can communicate with cloud servers using standard HTTP or its secure version, HTTPS. This is suitable for scenarios where web-based communication is required;
- *WebSockets:* Provide full-duplex communication channels over a single, long-lived connection. They are often used for real-time communication between IoT devices and cloud services (PubNub Inc., n.d.).

### Server Communication

- *REST (Representational State Transfer):* A widely used architectural style for designing networked applications. IoT devices can interact with servers through RESTful APIs, exchanging data in a stateless manner using standard HTTP methods (IBM, n.d.-a);
- *SOAP (Simple Object Access Protocol):* A protocol for exchanging structured information in web services. While less common in modern IoT applications, some legacy systems may use SOAP for communication (Gillis, n.d.);

[1] See Chap. 5, building block 18 "Data Storage: Data Lake, Data Warehouse, Data Lakehouse" in Table 5.2 and Chap. 6 Sect. 6.5.2

- *Message queues:* Devices can communicate with servers using message queue systems like RabbitMQ or Apache Kafka, where messages are sent to a queue and consumed by the server asynchronously. Message queues are essential components for IoT networks to accommodate a large number of connected devices effectively (IBM, n.d.-b).

## Device-to-Device Communication

- *Bluetooth:* Common for short-range communication between IoT devices. Bluetooth Low Energy (BLE) is often used for energy-efficient communication;
- *Zigbee and Z-Wave:* Wireless protocols designed for low-power, short-range communication between devices in home automation and industrial settings (Farahani, 2008; Z-Wave Alliance, 2024);
- *NFC (Near Field Communication):* Enables close-range communication between devices, often used for contactless payments and data exchange (Lawton, n.d.);
- *LoRaWAN (Long Range Wide Area Network):* Suited for low-power, long-range communication in scenarios like smart agriculture or asset tracking (LoRa Alliance, 2024);
- *6LoWPAN (IPv6 over Low-Power Wireless Personal Area Networks):* Optimises IPv6 for low-power, constrained devices in IoT applications (Lakshmi Devasena, 2016);
- *Mesh networks:* Devices can form mesh networks, allowing them to communicate with each other and relay messages within the network. This is often used in scenarios where direct communication with a central server may not be feasible.

In a typical IoT ecosystem, devices often use a combination of these communication methods based on factors such as range, power consumption, data size, and application requirements. The choice of communication protocol depends on the specific needs of the IoT deployment, considering factors like latency, reliability, and energy efficiency. Standardisation efforts and industry best practices continue to evolve to ensure interoperability and seamless communication in this complex and diverse domain.

Of particular importance are efficiency and device-to-device communication (Pawar & Trivedi, 2019). Instead of inundating a central server, devices share relevant information amongst themselves, optimising network bandwidth and curtailing latency. The collaborative decision-making that unfolds is not confined to centralised systems alone but is distributed across the interconnected devices, fostering a nimble and responsive decision-making process. Even if a central server falters, the city's digital twin retains its vitality as devices continue to communicate, ensuring the uninterrupted flow of essential functions. This decentralised approach instils a sense of reliability, fortifying the system against potential disruptions.

Through communication, devices share insights into their status, resource consumption, and operational conditions. This communion fosters a symbiotic relationship, where resources such as energy, bandwidth, and processing power are responsively allocated, contributing to the overall efficiency of the smart city. In addition, devices authenticate and verify each other's identity, erecting a digital barrier against unauthorised access and potential cyber threats. This layer of security is particularly crucial in scenarios involving critical infrastructure.

### 7.2.3 IoT Data Processing

IoT data processing can be performed at different places. The place where data is processed plays an essential role in how LDTs receive and handle the data. The data can generally be handled and processed using cloud, fog and edge computing. Each concept refers to the moment the (initial) data processing is performed. According to Syed et al. (2021), the edge computing model allows data processing via an 'edge node' that, in the case of IoT, can be done on the IoT 'thing' level itself. In the case of fog computing, data processing takes place on the level of network devices, such as a router. In the case of cloud computing, the data processing takes place on the computer network, where all the data comes together. Every model comes with its capabilities and limitations. It is also possible that some IoT devices use edge computing while others perform all the data processing in the cloud. In general, cloud computing allows heterogeneous data management from different devices at a high network cost with a high privacy risk but can also support more complex decisions. The edge computing model usually only accesses the data from the device itself, has a low network cost, and can enforce privacy protection on the device itself, but is less capable of processing multi-domain multi-sensor decisions.

On an LDT level, the IoT data processing is located on the middleware level, as depicted in Fig. 7.1. Data processing on the sensing and network layers is also possible but is considered outside the LDT. In the proposed LDT architecture (see Chaps. 5 and 6), the Data Query Service and Data Replication Client building blocks[2] are responsible for s providing a secure interface to access, explore, and understand the data within the digital twin and capturing the evolving changes from different asynchronous sources in a dynamic context.

### 7.2.4 Quality of IoT Devices and Data

The quality of data collected from an IoT device impacts its application and the role it can play in decision-making processes. Data quality can be measured using several metrics depending on the desired application. Three elements are important to the quality of IoT devices in a digital twin context.

[2] See building block 04 'Data Query Service' and building block 05 'Data Replication Client' in Table 5.2 and Chap. 6 Sect. 6.5.2

*Accuracy and precision:* Accuracy describes how close a measured value is to the true value, and precision describes how close multiple measurements of the same entity are to one another. Accuracy and precision are mainly influenced by the measurement principle of the sensor used to measure the data; however, overall accuracy and precision can be improved by the following data processing steps.

- *Data validation:* Checks of the quality and integrity of data sources prior to usage of data. A defect or tampered IoT sensor may produce inaccurate data, which could be identified by data validation;
- *Data cleaning:* Refers to the removal of outlier or corrupted data. IoT devices use simple sensing principles that may make raw sensor output prone to stochastic errors; such errors can be excluded by using data cleaning;
- *Data calibration:* Is performed by comparing the IoT device output to a traceable standard of known quality. The derived variables from this comparison are then used to build a parametrised model which can be used to improve the raw IoT device measurements in terms of data quality. Often, IoT devices rely on simple measurement principles where the sensor output can be sensitive to parameters other than the one of interest. Therefore, the device must be exposed to conditions similar to the operational conditions when acquiring data to build the calibration model.

*Timeliness:* IoT devices often aim to capture real-time or near-real-time data. It is important that the data transmission, processing, and access solutions allow the data to be accessible with a time delay that sufficiently serves the application.

*Completeness:* Ensures that the data points collected cover the time period required to derive meaningful insights.

Monitoring the data quality of IoT devices in an LDT context is located on the middleware layer. Processes like IoT sensor data calibration (see the example below), even if they use a wide range of algorithms and data analytic methods, usually seen as part of the business layer in many IT architectures, are located in the middleware layer (Fig. 7.1).

**Case: Dynamic Air Quality Data Calibration Process in the COMPAIR Project**

Using data from various sources on air quality with different geographical spreads and measurement methodologies and quality was one of the challenges of the COMPAIR project. In COMPAIR, results from citizen science sensors and professional sensors up to high-end official measuring stations were used to inform and evaluate local planning decisions (COMPAIR Consortium, 2024). Hofman et al. (2020) conclude that monitoring air quality in cities is challenging as a high resolution in space and time is required to assess population exposure accurately. Hofman et al. (2020) propose an

(continued)

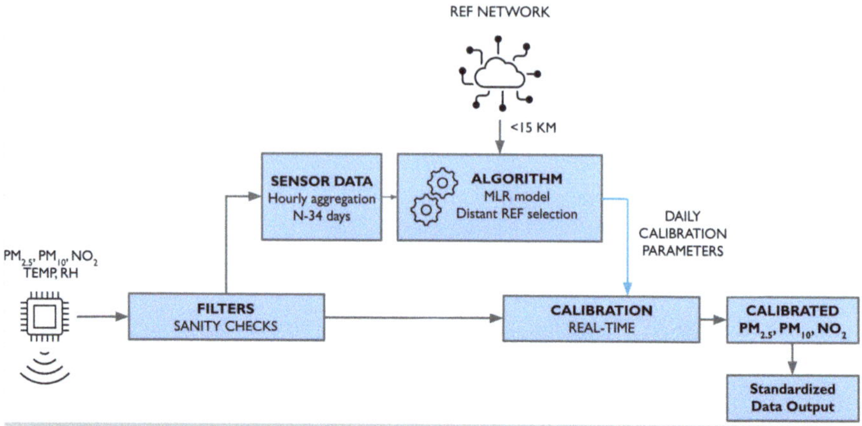


**Fig. 7.2** Cloud Calibration Pipeline for Citizen Science Air Quality Sensors (COMPAIR Consortium, 2024)

innovative IoT approach for highly granular air quality mapping in cities relying on (i) a combination of cloud-calibrated fixed and mobile air quality sensors, and (ii) machine learning approaches to infer the collected spatiotemporal point measurements in both space and time. This approach was integrated into a calibration pipeline, used and tested during the COMPAIR project to increase the data quality of Citizen Science sensors measuring particulate matter, and black carbon (Fig. 7.2).

The calibration pipeline combines raw (inaccurate) measurements from citizen science sensors with high-quality data from reference stations and uplifts the accuracy of the measurements in real-time. The advantages of the introduced approach are twofold. First, cloud-based calibration will not require the direct involvement and manual intervention of the citizens in dealing with the complex topic of sensor accuracy. Second, scientific validation and harmonisation will make the results more easily available for use in LDTs.

### 7.2.5 *IoT Metadata and Provenance*

Metadata describes data in a structured way so that systems and humans can find it. A recent paper considers metadata a crucial element in data driven decision-making because of the essential link between reliable data and the reliability of the decision outcome (Řezník et al., 2022). It plays an essential role during the data collection process regarding dataset characteristics, provenance, and data quality. The most used metadata standards to describe datasets are the Dublin Core (2004), Content Standard for Digital Geospatial Metadata published by the FGDC (1998), ISO

19115 Geographical Data—Metadata (ISO, 2014), Data Catalog Vocabulary (DCAT) (W3C, 2020). All these popular metadata formats and standards can describe the content of a dataset, varying from very basic information to a more extensive description, including data provenance.

Borgini focuses on another metadata level, not related to the dataset but to the IoT device (Borgini, 2023) and defines metadata as in-depth information about IoT measurements, such as the time they were generated, the system or device that generated them, and their format, amongst other relevant information related to the type of measurement. Ideally, metadata will provide a standard set of information about gathered data to make it easier to understand or categorise by various systems, applications and resources.

According to Borgini, metadata solves the interoperability challenge by quickly helping devices and systems that want to interact with IoT devices identify them and connect using the right communication protocol. Metadata also lets other devices know what data the IoT device can exchange. This type of information makes connecting to an IoT device more efficient and reduces time lag. So, metadata can help solve the interoperability problem, at least on a device level. And it can help standardise the data catalogue of an LDT, both at the level of fast-moving (from IoT devices) and slow-moving data (e.g. terrain or height models).

The provision of IoT metadata, including data provenance, is a capability of the LDT Model (and data) catalogue building block serving data and model discovery services[3] It is also related to the asset registry building block,[4] which is, in turn, more oriented to software-related building blocks like case and scenario management, data workflow, and component orchestration.

## 7.3 IoT Data Standards and Semantics: Towards Interoperability-By-Design

To understand how semantic interoperability makes IoT data usable in LDTs, we first need to understand which IoT data standards exist and what their purpose is. So, we will start by reviewing a number of key generic and geospatial IoT standards, before focusing on minimal interoperability requirements for sharing context information, data models and transactions.

[3] See building block 13 'Model Catalogue' in Chap. 5, Table 5.2 and Chap. 6, Sect. 6.5.3

[4] See building block 16 'Asset Registry' in Chap. 5, Table 5.2 and Chap. 6, Sect. 6.5.2

### 7.3.1 IoT Data Standards

Over the years, multiple IoT standards have been developed, covering areas like construction, agriculture, health and smart cities. IoT standards do not only include syntax and semantics but also elements like security. This overview focuses on IoT standards from well-known international standards-setting bodies like ISO[5]/IEC,[6] IEEE,[7] W3C,[8] and OGC.[9] Interested readers can also check the work done by the telecom players ITU[10] and ETSI.[11]

#### Generic Standards

ISO/IEC 30141: Internet of Things Reference Architecture

ISO/IEC 30141 (2018) provides a standardised IoT Reference Architecture using a common vocabulary, reusable designs and industry best practices. It uses a top-down approach, beginning with collecting the most important characteristics of IoT, abstracting those into a generic IoT Conceptual Model, and deriving a high-level system-based reference with subsequent dissection of that model into the four architecture views (functional view, system view, networking view and usage view) from different perspectives.

The reference architecture serves as a base from which to develop (specify) context-specific IoT architectures and, thence, actual systems. The contexts can be of different kinds but shall include the business context, the regulatory context and the technological context, e.g. industry verticals, technological requirements and/or nation-specific requirement sets (ISO/IEC, 2018). The architecture also highlights functional requirements such as data management, device management, security, confidentiality and privacy. It also emphasises non-functional requirements such as maintainability, reliability, usability, high availability, and scalability of a system.

ISO/IEC 30161-1 ED1: IoT Data Exchange Platform for IoT Services

The ISO/IEC 30161-1 (ISO/IEC, 2020) standard specifies requirements for an IoT data exchange platform for a variety of services in the technology areas of (1) middleware components of communication networks allowing the co-existence of IoT

[5] International Organization for Standardization, https://www.iso.org/home.html

[6] International Organization for Standardization - International Electrotechnical Commission, https://www.iec.ch/homepage

[7] Institute of Electrical and Electronics Engineers, https://www.ieee.org/

[8] World Wide Web Consortium, https://www.w3.org/

[9] Open Geospatial Consortium, https://www.ogc.org/

[10] International Telecom Union, https://www.itu.int/en/

[11] European Telecom and Standardisation Institute, https://www.etsi.org/

services with legacy services; (2) end-points performance across the communication networks among the IoT and legacy services; (3) IoT specific functions and functionalities allowing the efficient deployment of IoT services; (4) IoT service communication networks' framework and infrastructure and (5) IoT service implementation guideline for the IoT data exchange platform.

### ISO/IEC 30165: IoT Real-Time Framework

The ISO/IEC 30165 (ISO/IEC, 2021a) standard is a comprehensive framework for strategically deploying Real-Time Internet of Things (RT-IoT) systems, aiming to mitigate common pitfalls encountered in real-time system development. Emphasising the critical aspect of real-time capability, the standard extends beyond generic descriptions, recognising that deviations from precise timing constraints could lead to significant repercussions, potentially resulting in severe damage to the IoT system or its surrounding environment. Such consequences may include harm to individuals involved, underscoring the imperative nature of adherence to stringent timing requirements in RT-IoT system implementation.

### ISO/IEC 21823 1-4: IoT Interoperability

The ISO/IEC 21823 1-4 Interoperability for IoT standards comprise four parts. Part one (ISO/IEC, 2019) 'framework' addresses issues related to interoperability of the communications between IoT system entities. Part two (ISO/IEC, 2020), 'transport interoperability standard', specifies a framework and requirements for transport interoperability in order to enable the construction of IoT systems with information exchange, peer-to-peer connectivity and seamless communication both between different IoT systems and also among entities within an IoT system. Part three (ISO/IEC, 2021b) 'semantic interoperability standard', focuses on IoT semantic interoperability as the facet that enables data exchange between IoT systems using understood data information models. Part four (ISO/IEC, 2022b) specifies IoT interoperability from a syntactic point of view.

### ISO/IEC 27400 and 27402, 27402.2: Cybersecurity – IoT Security and Privacy – Guidelines

The ISO/IEC 27400 (ISO/IEC, 2022a) standard provides guidelines on risks, principles and controls for security and privacy of IoT solutions. ISO/IEC 27402 (ISO/IEC, 2023b) device baseline requirements provide guidance on a baseline set of information and communication technologies (ICT) requirements so that IoT devices are able to support security and privacy controls. A risk assessment is critical to develop a risk treatment plan that identifies the necessary IoT device features and countermeasures. The management of systems which use IoT devices depends on the capabilities of those devices. Upon the baselines, vertical markets (such as health, financial services, industrial, consumer electronics and transportation) can build additional requirements for the expected use and risks of IoT devices in their applications.

#### Institute of Electrical and Electronics Engineers (IEEE) IoT Standards

The Institute of Electrical and Electronics Engineers (IEEE) is a professional organisation founded in 1963 and responsible for a wide range of peer-reviewed journals. IEEE also publishes tutorials and standards produced by standardisation committees. The P1912 standard about Privacy and Security Architecture for Consumer Wireless Devices (IEEE SA, 2020a) defines a common communication architecture for diverse wireless communication devices. The P1451-99 Standard for Harmonisation and Security of IoT (IEEE SA, 2020b) utilises advanced capabilities of the XMPP protocol (IETF, 2024), such as providing authenticated identities, authorisation, presence, life cycle management, interoperable communication, IoT discovery and provisioning globally. The P2413—Standard for an Architectural Framework for IoT (IEEE SA, 2019a) defines an architectural framework for the Internet of Things (IoT), including descriptions of various IoT domains, definitions of IoT domain abstractions, and identification of commonalities between different IoT domains. The IEEE 802.15.4-2015—IEEE Standard for Low-Rate Wireless Networks (IEEE SA, 2015) focuses on the sensor connectivity domain and defines a protocol and compatible interconnection for data communication devices using low data-rate, low-power, and low-complexity short-range radio frequency (RF) transmissions in a wireless personal area network (WPAN).

### Geospatial-Oriented Standards

The OGC (Open Geospatial Consortium) has already defined in 2011 the first IoT standards. Today, OGC focuses on syntactically and semantically oriented standards and standardised services. Some of the OGC standards were designed in joint cooperation with the W3C. The standards below focus on IoT modelling SensorML (OGC, 2020), IoT observations and measurements—OMS (OGC, 2023), sensor observation service—SOS (OGC, 2012), sensor planning service—SPS (OGC, 2011), and common data and services—SWE (Robin, 2011).

#### OGC Sensor Model Language (Sensor ML)

The primary focus of the Sensor Model Language (SensorML) is to provide a robust and semantically tied means of defining processes and processing components associated with the measurement and post-measurement transformation of observations. This includes sensors and actuators as well as computational processes applied to pre-post measurements. The main objective is to enable interoperability, first at the syntactic level and later at the semantic level (by using ontologies and semantic mediation), so that sensors and processes can be better understood by machines, utilised automatically in complex workflows, and easily shared between intelligent sensor web nodes. The Sensor ML standard has been approved by the OGC in 2019 and published in 2020 (OGC, 2020).

#### OGC Observations, Measurements, and Samples (OMS)

The Observations, Measurements, and Samples standard—OMS (OGC, 2023; ISO/IEC, 2023a) defines a conceptual schema for observations, features involved in the observation process, and features involved in sampling when making observations. Models support the exchange of information describing observation acts and their results, both within and between different scientific and technical communities. The SensorThings API—STA (OGC, 2021), Sensor Observation Service SOS (OGC, 2012), Semantic Sensor Network—SSN (OGC & W3C, 2017) and Sensor Open Systems Architecture—SOSA (Janowicz et al., 2019) all use ISO19156 in their core. OMS was jointly prepared and published by the Open Geospatial Consortium and ISO as ISO19156:2023 (Schleidt & Rinne, 2023; ISO, 2023b).

#### OGC SensorThings API (STA)

The SensorThings API provides an open, geospatial-enabled and unified way to interconnect IoT devices, data, and applications over the Web. At a high level, the SensorThings API provides two main functionalities; each function is handled by a part. The two parts are the Sensing and the Tasking part. The Sensing part provides a standard way to manage and retrieve observations and metadata from heterogeneous IoT sensor systems and provides functions similar to the OGC SOS (OGC, 2012). The Tasking part provides functions similar to the OGC SPS (OGC, 2011). The standard was approved by the OGC in 2020 and published in 2021 (OGC, 2021).

#### OGC Sensor Observation Service (SOS)

The SOS standard applies to use cases in which sensor data needs to be managed in an interoperable way. This standard defines a web service interface that allows querying observations, sensor metadata, and representations of observed features. Further, the SOS standard defines means to register new sensors and to remove existing ones. It also defines operations to insert new sensor observations (OGC, 2012). The SOS standard became an approved OGC standard in 2016.

Sensor Planning Service (SPS)

The OpenGIS® Sensor Planning Service Interface Standard (SPS) defines interfaces for queries that provide information about the capabilities of a sensor and how to task the sensor. The standard is designed to support queries that have the following purposes: to determine the feasibility of a sensor planning request; to submit and reserve/commit such a request; to inquire about the status of such a request; to update or cancel such a request; and to request information about other OGC Web services that provide access to the data collected by the requested task (OGC, 2011). The SPS standard's most recent version 2.0 dates back to 2011.

Common Data and Services (SWE)

The Sensor Web Enablement (SWE) Common Data Model Encoding Standard defines low level data models for exchanging sensor related data between nodes of the OGC® Sensor Web Enablement (SWE) framework. These models allow applications and/or servers to structure, encode and transmit sensor datasets in a self-describing and semantically enabled way (Robin, 2011).

**Case: The Importance of OGC SensorThings API in the COMPAIR Project**

In the European citizen-science-related project COMPAIR, cooperation among several technical partners was essential to successfully integrate diverse systems into a unified solution. One of the challenges they face is reaching a consensus on the communication interfaces, as different partners may have their own systems. Moreover, the involvement of citizens adds another layer to these types of projects, as they may have access to segments of the solution.

A tool to address these challenges is standardisation. In particular OGC SensorThings API has played a key role. As a standard, it has established a common foundation in terms of concepts and terminology by providing precise interface definitions. Furthermore, it mandates structured storage of sensor metadata and links to ontologies within the measurements. This enables both the technical partners and citizens to gain a more comprehensive understanding of the data within the solution.

W3C/OGC Semantic Sensor Network Ontology (SSN)

The SSN ontology describes sensors in terms of capabilities, measurement processes, observations, and deployments in order to define the semantic interoperability of physical sensor networks. Its core concepts are sensors and their features, properties, observations, systems, measuring capabilities, operating and survival restrictions, and deployments (Rhayem et al., 2020).

### 7.3.2 LDT-IoT-Related Initiatives

Digital twin-related standards are difficult to define due to the lack of clarity in defining what a digital twin is, on the one hand, and due to the SoS approach, in which a large variety of applications, with specific standards, become part of a digital twin. The IoT-related digital twin standards almost all refer to DTs for industrial designs or digital twins in general, without specifying any particular domain. Nevertheless, the generic standardisation initiatives below related to digital twins are potentially useful for integrating IoT devices from the physical world into their LDT counterparts.

The ISO/IEC digital twin — Concepts and Terminology 30173:2023 initiative aims to define a common domain-overarching understanding (ISO/IEC, 2023c). Wang et al. (2022) propose a five-dimension digital twin model where each dimension consists of corresponding standards. The authors distinguish between physical entities, virtual entities, data, connections and services. Because of their specific relations in an LDT context, the physical and virtual entities need further elaboration.

- *Physical entities in a digital twin system have, according to Wang et al. (2022), two primary functions: data collection and device control:* The physical entities serve as data sources and actuating units for virtual entities.
- The IEEE also introduced standard series IEEE 2888 (IEEE, 2024). This standard series comprehensively defines an interface between the cyber world (digital twin) and the physical one. IEEE P2888.1 and IEEE P2888.2 define the vocabulary, requirements, metrics, data formats, and APIs necessary for acquiring information from sensors and commanding actuators, providing the definition of interfaces between the two worlds. P2888.3 is a standard on the "Orchestration of Digital Synchronisation between the Cyber and Physical World." IEEE P2888.4 is a standard on Architecture for Virtual Reality Disaster Response Training Systems, while P2888.5 and P2888.6 focus on Evaluation Methods of Virtual Training Systems and Holographic Visualisation for Interfacing Cyber and Physical Worlds;
- *Virtual entities in a digital twin system can be seen as virtual entities that serve as the digital representation of physical entities:* Virtual entities are composed of models that describe physical entities via multi-temporal, multi-spatial scales (Wang et al., 2022). However, the IEEE Standard on System Architecture of Digital Representation for Physical Objects in Factory Environments (IEEE SA, 2019b) assumes a non-smart city digital twin environment. It is a good example of how physical objects influence virtual entities in terms of objectives, components, data resources and procedures.

The ISO TC184/SC4, IEC/TC65/WG24 are developing standards to provide guidance for an Asset Administration Shell (AAS). The concept of AAS aims to convert a physical entity into a digital twin. The AAS offers a semantic model that consists of a number of domain-specific sub-models in which all the information and functionalities of a given asset—including its features, characteristics, properties, statuses, parameters, measurement data and capabilities—can be described (Dossogne, 2022). The asset registry is also considered a base feature of an LDT, which needs an index to catalogue all of the LDT assets. While the asset documentation can exist external to an LDT instance, the registry is integral for traceability and discoverability. The Asset Registry provides an encompassing overview of the available datasets, schemas, vocabularies, algorithms, and other usable assets.

### *7.3.3 Minimal Interoperability Mechanisms for IoT and Digital Twins*

The OASC[12] Minimal Interoperability Mechanisms (MIM) aim to unite cities and communities in a global market for solutions, services, and data based on their needs. To achieve these goals, the MIMs define a set of practical capabilities based on open technical specifications to enhance the replicability and scalability of solutions (OASC, 2023a). The MIMs cover a wide field of interoperability topics, where many are touching IoT-related topics. The most mature are MIM 1 (Context Information Management), MIM 2 (Shared Data Models) and MIM 3 (Ecosystem Transaction Management).

#### MIM 1: Context Information Management

Context Information Management ensures comprehensive and integrated access, use, sharing, and management of data across different solutions and purposes. It manages the context information coming from IoT devices and other public and private data sources, providing cross-cutting context data and access through a uniform interface (OASC, 2023b). MIM 1 offers the following capabilities: status information provision, access enabling multiple data sources, context information provision, information discovery and querying, and change and update management. An example of a MIM 1 implementation is NGSI-LD (ETSI-CIM, n.d.-a).

#### MIM 2: Shared Data Models

MIMS of the Shared Data Models comprise guidelines and a catalogue of minimum common data models in different domains to enable interoperability for applications and systems among different cities. MIM 2 (OASC, 2023c) focuses on a harmonised representation of data formats and semantics, usable by applications that both consume and publish data. MIM 2 uses the concept of Smart Data Models to

[12] Open Agile Smart Cities, https://oascities.org/

ensure interoperability and replicability in multiple sectors, including all smart city domains. The main capabilities of MIM 2 are related to the definition of clearly defined data models, capturing the complete context and allowing applications to request well-specified attributes. MIM 2 recommends the following specifications: NGSI-LD (ETSI, n.d.-a), ETSI/oneM2M (ETSI, n.d.-b) and SAREF (Daniele et al., 2020).

**MIM 3: Ecosystem Transactions Management**

The Ecosystem Transaction Management MIM 3 is about scaling data services within cities and communities, including IoT- and AI-enabled services. MIM 3 requires easy and risk-free access to suitable local data sources available within those communities. A local data marketplace allows for easy and risk-free access to relevant and available local data, solutions, and other resources so that new and valuable services and solutions, many of which have already been deployed in other cities, can easily be implemented within the local area (OASC, 2023d). The MIM 3 marketplace concepts offer the following capabilities: exposure of data and data set offerings built on standard interoperability mechanisms; access to services offerings; ecosystem transaction management, including effective matchmaking of relevant data sources (e.g. urban IoT data) from providers with respective data consumers, as well as trusted exploitation based on enforceable data usage agreements and secure value flow. A set of MIM 3 specifications is part of the SynchroniCity[13] project Marketplace Enablers Report (SynchroniCity, 2018a), and the Reference Architecture for IoT Enabled Smart Cities (SynchroniCity, 2018b).

## 7.4 Sustainable IoT Sensor Networks as Part of an LDT

Čolaković and Hadžialić (2018) define Sensor Networks as a collection of sensors which communicate with each other and/or transmit data to some other infrastructure (e.g. Fog, Cloud). Sensor networks consist of the sensors, actuators, firmware and a thin layer of software framework. All these capabilities enable objects to be aware of their environment and to exchange data, which is one of the goals of IoT.

IoT systems typically exhibit complexity, primarily attributed to their influence on diverse facets of human existence and the deployment of a range of technologies facilitating autonomous data exchange among embedded devices. The evolution of IoT significantly affects multiple dimensions of human life, including but not limited to security, safety, health, mobility, energy efficiency, and environmental

[13] Delivering an IoT enabled Digital Single Market for Europe and Beyond (SynchroniCity), EU H2020 project, https://cordis.europa.eu/project/id/732240

sustainability. Consequently, it becomes imperative to address issues and challenges related to IoT from a comprehensive perspective, encompassing enabling technologies, services and applications, and business models, all while considering social and environmental impacts. Many of the challenges related to this comprehensive perspective are very similar to the challenges LDTs as an end user-oriented solution want to overcome. This subchapter will proceed by reviewing two different sensor networks: professional and community driven. We will then present several use cases to show how the networks can be combined in an LDT environment.

### 7.4.1 Professional Sensor Networks

Professional IoT sensor networks, as listed below, can assure a constant stream of qualitative input data from the physical reality to the virtual world. An LDT can integrate multiple sensor networks into one environment to support complex processes and use cases that benefit from multiple cooperating sensor networks. Syntactic and semantic interoperability on the data and metadata level are two conditions sine qua non for a joint, multi-sensor knowledge creation. The following are examples of professional IoT networks in cities with potential in an LDT operational and policy context.

- *Building management:* Digital twins of buildings can integrate sensor data to monitor and optimise energy usage and ventilation depending on building occupancy and outside conditions;
- *Traffic management:* Data from cameras, sensors and IoT-connected vehicles can be used to simulate and optimise traffic flow, improve road safety, and provide input for traffic planning;
- *Environmental monitoring:* Water quality, flow and levels can be used to detect leaks and improve water distribution. Flooding and drought prevention and management are other use cases. Air quality monitoring, measuring different pollutants, provides information in combination with weather data for, e.g. smog prevention and can also be used in traffic and spatial planning;
- *Waste management:* Waste management systems can use sensor data to monitor bin levels and optimise waste collection routes for the city waste authorities;
- *Smart grids:* An LDT of the electrical grid can be generated using real-time data from smart meters in buildings and sensors on power lines and substations to monitor energy consumption, identify and predict faults and facilitate energy distribution.

An important issue to consider in the context of ubiquitous IoT deployment is the sheer volume of generated data. Cities are being flooded with large quantities of information coming from different directions, a phenomenon commonly referred to as data tsunami. Today, a single smart building can have several thousand sensors measuring everything from temperature to energy consumption. A case in point is

Edge in Amsterdam, which has 28,000 sensors.[14] Scale this to the city level by adding all buildings, lamp posts, waste bins, parking lots and other urban activities, and the number and variety of potential nodes in a master network becomes very large. In practice, however, such implementation is challenging in more ways than one. Besides integration requirements, big data places considerable demands on storage, computing power, privacy safeguards, and environmental sustainability of data centres and supercomputers used to process all the incoming data streams.

In addition, the hype surrounding big data has been questioned on relevance grounds. Critics point out that for "many problems and questions, small data itself is enough" (Pollock, 2013). In the context of IoT, small data refers to information on specific attributes of the current state and/or conditions being measured (Kavis, 2015). Small datasets can cover things like location, temperature, vibration, movement, and so on and are often enough to trigger events in, and communication between, physical assets. Small data packets can be transferred over long distances using a variety of technologies, including the Narrowband IoT (NB-IoT) (Narrowband.com authors, 2024), LTE-M and LTE-MTC (Rosende, 2024), which are often found in devices used for citizen-led monitoring.

### 7.4.2 User-Generated Content and Citizen Science IoT Networks

The use of Citizen Science IoT devices to connect the physical reality from volunteers to the digital world is relatively new. One of the earliest and most successful examples of a DIY IoT citizen science air quality sensor was the community grassroots Luftdaten initiative (Luftdaten, n.d.) in Germany in 2015. Luftdaten was succeeded by the multi-measurement sensor community (sensor.community, n.d.), with a user base of more than 10,000 users all over the world. A large-scale example of a quadruple helix IoT initiative is the CurieuzeNeuzen Garden (n.d.) project in Flanders, Belgium. An NB-IoT soil sensor was rolled out in 5000 places (selected out of more than 50,000 candidates), most of them private gardens, to measure heat and drought. The initiative received broad coverage thanks to a consortium of research institutes, the Flemish government, newspaper media, private companies including telecom providers and the leading nature conservation organisation. The availability of the data as open data and, in the case of CuriezeNeuzen Garden, strong scientific support also makes the data interesting for integration in an LDT. In the COMPAIR project (COMPAIR Consortium, 2024), the sensor.community is part of a dynamic calibration process that post-calibrates the measurement results (see case: Dynamic Air Quality Data calibration process in part 6.2).

[14] https://neuroject.com/smart-building-examples/

### 7.4.3 Citizen Science IoT Data for Policy-Making: New Possibilities and Potential Risks

There are multiple arguments and risks to consider when deciding whether citizen science is a valuable new data source comparable to government and private sector data and whether it has significant potential to power LDTs and associated policy-making processes. Using an IoT network with the framework of citizen science comes with new possibilities and risks. Based on the COMPAIR project experiences in five pilot locations spanning Belgium, Bulgaria, Germany and Greece, we summarise these as follows.

**Opportunities**

- *Access to a new range of locations:* Gardens, facades (access to private spaces, places where people effectively live or work);
- *High network density:* A high number of measurement spots at a reasonable cost, with a high potential variability or a high spatial concentration;
- *Lower operation costs:* External management of the sensors by volunteers, efficient continuous data collection;
- *Citizen involvement:* Participants feel involved and are highly interested in the measurement results and the outcome of related policy decisions.

**Risks**

- *None or lower control over the devices*: e.g. disconnecting devices or malfunctioning sensors;
- *Increased chance of failure*: e.g. connecting issues like unstable network connections;
- *Increased chance of incorrect measurement*: e.g. by change of location, measurement direction;
- *Drop out of volunteers*;
- *Unequal spread*: e.g. difficulties setting up a network due to a lack of interest or installation options in certain areas.

An important finding of COMPAIR was that network connectivity varies across the EU. In most European countries, coverage for NB-IoT and LTE-M is available. But country-wide availability is not guaranteed everywhere. In Europe, availability in the Balkans is, for example, poor, hindering the rollout of IoT networks. There are also noticeable differences between good availability in (big) cities and the lack of coverage in the countryside. If the necessary IoT infrastructure is lacking, data collection will not be possible, which will have a knock-on effect on citizen participation. Projects are therefore encouraged to do a thorough (connectivity) risk assessment before deciding what is to be measured, where, and how (using which sensor).

## 7.5 IoT Use Cases in an LDT Context

Getting insights into the availability of smart city sensors in the public domain and getting open access to the measurements are usually rare. If data is available, you have to find your way to the theme and device type-specific platforms. An LDT can offer solutions to bring relevant IoT sensor data together and can provide access via different tools like 3D map visualisations, data dashboards and immersive technologies like Augmented Reality (AR) and Virtual Reality (VR). The European Commission launched CitiVerse (Gil, n.d.) as a concept to integrate LDT and immersive technologies and make the results available to local authorities and citizens. Integrating multi-sensor IoT data, including calibrated citizen science data, into an LDT to support evidence-informed decision-making shows how local policies can benefit from multiple IoT data streams, including data streams coming from Citizen Science projects and initiatives.

The three implementation examples below go beyond the current state of the art, where IoT devices and network-specific web interfaces are prevalent, providing single-sensor and single-business domain data and information. The first case is about how Citizen Science IoT data and official traffic counting data can be visualised in a 3D digital twin environment, showing historical and live sensor information. The data can be further combined with predictive traffic modelling data or air quality data.

The second and third cases provide insight into how the different types of IoT data can be visualised in other visualisation environments. A multi-sensor dashboard view allows users to group and compare sensors for policy evaluation purposes. A second innovative visualisation is intended for use on the terrain. It combines IoT network data and augmented reality (AR) to visualise air pollution in one's immediate surroundings.

**Case: Telraam Traffic Count Data Visualisation in a Digital Twin (DUET[15] and COMPAIR Projects)**

The Telraam (Rear Window BV, 2024) sensor continuously monitors a street from a citizen's window, providing crucial data on various modes of transport, including motorised vehicles, cyclists, pedestrians, and more. Telraam devices were used at several locations during the COMPAIR and DUET projects to create opportunities for dialogue between traffic planners, local authorities and their most affected communities: the citizens who live in—and use—these streets by turning traffic counting into an open and accessible citizen science project. The data was integrated into the DUET digital twin, where it can be visualised together with the traffic loop data, traffic model data and air quality sensors for a holistic assessment of urban dynamics (Fig. 7.3).

[15] Digital Urban European Twins (DUET), EU H2020 project, https://cordis.europa.eu/project/id/870697

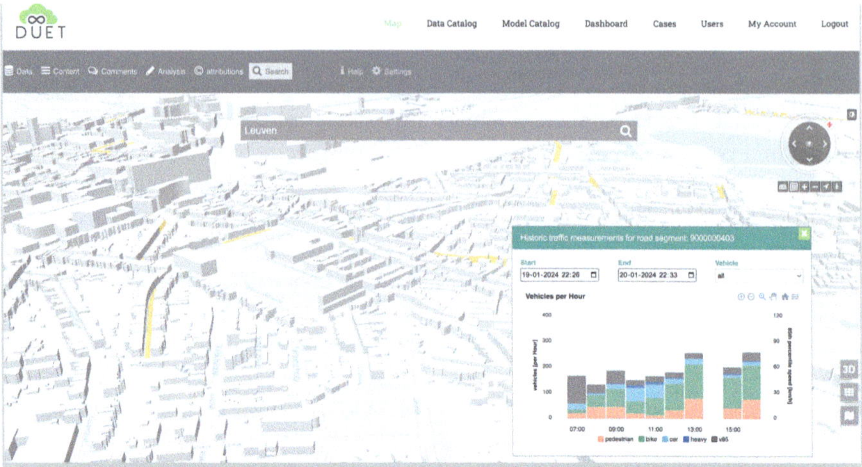


**Fig. 7.3** DUET Digital Twin—Telraam Citizen Science sensor data visualisation (DUET, 2023)

**Case: IoT Policy Monitoring Dashboard (COMPAIR Project)**

During the COMPAIR project, Telraam Citizen Science sensors have been rolled out at more than 20 locations in the local community of Herzele (Belgium) to measure the effect of a school street, a street along the school that is closed for motorised traffic during children drop-off and pick-up times. The Telraam data provided insights into the traffic difference before and after the school street implementation. The results are displayed in a publicly available dashboard that complements the digital twin 3D visualisation. The teachers and schoolchildren have used the digital twin and the dashboard during the classes to analyse and discuss the implementation results with the local city council.

The results of the Herzele school street case were available via a Policy Monitoring Dashboard (PMD) (COMPAIR, 2024) providing public access to multiple sensor networks varying from high fidelity official measurement stations to calibrated citizen science data (Fig. 7.4). The PMD dashboard below offers a combination of unique features, providing open access to policy related data, information and knowledge.

Dashboard users can select and visualise different groups of sensors (e.g. sensors near the school street versus sensors further afield) to study the difference between them. This can be particularly useful when trying to analyse policy impacts, such as roadblocks or traffic calming measures, as the dashboard can compare multiple periods, e.g. before and after a measure was implemented. Another useful functionality is the implementation of thresholds to measure the evolution towards a policy goal. A built-in download option allows users to download raw standardised data, which is helpful for further in-depth expert analysis. Another option is creating browsable fixed map views that can be used for storytelling to provide insights. Due to its high level of standardisation, users can create dashboards by combining different sensor setups.

Fig. 7.4 Policy Monitor sensor visualisation (COMPAIR, 2024)

**Case: Dynamic Exposure Visualisation via AR APP (DEVA) and dashboard (DEV-D) in the COMPAIR project**

Due to the proliferation of air quality sensors and the broad availability/accessibility of air quality model data, there is already a decent coverage of (IoT) air quality data in urban areas across Europe. Augmented Reality is a relatively new visualisation technique in the field of air quality monitoring. It offers a more intuitive way to explore the surrounding sensor and model data on environmental conditions. By using a smartphone or tablet, the user can see a visual overlay of environmental information such as air quality or traffic information. Using advanced visualisation in the 3D AR space, the user can explore and monitor the current state of air pollution directly in the surroundings (Fig. 7.5). In the context of the COMPAIR project, a novel AR app was developed. It offers real-time visualisation of air quality and traffic data based on publicly available environmental sensor data and model data mapped on a grid. The app also combines DIY IoT data, calibrated citizen science data and high-fidelity government sensor data. The overall framework of the application follows a flexible and dynamic software concept, which can be extended

(continued)

with additional functionality according to user needs and the availability of new sensor data.

Another approach to monitoring dynamic exposure involves combining data from mobile air quality sensors and GPS tracking devices (such as the DEVA trip recorder) within a data management system. This method allows for the integration of positioning and air quality information, which can then be processed and presented in a user-friendly manner to citizens and other stakeholders. During the COMPAIR project, bicycle and walking trips were monitored using mobile SODAQ fine-dust sensors alongside the DEVA trip recorder. The data collected from these devices were analysed and visualised using the DEV-D (Fig. 7.6). This dashboard provides citizens with detailed information about the air quality along their routes. Users can filter the data, visualise the evolution of air quality on a colour-coded map and various graphs, measure their exposure or inhaled dose (dynamically adjusted based on activity level, gender, and age) of pollutants and relate data to the WHO[16] guidelines. Additionally, the DEV-D allows for the comparison of different trips, helping users identify the best alternative routes, locate sources of contamination, investigate temporal effects, and compare similar sites across different countries or cities.

For both DEVA and DEV-D, the awareness of environmental conditions in the local surroundings can have an impact on user behaviour, such as taking a bike or bus instead of a car. When mixed with gamification elements (e.g. competitions between students to follow less polluted routes), AR-based apps can influence change in attitudes and behaviour within groups, thus scaling impact from individual- to community level.

**Fig. 7.5** Dynamic Exposure Visualisation App using Augmented Reality (COMPAIR, 2024; Renault et al., 2024)

[16] World Health Organization, https://www.who.int/

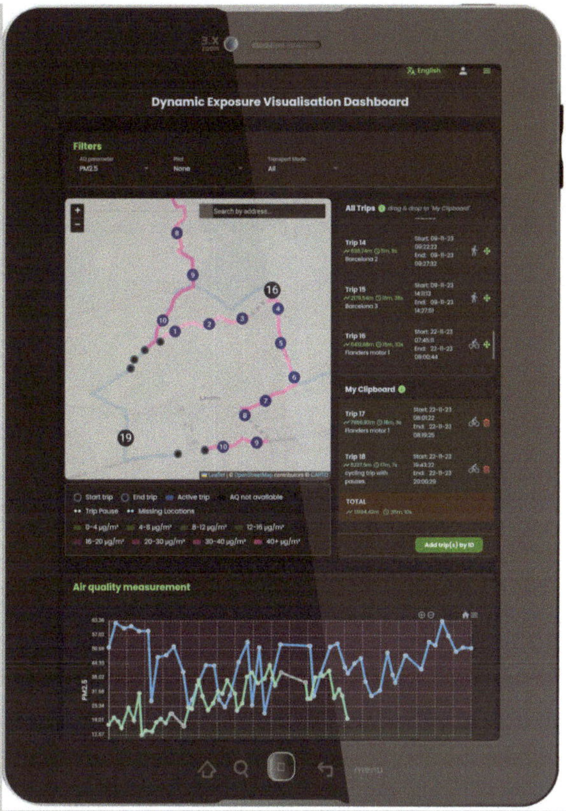


**Fig. 7.6** The Dynamic Exposure Visualisation Dashboard (DEV-D)

## 7.6 Conclusions

Internet of Things (IoT) networks provide an indispensable building block for translating physical conditions into the digital representation of a city. New network technologies and a broadening range of IoT devices, which increasingly become smaller and cheaper, create conditions for change in the way cities are monitored and managed. The chapter provided an overview of the standardisation needs and options for rolling out integrated IoT networks in a Local Digital Twin (LDT) context, including the need for and applicability of Minimal Interoperability Mechanisms (MIMs). These MIMs are essential to interoperability, and without them, the vision of a truly connected smart city would be hard to achieve. By studying concrete implementation examples, readers of this chapter can learn how to address differences in data quality and how to avail of the opportunities for stakeholder engagement, policy evaluation and behavioural change provided by recent advances in IoT, citizen science, Augmented Reality (AR), data analytics, and digital twins.

## References


Akyildiz, I. F., Su, W., Sankarasubramaniam, Y., & Cayirci, E. (2002). Wireless sensor networks: A survey. *Computer Networks, 38*(4), 393–422.

Atzori, L., Iera, A., & Morabito, G. (2010). The internet of things: A survey. *Computer Networks, 54*(15), 2787–2805.

Bélissent, J., Mines, C., Radcliffe, E., & Darashkevich, Y. (2010). *Getting clever about smart cities: New opportunities require new business models*. Cambridge.

Borgini, J. (2023, April 14). Use metadata for IoT data organization. *TechTarget*. https://www.techtarget.com/iotagenda/tip/Use-metadata-for-IoT-data-organization

Bormann, C. (2016). COAP – RFC 7252 Constrained Application Protocol. *COAP*. https://coap.space/

Carfantan, G., Daniel, F., d'Orazio, L., Le, T.-D., Marin, X., Peau, O., & Rannou, H. (2020). Think Cities: The accelerator for sustainable planning. In *2020 IEEE 36th International Conference on Data Engineering Workshops (ICDEW)* (pp. 64–70).

Choi, A. J. (2014). Internet of Things: Evolution towards a hyper-connected society. *IEEE Asian Solid-State Circuits Conference (A-SSCC), 2014*, 5–8. https://doi.org/10.1109/ASSCC.2014.7008846

Čolaković, A., & Hadžialić, M. (2018). Internet of Things (IoT): A review of enabling technologies, challenges, and open research issues. *Computer Networks, 144*, 17–39. https://doi.org/10.1016/j.comnet.2018.07.017

COMPAIR consortium. (2024). *Together we can achieve clean air for all—Join COMPAIR and participate in measuring and reviewing air quality against other city data sources*. https://monitoring.wecompair.eu/

CurieuzeNeuzen. (n.d.). *Meer dan 50.000 CurieuzeNeuzen schreven zich in om de hitte en droogte te meten*. https://sensor.community/en/

Daniele, L., Garcia-Castro, R., Lefrançois, M., & Poveda-Villalon, M. (2020). *SAREF: The Smart Applications REFerence ontology*. ETSI. https://saref.etsi.org/core/v3.1.1/

Dossogne, V. (2022, November). A look at the latest standardisation projects in the field of digital twins. *S Innovation Forward*. https://www.sirris.be/en/inspiration/look-latest-standardisation-projects-field-digital-twins

Dublin Core. (2004). Dublin core metadata initiative. *Dublin Core Metadata Initiative*. https://www.dublincore.org/

ETSI-CIM. (n.d.-a). *Industry specification group (ISG) cross cutting context information management (CIM)*. ETSI. https://www.etsi.org/committee/cim

ETSI-CIM. (n.d.-b). *One machine-to-machine partnership project (ONEM2M)*. ETSI. https://www.etsi.org/committee/1419-onem2m

Farahani, S. (2008). ZigBee and IEEE 802.15.4 Protocol Layers. In *ZigBee Wireless Networks and Transceivers* (pp. 33–135). Elsevier. https://doi.org/10.1016/B978-0-7506-8393-7.00003-0

FGDC, J. (1998). *Content standard for digital geospatial metadata (revised June 1998)*. FGDC-STD-001-1998, 78 pgs.

Gil, G. (n.d.). Development of the CitiVerse call. *Living-in.Eu*. https://living-in.eu/news/development-citiverse-call

Gillis, S. (n.d.). SOAP (Simple Object Access Protocol). *TechTarget*. https://www.techtarget.com/searchapparchitecture/definition/SOAP-Simple-Object-Access-Protocol

Hofman, J., Nikolaou, M. E., Huu Do, T., Qin, X., Rodrigo, E., Philips, W., Deligiannis, N., & La Manna, V. P. (2020). Mapping air quality in IoT cities: Cloud calibration and air quality inference of sensor data. In *2020 IEEE SENSORS* (pp. 1–4). https://doi.org/10.1109/SENSORS47125.2020.9278941

IBM. (n.d.-a). *What is a REST API?* https://www.ibm.com/topics/rest-apis

IBM. (n.d.-b). What is a message queue? IBM. https://www.ibm.com/topics/message-queues

IEEE SA. (2015). *IEEE 802.15.4-2015 Standard for Low-Rate Wireless Networks*. IEEE. https://standards.ieee.org/ieee/802.15.4/5788/

IEEE SA. (2019a). *IEEE 2413-2019 Standard for an Architectural Framework for the Internet of Things (IoT)*. https://standards.ieee.org/ieee/2413/6226/

IEEE SA. (2019b). *P2806 System Architecture of Digital Representation for Physical Objects in Factory Environments*. IEEE. https://standards.ieee.org/ieee/2806/7524/

IEEE SA. (2020a). *P1912 Standard for Privacy and Security Framework for Consumer Wireless Devices*. IEEE. https://standards.ieee.org/ieee/1912/10174/

IEEE SA. (2020b). *P1451.99 Standard for Harmonization of Internet of Things (IoT) Systems Interactions*. IEEE. https://standards.ieee.org/ieee/1451.99/11634/

IEEE SA. (2024). *IEEE 2888*. https://sagroups.ieee.org/2888/

IETF. (2024). XMPP Specifications. *Internet Engineering Task Force – XMPP*. https://xmpp.org/extensions/

ISO. (2014). *ISO 19115-1:2014(en) Geographic information—Metadata—Part 1: Fundamentals*. ISO. https://www.iso.org/obp/ui/en/#iso:std:iso:19115:-1:ed-1:v1:en

ISO/IEC. (2018). *ISO/IEC 30141:2018(en) Internet of Things (loT)—Reference Architecture*. ISO. https://www.iso.org/obp/ui/en/#iso:std:iso-iec:30141:ed-1:v1:en

ISO/IEC. (2019). *ISO/IEC 21823-1:2019(en) Internet of things (IoT)—Interoperability for internet of things systems—Part 1: Framework*. ISO. https://www.iso.org/obp/ui/en/#iso:std:iso-iec:21823:-1:ed-1:v1:en

ISO/IEC. (2020). *ISO/IEC 21823-2:2020(en) Internet of things (IoT)—Interoperability for IoT systems—Part 2: Transport interoperability*. ISO. https://www.iso.org/obp/ui/en/#iso:std:iso-iec:21823:-2:ed-1:v1:en

ISO/IEC. (2021a). *ISO/IEC 30165:2021(en) Internet of Things (IoT)—Real-time IoT framework*. ISO. https://www.iso.org/obp/ui/en/#iso:std:iso-iec:30165:ed-1:v1:en

ISO/IEC. (2021b). *ISO/IEC 21823-3:2021(en) Internet of things (IoT)—Interoperability for IoT systems—Part 3: Semantic interoperability*. ISO. https://www.iso.org/obp/ui/en/#iso:std:iso-iec:21823:-3:ed-1:v1:en

ISO/IEC. (2022a). *ISO/IEC 27400:2022(en) Cybersecurity—IoT security and privacy—Guidelines*. ISO. ISO/IEC. (2020a). *ISO/IEC 30161:2020(en) Internet of Things (IoT)—Requirements of IoT data exchange platform for various IoT services*. ISO; 17-1-2024. https://www.iso.org/obp/ui/en/#iso:std:iso-iec:30161:ed-1:v1:en

ISO/IEC. (2022b). *ISO/IEC 21823-4:2022(en) Internet of things (IoT)—Interoperability for IoT systems—Part 4: Syntactic interoperability*. ISO. https://www.iso.org/obp/ui/en/#iso:std:iso-iec:21823:-4:ed-1:v1:en

ISO/IEC. (2023a). *ISO 19156:2023(en) Geographic information—Observations, measurements and samples*. ISO. https://www.iso.org/obp/ui/en/#iso:std:iso:19156:ed-2:v1:en

ISO/IEC. (2023b). *ISO/IEC 27402:2023(en) Cybersecurity—IoT security and privacy—Device baseline requirements*. ISO. https://www.iso.org/obp/ui/en/#iso:std:iso-iec:27400:ed-1:v1:en

ISO/IEC. (2023c). *ISO/IEC 30173:2023(en) Digital twin—Concepts and terminology*. ISO. https://www.iso.org/obp/ui/en/#iso:std:iso-iec:30173:ed-1:v1:en

Janani, R. P., Renukak, K., Aruna, A., & Lakshmi Narayanan, K. (2021). IoT in smart cities: A contemporary survey. *Global Transitions Proceedings, 2*(2), 187–193. https://doi.org/10.1016/j.gltp.2021.08.069

Janowicz, K., Haller, A., Cox, S. J. D., Le Phuoc, D., & Lefrançois, M. (2019). SOSA: A lightweight ontology for sensors, observations, samples, and actuators. *Journal of Web Semantics, 56*, 1–10. https://doi.org/10.1016/j.websem.2018.06.003

Kavis, M. (2015). Forget big data—Small data is driving the internet of things. *Forbes*. https://www.forbes.com/sites/mikekavis/2015/02/25/forget-big-data-small-data-is-driving-the-internet-of-things/

Khan, R., Khan, S. U., Zaheer, R., & Khan, S. (2012). Future internet: The internet of things architecture, possible applications and key challenges. In *2012 10th International Conference on Frontiers of Information Technology* (pp. 257–260).

Lakshmi Devasena, C. (2016). IPv6 Low Power Wireless Personal Area Network (6LoWPAN) for Networking Internet of Things (IoT) – Analyzing its Suitability for IoT. *Indian Journal of Science and Technology, 9*(30). https://doi.org/10.17485/ijst/2016/v9i30/98730

Lawton, G. (n.d.). Definition—Near-field communication (NFC). *TechTarget Mobile Computing*. https://www.techtarget.com/searchmobilecomputing/definition/Near-Field-Communication

LoRa Alliance. (2024). What is LoRaWAN® Specification. *LoRa Alliance*. https://lora-alliance.org/about-lorawan/

Luftdaten. (n.d.). *Luftdaten, Measure Air Yourself*. https://luftdaten.info/

Lynn, T., Endo, P. T., Ribeiro, A. M. N. C., Barbosa, G. B. N., & Rosati, P. (2020). The Internet of Things: Definitions, key concepts, and reference architectures. In T. Lynn, J. G. Mooney, B. Lee, & P. T. Endo (Eds.), *The Cloud-to-Thing Continuum* (pp. 1–22). Springer International Publishing. https://doi.org/10.1007/978-3-030-41110-7_1

Madakam, S., Ramaswamy, R., & Tripathi, S. (2015). Internet of Things (IoT): A literature review. *Journal of Computer and Communications, 03*(05), 164–173. https://doi.org/10.4236/jcc.2015.35021

MQQT.org. (2022). MQTT: The Standard for IoT Messaging. *MQQT*. https://mqtt.org/

Narrowband.com authors. (2024). What is narrowband IoT. *Narrowband*. https://www.narrowband.com/what-is-narrowband-iot

OASC. (2023a). *Minimal Interoperability Mechanisms – MIMs*. https://oascities.org/minimal-interoperability-mechanisms/

OASC. (2023b). *OASC MIM1: Context Information Management*. OASC. https://mims.oascities.org/mims/oasc-mim-1-context

OASC. (2023c). *OASC MIM2: Shared Data models*. OASC. https://mims.oascities.org/mims/oasc-mim-2-data-models

OASC. (2023d). *OASC MIM3: Ecosystem Transactions Management*. OASC. https://mims.oascities.org/mims/oasc-mim-3-contracts

OGC. (2011). *OGC® Sensor Planning Service Implementation Standard Version 2.0*. OGC. https://portal.ogc.org/files/?artifact_id=38478

OGC. (2012). *OGC® Sensor Observation Service Interface Standard Version 2.0*. OGC. https://portal.ogc.org/files/?artifact_id=47599

OGC. (2020). *OGC® SensorML: Model and XML Encoding Standard Version 2.1*. OGC. https://docs.ogc.org/is/12-000r2/12-000r2.html

OGC. (2021). *OGC® SensorThings API Part 1: Sensing Version 1.1*. OGC. https://docs.ogc.org/is/18-088/18-088.html

OGC. (2023). *OGC Abstract Specification Topic 20: Observations, measurements and samples* (3.0) [Abstract Specification]. OGC. https://www.ogc.org/standard/om/

OGC & W3C. (2017). *Semantic Sensor Network Ontology—W3C Recommendation 19 October 2017*. W3C. https://www.w3.org/TR/vocab-ssn/

Pal, A., Mukherjee, A., & Dey, S. (2016). Future of healthcare—Sensor data driven prognosis. In *Wireless world in 2050 and beyond: A window into the future!* (pp. 93–109).

Pawar, P., & Trivedi, A. (2019). Device-to-device communication based IoT system: Benefits and challenges. *IETE Technical Review, 36*(4), 362–374. https://doi.org/10.1080/02564602.2018.1476191

Phuyal, S., Bista, D., & Bista, R. (2020). Challenges, opportunities and future directions of smart manufacturing: A state of art review. *Sustainable Futures, 2*, 100023. https://doi.org/10.1016/j.sftr.2020.100023

Pollock, R. (2013). Forget big data, small data is the real revolution. *The Guardian*. https://www.theguardian.com/news/datablog/2013/apr/25/forget-big-data-small-data-revolution

PubNub Inc. (n.d.). PubNub Guide, What are WebSockets? *PubNub*. https://www.pubnub.com/guides/websockets/

Radoglou Grammatikis, P. I., Sarigiannidis, P. G., & Moscholios, I. D. (2019). Securing the Internet of Things: Challenges, threats and solutions. *Internet of Things, 5*, 41–70. https://doi.org/10.1016/j.iot.2018.11.003

Raes, L., Michiels, P., Adolphi, T., Tampere, C., Dalianis, A., McAleer, S., & Kogut, P. (2022). DUET: A framework for building interoperable and trusted digital twins of smart cities. *IEEE Internet Computing, 26*(3), 43–50. https://doi.org/10.1109/MIC.2021.3060962

Rear Window BV. (2024). *Telraam—Your window on local traffic*. https://telraam.net/en/what-is-telraam

Renault, S., Feldmann, I., Raes, L., Silence, J., & Schreer, O. (2024, May). *Dynamic exposure visualization of air quality data with augmented reality*. 14th Int. Conf. on Geographical Information Systems Theory, Application and Management, Angers, France. https://www.insticc.org/node/TechnicalProgram/gistam/2024/presentationDetails/125867#:~:text=Book%20of-,Abstracts,-Schedule

Řezník, T., Raes, L., Stott, A., De Lathouwer, B., Perego, A., Charvát, K., & Kafka, Š. (2022). Improving the documentation and findability of data services and repositories: A review of (meta)data management approaches. *Computers & Geosciences, 169*, 105194. https://doi.org/10.1016/j.cageo.2022.105194

Rhayem, A., Mhiri, M. B. A., & Gargouri, F. (2020). Semantic Web Technologies for the Internet of Things: Systematic Literature Review. *Internet of Things, 11*, 100206. https://doi.org/10.1016/j.iot.2020.100206

Robin, A. (Ed.). (2011). *OGC® SWE Common Data Model Encoding Standard. Version 2.0.0.* [207pp.]. https://doi.org/10.25607/OBP-629

Rosende, J. (2024, February 7). Cellular Networks—A complete guide to LTE-M for IoT. *Onomondo*. https://onomondo.com/blog/lte-m-iot-guide/

Schleidt, K., & Rinne, I. (2023). *OGC® Abstract Specification Topic 20: Observations, measurements and samples*. OGC. https://docs.ogc.org/as/20-082r4/20-082r4.html

Sensor.Community. (n.d.). *Sensor.community is a contributors driven global sensor network that creates Open Environmental Data*. https://sensor.community/en/

Sharma, P. (2023, May). Smart homes and IoT: How technology is revolutionizing architecture? *Parametric Architecture*. https://parametric-architecture.com/smart-homes-and-iot-how-technology-is-revolutionizing-architecture/

Stock, O. (1997). *Spatial and temporal reasoning*. Kluwer Academic Publishers.

Syed, A. S., Sierra-Sosa, D., Kumar, A., & Elmaghraby, A. (2021). IoT in smart cities: A survey of technologies, practices and challenges. *Smart Cities, 4*(2), 429–475. https://doi.org/10.3390/smartcities4020024

SynchroniCity Consortium. (2018a). *D2.4. Basic data market place enablers*. Synchronicity Consortium. https://oascities.org/wp-content/uploads/2022/08/SynchroniCity_D2.4.pdf

SynchroniCity Consortium. (2018b). *D2.10. Reference Architecture for IoT Enabled Smart Cities, Update*. Synchronicity Consortium. https://oascities.org/wp-content/uploads/2022/08/SynchroniCity_D2.10.pdf

W3C. (2020). *Data catalog vocabulary (DCAT)*. https://www.w3.org/TR/vocab-dcat-1/

Wang, K., Wang, Y., Li, Y., Fan, X., Xiao, S., & Hu, L. (2022). A review of the technology standards for enabling digital twin [version 2; peer review: 2 approved]. *Digital Twin, 2*(4), Article 4. https://doi.org/10.12688/digitaltwin.17549.2

Wi-Fi Alliance authors. (2024). Discover Wi-Fi security. *Wifi Alliance*. https://www.wi-fi.org/discover-wi-fi/security

XChange. (2020, February). Smart Container | Advantages, Use Cases and Impact on Container Logistics. *Container Logistics*. https://www.container-xchange.com/blog/smart-containers/

Z-Wave Alliance. (2024). Learn about Z-Wave. *Z-Wave*. https://www.z-wave.com/learn

# Chapter 8
# Future Ready Local Digital Twins and the Use of Predictive Simulations: The Case of Traffic and Traffic Impact Modelling

**Chris Tampère, Paul Ortmann, Karel Jedlička, Walter Lohman, and Stijn Janssen**

## Contents




C. Tampère (✉) · P. Ortmann
Centre for Industrial Management, Traffic & Infrastructure, Katholieke Universiteit Leuven, Leuven, Belgium
e-mail: chris.tampere@kuleuven.be; paul.ortmann@kuleuven.be

K. Jedlička
Department of Geomatics, University of West Bohemia, Pilsen, Czech Republic
e-mail: smrcek@kgm.zcu.cz

W. Lohman
Nederlandse Organisatie voor Toegepast-Natuurwetenschappelijk Onderzoek, Delft, The Netherlands
e-mail: walter.lohman@tno.nl

S. Janssen
Vlaamse Instelling voor Technologisch Onderzoek, Mol, Belgium
e-mail: stijn.janssen@vito.be





L. Raes et al. (eds.), *Decide Better*,
https://doi.org/10.1007/978-3-031-81451-8_8

## 8.1 Introduction

Local Digital Twins (LDT) support evidence-based cross-domain decision-making by integrating domain-specific data sources and models in a single environment and making these available to policymakers, civil servants, investors, developers, and creative citizens to engage the community to enrich the data and develop new services. It supports monitoring and exploring what-if simulations but is also a tool for measuring effects. Providing insight into data and cross-domain data analysis is also an opportunity for the LDT to be a communication tool for citizens.

As a digital twin of a smart city, the LDT should ideally cover various smart city domains and their interactions. Figure 8.1 depicts interacting domains from two different sources. While for most of the individual domains, models, data, technology, and KPI dashboards exist that allow stakeholders within that domain to understand the current status and what-if scenarios, the strength of a digital twin lies in making these uniformly available to more stakeholders and addressing cross-domain challenges for which an integrated analysis and exploration is required.

While LDTs are driven by data, simulation models play an equally important, central role in the digital twin to:

- Interpolate (e.g., spatially or temporally) where no direct measurement data is available;

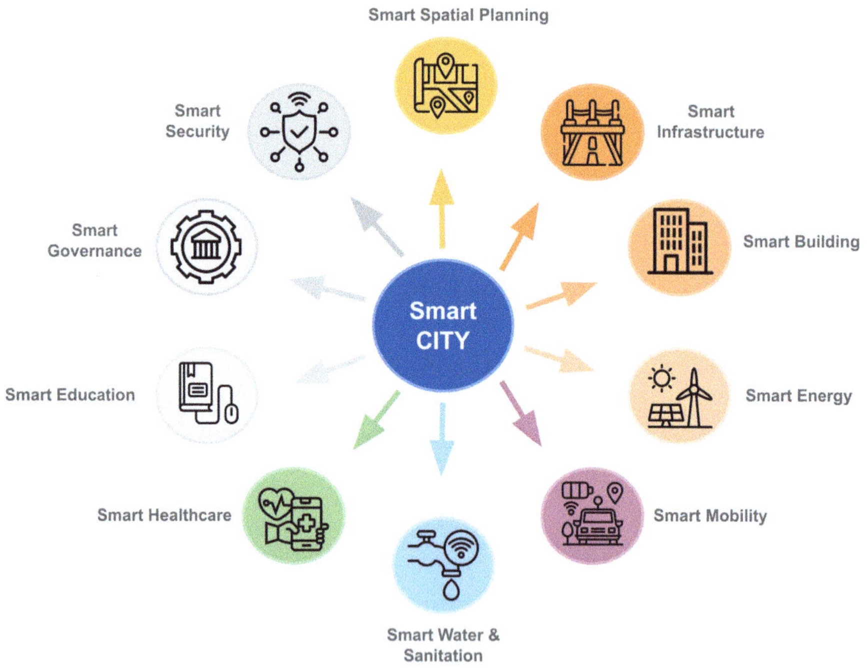


**Fig. 8.1** Smart city domains

- Integrate the presentation and analysis of complementary data sets;
- Cross-correlate data from different domains;
- Infer properties/attributes that are not directly measured;
- Convert measurements and state information into KPIs;
- Extrapolate (predict) business as usual (BAU) and what-if scenarios.

For most of the domains depicted in Fig. 8.1, domain-specific models exist to support decision-making by domain-specific stakeholders. However, most domain-specific decision support models disregard interactions with other smart city domains. The essential difference with an LDT is that the latter should be suited to support a much more diverse variety of users from different domains in a more integrated evaluation, scenario exploration and decision-making approach. As a result, for setting up an LDT, the domain boundaries are not a priori known, and neither are the types of explorations and decisions. This knowledge sets new challenges to models embedded in an LDT. The fact that existing domain-specific models are developed to support a relatively narrow range of use cases offers modellers a rationale to decide which model abstractions, simplifications, delineations, et cetera can be justified. Such parsimony is the mere concept of modelling: it is not the intention to recreate in a model an exact digital copy of the modelled city, but only those domain objects, boundaries and relationships that matter for its application (Occam's razor: "Entities must not be multiplied beyond necessity" (Mueller & Axhausen, 2011)). This concept is challenged in an LDT where the much broader range of potential applications may render formerly justifiable abstractions and delineations of the individual subdomain models that we would like to integrate into the LDT inappropriate.

In fact, delineations in stand-alone models may be replaced in an LDT setting by boundaries predicted by interconnected models of other subdomains or by synchronisation with interconnected data.

In this chapter, we further explore these abstract modelling considerations by reporting and generalising lessons from the traffic-centred model integration we achieved in the LDT pilot project DUET[1] (Raes et al., 2022) to the generic case of LDTs for smart cities.

To learn about predictive domain models' roles and interactions, we discuss our experiences integrating traffic-centred models in the DUET LDT prototype. Before discussing the integrated traffic simulation and traffic impact models, we address some important issues concerning conceptual matching these models' scope and resolution levels to the intended application. While the original stand-alone domain models were appropriate for the stakeholders that used to consult them, their scope and resolution may no longer be sufficient to address all use cases desired by the much more diverse users of an LDT. Nevertheless, integrating existing models is a head-start while developing the interacting models needed in a digital twin. Based on the DUET experience and the strengths and weaknesses of the integrated

[1] Digital Urban European Twins (DUET), EU H2020 project, https://cordis.europa.eu/project/id/870697

models, we discuss some lessons for the future development of LDT models. Before identifying the many interacting smart city domains whose models could and should be integrated into an LDT, we also discuss how the already integrated models need further development to make their level of detail, temporal scope and outputs more useful for the diverse LDT users. We identify a broad and detailed ontology of smart city entities as an indispensable tool for the conceptual integration of multiple domain models and data sources in an LDT and re-formulate the role of domain models and calibration techniques as tools to consistently maintain the properties of smart city entities in this ontology. Finally, we list a set of services that an LDT should provide to assist its users in developing, managing, and optimising what-if scenarios.

In the second part of this chapter, we discuss the integration of the traffic-centred model as implemented in the DUET project. In contrast, in part three, we focus on more generic user lessons learned and user needs related to cross-domain cooperating multi-model simulations beyond DUET.

## 8.2 A Case Study of Domain Prediction Models in an LDT Context: The Case of DUET Model Integration

### *8.2.1 Integrating Models in a Traffic-Centred LDT*

#### Traffic-Centred Focus in the DUET Digital Twin

Figure 8.1 shows how smart mobility or transportation is among the main domains of a smart city, along with environment, spatial planning, energy and resource management, etc. During the various DUET project co-creation sessions in Athens, Flanders and Pilsen, mobility-related use cases linked to environmental impact were one of the most important concerns of the various participants. DUET selected traffic and traffic-related impacts as the first domain to be integrated into an LDT concept for smart cities. At the same time, it was acknowledged how such traffic-centred delineation can only be considered as the start of a more encompassing development that should evolve towards including all related smart city domains of Fig. 8.1.

As a component of a smart city, the transportation system is an open system, where travellers of different population segments interact in different transportation modes to enable different types of activities. There exists no single all-encompassing way of modelling all these interactions. Rather, a multitude of model components exist that can be combined into a whole range of transport models.

Figure 8.2 brings some structure into the cause-and-effect relationships within transportation systems and, therefore, in the many existing domain-specific models and model components that aim to 'isolate' the transportation system from its boundaries and interconnected systems for decision-making in transport. It shows how the demand for mobility is linked to interactions at the socio-demographic level. A whole series of decisions converts the demand for mobility into specific

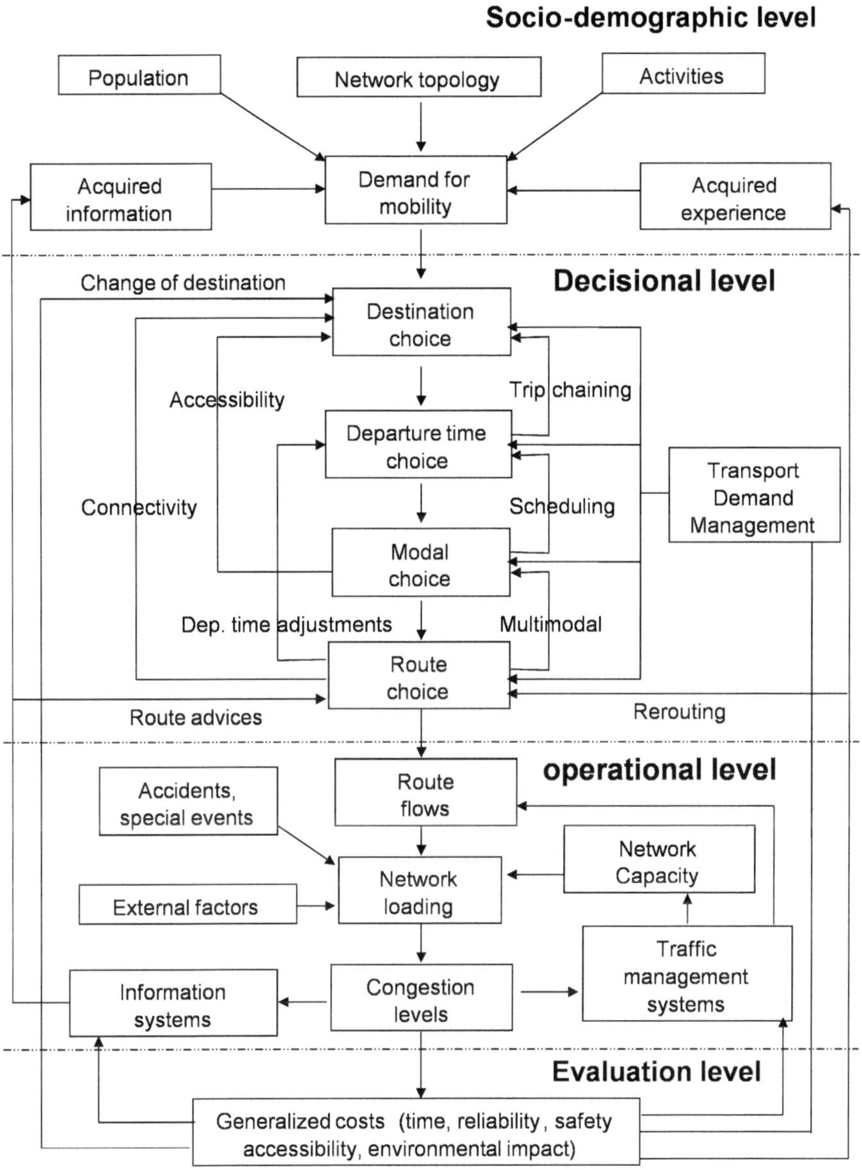


**Fig. 8.2** Transportation system structure and model components

demands for trips along particular routes. At the operational level, these trips finally come together in the transport infrastructures, which determines the locally observed flows and delays along every road and intersection in the network. The stakeholders involved in transportation can evaluate the resulting traffic patterns from various perspectives, like the time cost, environmental impact, safety cost, etc. Note how many feedback mechanisms connect phenomena on one level in the transportation system to other levels, which creates dynamic interactions in the short, medium, and long term. Also, it means that typically, the impact of any change within the transportation system or one of its boundary conditions does not remain local but trickles down or up to many related parts of the transportation system.

The open character of the transportation system appears from the fact that some blocks in Fig. 8.2 that are considered inputs to the transportation system can actually be elaborated into full models as well. For instance, the population and its activities could be modelled as a synthetic population of agents who make many decisions about which activities to perform, where to live and do activities, which vehicles or transport service subscriptions to own, et cetera. Likewise, the transportation network topology, which consists of physical infrastructure objects like roads, sidewalks and bicycle paths, and the service network topology, which consists of public transport lines and timetables, ride-hailing service zones and car-sharing stations, is assumed to be a given. But these could also be modelled with a digital twin component representing city authorities (to set regulations, develop infrastructure, etc.), public or private transportation service agencies.

## Scope and Resolution Levels in Traffic-Centred LDTs

Depending on the socio-demographic level of interest and the evaluations the analyst is interested in, the abstraction of models that aim to capture the traffic-centred interrelations sketched in Fig. 8.2 can differ substantially. For instance, one could distinguish the decision level into multiple decisions related to different types of activities for which the decision-making may differ.

Traditional transport models distinguish between different trip purposes, e.g., homework, homeschooling, leisure, social activities, and commercial trips. Likewise, the operational level is, in reality, multi-layered and might distinguish operations on various infrastructural levels like the road network, rail network, underground network, airspace, and pedestrian or cycling infrastructure, some of which may be partly separated or partly shared spaces.

On top of that, Table 8.1 lists some additional dimensions along which transportation analyses can be categorised. It shows that the scope and resolution level are usually connected. The spatial scope defines the spatial extent of the region that is modelled. As shown in Fig. 8.3, the more local the interest, the smaller the zone of influence and the higher the level of detail of the spatial units (discrete building/POI (point of interest), borough, municipality, region, province, country) and traffic units, e.g. discrete agent, discrete vehicle, distributions of vehicular states, expectation values (also continuum approximation) of the vehicular flow, zonal averages of vehicular flow. It is obvious that radically different transport models are required to investigate the short-term impact (e.g., the next day) of a local deviation in a residential neighbourhood versus, for example, a 10-year impact assessment of a road charging scheme on lower-income groups in a metropolitan region. Not only will the data requirement (resolution/aggregation level) differ substantially, but the

**Table 8.1** Dimensions for transport analyses

| Dimension | Category | Example |
|---|---|---|
| Space | Scope | Terminal, city block, city, metropolitan area, region, country, continent, world |
| | Resolution | Single building, neighbourhood, municipality |
| Time | Scope | Historical, real-time, short-term forecast, long-term scenario forecast |
| | Resolution | Seconds, minutes, hours, peak/off-peak, day, month, year |
| Population | Resolution | Individual agents, households, socio-demographic segments (e.g. income percentiles, age groups), population |
| Activity space | Purpose | Social, leisure, home-work, home-school, professional, freight |

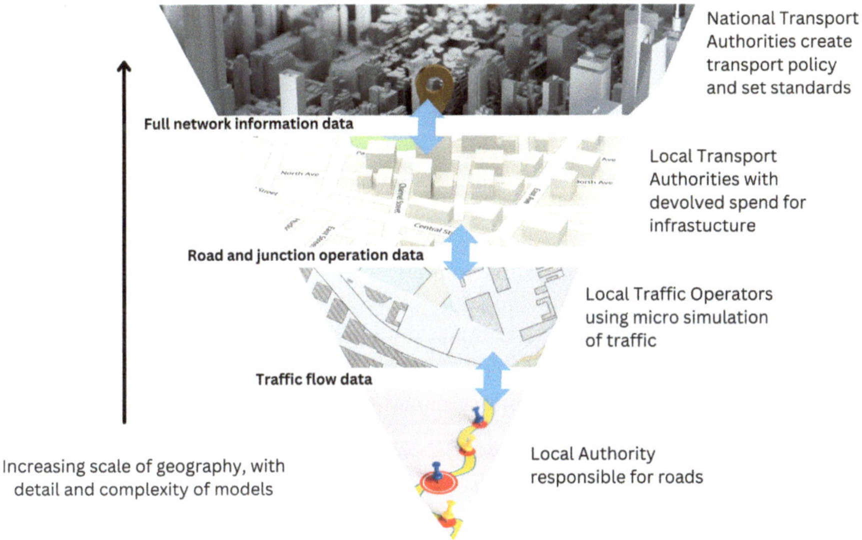


**Fig. 8.3** Spatial scope and aggregation levels in traditional traffic models

behaviour affecting the evaluation criteria of interest will differ significantly. This fact may range from coarse, aggregate regressions of how a population shifts between travel options to stochastic simulation of detailed decision-making models of individual travellers.

One needs to be aware that the accuracy of transportation models cannot be infinitely increased by refining the resolution level. These are, in fact, different things that often need clarification. A high-resolution level means that the description of the processes allows more details to be recognised (e.g. individual vehicles or even passengers inside vehicles, called 'agents'). However, this does not guarantee that all of these details are valid. In many cases, agent-based simulations are valid on the level of distributions (i.e. their average and covariances may be valid, not the individual samples). They are often calibrated against the same aggregate data as continuous-flow approaches.

It is important to realise that, as user needs may be focused on individual streets and local districts, flows may be so thin that a discrete approach feels natural. While simulators exist with a resolution onto that level (whether using discrete or continuous data aggregation), the behaviour that drives these local decisions can only be described in stochastic terms (e.g., expectation values, either of multiple simulations of discrete agents or as direct variables). Inevitably, however, the accuracy of more aggregate variables (or, more precisely, the validity) will always be higher than that of local, more disaggregated variables.

In other words, no matter the resolution at which the simulation is described, it will always be more valid in describing arterials and motorways that collect large flows, as compared to local streets, where the prediction of subtle local influences will always remain problematic. Data driven approaches with detailed local data may be superior.

As Fig. 8.3 shows, specific instances of the wide range of potential transportation models have been developed—and in many cases fine-tuned over the years or even decades—by specific stakeholders in the domain (e.g. departments of transport, transit agencies). The temporal level of detail is related to the spatial scope and level of detail. A national transportation authority would develop and maintain region- or even nation-wide strategic models (highest level in Fig. 8.3) for average traffic loads during peak periods in all transportation modes and infrastructures in their jurisdiction, albeit on a relatively coarse resolution of municipalities or other aggregate 'traffic analysis zones' (e.g. corresponding to statistical sectors in public databases). Such models support, for instance, scenario and cost-benefit analyses related to large infrastructure projects or tax scenarios. Local traffic controllers would develop detailed second-to-second local microsimulation models of traffic operations on a signalised corridor in which they are operating (lowest level in Fig. 8.3). They may explore what-if scenarios for better incident response (e.g. prioritise emergency services) or real-time optimisation of delays for different traffic types.

As discussed in the introduction to this chapter, the use cases of an LDT may be much more diverse and not all known a priori and may, therefore, not be captured by a single (spatial) scope or the level of detail. To serve the different needs of all LDT users, such tools may develop towards a library of various integrated traffic and smart city-related domain models, including a complete ontology and tools to convert between different aggregation levels of time, space, population, et cetera. Moreover, these models should be compatible and consistent; for example, finer-resolution models (along all dimensions of Table 8.1) should be disaggregated into lower-resolution versions and vice versa.

## Synchronisation of an LDT

Since a digital twin is a parallel version of a part of the real world, it needs to be synchronised with how that world evolves. Models synchronise with the real world through data through a process called data assimilation or calibration. Focusing on traffic-centred digital twins (which can be generalised to other domains), an important design issue is how synchronised the digital twin should be and how that calibration is obtained (externally or internally).

The first issue is one of time scales.

- *Real-time/short-term prediction:* Traffic evolves from second to second; for applications such as traffic information or real-time traffic control, a digital twin (used, for instance, in a traffic control centre) would have to track reality on the scale of seconds or minutes. For this type of use case, predictions are relevant over a horizon of the next few minutes up to one hour, known as short-term traffic prediction. Data driven (Yuan & Li, 2021) or model-driven predictions (Gentile & Meschini, 2011) and data assimilations (Tampere & Immers, 2007) have been proposed for such real-time decision support;
- *Day-to-day / next-day prediction:* Because of the daily rhythm of traffic, both travellers and traffic or transport system operators have daily strategies that may be updated after every experience. For example, traffic management around a work zone may need daily fine-tuning, or the management of electric charging networks may require daily predictions of electricity demand by traffic. An LDT supporting such use cases should synchronise daily to evaluate the latest experience and predict conditions for the next day or days. Data driven approaches are dominant in this domain (Ma et al., 2021);
- *Slow-moving changes:* On a scale of months/years, both the structural demand pattern, the transportation services, and transport infrastructures will evolve slowly. Even if an LDT would only be used to predict, over the years or even decades, the impact of what-if scenarios on a strategic level (i.e. which does not require daily nor real-time updating), any traffic model configured for a base year would soon be outdated if it is not synchronised with living data reflecting the slow-moving changes in demand and infrastructure. This problem resembles the challenge of initially setting up such a strategic model. Whereas in consulting, it was customary to adopt an existing traffic model of the region of interest and apply manual changes to update it to a new base year, deployment of strategic traffic models in a digital twin requires the model set-up and updating to be structurally connected to permanently updated, 'living' data sources like geographical databases of infrastructure, timetables, POI, land-use databases, population statistics, regional economic databases etc.

The second issue of the *calibration method* is a complicated but crucial one. After all, if models are not well calibrated, one can never expect their predicted outputs to be reliable (*garbage in, garbage out* problem). The state-of-the-art in (traffic) model calibration offers a wide variety of automated, semi-automated and—very often—manual manipulations of parameters aimed at validly reproducing model outputs of a known reference case and validly predicting changes to this reference case. (Actually, some refer to the former as *calibration* and the latter as *validation* of the model.) The more complicated the model (e.g. higher dimensionality of input parameter space, higher non-linearity and/or non-convexity of the model's transformation of inputs into outputs and into a calibration objective function), the less successful automated calibration gets, and expert intervention is inevitable.

For LDTs that need systematic synchronisation with living data, it is inconvenient that calibration often requires manual intervention, and no generically applicable automated calibration methods exist. At best, calibration can be automated for specific characteristics of the network and specific combinations of available data sources, but this transfers badly to other cases and is inconvenient. The fact, however, that the LDT platform integrates data sets in a standardised way according to a consistent ontology could significantly increase the feasibility of automated calibration procedures. Despite progress made in DUET on automatically updating aggregate travel demand input for regional transport models (Notelaers et al., 2024), it remains an essential avenue of LDT research and development.

### *8.2.2 Traffic-Centred Models in the DUET Digital Twin*

In the DUET digital twin, seven different traffic or traffic impact models were integrated, and they all communicated with the generic data sources and each other. All models had been developed before for other purposes, such as integrated modelling frameworks, web services, open-source toolkits, or research and educational toolkits. They were all modified and provided dedicated interaction interfaces to exchange data with and receive computation triggers from the DUET integration platform. Table 8.2 overviews the models' scope, time horizon, transport modes and impact KPIs. Each model and their data exchange mechanisms are briefly described hereafter.

#### **Traffic and Traffic Impact Models Integrated in DUET**

Dyntapy Static and Dynamic Assignments

Dyntapy (Ortmann & Tampère, 2022) is an open-source traffic modelling toolkit that integrates the educational and research Matlab traffic toolbox (Himpe, n.d.) in Python, which provides traffic modelling services in the DUET LDT. It has operational algorithms for deterministic static assignment in road traffic networks Method of Successive Averages (MSA), FW Frank-Wolfe, and Dial-B (Dial, 2006), stochastic traffic assignment (MSA, Dial (1971), recursive logit (Verstraete & Tampère, 2018), and dynamic traffic assignment Link Transmission Model (LTM) (Himpe et al., 2016)).

Through specific parsing and graph construction modules, dyntapy autoconfigures the road traffic network model into a connected routable graph for a given study area using living data sources in the case of OpenStreetMap (OSM). This approach is not only used to configure a new traffic model instance for an LDT in a new study area, but it also updates the traffic model for an existing LDT whenever the road network changes. Likewise, dyntapy integrates with an external demand generation module named Poidpy (Notelaers et al., 2024) that

**Table 8.2** Properties of the models available in DUET

| Model | Spatial scope | Time horizon | Transport mode | Air quality impact | Noise impact |
|---|---|---|---|---|---|
| Dyntapy Static Unimodal Assignment KUL[a] | Regional (inner city + satellites) | Strategic planning | Car | No | No |
| Dyntapy Dynamic Traffic Assignment KUL | Regional (inner city + satellites) | Tactical and strategic planning | Car | No | No |
| Static Multimodal Assignment Model P4A[b] | Regional (inner city + satellites) | Strategic planning | Car, PT | No | No |
| CityFlows Local Traffic Model imec[c] | Inner city districts | Real-time state estimation | Car, cycle, walk | No | No |
| Urban Strategy Air quality and Noise Model TNO[d] | Inner city or regional (inner city + satellites) | Strategic planning | Car | Yes | Yes |
| ATMO Air Quality Model VITO[e] | Regional (inner city + satellites) | Strategic planning | Car | Yes | No |
| NoiseModelling P4A | Inner city | Strategic planning | Car | No | Yes |

[a]Katholieke Universiteit Leuven, https://www.kuleuven.be/english/kuleuven
[b]Plan4All, https://www.plan4all.eu/
[c]Interuniversitair Micro-Electronica Centrum, https://www.imec-int.com/en
[d]Nederlandse Organisatie voor toegepast-natuurwetenschappelijk onderzoek, https://www.tno.nl/en/
[e]Flemish Institute for Technological Research, https://vito.be/en

auto-configures an origin-destination (OD) trip demand matrix for any desired zoning, and it automatically connects the traffic analysis zone centroids (i.e. its gravity centre) to the road network graph. Also, this demand generation module reads its source data from OSM, allowing for auto-configuring trip demand in a new study area or updating an existing LDT whenever the land use and POI in the zones change.

### Traffic Modeller Static Traffic Model

This open source model traffic model as a web service (Jedlička et al., 2020) allows exploration and analysis of past traffic or real-time information on the traffic network status and performance of what-if scenarios of city traffic on the tactical level (e.g., planned cultural or sports events) or strategic level (new or modified infrastructure). It generates updated travel demand based on socio-demographic data of the traffic analysis zones. It assigns traffic to the network through parallelised equilibration algorithms for fast computations in a digital twin environment (Potuzak & Kolovsky, 2021).

NoiseModelling

Traffic noise in cities affects the lives and health of many people. The European Commission requires major EU cities to produce noise maps and corresponding noise-exposure distributions of their inhabitants to regulate and control the effects of urban traffic noise. Generating traffic-based noise maps delivers the output from which noise-exposure distributions can be derived. In the Netherlands, it is also used as a policy-making tool to see the effect of different planning scenarios for infrastructure, buildings and sound barriers. Since noise and air quality are essential factors for the liveability of cities and use similar data about traffic volumes and the morphology of public space, both are important to integrate into a digital twin. Two different types of noise models were integrated and tested in the DUET project. Both models start from a traffic model and the public space morphology.

In Pilsen, a NoiseModelling library[2] and a tool capable of producing noise maps of cities (Bocher et al., 2019) were used. This tool is almost compliant with the CNOSSOS-EU standard method for noise emission (only road traffic) and noise propagation. Integrating the NoiseModelling library, available under open source GPL v3 licence, in DUET entails optimising the library and tokenisation, as the library was prepared for connection to the DUET central message brokering component.

The first important step was discussing, designing, and defining the brokering message structure. The next challenge was evaluating a what-if scenario's effectiveness in calculating noise propagation, which is a time-consuming three-dimensional calculation process. Therefore, preprocessing was necessary to speed up demand recalculation later on. The preprocessing is repeated each time a 3D model of the area of interest is added or altered: namely, all the noise propagation paths, including the noise refraction, produced by the 'typical traffic' scenario are precalculated. The follow on-demand and recalculation of the what-if scenario consists only of calculating delta noise emission, following precalculated noise propagation paths, delivering results in a reasonable time.

In Flanders and Athens, a noise model from Urban Strategy Noise based on road traffic was used. The TNO model is also capable of capturing rail traffic and industry, but this wasn't applied in the LDT. The calculation follows the Dutch statutory methods for noise calculations based on the "Standaard RekenMethode 2/Standard Calculation method 2 (SRM2)" version for Noise. In general, the noise module is used to calculate noise levels on receptors. These receptors are placed evenly within the study area, on the facades of buildings and next to roads. From these receptors, a continuous noise map can be generated. This approach can be leveraged for large areas up to 30 km2. Typically, about three million receptors would be used for such an area, which can provide a detailed noise map of the street level.

[2] NoiseModelling library, https://noise-planet.org/noisemodelling.html, https://github.com/Universite-Gustave-Eiffel/NoiseModelling, https://noisemodelling.readthedocs.io/en/latest/

### Urban Strategy Air Quality and Noise Models

The TNO Urban Strategy air quality model calculates the $NO_2$ and PM concentrations emitted by traffic (Borst et al., 2009). It uses the Dutch SRM1 and SRM2 (Standaard RekenMethode/standardised calculation methods) as described in the RBL 2007 (Dutch regulation for air quality (Koninkrijksrelaties, n.d.)). The Urban Strategy Noise Module focuses on generating Noise maps and delivers the output from which noise-exposure distributions can be derived. In the Netherlands, it is also used as a policy-making tool to see the effect of different planning scenarios for infrastructure, buildings and sound barriers (Borst, 2010). The air quality calculation combines different air quality models with specific functions. The TNO model starts by calculating the background levels derived from the GCN (Grootschalige Concentratie Nederland or Large-scale Concentration in the Netherlands). These background concentrations are based on meteorological data and data about the terrain roughness.

The local contribution by traffic is based on the interplay of two additional models: The SRM2 Gaussian plume model calculates the emission dispersion from motorways and major roads, and the SRM1 CAR model calculates street concentrations (with buildings along the road). Both models rely on data on current and future emission estimations of the fleet (how much substance is emitted by a specific type of vehicle), as well as estimates of background concentration. Emissions and background concentrations change over time. Because of type approval regulations and the introduction of new technologies, like PM filters and automatic driving, emission values are becoming smaller. Because of this and similar actions on other emitters, background values will likely decrease. Therefore, emission and background scenarios are implemented. Based on the year developments are planned, appropriate emission factors and background values are taken from the database. These emission and background values are updated annually. Each model takes other parameters into account. The SRM1 'city model' takes the following conditions into account: (1) the road is in an urban environment; (2) the maximum calculation distance is the distance to the buildings, with a maximum of 30 or 60 metres from the road axis, depending on the street type; (3) there is little difference in height between the road and the surroundings; (4) there are no shielding structures along the road. The SRM2 model calculating the impact of motorways and open roads takes the following elements into account:

1. The presence and width of a central reservation;
2. The configuration of the carriageways where the following configurations are possible:
    a. one direction of travel consisting of one or more lanes;
    b. two driving directions consisting of one or more runways.
3. The height of the road in relation to ground level;

4. The presence of screens or ramparts, the location (one-sided/two-sided), the height and the distance to the road edge, where h has a minimum value of 1 metre and a maximum value of 6 metres, and for l a maximum value of 50 metres;
5. The presence of a tunnel, whereby there are no openings in the top or sides of the tunnel.

VITO delivers with ATMO-Plan (VITO, n.d.-a) and ATMO-Street (VITO, n.d.-b), two products for simulating air quality concentrations that integrate into digital twins. Like the TNO models, several underlying simulation models are also integrated to calculate NO2, PM10, PM25 and Black Carbon pollution. VITO's ATMO-street model calculates air pollutant concentrations across a region, considering the regional and urban background and capturing so-called street canyon effects into a single high-resolution air quality map. This calculation allows for estimating the health impact of air quality. It enables policymakers to take action to reduce concentration levels at pollution hotspots. The data can also be used in applications that can help citizens, for example, to choose the 'healthiest' route to cycle or walk to work. An interesting feature of an LDT is the capability to estimate the effects on the local air quality of traffic scenarios (both in terms of traffic volumes and fleet composition via, e.g. Low Emission Zones (LEZ's), urban development plans or industrial mitigation strategies.

#### CityFlows Local Traffic Visualisation

CityFlows supports mobility experts in interpreting homogeneous mobility data sources (imec, n.d.). Based on different mobility data sources (i.e. telco signalling data, Wi-Fi scanning data, Automatic Number-Plate Recognition (ANPR) camera data, Telraam data (Rear Window BV., n.d.), counting loops, speed radar data, bike sharing data, etc.). CityFlows distributes a unified density of traffic and discriminates between different modalities, such as bikes, pedestrians and non-motorized traffic, in the streets of a certain area. This unified unit (i.e. density) enables mobility experts to compare multimodal traffic business in time and geography. Next to this, CityFlows provides an accuracy score, enabling mobility experts to know when to trust the output data and when not.

### Interaction Mechanisms in DUET

#### Between the Domain Models

The traffic and traffic impact models of the previous section interact through a Message Broker in the DUET core based on a T-cell architecture. Each computational model (air, noise, traffic) was connected to the DUET T-Cell by means of a suitable Application Programming Interface (API). This API enables the DUET system to control the models, including starting and stopping simulations, initiating calibration and validation, and exchanging necessary data and results. The API is accessible using a gateway to the Apache Kafka Platform (Apache Software Foundation, 2023) and relays messages between Kafka and the models. Kafka functions as the main message streaming platform in the DUET T-Cell architecture.

The availability of the individual models is realised using Docker containers. The individual models have been packaged inside a Docker container enabling deployment anywhere in the available cloud, thus forming a cloud of available models. The models run outside the DUET T-Cell and are interconnected using the API. A Docker Orchestrator has been implemented to start up, retrieve status and terminate the individual model Docker containers. More technical details are provided by Schreuder and Lohman (2020).

#### Interaction of DUET Models with Data: Towards Automated Model Configuration and Recalibration

Configuration is the process of setting up the model's input parameters for a given region of interest, say a city and its surrounding influence area. Setting up means that the entities and their properties relevant for traffic modelling in that region of interest need to be identified and quantified. Traffic models typically split their total entity set into supply and demand entities. Supply entails the road network, intersections and all relevant infrastructure and controls that determine how traffic propagates in the network.

The supply-side of traffic and its physical infrastructure are the layers of entities that are most developed in DUET so far: entities like 3D buildings, streets, squares, etc., have been the first to be defined in DUET's ontology and are used for validation and as input to the domain models for traffic and emission and noise propagation. The dyntapy module of DUET (Ortmann & Tampère, 2022) selects relevant entities within the modelled region and some relevant properties (like: number of lanes, road type, speed limit) from generic infrastructure data sources like OSM and OpenTransportNet,[3] which are automatically complemented by properties that the traffic models require e.g. capacity and travel time function parameters, zone connectors.

Since travel demand results from socio-economic activities, data for the demand-side of traffic models is traditionally inferred from three main complementary data types: land use data, population data, and behavioural surveys. Especially for the latter, no generic data sources exist, although there is a trend trying to substitute survey data in demand generation by passive tracking of a population sample on the aggregate level (e.g. telecom cell-handover data) or disaggregate level, e.g. life tracking apps, telecom customer records (MOMENTUM[4] consortium, 2020). Such

[3] Spatially Referenced Data Hubs for Innovation in the Transport Sector (OpenTransportNet), EU CIP Project, https://cordis.europa.eu/project/id/620533

[4] Modelling Emerging Transport Solutions for Urban Mobility (MOMENTUM), EU H2020 Project, https://cordis.europa.eu/project/id/815069

techniques, which automatically estimate aggregate travel demand (OD trip matrices) solely from land use data in OSM (Notelaers et al., 2024), were not integrated into DUET.

Although the state of the art offers no methods to automatically perform an initial in-depth calibration of traffic or traffic-impact models, the auto-configuration modules for traffic supply and demand of DUET are, in principle, suited for an automatic recalibration of these models whenever ('slow') changes occur to the road network infrastructure or land use. Such 'slow' changes can originate from two sources: they may have actually occurred in reality and are reflected in an update of the underlying 'living' data source, or a user may enter changes to explore a scenario of infrastructure or lane use.

### *8.2.3 User Needs in the DUET Digital Twin*

Upon the formation of the DUET project consortium and thus selection of the modelling expertise reflected in the list of available models of Table 8.2, a preliminary inquiry into user needs suggested that users, just like traditional transport agencies, would desire analyses of peak period flows on the regional level (= the inner city + the surrounding land and satellite municipalities from which the majority of commute traffic is attracted) and on the strategic time horizon. As a result, the first generation of models interacting in DUET has a regional, strategic scope (Table 8.2). Moreover, they are largely oriented towards motorised road traffic (with no explicit behavioural models for freight or logistics, hence labelled in the Table as 'car' traffic, where trucks are converted into person car equivalents). The traffic impact models capture exhaust gas and noise emissions by motorised traffic on a local scale and over a broad spatial scope ranging from districts to entire regions; their time resolution is coarse (annual and daily profiles), corresponding to strategic planning needs.

Interestingly, while the consortium developed the platform and as mock-up and pilot versions of it became available, discussed in interviews and workshops its potential use cases with a broader range of future users (Walravens et al., 2021), it appeared that many user needs had a different scope. Indeed, as Table 8.3 summarises, most users would like urban digital twins to address strategic planning problems, but they zoom in on a more local inner-city scale than most of the first-generation DUET traffic models of Table 8.2 do (Silence et al., 2020). Given this more local scope, many user stories involve, in addition to cars, public transport and/or active travel models like cycling and walking and related personal micromobility solutions like scooters. They also demanded the integration of parking, modal shift and multimodal trip making decisions by the population (urban residents, visitors and commuters). The traffic impact models match very well the scope, time horizon and impact that users expressed interest in, and users highly valued the integrated consultation of (multiple) traffic models with local traffic impact models.

**Table 8.3** Summary of user story types collected from interviews with stakeholders (Silence et al., 2020; Walravens et al., 2021)

| Epic/User Story | Spatial scope | Time horizon | Transport mode | Air quality impact | Noise impact |
|---|---|---|---|---|---|
| Controlled Parking / Promote Use of Public Transport | Regional (inner city + satellites) | Daily + strategic planning | Car, PT | | |
| Stimulating Combined Use of Car, PT and Active Modes | Regional (inner city + satellites) | Strategic planning | Car, PT, cycle, walk | | |
| Green Routes to Reduce Pollution | Regional (inner city + satellites) | Strategic planning | Car | Yes | |
| Parking Management Application | Inner city districts | Daily management | Car | | |
| Analyse Trends in Noise Levels | Inner city districts | Strategic planning | Car | | Yes |
| Analyse Trends in Air Pollution Levels | Inner city districts | Strategic planning | Car | Yes | |
| Insights into Mobility Flows at the Neighbourhood Level | Inner city districts | Strategic planning | Car, PT, cycle, walk | | |
| Impact of LEZ on Mobility and Air Pollution | Inner city districts | Strategic planning | Car | Yes | |
| Healthy and Safe Routes for Vulnerable Road Users | Inner city districts | Strategic planning | Cycle, walk | Yes | |
| Impact of New Buildings and Activities | Regional (inner city + satellites) | Strategic planning | Car (PT, cycle, walk) | | |
| Match Demand and Supply of Public Space | Inner city districts | Strategic planning | Car, PT, cycle, walk | Yes | Yes |

Apart from these traffic-centred issues, as more data becomes available and more stakeholders embrace the use of the digital twin to support their decision-making or communication of plans towards the broader public, the further development of LDTs will require expansion and inclusion of other smart city domains (whether or not in transport).

## 8.3 Lessons Learned from DUET Model Integration for the Future Development of LDTs

### *8.3.1 LDT User Needs Beyond DUET*

The DUET LDT case study showed that while the integrated traffic-centred domain models are indispensable, they are as yet insufficient to address all needs of the users. On the one hand, users express needs that require further refinement and/or development of the traffic-centred domain models. Other user needs require models of complementary smart city domains to be integrated.

#### Development Directions of Mobility, Traffic & Traffic Impact Models

An important lesson from prototype LDT cases like DUET is that while it gives a head-start to integrate already existing domain models, such models, on the other hand, bear the legacy of a development history where the isolated use within a smart city subdomain may have resulted in different requirements set by such specialised users, as compared to the more diverse use cases of an LDT. For example, traffic and transport models traditionally focus on regional, strategic policy that primarily concerns peak periods when pressure on the transportation system is at its maximum. LDTs, however, are targeted to a much wider and more diverse range of stakeholders whose needs may not be (fully) addressed by the integration of existing traffic models, for instance:

- *Finer-grained local traffic impact scenario predictions:* Current models are sensitive mainly to strategic/structural mobility measures (e.g. infrastructure development, urban planning, congestion charging, multimodal accessibility), whereas city stakeholders are faced with many local measures too (e.g. local mobility impact studies of new buildings or even the way in which access structures are connected, parking, fine-grained traffic management, solving local conflicts between motorised and slow traffic, curb management, temporary measures such as closed streets around schools). As a result, there is a need for finer demand and (re)routing modelling; it also calls for additional components of the mobility, logistics, and traffic system to be integrated into the traffic models;
- *Multi-period models:* Current models focus on peak periods; impact on city (e.g. liveability) is often equally or even more important during off-peak and on weekends/holidays that traffic agencies rarely model;
- *Additional output:*
  - The main outputs of existing traffic models are link flows and average speeds that deliver *input for the traffic impact models* (noise and air quality emissions). The digital twin graphically often presents model outputs on a highly detailed, 3D physical world (e.g. 3D building shapes), which suggests that model outputs would be equally trustworthy on this detailed resolution level.

However, existing traffic models are based on average relationships, correlations, and empirical rules that are only valid on the aggregate level but get noisier and more unreliable on the disaggregate, local level. The users cannot see this distinction and may create false expectations about prediction accuracy;

- It is therefore recommended that the following *metadata* on the outputs be available: how certain are the results, how stable or variable can actual values be expected around their mean? This recommendation calls for additional distributional characteristics to the model outputs (i.e. confidence intervals and percentiles). Even though such subtle information might be challenging to interpret by the non-expert user, such distributional data might be exploited by the LDT platform to select which information to present at which level (e.g. while zooming in too closely, remove or gradually blur details that have too high a variance at this level) as an indirect way of making the user aware of the confidence bounds and limited disaggregate validity of model outputs;
- By only providing link-based outputs, many dimensions and alternative aggregation levels that can be meaningful to users might be lost. It is recommended for models to deliver to the LDT *additional outputs* like cordon analysis, selected link analysis, watershed analysis, accessibility, access and reachability measures, isochrone maps, route analysis, OD analysis, and skim matrices.

Even more fundamentally, users express interest in use cases that involve components of the transportation system that are often disregarded in domain models used for transport planning. Some examples of mobility and transport model components that can complement future digital twins are parking models, pedestrian models, cycling models (and other light vehicles), vehicle fleet models, mass transit models, shared-mobility and MaaS (mobility-as-a-service) system models, microscopic travel demand model (including tour-based correlations, vehicle and mobility tool ownership), modal choice and multimodal trip behavioural modelling, traffic management and control models, mobility and traffic signposting, dynamic information provision models, behavioural models in non-recurrent conditions (incidents, accidents, manifestations, events, disasters, evacuation etc.) and finally safety, social and fiscal impact models.

### Development Directions of Other Smart City Domain Models

The previous section discussed future development directions for the person-mobility domain. Many users also express needs related to other smart city domains that may be worth adding to an LDT:

- Synthetic population model distinguishing relevant subsections of the population:
  - Age groups, socioeconomic strata, gender, people with special needs;
  - Activity-based demand model;

  - Tourism model;
  - Social network and interaction model;
  - Economic interaction model;
  - Labour market model;
  - Health model.

- Weather and climate modelling;
- City logistics model (including reverse logistics like waste collection and returns);
- (Transport) infrastructure and infrastructure maintenance model;
- Construction activity model (including road works);
- Housing market and land-use model;
- Energy and water distribution model;
- Sewer and water management;
- Biodiversity model;
- Governance and policy model;
- Crime modelling (Leitner, 2015).

## Ontology for Urban Digital Twins: Towards a Deeper Integration of LDT Models and Data

Most existing smart city domain models and data processing procedures that are candidates for integration in an LDT have originally yet to be conceived for deployment in a data-rich, living digital twin platform where many other data procedures and models coexist. Their systematic integration requires:

### Development of an Urban Digital Twin Ontology

An ontology is a formal naming and definition of the entity types, properties, and interrelationships that really or fundamentally exist in the smart city domains of interest (e.g. traffic and transportation).

Properties of entities are time-dependent: they have unique historical values (retrocasts), estimates of their current values (state estimation), and (possibly multiple) predictions of their future values (forecasts) under various scenario boundary conditions and according to different prediction models.

Moreover, many properties may be considered in an LDT at various aggregation levels, e.g., the demand for travel may be known as activity tours of a synthetic population and as a zonal aggregated OD table. An ontology also describes such hierarchical or aggregation relationships and methods should be provided in the LDT to sustain consistency between differently aggregated versions of the same properties; this may entail dedicated aggregation (e.g., the sum of individual trips of synthetic residents of a zone should correspond to the zonal trip production of that zone in the OD table) or disaggregation methods (e.g., the cost of a public transport trip between two zones may be disaggregated over individual travellers willing to use public transport between two locations within those zones).

### Rethinking the Role of Domain Models

Essentially, models relate properties of entities to each other based on theoretical or empirical knowledge that the modeller expressed as analytical, statistical, or procedural relationships. They can set values of certain properties based on registration to other properties present in the ontology. Using this perspective, we can distinguish different types of services that models may provide in a digital twin:

- *Property transformations:* Examples are (dis)aggregation over any relevant dimension like space, time, or population subgroups;
- *Estimation/fusion/inference of latent variables:* While no direct empirical observation may exist of a latent property of an entity, its value may be inferred from observed data through some form of statistical inference or fusion of multiple heterogeneous data sources; a so-called measurement model then relates the latent, unobservable and so far, unknown property to observable properties (data) or to other latent properties that have been inferred before;
- *Extrapolation/prediction:* When a model relates historical and/or current state estimates to future properties of the entities, forecasts are produced. These are inherently uncertain and subject to assumptions on scenario boundary conditions and decision variables (some of which may be controlled by the user).

### Exploit the Living Digital Twin Context for Permanent Training of Models

As a digital twin is a living representation of reality that permanently acquires updated data, its properties migrate over time from being forecasts to current state to retrocast. During this process, the property evolves from a mere extrapolation, an over-inferred property conditioned on earlier and current observations, into a retrocast conditioned on earlier and as later observed data. Being conditioned on ever more data, the uncertainty decreases during this process. Hence, the retrocasts can be seen as ex-post ground truth and allow for permanent training or calibration of the state estimation and forecasting models.

### 8.3.2 *Broader Support of Case and Scenario Management and Control*

#### (Semi-)Automated Set Up and Calibration of LDT Models/Cases

Model/Case Setup

Within DUET, it was described how traffic networks could be automatically extracted and set up as part of the dyntapy traffic modelling toolbox; traffic demand OD-matrices can be extracted and set up through the Poidpy toolkit. Any LDT needs such procedures, but they even need to go beyond configuring entities and properties that need to be known for traffic modelling. LDT configuration requires support for a more encompassing and systematic setup of all related modelling entities and their properties, respecting the digital twin ontology proposed in the previous section. Such configuration should be automated with minimal human intervention during configuration.

Model Calibration

At present, the state of the art offers no automated calibration procedures or generally applicable guidelines on which data is minimally required to guarantee a certain level of validity of model outputs. We witnessed in the DUET LDT prototype that integration of models and data with advanced visualisation can easily raise unrealistic expectations about validity. Models were integrated as generic computational services that can run on any network. Therefore, visualisations of model outputs can be produced for any territory configured and look just as convincing to a non-expert user, whether those outputs were empirically validated or not. Modellers will stress that model outputs can only be trusted for networks for which substantial calibration efforts have been performed in the context of specific pilot use cases using dedicated data sources. Any output of non-calibrated use cases needs to be distrusted, as the garbage-in-garbage-out principle applies.

Integration of models in an LDT context, however, may spark new opportunities to automate the tedious process of model calibration, which is an important avenue for future LDT development. Indeed, an LDT forms the ideal platform to host automated calibration procedures, given the standardised data models that offer an agreed description of the network and all objects (e.g. buildings) with shared properties. This description of the physical world is shared with the data sources that connect to the LDT, which facilitates a direct comparison between calibration/validation data and model states computed by the integrated domain models without the inconvenience that used to exist when mapping models and data sources that each had their own data model, indexing, and properties definitions. A calibration/validation module will act as any other model that subscribes to and publishes properties of the physical world that is virtualised in the LDT. In this particular case, it would subscribe to model outputs for which corresponding reference data exists, compute adjusted parameter settings based on observed mismatches between model output and data, and publish the adjusted parameters for updating the model. This procedure could iteratively improve the model's calibration.

Enhanced Scenario Management, Optimisation, Control, and Analysis

Using the DUET LDT prototype, we detected a lack of semantic description of cases and scenarios and a schema or standard API for its management. As digital twin technology matures, such a standardisation may foster further interoperability between digital twin building blocks. DUET already allowed developers to describe definitions of cases and scenarios and provided interfaces through which users can set up, manage and orchestrate interactions between data, models and scenarios.

In addition to such interfaces, users would benefit from additional tools to manage, optimise, control and analyse scenarios. A typical use case of a digital twin is to assist a stakeholder in exploring how they might change the outcome of some KPIs of interest by changing the decision variables through which they control part of the world modelled in the LDT. Exploration of options can be supported by offering, for example:

- Sensitivity information of KPI for changes in the decision variables;
- *Optimisation (goal-seeking) of KPIs:* Which combination of decision variables maximises given objectives;
- *Pareto-front exploration:* While some KPIs can be simultaneously improved (i.e. when they are aligned), others are conflicting and form a so-called Pareto-front (i.e. the collection of point for which improvement of one KPI can only be achieved by negatively affecting at least one of the other KPIs of interest). For decision-makers, it is very helpful when a modelling tool assists in (semi-)automatically finding the Pareto front, herewith revealing the trade-offs in the user's decision-making (Possel et al., 2018).

### *8.3.3 LDT Model and Data Interaction Mechanisms*

LDT data and model orchestration are essential to creating an interoperable policy domain overarching solution, as described in Chap. 5. However, the data and model interaction mechanisms, designed and tested in DUET, are only part of the basic architecture. DUET used an Apache Kafka-based message streaming platform to exchange events and data. The Kafka broker component is responsible for the communication and Data Exchange with the T-Cell; thus, other parts of the DUET system are done using the Kafka platform. The models define their own 'channels or topics' for exchanging information with the system. The data to be exchanged with the model or the Docker Orchestrator will be formalised in a minimal required API. Figure 8.4 depicts the cloud-based interaction model.

The models in the cloud are controlled by a Model Agent and corresponding API and deployed upon request. An Orchestrator is responsible for deploying models taking platform and resource requirements into account. The Docker technology will use scripts based on Kubernetes or similar. The Orchestrator receives messages indirectly through the Model Agent API and executes the requests to Start (Deploy), Stop (Delete) the models. The start request received from the DUET system will include a model context (parameters, data) to be pushed and passed on to the model. Response messages from the model include a unique instance ID to control or get information from the specific model optionally. When a model is deployed, it should listen for command messages from the Orchestrator/Model Agent API and handle data through the DATA API. Necessary properties, data or links to data sources can be passed in the context section included with the startModel request (Fig. 8.5).

The DUET T-Cell has two major RESTful APIs: The Model API and the Data API. RESTful APIs provide a standardised way of communicating with data sources on the web.

The DUET T-Cell architecture and its modular approach enable dynamic and on-demand attachment of models to the DUET system. Using a message streaming platform allows the DUET system NOT to set a fixed sequenced chain of models. Models will be signalled to run when changed data or event messages instruct a model to perform a 'run'. This topic needs further exploration. During the DUET design, it became apparent that a lack of semantic interoperability and standards allows models to communicate. Almost no standardisation work has been done in this field. Some standardisation attempts, like the OGC OpenMI (Harpham et al., 2019), aren't widely adopted and require that models know about each other, which is not favourable. Model interaction standardisation has the potential, thanks to

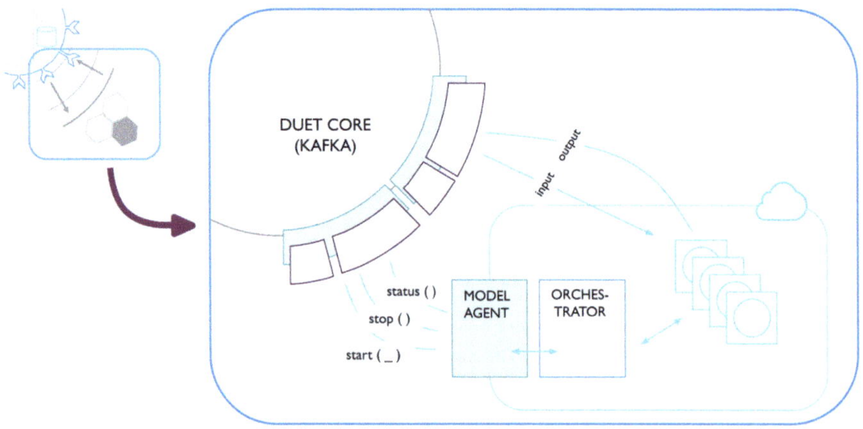


**Fig. 8.4** DUET T-Cell architecture cloud design for models (Schreuder et al., 2020)

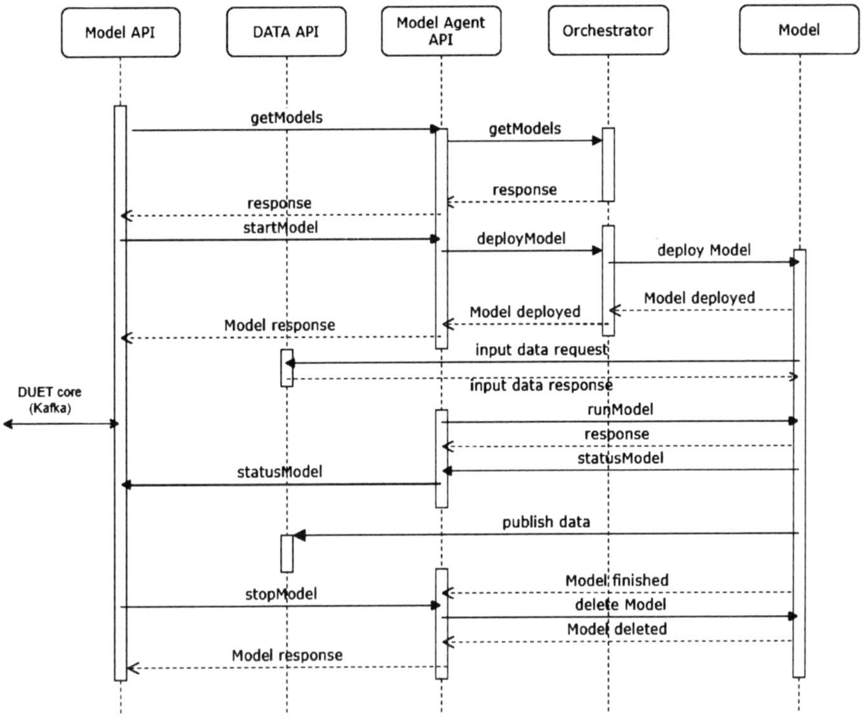


**Fig. 8.5** DUET Model activation & execution sequence (Schreuder et al., 2020)

LDTs, to become a new field where model specialists and ICT integrators need to cooperate in the future.

## 8.4 Conclusion

It is the ambition of a Local Digital Twin (LDT) to provide its users with a virtual version of their city in support of better management and exploration of future scenarios. To this end, models should mimic the many interactions and temporal evolution of many entities and their properties in a smart city. It is logical to avoid reinventing the wheel and to reuse the many existing domain-specific models that the state-of-the-art offers of many subdomains of a smart city.

However, the requirements of models deployed in an LDT context may differ from the stand-alone, domain-specific applications. We illustrate this fact in this chapter based on our experiences integrating several existing traffic and traffic impact models into the DUET LDT prototype in Athens, Flanders and Pilsen. While it appeared that technical and conceptual integration could be achieved between the models and a set of generic data sources, the resulting LDT functionality only partly covered the many user needs of the more diverse users that an LDT attracts compared to domain specialists who usually interact in more uniform ways with the stand-alone domain models.

Not only should the domain models themselves be further developed to be more encompassing and more versatile tools, but the use cases and scenarios in LDT also call for a more dynamic response of many more smart city components that stand-alone domain models can assume to be invariant boundaries of the narrowly scoped subdomain. The concept of a detailed and broadly defined ontology of smart city entities and their variable properties is identified as an indispensable tool to support the correct modelling of interrelationships between these entities, with the role of models and data sources redefined as instruments that sustain in a systematic and consistent way the conceptual and temporal relationships between these entities.

Another important LDT requirement is the synchronisation of the configuration data to the real world. While data-assimilation techniques to synchronise short-term traffic prediction models to online traffic data sources exist, similar techniques for transport models on slower time scales (with automatic calibration of supply and demand data) and for automatic configuration and calibration of other domain models are largely lacking. However, in many smart city domains, the abundance of big data has sparked research to configure models ever more automatically. The development of LDTs could benefit from such ongoing efforts and might be a stimulus to accelerate them.

## References

Apache Software Foundation. (2023). Apache Kafka—Apache Kafka is an open-source distributed event streaming platform used by thousands of companies for high-performance data pipelines, streaming analytics, data integration, and mission-critical applications. *Kafka*. https://kafka.apache.org/

Bocher, E., Guillaume, G., Picaut, J., Petit, G., & Fortin, N. (2019). NoiseModelling: An open source GIS based tool to produce environmental noise maps. *ISPRS International Journal of Geo-Information, 8*, 130. https://doi.org/10.3390/ijgi8030130

Borst, J. (2010). Urban strategy: Interactive spatial planning for sustainable cities. In *Next generation infrastructure systems for eco-cities*. Presented at the Next generation infrastructure systems for eco-cities, pp. 1–5. https://doi.org/10.1109/INFRA.2010.5679227

Borst, H. C., Salomons, E. M., Lohman, W. J. A., Zhou, H., Miedema, H. M. E., & Ondergrond, T. B. (2009). Urban strategy: Noise mapping in instrument for interactive spatial planning. In *8th European Conference on Noise Control 2009, EURONOISE 2009*, 26–28 October 2009, Edinburgh, Scotland, UK 31.

Dial, R. B. (1971). A probabilistic multipath traffic assignment model which obviates path enumeration. *Transportation Research, 5*, 83–111. https://doi.org/10.1016/0041-1647(71)90012-8

Dial, R. B. (2006). A path-based user-equilibrium traffic assignment algorithm that obviates path storage and enumeration. *Transportation Research Part B: Methodological, 40*, 917–936.

Gentile, G., & Meschini, L. (2011). Using dynamic assignment models for real-time traffic forecast on large urban networks. In *Proceedings of the Second International Conference on Models and Technologies for Intelligent Transportation Systems, Leuven, Belgium*. Presented at the MT-ITS, Leuven, Belgium.

Harpham, Q. K., Hughes, A., & Moore, R. V. (2019). Introductory overview: The OpenMI 2.0 standard for integrating numerical models. *Environmental Modelling & Software, 122*, 104549. https://doi.org/10.1016/j.envsoft.2019.104549

Himpe, W. (n.d.) *Matlab traffic toolbox [WWW Document]*. https://gitlab.kuleuven.be/ITSCreaLab/public-toolboxes/matlabtraffictoolbox (accessed 11.12.18).

Himpe, W., Corthout, R., & Tampère, M. J. C. (2016). An efficient iterative link transmission model. *Transportation Research Part B: Methodological, Within-day Dynamics in Transportation Networks, 92, Part B*, 170–190. https://doi.org/10.1016/j.trb.2015.12.013

Imec. (n.d.). *CityFlows | imec Vlaanderen [WWW Document]*. https://www.imec.be/nl/vlaamse-innovatiemotor/impactdomeinen/smart-cities/cityflows (accessed 4.29.23).

Jedlička, K., Beran, D., Martolos, J., Kolovský, F., Kepka, M., Mildorf, T., & Shánĕl, J. (2020). Traffic modelling for the smart city of Pilsen. In *8ICCGIS*. Presented at the 8th International Conference on Cartography and GIS, Bulgarian Cartographic Association, Nessebar, Bulgaria.

Koninkrijksrelaties, M. van B. Z. (n.d.). *Regeling beoordeling luchtkwaliteit 2007 [WWW Document]*. https://wetten.overheid.nl/BWBR0022817/2021-04-03 (accessed 4.29.23).

Leitner, M. (Ed.). (2015). *Crime modeling and mapping using geospatial technologies* (2013th edition. ed.). Springer.

Ma, D., Song, X., & Li, P. (2021). Daily traffic flow forecasting through a contextual convolutional recurrent neural network modeling inter- and intra-day traffic patterns. *IEEE Transactions on Intelligent Transportation Systems, 22*, 2627–2636. https://doi.org/10.1109/TITS.2020.2973279

MOMENTUM consortium. (2020). MOMENTUM Deliverable 3.3: Methodologies and Algorithms for Mobility Data Analysis.

Mueller, K., & Axhausen, K. W. (2011). *Occam's Razor and some randomness: Generating a synthetic population for Switzerland*. Presented at the European Transport Conference 2011Association for European Transport (AET)Transportation Research Board.

Notelaers, L., Verstraete, J., Vansteenwegen, P., & Tampère, C. M. J. (2024). A travel demand modeling framework based on OpenStreetMap. *Discover Civil Engineering, 1*, 26. https://doi.org/10.1007/s44290-024-00020-y

Ortmann, P., & Tampère, C. M. (2022). dyntapy: Dynamic and static traffic assignment in Python. *Journal of Open Source Software, 7*, 4593. https://doi.org/10.21105/joss.04593

Possel, B., Wismans, L. J. J., Van Berkum, E. C., & Bliemer, M. C. J. (2018). The multi-objective network design problem using minimizing externalities as objectives: Comparison of a genetic algorithm and simulated annealing framework. *Transportation, 45*, 545–572. https://doi.org/10.1007/s11116-016-9738-y

Potuzak, T., & Kolovsky, F. (2021). Parallelization of the B static traffic assignment algorithm. *Ain Shams Engineering Journal*. https://doi.org/10.1016/j.asej.2021.09.003

Raes, L., Michiels, P., Adolphi, T., Tampere, C., Dalianis, A., McAleer, S., & Kogut, P. (2022). DUET: A framework for building interoperable and trusted digital twins of smart cities. *IEEE Internet Computing, 26*, 43–50. https://doi.org/10.1109/MIC.2021.3060962

Rear Window BV. (n.d.). Telraam, Your window on local traffic. *Telraam*. https://telraam.net/en/what-is-telraam

Schreuder, M., & Lohman, W. J. A. (2020). DUET D3.5 Cloud design for model calibration and simulation (No. D3.5), DUET project deliverables.

Schreuder, M., Lohman, W., & Cornelissen, H. (2020). *DUET D3.5 Cloud design for model calibration and simulation*. https://cordis.europa.eu/project/id/870697/results

Silence, J., Walravens, N., Malik, Z., & Tsakanika, D. (2020). DUET D2.3 Final list of user requirements for the DUET solution (No. D2.3), DUET project deliverables.

Tampere, C. M. J., & Immers, L. H. (2007). An extended Kalman filter application for traffic state estimation using CTM with implicit mode switching and dynamic parameters. In *IEEE Intelligent Transportation Systems Conference, 2007. ITSC 2007. Presented at the IEEE Intelligent Transportation Systems Conference, 2007. ITSC 2007* (pp. 209–216). https://doi.org/10.1109/ITSC.2007.4357755

Verstraete, J., & Tampère, C. M. (2018). Implicit acyclic full route set for stochastic traffic assignment. In *Mathematics applied in transport and traffic systems. Presented at the Mathematics Applied in Transport and Traffic Systems*. Delft, The Netherlands.
VITO. (n.d.-a). ATMO-PLAN – A web-based software application to assess the impact of emission reductions on pollutant concentrations. *VITO Atmosys*. https://atmosys.vito.be/en/atmo-plan
VITO. (n.d.-b). ATMO-STREET – Mapping air quality to street level. *VITO*. https://vito.be/en/atmo-street
Walravens, N., Raes, L., & D'Hauwers, R. (2021). DUET D2.2 Scenario specifications of the DUET solution (No. D2.2), DUET project deliverables. https://cordis.europa.eu/project/id/870697/results
Yuan, H., & Li, G. (2021). A survey of traffic prediction: From spatio-temporal data to intelligent transportation. *Data Science and Engineering, 6*, 63–85. https://doi.org/10.1007/s41019-020-00151-z

# Part III
# Maximising Impact of Local Digital Twins

# Chapter 9
# Local Digital Twins for Cities and Regions: The Way Forward

**Yannis Charalabidis, Gerasimos Kontos, and Dimitrios Zitianellis**

**Contents**



## 9.1 Introduction

Digital solutions promise significant value that was impossible to realise before the advent of connected, intelligent technologies. The idea of a digital twin, which is at the forefront of the fourth industrial revolution, seems to have been particularly intriguing of late and, in simple terms, is a near real-time digital image of a physical object or process that helps improve performance in different areas to optimise sectors. Academia and organisations define digital twins in different ways, but the first definition was suggested by Grieves in his article titled "Digital Twin: Manufacturing Excellence through Virtual Factory Replication". Specifically, Grieves defines the digital twin as a set of virtual information constructs that fully describe a potential or actual physically manufactured product from the micro (atomic) to the macro

Y. Charalabidis (✉)
Department of Information and Communication Systems Engineering, University of Aegean, Samos, Greece
e-mail: yannisx@aegean.gr

G. Kontos
Abu Dhabi University, Abu Dhabi, UAE
e-mail: gerasimos.kontos@adu.ac.ae

D. Zitianellis
University of the Aegean, Samos, Greece



L. Raes et al. (eds.), *Decide Better*,
https://doi.org/10.1007/978-3-031-81451-8_9

(geometric) level. Optimally, all the information that could be gleaned from inspecting a physically manufactured product can be gleaned from its digital twin (Grieves, 2014). This paper was the basis for the development of digital twins in the next few years. Digital twin implementations are growing rapidly with advances in the Internet of Things (IoT) and Artificial Intelligence (AI), which can accelerate this growth. In this phase, the areas of interest are manufacturing, automotive, aerospace, healthcare, smart cities, etc. Focusing on smart cities, we encounter digital twins in an urban setting, which are digital representations of the physical built environment in our cities, including urban transport networks, buildings and infrastructure connected to the data in and around them. A Local Digital Twin (LDT) is rendered in Virtual Reality (VR) (3D virtual replicas). Using powerful supercomputers, electronic sensors and cutting-edge data analysis and visualisation technologies, LDTs integrate both visible and invisible features of the built environment in an interactive format. LDTs allow users to aggregate complex data from many sources at scale and simulate future outcomes ($CO^2$ emissions, temperatures, energy consumption, pedestrian flows, traffic, financial revenues). As the world prepares to tackle climate change, we need tools like this more than ever to better understand, plan, predict and implement our sustainability, social and economic goals while responding in real-time to the changing world around us.

Within the context, the present chapter aims to elicit new pathways for the LDTs of the future, offering new functionalities and maximising their potential both in Local Administration governance but also towards better quality of life for all.

## 9.2 Background

### *9.2.1 Digital Twins: From Inception to Evolution*

The concept of a 'digital twin' gained recognition in 2002 after Challenge Advisory hosted a presentation on technology for Michael Grieves at the University of Michigan (Durão et al., 2018; Miskinis, 2019). The subject of the presentation was the development of a Product Lifecycle Management Center. It contained all the elements required for the digital twin, including the real space, the virtual space, and the spread of data and information flow between the real and virtual space. While the terminology may have changed over the years, the concept of creating a digital and physical twin as one interconnected entity has remained the same since its inception. While generally believed to have been developed in 2002, digital twin technology itself is a concept that has been practised since the 1960s. NASA would use basic twinning ideas for space programming during this time. They did this by physically creating duplicate systems at ground level to match the systems in space. One example is NASA's development of a digital twin to assess and simulate conditions aboard Apollo 13 (Glaessgen & Stargel, 2012).

Although the concept of digital twins has existed for a few decades, it emerged as one of the most important strategic technology trends only in 2017. Technologies like the IoT enabled digital twins to become cost-effective, making them as imperative to different sectors as they are today (Grieves & Vickers, 2017).

As illustrated in Fig. 9.1, the concept of the digital twins revolves around the intersection of the Physical and Digital World, as a system operating in a cycle. The original digital twin is obtained through analysing, modelling and getting data from the real-world system. The resulting digital twin can then operate in the Digital World, acting as a source of information to be visualised, offering new ways to understand and manage complex phenomena, but also as a destination of information to be stored.

Then, through further modelling and simulation, including AI-enabled scenario building and decision support functionality, the evolving digital twin can now support complex decision-making through forecasting and prognosing future behaviour of the original system(s). In a way, the proposals of the digital twin can then be put into practice in the Real World again, thus closing the circle.

Digital twins continue to be the top trend in recent years (Barricelli et al., 2019). It is estimated that billions of things will be represented by either digital twins, software models or physical systems in the next few years (Fuller et al., 2020). Digital twins are predicted to be used by half of major industrial companies and about 21 billion digitally connected sensors, potentially saving billions in maintenance, repair and operations (Fuller et al., 2020; Li et al., 2021). It is also predicted that up to 60% of manufacturers will monitor product performance and quality using digital twins. Up to 60% of global businesses will also use digital twins to provide better customer service experiences. The use of digital twins is fueled by the rise of IoT-engineered sensors, with the future of both going hand-in-hand. Sensors can provide data on how an object is operating and how it responds to the environment, while implementing digital twins can improve analysis, state

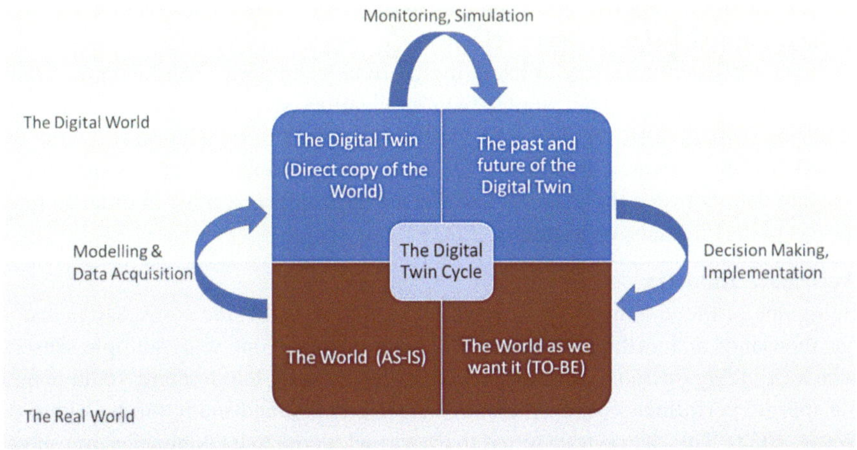


**Fig. 9.1** The concept of a digital twin

simulation, operation and decision-making. Given the obvious importance of digital twins and their potential growth, their value will be effective for several years to come (Rosen et al., 2015).

### 9.2.2 *Digital Twins: Lessons from the Industry*

This part aims to identify the potential of digital twins in each sector and the purpose of its implementation for the right application. It also aims to understand what may prove to be beneficial for researchers, companies, or sectors before investing in the technology to unleash its true potential.

**Manufacturing**
Historically, among the first applications of digital twins happened in the manufacturing environment. Industries are systematically looking for ways to track and monitor machines and products, to predict and maintain in due time, ultimately saving enough time and money to justify the immense investment needed to connect and model everything (Rosen et al., 2015).

Digital twins have the potential to provide real-time machine information and allow for managing the performance of any tiny bit of any production line. AI algorithms coupled with digital twins have the potential to provide predictive analytics for a variety of manufacturing, development, or construction issues, while product testing becomes an instant process at a simulation level (Tao et al., 2018).

**Car Industry**
The automobile industry has changed over time as new technologies are constantly entering the field. The industry keeps part of its traditional infrastructure but is constantly enriched with new digital services based on sensors and devices with AI that mainly work after the product has entered the market. The involvement of the digital twins is an ally in improving the vehicle aid in its life cycle value creation and also in the optimised design of future vehicles.

Tesla is allegedly heavily utilising digital twin technology. Thinkwik, the company that developed Tesla's digital twin application, states that even mechanical issues in Tesla motors, regardless of their magnitude, can be fixed in real-time by downloadable software components. Of course, the continuous transmission of the relevant data between the vehicles and the manufacturer is a must in order to feed the car twin (Piromalis & Kantaros, 2022).

**Aerospace Industry**
Being one of the first application domains for digital twins, the aerospace industry has thousands and millions of pieces of equipment, each one with multiple sensors which can relay operational data, tracking energy output, temperature, rotation and air speeds, performance and efficiency measurements, and many more (Xiong & Wang, 2022). This data is transferred to the virtual model to let companies run simulations to study performance over time, the impact of small changes, and what can

be done to increase performance and efficiency. The goal of a digital twin is to have access to data that provides insights into the effectiveness of current practices and to provide a place for businesses to try new things without impacting productivity (Bisanti et al., 2023).

Examples of digital twin applications include all manufacturers and many airline operators. Boeing saw a 40% improvement in first-time quality of parts, by using digital twins throughout the life cycle. Aerospace manufacturers can now use digital twins to improve the design and engineering of new parts by simulating their performance under a variety of conditions (Xiong & Wang, 2022). How will an engine fare in harsh weather? How is performance affected after 300+ flights? This knowledge can now be obtained and used to improve parts, predict when maintenance is needed, and extend the lifespan of machinery, vehicles, and more (Li et al., 2021).

**Healthcare**

The healthcare sector is another area related to the digital twin technology. The impact of enabling technology on healthcare is extraordinary since previously impossible tasks are becoming achievable. The increase in connectivity is due to the fact that IoT devices are cheaper and easier to integrate. The increased connectivity is growing the potential application of digital twins within the healthcare sector. A digital twin of a human, which provides real-time body analysis, is used by many drug manufacturers in order to simulate the effects of certain treatments (Erol et al., 2020). Digital twins can also be used to plan and perform surgical treatments. In healthcare as a whole, the digital twin technology gives researchers, physicians, hospitals and healthcare providers the ability to simulate environments that suit their needs, whether in real-time or in anticipation of future developments and applications. In addition, the digital twin can be used simultaneously with AI algorithms to make smarter predictions and decisions. Many healthcare applications do not directly involve the patient but are beneficial to ongoing care and treatment; hence the key role such systems play in patient care. (Alazab et al., 2022). The digital twin of the healthcare system is still in its infancy, but the potential is huge, from use for bed management to managing large wards and hospitals. The ability to simulate and act in real-time is even more important in healthcare as it can mean the difference between life and death. The digital twin could also help with predictive maintenance and ongoing repair of medical equipment. The digital twin in the medical environment, coupled together with AI algorithms, has the potential to support life-saving decisions based on real-time and historical data (Liu et al., 2019).

## 9.3 LDTs

In the following paragraphs, the concept of LDTs is discussed, including application areas and use cases.

### 9.3.1 The Concept of LDTs

Within the overall idea of digital twins, an LDT is an infrastructure that aims at gathering and processing information at city or regional level in order to support decision-making and provide new means for advanced services towards citizens and businesses. An LDT typically provides services such as (Deng et al., 2021; Mylonas et al., 2021):

- Digital representation of the physical and technical background, such as land, plots, streets, buildings and other technical infrastructure;
- Sensing of various indicators that may include air and water quality, noise and $CO_2$ emissions, vehicles and people circulation, temperature, light and more;
- Representation of the status of various systems, operating in the public and connected enterprises;
- Storing, filtering and processing of vast amounts of sensor- or citizen-generated information;
- Additional systems and services for citizen interaction with the digital twin;
- Advanced AI-based, algorithmic or other dynamic simulation of events and scenarios and further validation of real-time decision support systems.

As depicted in Fig. 9.2, the LDT cycle of operation consists of four different steps/transitions:

- Initial creation of the LDT, through modelling and data acquisition from the physical world;
- Monitoring and management of the LDT, as a way to monitor and manage the physical infrastructures;
- Further simulation, based on vast amounts of historical data, in order to test innovative scenarios for the city or region evolution;
- Implementation of the city or region transformation actions and further enhancement of the LDT.

A high-level architecture for a city-scale LDT, including the key technologies, main components, main data sources and application domains, is presented in Fig. 9.3, adopted from Mylonas et al. (2021). As shown, a typical LDT has several layers:

- The Data Acquisition Layer, where real-time information is gathered via sensors and interactive systems from the physical world, and this includes data from buildings, citizens, transportation modes and other infrastructures;
- The Data Processing and Simulation Layer where data is curated, filtered and stored, information is analysed, simulations are performed, and other decision support models and subsystems reside;
- The Visualisation and real-time applications layer include various means for inspecting and visualising data and systems in real-time (maps, 3D models, VR, graphical representations) as well as means for providing specific output and suggested action plans and decisions on key public sectors, including Energy and

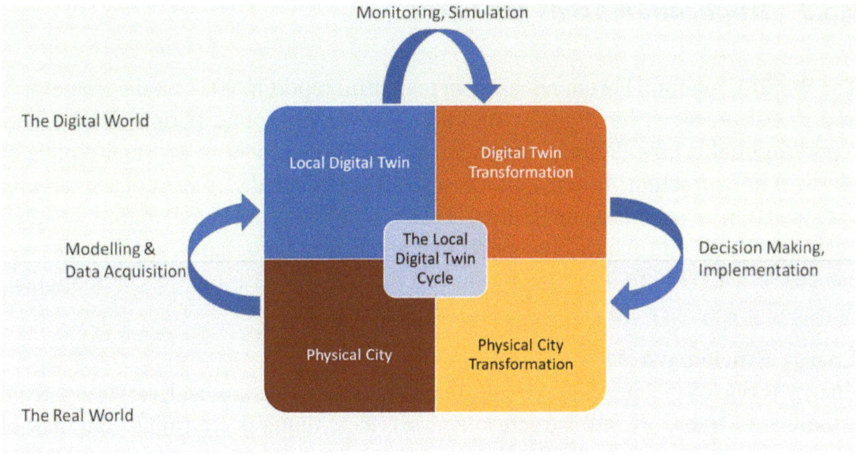


**Fig. 9.2** The Local Digital Twin Cycle, from modelling to transformation

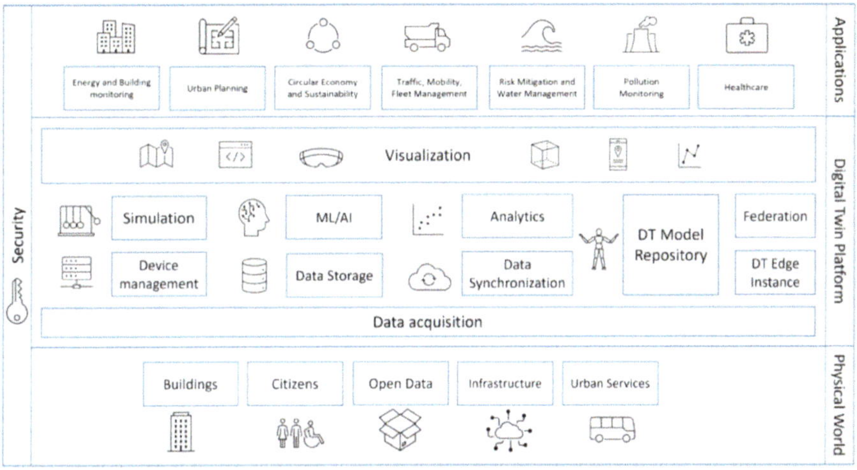


**Fig. 9.3** A high-level overview of a city-scale digital twin (Mylonas et al., 2021)

Building monitoring, Urban planning and Traffic Mobility, Sustainability and Pollution Monitoring as well as Healthcare and medical treatment.

The above core layers of an LDT are also supported by infrastructures for data security and interoperability, which enable real-time interactions with users, and direct control and decision-making over critical public infrastructures.

### *9.3.2 Application Areas for LDTs*

The World Economic Forum released an insightful report in 2022 on the framework and global practices for digital twin cities (World Economic Forum, 2022). This report highlights how digital twins facilitate the development of a virtual replica of physical infrastructure, systems, processes and sensors in the context of a smart city and envision a seamless integration between the physical and digital context, enabling direct control over city operations. In the next paragraphs, applications and use cases of LDTs are discussed, followed by a review of future research applications and a way forward for the promising technology.

**Energy Efficiency & Management**

Energy is one of the most important resources for city operations. Everything, from buildings to transport, infrastructure and services, requires enormous amounts of energy (Bortolini et al., 2022). Taking advantage of best practices and lessons learned from the manufacturing industry, smart energy management appeared as a natural evolution in the LDT context (Testasecca et al., 2023). Interest in building and grid energy efficiency and the availability of smart energy metering devices have certainly led to new digital twin approaches in the energy sector. The large amount of available real-time data on building energy performance through the spread of IoT technologies is providing the necessary basis for energy efficiency calculations. Building Information Modelling (BIM) technologies are used as a means of visualising the energy performance of buildings, offering energy managers and officials more user-friendly platforms on which to base their decision-making, while enhancing citizen participation and raising awareness on energy-related issues (Bortolini et al., 2022). In addition, big data analysis frameworks reveal patterns and trends that can lead to improved sustainability and energy efficiency.

**Urban Planning**

The increasing number of inhabitants in metropolitan areas, as well as the limited space and resources for urban expansion, make urban planning and simulation of proposed measures and buildings essential for sustainable city functioning. Urban planning procedures represent challenging tasks for city officials regarding optimal decision-making, selecting sets of measures that produce the least amount of disturbance and negative impact on other aspects and citizen involvement and acceptance. LDTs offer the decision support needed for this complex planning process. Representation of city environments is performed dynamically through point-cloud technologies. This allows for an actual visual presentation of city structures that are planned to undergo changes long before anything is actually implemented (Caprari et al., 2022). Scenario simulation produces results for both officials and citizens on positive and negative outcomes of planned interventions.

**Circular Economy and Sustainability**

Traditionally, digital twin applications for circular economy were limited or performed indirectly through other domains (Caprari et al., 2022). However, we are beginning to see more and more use cases involving digital twins, particularly in areas where remanufacturing and sustainable production are the goal. Other promising application domains include the sustainability assessment of buildings and urban waste management.

**Traffic, Mobility and Fleet Management**

It could be argued that the journey of urban digital twins started as part of an effort to create mapping services (Google Maps, HEREWeGo, etc.), since the creation of detailed city maps essentially involves the extraction of features from the real world and their transformation into digital ones, also updating them regularly. In essence, the digital twins can provide a basis for the development of services from either a private company perspective or a city authority perspective. From the private sector's point of view, the currently prevailing business model involves building a closed-source digital twin of the physical world in order to utilise it to provide mobility-focused features. The rise of autonomous driving has pushed this direction further, either through the availability of such features in passenger cars or through the efforts of companies aiming to produce fleets of self-driving taxis, like Waymo and Uber. A digital twin of the urban space can help to provide more advanced autonomous driving functions, better passenger mobility and timetable planning, among others. Essentially, in the case of simulating autonomous driving features in virtual environments that match those of the real world, digital twins are a direct response to this real-world business use case in the automobile industry. Digital twins can also support parking optimisation and city logistics both for freight and citizen parking (Liu et al., 2021). Smart parking systems that leverage sensors and mobile applications can provide real-time information on parking slot availability and offer guidance to vacant parking positions. By reducing the time spent searching for parking, cities can reduce traffic congestion, enhance urban accessibility and improve the overall parking experience for freight and citizen drivers (Faliagka et al., 2024). Digital twin technologies appear well-timed to utilise the advances in autonomous vehicles and appear to align well with the current ongoing wave of mobility electrification. There is an obvious interest from both private and public entities in using such approaches to advance the autonomous driving vision and implement better traffic management, and at the moment, this seems to be a strong application scenario for using digital twins. Since the field is still fairly new, some of the challenges we see in most digital twin applications are also evident in traffic and fleet management. These include standardisation, scaling, security and privacy (Faliagka et al., 2024). However, it also seems likely that advances in smart cities, vehicle electrification and digital transformation of the car industry will help speed things up in these aspects (MarketsandMarkets.com, 2023).

**City Resilience**

Over the past 20 years, we have witnessed the effects of climate change in the form of an increasing number of extreme weather events and their associated costs worldwide. A large part of such events is related to water, in the form of either droughts or floods, while the current projections for sea level rise in the coming decades are a cause of great concern. At the same time, we are witnessing the effects of the

COVID-19 pandemic, which has to some extent exposed the deficiencies in disaster risk management in many parts of the world. The word 'resilience' has entered the public debate surrounding cities and communities, indicating an awareness of the magnitude of the impact such events can have and the importance of risk mitigation mechanisms. To a large extent, these events have fuelled a renewed interest in using recent technologies to develop smart city solutions for crisis management. However, some authors have noted that real-world digital twin implementations for disaster response remain limited, which may be explained by the large hidden costs and complexities involved (Valverde-Pérez et al., 2021).

**Fighting Pollution**

Pollution monitoring is vital in any city as reducing pollution is a key factor in ensuring the health and well-being of citizens. We are starting to see digital twin applications deployed in this area, with a clear focus primarily on-air quality and secondarily on noise pollution in urban environments. The collection of air pollution data from sensors coupled with the model's ability to apply computational fluid dynamics algorithms provides the ability to visualise air pollution levels throughout the city. The propagation of noise through city structures can also be simulated using a 3D Geospatial Information System (GIS) layer (Rasheed et al., 2020). Providing publicly available digital twin-based visualisation options of these common urban issues could also aid in raising citizen awareness on environmental issues and adopt a greener approach to the use of polluting resources and operations. Smart cities can use digital twins to respond to potential and actual dangerous situations regarding health, e.g., air pollution affecting the health of citizens living in a certain urban area (Fuller et al., 2020).

**Smart Cities and Citizens Medical Treatment**

In healthcare and medical treatment, a digital twin can be considered as a virtual copy of a physical object or process, such as a patient or a hospital environment. Currently, digital twins in healthcare are able to dynamically reflect data sources such as electronic health records and disease registries, as well as demographic, societal and lifestyle data over time for an individual patient (Armeni et al., 2022). Thanks to the evolution of underlying technologies (e.g., IoT, AI) and increasingly diverse, accurate, and accessible data (e.g., biometric, behavioural, psychological), research and potential applications of digital twins in healthcare have seen increasing interest. Applications in healthcare can contribute to the broad trend of precision medicine, replacing the 'one-size-fits-all' approach (Liu et al., 2019; Sun et al., 2023). Specific use cases, such as digital twins of human organs, can help to simulate the effect of different treatments while taking into account a patient's medical history and current condition. If their potential is to be fully realised, digital twins will facilitate the possibility of interconnected personalised care and alter the way lifestyle, health, wellness, and chronic diseases will be managed in the near future. Such digital twins would need to be 'fed' with diverse information obtained by wearables and other sources of self-reported data, like mobile health applications. Finally, another possible application in healthcare is the optimisation of hospital operations and management. Different possible solutions and scenarios can be tested in virtual environments before implementing them in a real-world setting (e.g., patient bed planning, staff schedules and rotation, surgical simulation, and virtual drug experiments). By applying simulations and analytics, hospitals can significantly improve patient service, safety, experience, and activity volume (Armeni et al., 2022). When optimised for healthcare, digital twins can help hospital management to better respond to challenges such as growing patient demand, increasing clinical complexity, ageing infrastructure, lack of space and increasing waiting times (Alazab et al., 2022). In terms of the challenges involved, the most frequently cited challenges are privacy and ethics, as health data is inherently very sensitive, followed by challenges related to implementation.

### *9.3.3 Existing LDT Projects and Prototypes*

There is a growing number of research projects in city-scale digital twins utilising the approach presented above. In the examples reviewed below, we will cover projects that focus primarily on 3D representations of the built environment and urban planning, as well as those with a pronounced focus on co-creation and collaborative activities.

**The DUET Project**
Digital Urban European Twins is an innovation project that aims to leverage the advanced capabilities of cloud and High Performance Computing (HPC) to make public sector decision-making more democratic and effective, by developing digital twins for policy exploration and experimentation across entire cities and regions. The DUET[1] project focused on improving day-to-day city operations by helping managers respond quickly to real-time events and more easily harness the collective intelligence of all policy stakeholders to tackle complex, systemic policy issues that require innovative thinking to develop transformative solutions (Raes et al., 2022).

Motivated by the above objectives, the DUET project developed a prototype LDT infrastructure, covering different aspects of operation in three pilot cases:

- *Athens*: Improving the effectiveness of policy design and implementation through citizen participation and service co-creation;
- *Pilsen*: Developing a set of tools for policy support in urban design, including traffic and noise pollution modelling, visualisation tools, and a sensor data orchestrator;
- *Flanders*: Creating a Smart region where everyone can access services and data.

**The Barcelona City Digital Twin**
Barcelona is one of the latest cities to start building a digital twin of itself. The data driven replica of the city, currently in a testing phase, is expected to be operational

[1] Digital Urban European Twins (DUET), EU H2020 project, https://cordis.europa.eu/project/id/870697

by 2027, when it will be used as an urban design tool to shape the city's future development (Hernandez-Morales, 2022). The digital twin will be housed in the Mare Nostrum supercomputer, one of the most powerful data processors in the world, located in the chapel of the city of Torre Girona (Barcelona Supercomputing Center, 2022).

The Barcelona digital twin will offer urbanists, architects, and planners the opportunity to test urban theories and projects before implementation in order to understand their impact without physically disrupting the city. The use of HPC gives the opportunity to get certainty that urban planning isn't just based on clever ideas and good intentions but on data that allows city stakeholders to anticipate impacts and mitigate negative impacts in advance (Hernandez-Morales, 2022).

A recent relevant application in Barcelona is found in the project of city superblocks (Fig. 9.4). The city had begun developing superblocks as car-free mini-neighbourhoods around which traffic would flow. Launched in response to the city's deadly struggle with air pollution, the plan sought to ultimately reduce vehicular traffic by 21%, freeing almost 60% of the streets from cars.

However, despite promising impacts on air quality within the superblocks themselves, an analysis by the supercomputer found that the impact on emissions in the wider area was negligible. In conclusion, the air quality within the superblocks improved, but pollution has grown in the adjacent streets to which the displaced car traffic has shifted. The result highlights the need for additional measures to effectively tackle displaced emissions.

The supercomputer is now being used to inform Barcelona's vision of a 15-minute city, which would give citizens access to all daily services within a 15-minute walk or bike ride from their homes. Analyses conducted using the digital twin could include gentrification trends, transportation access, or highlight higher populations of elderly people in need of particular health, social or transport infrastructure. The project will allow the city to make rapid planning decisions to combat climate change. The goal for Barcelona is to be climate-neutral by 2050 (Barcelona Supercomputing Center, 2022).

**The Slovenian National Digital Twin**

Governments worldwide are realising the potential of digital twins and are making it a critical part of their national strategic agenda (Grübel et al., 2022). One of the most prominent examples is the Slovenian government, which has positioned Slovenia as a True AI Maverick (Atlantis, 2022), shaping a new Human Centric Society.

The Slovenian International Research Center on Artificial Intelligence (IRCAI) is currently developing a national-wide digital twin model, incorporating a novel AI model capable of constructing a nation's digital flow vis-a-vis situational awareness, to augment decision-making processes on the enterprise and government levels (Minevich, 2020).

The Slovenian digital twin consists of five critical AI-powered components: (i) nowcasting, (ii) root cause analysis, (iii) causal modelling, (iv) prediction, and (v) anomaly detection. Collectively, these components provide a real-time digital

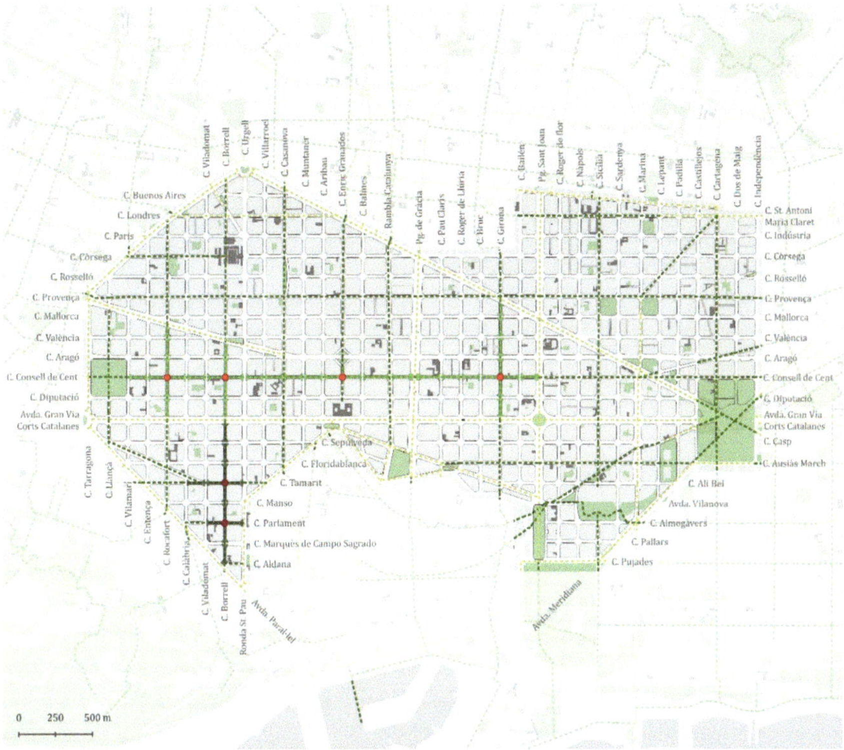


**Fig. 9.4** Barcelona creating car-free 'superblocks' (Magrinyà et al., 2023)

replica of critical public infrastructures, which enables policy and decision-makers to experience a never-seen-before level of intelligence optimisation and real-time decision-making (Minevich, 2020; Atlantis, 2023). The digital twin model of situational awareness is robust and hence provides a number of critical use cases. According to the government's spokesperson, the most relevant applications of the digital twin include healthcare and city logistics optimisation (Minevich, 2020).

A prime example of an automated situational awareness system that Slovenia has developed includes the IRCAI's Events Registry System, which aims to map and analyse the social dynamics of various global challenges. In combination with the Slovenian Large-Scale Pilot 1 (LSP1) ecosystem for transport, energy and telecommunications optimisation, the initial set of weather and traffic data has been prepared (Atlantis, 2023). The government's expectation is that this integration will enhance situational awareness, foster more effective risk management, and serve as a proactive tool for policymakers to predict and respond to challenges swiftly. Insights from predictive analysis are expected to enable policymakers to evaluate and manage cross-sector systemic risks more efficiently (Grübel et al., 2022).

**The New Mexico Digital Twin**
New Mexico is located in the southwest of the United States, covering an area of about 314,900 square kilometres. It is the fifth-largest state in the United States, with a population of about 2,097,000. In 2019, the state passed the Energy Transition Act (ETA), which proposes that the state shall become a clean energy leader and achieve 100% clean energy by 2050. Founded in 2009, Cityzenith, a US software company, proposed to transform cities through digital twin technology to make them cleaner and healthier and contribute to the 'Clean Cities—Clean Future' vision. As a result, the State of New Mexico has partnered with Cityzenith to develop SmartWorldPro, a digital twin city platform, to help build new 'smart infrastructure' and achieve carbon neutrality goals (Dubey, 2020). The expectation is that, by deploying the digital twin platform, the city could reduce operating costs by 35%, increase productivity by 20%, and reduce carbon emissions by 50–100% (World Economic Forum, 2022).

**Digital Twins in Australia**
The New South Wales (NSW) Government, in partnership with the Data61 department of the Commonwealth Scientific and Industrial Research Organisation (CSIRO), has developed the digital twin proof-of-concept model: a complete, real-time, accurate and reliable 4D framework model that projects a physical environment that can enable real-time, spatial-based data sharing and collaboration to help policy planners and project developers better design and manage the future of cities.

The digital twin platform is the largest 3D modelling project in Australia's history. It uses sensor-equipped fixed-wing platforms to capture images of large areas with high accuracy, with the end result expected to cover 3392 square kilometres and include a 3D grid map of Sydney's western region captured at less than 6 cm pixel resolution. The platform extensively aggregates data from multiple sources; visualises historical data from government, industry and communities; and models buildings and natural resources above and below ground using data obtained from water, energy and telecom utilities.

NSW's spatial digital twin project can now produce an online Western Sydney map of 22 million trees with height and canopy attributes, more than 540,000 buildings, nearly 20,000 kilometres of 3D roads and 7000 3D strata plans. This can effectively help infrastructure builders to plan soundly and digitally before projects are implemented and to facilitate regional economic activity (World Economic Forum, 2022).

## 9.4 Future Research Directions for LDTs

The analysis of the initiatives, trends, and application experiments in the area of LDTs, as presented and discussed in the previous chapters, enables the formation of the next waypoints in the roadmap of these semantically rich and prominent intelligence systems.

Such new possibilities, capabilities or features will be presented under two different categories (see Fig. 9.5), relating to the nature and span of each new direction and operation:

- *Directions for extension of the functionality of the LDT:* By means of indicating specific sub-objectives and future research goals (short to medium-term improvements);
- *Directions for a broader expansion of the LDT concept:* Depicting a few forward-looking scenarios for their use in the future (long-term improvements).

## *9.4.1 Extension Directions for LDTs*

**More Intelligence**

This research and application direction for LDTs aims towards more intelligent LDT systems that will ultimately have the ability to analyse the past and forecast the future on important city problems.

While smart city activities and technologies have commonly been about producing data and gaining new knowledge on the complexity and dynamics of a city, AI takes cities to the next step of utilising the data and knowledge to support decision-making. The concept of urban AI can be defined as: "Artefacts operating in cities, which are capable of acquiring and making sense of information on the surrounding urban environment, eventually using the acquired knowledge to act rationally according to predefined goals, in complex urban situations when some information might be missing or incomplete" (UNCRD, 2022). By 2025, AI is expected to enable over 30% of smart city applications, among which urban mobility solutions, significantly contributing to resilience, sustainability, social welfare and vitality of urban life. AI applications in smart cities can be categorised in the following seven dimensions:

- *AI for governance:* Urban planning, tailored subsidy provision, disaster prevention and management;
- *AI for living and liveability, safety, security and healthcare:* Smart policing, personalised healthcare, noise and nuisance management and improved cyber security;
- *AI for education and citizen participation:* Locally accurate, validated and actionable knowledge supporting decision-making;
- *AI for economy:* Resource (cost and time) efficiency and improved competitiveness, sharing services, efficient supply chains and customer-tailored solutions;
- *AI for mobility and logistics:* Autonomous and sustainable mobility, smart routing and parking assistance, supply chain resiliency and traffic management;
- *AI for infrastructure:* Optimised infrastructure deployment, use and maintenance, including waste and water management, transportation, energy grids, and urban lighting;

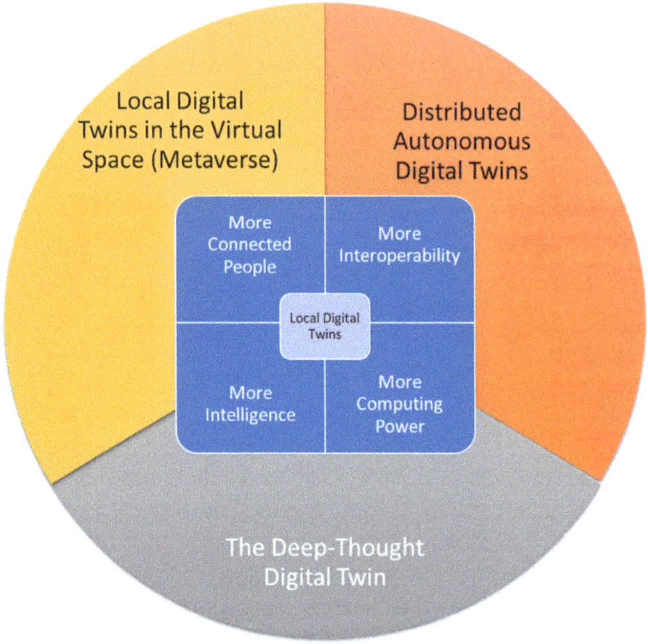


**Fig. 9.5** Extending and Expanding LDTs

- *AI for the environment:* Biodiversity preservation, urban farming and air quality management.

Among others, AI applications can improve and innovate water and energy infrastructures, urban services and promote empowered and resilient communities in smart cities (European Parliament Think Tank, 2021).

**More Sensors, but in a Humane Way**

Advances in the use and implementation of sensors and IoT devices and their application for the development of smart cities will allow residents to access a better quality of life (Al-Ali et al., 2020). Even though the use of wireless sensor networks provides valuable data that are used for better management of resources, there are still areas for improvement, such as finding new approaches to the problem of detection, prevention, or anticipation of the dangers that future smart cities can face. A major challenge in health applications is privacy and the secure transmission of data. Low-cost wireless sensor networks also help to achieve direct communication between a user's mobile terminals and wearable medical devices while enforcing privacy-preserving strategies (Ramírez-Moreno et al., 2021).

**More Computing Power**

LDTs rely heavily on computing power to process large amounts of data and run complex simulations. As the demand for digital twins grows, so does the need for more computing power. HPC can handle complex simulations and large amounts of data. HPC systems use multiple processors and parallel processing techniques to perform computations quickly and efficiently.

Another way to address this requirement is to use Cloud Computing. Cloud computing allows digital twins to access computing resources on demand, enabling them to scale up or down as needed. Cloud computing also provides access to powerful computing resources that would otherwise be too expensive to purchase and maintain (Ramu et al., 2022).

For LDT applications requiring low latency and/or robust data security and privacy, edge computing provides a convenient model for analysing and processing a portion of data using the network resources distributed on the paths between data sources and the cloud computing centre (Protner et al., 2021).

Another area of opportunity is quantum computing. Once fully implemented, the technology aims to create more performance benefits than current supercomputing applications (Wu et al., 2021). As all these technologies continue to evolve, we can expect LDTs to become even more powerful and capable of simulating complex urban environments in greater detail.

**More Connectivity**

The benefits of next-generation mobile networks (5G, 6G, and beyond) are significant for urban societies. 5G could improve ongoing operations by continuously monitoring the real physical systems and using Big Data analytics and machine learning to predict any issues before they happen in the real world. The implementation and automation of IoT could benefit from 5G to reduce maintenance issues and optimise production. 5G is seen as an enabler of new emerging services including city management tools that could help governments, especially in developing countries, to address critical challenges related to traffic control, water and sanitary management and urban security. This could be done by creating a digital twin containing the 3D model of a city and overlaying it with data from the 5G network along with other information such as transportation networks, street grids, buildings, IoT data, as well as people's movements. Even though 5G is still being deployed, work is being carried out to define the next 6G networks. The idea behind 6G is to enhance even further all the applications and vertical use cases of the 5G network by bringing intelligence to the edge of the network (Nguyen H et al., 2021). Consequently, what lies beyond the 5G would be an intelligent, interconnected system of digital twins that enables the creation of a real-time digital world where policymakers can have real-time interaction and decision-making capabilities with critical city infrastructures. Thus, 6G will be represented by connected and augmented intelligence that will change the way data is created, processed and consumed.

**More Interconnection**

Connecting and making large volumes of structured and unstructured data smart as an output of different processes (e.g. terrain measurements, sensor measurements, algorithm outcomes, AI modelling) and making them universally accessible, reusable and comprehensible by all transaction parties (in a human-to-machine and machine-to-machine) are important requirements for maximising interoperability (Gürdür & Asplund, 2018). With the recent explosive growth of AI and big data, it has become vital to organise and represent the enormous volume of knowledge appropriately. Knowledge models and knowledge graphs, as a collection of interlinked descriptions of concepts, entities, relationships and events, put data in context via semantic embeddings and provide a framework for data integration, unification, analytics and sharing (Ontotext, n.d.). As graph data, knowledge graphs accumulate and convey knowledge of the real world. Through knowledge graph embeddings, knowledge acquisition, knowledge graph completion, knowledge fusion, and knowledge reasoning (Peng et al., 2023), knowledge graphs help to ensure that information from multiple domains of expertise can be accumulated into multi-facet policy prediction outcomes produced by an LDT. Knowledge graphs can be seen as the 'Enhancers of the Intelligent Digital Twins' (Sahlab et al., 2021).

### *9.4.2 Expansion in New Directions*

Leveraging advances in AI, IoT, 6G and HPC, three scenarios for the evolution of LDTs are presented below using a combination of said technologies and some innovative business or operational models. These directions of possible expansion of LDT abilities are as follows:

- Distributed autonomous digital twins;
- Digital twins in the virtual sphere (Metaverse);
- The deep-thought digital twin.

**Distributed Autonomous Digital Twins**

Interconnected digital twins (IDTs) are shared and connected across organisations with the objective of creating holistic simulation and decision models of an entire physical system (Van Dyck et al., 2023). IDTs can be conceptualised as a network of virtual representations of physical objects or systems for communicating and exchanging information and resources across lifecycles in real-time in order to optimise performance and decision-making through simulation models on the operational level (CDBB, 2022). In this context, new possibilities can be explored, such as the sharing of historical data and values, the online interconnection of transportation and city logistics models, and the joint simulation of societal, green and built environments (CDBB, 2022). According to Van Dyck et al. (2023), the main characteristics of IDTs are (i) transparency and decentralised structure of its technical data exchange, and (ii) fully automated AI-assisted decision-making, and (iii) real-time bidirectional data flows that enhance operational efficiency.

One of the first approaches for IDTs is being developed by the University of Amsterdam together with the Dutch research consortium LTER—LIFE (NIOO–KNAW, 2023). This initiative is setting up a virtual interconnected environment that will provide comprehensive and diverse ecological and environmental data, advanced modelling tools and high-performance computing techniques (NIOO–KNAW, 2023). With this interconnected infrastructure, researchers can link long-term data on plants, animals and the environment and investigate multiple scenarios of how global change will affect ecosystems, both natural and man-made (NIOO–KNAW, 2023).

**Digital Twins in the Virtual Sphere (Metaverse)**

The integration of metaverse into an LDT can ensure that urban planners, developers, administrators, and other stakeholders will have equal opportunities to interact and collaborate within the digital realm as they make plans and seek solutions for various urban issues (Allam et al., 2022). The results can be used for collaborative testing of different scenarios and policies concerning urban development, infrastructure investments, and resource allocation in urban domains ranging from transport to public spaces (Allam et al., 2022; Bibri, 2022; Bibri et al., 2022). The development of the metaverse is still in its early stages, however, and there are many concerns over privacy and ethics that still need to be addressed before this virtual platform will become mainstream (Al-Ghaili et al., 2022).

**The Deep-Thought Digital Twin**

Isaac Asimov, the science fiction writer and thinker, introduced a concept called Psychohistory in his famous 'Foundation trilogy' novel series. The Psychohistory combined history, sociology, and mathematical statistics to make general predictions about future events and behaviours of the human race in the interstellar Galactic Empire in his stories. The use of this science only worked with large populations of individuals and for long periods of time. In addition, it could only handle a limited number of independent variables; it worked best when freedom of action was strongly restricted and only when its findings were kept secret.

Asimov used the analogy with gas to explain it: an observer has great difficulty predicting the movement of a single gas molecule but can predict the action of the mass of the gas with a high level of precision (kinetic theory) (Magazine Factor Tomorrow, 2018). Obviously, this 'science' is part of the science fiction realm but might be considered the first theory of using Big Data and AI for prediction purposes. The central notion of psychohistory is still cited as both a motivation and model for many contemporary attempts to leverage massive computing power and vast datasets for predictive ends.

Building on Asimov's Psychohistory, one could postulate several ways in which an LDT could be expanded.

- *Real-time operational control and monitoring:* A digital twin, given its virtual nature, is accessible and controlled in real-time from anywhere. Given the complexity and resources required for such processes in a physical world, this provides significant benefits over monitoring physical systems;
- *Human safety and operational efficiency:* Digital twins are envisioned to enable greater autonomy with humans in the loop as and when required. This will ensure that the dangerous, dull and dirty jobs are allocated to robots with humans controlling them remotely. This way, humans will be able to focus on more creative and innovative jobs;
- *Predictive maintenance, repair, and operations:* An integrated digital twin system will ensure that multiple sensors monitoring the physical infrastructure gen-

erate operational big data in real-time. Through smart filtering and data analysis, faults in the system can be detected in advance. This will enable more accurate predictive maintenance and more efficient operation scheduling;

- *Risk assessment and risk mitigation:* Digital twins enable what-if analyses for different scenarios in real-time, thus producing a more efficient risk assessment. With the support of quantum computing and 5G/6G networks, it will be possible to formulate unexpected scenarios and study the system's response as well as the corresponding mitigation strategies;
- *Better intra- and inter-team synergy and management:* With accurate and real-time information available, project teams distributed worldwide can experience enhanced collaboration, leading to greater productivity;
- *Personalised and tailor-made products and services:* With detailed personalised requirements and preferences of various stakeholders and evolving market trends and competition, the demand for personalised products and services is constantly increasing. A digital twin will enable faster and more efficient development of personalised products and services;
- *Improved communication, transparency, and decision-making:* Readily available information combined with automated feedback enables stakeholders to keep abreast of ongoing processes, opportunities, and outcomes, creating a more transparent environment for decision-making.

## 9.5 Conclusions

Digital twins are virtual replicas of physical systems or processes that use data and algorithms to simulate real-world conditions. They have become increasingly important in industries such as manufacturing, healthcare, and transportation, as they can help companies optimise operations, reduce costs, and improve overall performance. By creating a virtual representation of a physical system, companies can conduct simulations, test new designs, and troubleshoot potential issues before implementing changes in the real world. This not only saves time and money but also helps to minimise risks and improve the accuracy of decision-making. Overall, digital twins are essential tools for companies looking to stay competitive in an increasingly digital world.

A Local Digital Twin (LDT) is a type of digital twin that represents a city or urban area in a virtual environment. It is a digital replica of a city, town, village etc., that uses real-time data from sensors, cameras, and other sources to model the behaviour of the infrastructure, systems, and people. LDTs are used to simulate different scenarios and test the impact of changes in the area's infrastructure and policies. They can help urban planners, local government and other stakeholders to make informed decisions about urban development, transportation, energy use and emergency response. In addition, they can be used to improve citizens' quality of life, enhance sustainability, and optimise resource allocation.

In the final chapter, after analysing several types and projects of LDTs, a set of directions for their extension and expansion is presented.

### 9.5.1 Extending LDTs

One of the key extensions of LDTs is that they enable *greater connectivity between people and the built environment.* By collecting and analysing data from sensors, cameras and other sources, an LDT can provide real-time information about traffic, air quality, energy usage, and more. This information can be used to optimise services, improve public safety and enhance the overall quality of life in various areas of urban governance. In addition, it can also facilitate greater connectivity between people themselves. For example, by integrating social media and other digital platforms into the twin, area officials can gain a better understanding of how people use and interact between them and with the local area too. This information can be used to improve public engagement and encourage greater civic participation. Overall, LDTs have the potential to create a more connected and sustainable urban environment. By leveraging data and technology to optimise operations and enhance the quality of life for residents, these digital replicas can help create more liveable and resilient areas for the future.

*Interoperability is a key challenge in creating effective LDTs,* as these systems need to be able to integrate data from a wide range of sources in order to provide a comprehensive view. Greater interoperability can help ensure that digital twins are able to operate effectively and provide the insights and benefits that the area needs. One way to improve interoperability is to develop common data standards and protocols. This can help ensure that data from different sources can be easily integrated and analysed, making it easier to identify patterns and trends and make informed decisions about regional operations. Another approach is to use open APIs (Application Programming Interfaces) that enable different systems to communicate and share data. This can help to reduce the need for complex and proprietary integrations and make it easier for regions to access and analyse data from a wide range of sources. In addition, developing a common ontology or data model can help ensure that different systems are able to share data in a consistent and standardised way. This can help to reduce the risk of data inconsistencies and errors and ensure that the local government can make informed decisions based on accurate and reliable data. Improving interoperability in LDTs is essential for creating effective and sustainable smart areas. By developing common data standards and protocols, using open APIs, and developing a common ontology or data model, regions can create digital twins that are able to provide a comprehensive view of what is happening within them, and to enable effective decision-making.

*Intelligence is a key feature of LDTs,* as these systems are designed to provide real-time data and insights to optimise operations, enhance services, and improve the overall quality of life for residents. There are several ways that intelligence can be enhanced in digital twins. First, machine learning and Artificial Intelligence (AI) can be used to analyse data and identify patterns and trends that may be difficult to detect through traditional data analysis methods. By using algorithms to analyse large volumes of data, digital twins can help area officials identify potential issues and opportunities more quickly and accurately. Second, predictive analytics can be used to anticipate future trends and events, helping officials to plan and allocate resources more effectively. For example, predictive analytics can be used to forecast demand for public services, such as transportation or energy. Third, intelligent automation can be used to improve the efficiency and effectiveness of an area's operations. For example, autonomous vehicles and drones can be used to perform routine tasks, such as maintenance or inspections, reducing the need for human intervention and freeing up resources for more complex tasks. Finally, intelligent user interfaces can be developed to make it easier for residents and local officials to interact with digital twins and access the insights and data they need. These interfaces can use natural language processing and other AI technologies to provide more intuitive and user-friendly experiences, enabling more effective decision-making. Enhancing intelligence in LDTs can help cities become more responsive, efficient, and sustainable. By leveraging machine learning, predictive analytics, intelligent automation, and intelligent user interfaces, digital twins can provide a comprehensive view of the city and enable effective decision-making.

Digital twins require significant *computing power to process and analyse large volumes of data* generated by a wide range of sensors and other data sources. One way to increase computing power in digital twins is to leverage cloud computing technologies. By using cloud-based infrastructure, LDTs can access scalable computing resources that can be quickly provisioned and de-provisioned as needed. This can make urban areas manage spikes in demand for computing resources and ensure that digital twins are able to process data efficiently. Another approach is to use distributed computing technologies, such as edge computing or fog computing, to enable data processing and analysis closer to the source of data. This can help reduce latency and improve the speed and accuracy of data processing, which is particularly important for applications that require real-time or near-real-time processing. In addition, advances in hardware technology, such as the development of specialised processors for AI and machine learning workloads, can also help to increase computing power in digital twins. These specialised processors can accelerate data processing and analysis, making it possible to analyse larger volumes of data more quickly. Increasing computing power in urban digital twins is essential for enabling cities to make effective use of data and optimise city operations. By leveraging cloud computing, distributed computing, and specialised hardware technologies, urban areas can ensure that their digital twins have the computing power needed to process and analyse large volumes of data and provide insights needed to create more sustainable and liveable cities.

### 9.5.2 Expanding LDTs

LDTs in the virtual space (metaverse) refer to the use of digital replicas of real-world urban environments, infrastructure, and services within virtual worlds. The goal of LDTs is to provide a high-fidelity representation of urban areas that can be used for a range of purposes, such as urban planning, design, simulation, and management.

In the metaverse, digital twins can enable immersive experiences that allow users to explore, interact with, and modify urban environments in a virtual setting. For example, a digital twin could be used to test out different scenarios for urban development, transportation systems, or environmental policies. Users could then visualise the potential impacts of these scenarios in a highly realistic and interactive environment. The metaverse in an LDT context can facilitate greater collaboration and communication among stakeholders involved in urban planning and management. By providing a shared platform for data, analysis, and visualisation, the integration of the two systems can enable more informed decision-making and support greater participation and engagement among citizens.

However, there are also challenges to developing and using digital twins in the metaverse. These include issues related to data privacy, ownership, and security, as well as the need to ensure that the digital twin accurately reflects the real-world environment and is accessible to a broad range of users. LDTs in the metaverse represent an exciting area of technology that has the potential to transform how we plan, design, and manage urban areas, and enable more sustainable and equitable urban environments.

A deep thought prognosing digital twin could be used to simulate system behaviour and performance in various scenarios. Such an LDT would require a multidisciplinary foundation combining AI, computer science, and philosophy, among others.

Interconnected digital twins (IDTs) are digital replicas of physical assets, processes or systems that are linked to each other and can interact with their real-world counterparts autonomously. They are built using advanced technologies such as artificial intelligence, machine learning, the Internet of Things (IoT), and Blockchain. They are capable of simulating and predicting real-world events and can be used for a variety of applications, such as predictive maintenance, quality control, and asset optimisation. They can also be used for monitoring and controlling complex systems, such as power grids or traffic networks. One of their key advantages is that they can operate in a decentralised and distributed manner. This means that multiple digital twins can interact with each other without the need for centralised control. This makes them more resilient, flexible, and adaptive than traditional centralised systems. Distributed autonomous digital twins represent a promising new approach to managing and optimising complex systems and are expected to play an increasingly important role in smart cities and allied industries such as energy and transportation.

## References

Alazab, M., Khan, L. U., Koppu, S., Ramu, S. P., Iyapparaja, M., Boobalan, P., et al. (2022). Digital twins for healthcare 4.0—Recent advances, architecture, and open challenges. *IEEE Consumer Electronics Magazine, 12*(6), 29–37. https://ieeexplore.ieee.org/abstract/document/9900390

Allam, Z., Sharifi, A., Bibri, S. E., Jones, D. S., & Krogstie, J. (2022). The metaverse as a virtual form of smart cities: Opportunities and challenges for environmental, economic, and social sustainability in urban futures. *Smart Cities, 5*(3), 771–801. https://doi.org/10.3390/smartcities5030040

Al-Ali, A. R., Gupta, R., Zaman Batool, T., Landolsi, T., Aloul, F., & Al Nabulsi, A. (2020). Digital twin conceptual model within the context of internet of things. *Future Internet, 12*(10), 163. https://www.mdpi.com/1999-5903/12/10/163/pdf

Al-Ghaili, A. M., Kasim, H., Al-Hada, N. M., Hassan, Z. B., Othman, M., Tharik, J. H., et al. (2022). A review of metaverse's definitions, architecture, applications, challenges, issues, solutions, and future trends. *IEEE Access, 10*, 125835–125866. https://ieeexplore.ieee.org/iel7/6287639/6514899/09966605.pdf

Armeni, P., Polat, I., De Rossi, L. M., Diaferia, L., Meregalli, S., & Gatti, A. (2022). Digital twins in healthcare: Is it the beginning of a new era of evidence-based medicine? A critical review. *Journal of Personalized Medicine, 12*(8), 1255. https://doi.org/10.3390/jpm12081255

Atlantis. (2022). *Improved Resilience of Critical Infrastructures against large scale transnational and systemic risks*. EU Horizon 2020 funded project under grant agreement No. 101073909. https://www.atlantis-horizon.eu/pilots/

Atlantis. (2023). Improved Resilience of Critical Infrastructures against large scale transnational and systemic risks. EU Horizon 2020 funded project under grant agreement No. 101073909. *Digital Twin for LSP1 in Slovenia Begins Data Integration*. https://www.linkedin.com/pulse/digital-twin-lsp1-slovenia-begins-data?trk=public_post_main-feed-card_feed-article-content

Barcelona Supercomputing Center. (2022, July 08). *BSC agreement with CINECA and the city councils of Barcelona and Bologna to develop digital twins*. BSC. https://www.bsc.es/news/bsc-news/bsc-agreement-cineca-and-the-city-councils-barcelona-and-bologna-develop-digital-twins

Barricelli, B. R., Casiraghi, E., & Fogli, D. (2019). A survey on digital twin: Definitions, characteristics, applications, and design implications. *IEEE Access, 7*, 167653–167671. https://ieeexplore.ieee.org/iel7/6287639/8600701/08901113.pdf

Bibri, S. E. (2022). The social shaping of the metaverse as an alternative to the imaginaries of data driven smart cities: A study in science, technology, and society. *Smart Cities, 5*(3), 832–874. https://www.mdpi.com/2624-6511/5/3/43

Bibri, S. E., Allam, Z., & Krogstie, J. (2022). The Metaverse as a virtual form of data driven smart urbanism: Platformization and its underlying processes, institutional dimensions, and disruptive impacts. *Computational Urban Science, 2*(1), 24. https://link.springer.com/article/10.1007/s43762-022-00051-0

Bisanti, G. M., Mainetti, L., Montanaro, T., Patrono, L., & Sergi, I. (2023). Digital twins for aircraft maintenance and operation: A systematic literature review and an IoT-enabled modular architecture. *Internet of Things*, 100991. https://doi.org/10.1016/j.iot.2023.100991

Bortolini, R., Rodrigues, R., Alavi, H., Vecchia, L. F. D., & Forcada, N. (2022). Digital twins' applications for building energy efficiency: A review. *Energies, 15*(19), 7002. https://doi.org/10.3390/en15197002

Caprari, G., Castelli, G., Montuori, M., Camardelli, M., & Malvezzi, R. (2022). Digital twin for urban planning in the green deal era: A state of the art and future perspectives. *Sustainability, 14*(10), 6263. https://doi.org/10.3390/su14106263

Center of Digital Build Britain (CDBB). (2022). *Gemini papers: What are connected digital twins*. White paper. https://www.cdbb.cam.ac.uk/files/gemini_papers_-_what_are_connected_digital_twins.pdf

Deng, T., Zhang, K., & Shen, Z. J. M. (2021). A systematic review of a digital twin city: A new pattern of urban governance toward smart cities. *Journal of Management Science and Engineering, 6*(2), 125–134. https://doi.org/10.1016/j.jmse.2021.03.003

Dubey, P. (2020, October 19). Digital Twin platform powers the State of New Mexico in transitioning to a carbon neutral future, Informed Infrastructure.

Durão, L. F. C., Haag, S., Anderl, R., Schützer, K., & Zancul, E. (2018). Digital twin requirements in the context of industry 4.0. In *Product lifecycle management to support industry 4.0: 15th IFIP WG 5.1 international conference, PLM 2018, Turin, Italy, July 2-4, 2018, proceedings 15* (pp. 204–214). Springer. https://doi.org/10.1007/978-3-030-01614-2_19

Erol, T., Mendi, A. F., & Doğan, D. (2020, October). The digital twin revolution in healthcare. In *2020 4th international symposium on multidisciplinary studies and innovative technologies (ISMSIT)* (pp. 1–7). IEEE. https://doi.org/10.1109/ISMSIT50672.2020.9255249

European Parliament Think Tank. (2021, July 23). *Artificial Intelligence in smart cities and urban mobility*. https://www.europarl.europa.eu/thinktank/en/document/IPOL_BRI(2021)662937

Faliagka, E., Christopoulou, E., Ringas, D., Politi, T., Kostis, N., Leonardos, D., et al. (2024). Trends in digital twin framework architectures for smart cities: A case study in smart mobility. *Sensors, 24*(5), 1665. https://doi.org/10.3390/s24051665

Fuller, A., Fan, Z., Day, C., & Barlow, C. (2020). Digital twin: Enabling technologies, challenges and open research. *IEEE Access, 8*, 108952–108971. https://ieeexplore.ieee.org/iel7/6287639/6514899/09103025.pdf

Glaessgen, E., & Stargel, D. (2012, April). The digital twin paradigm for future NASA and US Air Force vehicles. In *53rd AIAA/ASME/ASCE/AHS/ASC structures, structural dynamics and materials conference 20th AIAA/ASME/AHS adaptive structures conference 14th AIAA* (p. 1818). https://doi.org/10.2514/6.2012-1818

Grieves, M. (2014). Digital twin: Manufacturing excellence through virtual factory replication. *White paper, 1*(2014), 1–7. https://www.researchgate.net/publication/275211047_Digital_Twin_Manufacturing_Excellence_through_Virtual_Factory_Replication

Grieves, M., & Vickers, J. (2017). Digital twin: Mitigating unpredictable, undesirable emergent behavior in complex systems. In *Transdisciplinary perspectives on complex systems: New findings and approaches* (pp. 85–113). Springer. https://doi.org/10.1007/978-3-319-38756-7_4

Grübel, J., Thrash, T., Aguilar, L., Gath-Morad, M., Chatain, J., Sumner, R. W., et al. (2022). The hitchhiker's guide to fused twins: A review of access to digital twins in situ in smart cities. *Remote Sensing, 14*(13), 3095. https://doi.org/10.3390/rs14133095

Gürdür, D., & Asplund, e. F. (2018). A systematic review to merge discourses: Interoperability, integration and cyber-physical systems. *Journal of Industrial Information Integration, 9*, 14–23. https://doi.org/10.1016/j.jii.2017.12.001

Hernandez-Morales, A (2022, April 19). Barcelona bets on 'digital twin' as future of city planning. *POLITICO*. https://www.politico.eu/article/barcelona-digital-twin-future-city-planning/

Li, L., Aslam, S., Wileman, A., & Perinpanayagam, S. (2021). Digital twin in aerospace industry: A gentle introduction. *IEEE Access, 10*, 9543–9562. https://doi.org/10.1109/ACCESS.2021.3136458

Liu, Y., Zhang, L., Yang, Y., Zhou, L., Ren, L., Wang, F., et al. (2019). A novel cloud-based framework for the elderly healthcare services using digital twin. *IEEE Access, 7*, 49088–49101. https://doi.org/10.1109/ACCESS.2019.2909828

Liu, Y., Folz, P., Pan, S., Ramparany, F., Bolle, S., Ballot, E., & Coupaye, T. (2021). Digital twin-driven approach for smart city logistics: The case of freight parking management. In *Advances in production management systems. Artificial intelligence for sustainable and resilient production systems: IFIP WG 5.7 International Conference, APMS 2021, Nantes, France, September 5–9, 2021, Proceedings, Part IV* (pp. 237–246). Springer. https://minesparis-psl.hal.science/hal-03388874/file/520761_1_En_25_Chapter.pdf

Magazine Factor Tomorrow. (2018, Spring). *Making Asimov's psychohistory a reality - Using big data to predict the future*. https://magazine.factor-tech.com/factor_spring_2018/making_asimov_s_psychohistory_a_reality_using_big_data_to_predict_the_future

Magrinyà, F., Mercadé-Aloy, J., & Ruiz-Apilánez, B. (2023). Merging green and active transportation infrastructure towards an equitable accessibility to green areas: Barcelona green axes. *Land, 12*(4), 919. https://doi.org/10.3390/land12040919

MarketsandMarkets.com. (2023). *Digital twin market size, share, statistics and industry growth analysis report.* https://www.marketsandmarkets.com/Market-Reports/digital-twin-market-225269522.html?gad_source=1&gclid=EAIaIQobChMI9enY4orohAMVf5KDBx37dgAVEAAYASAAEgJU3PD_BwE

Minevich, M. (2020, April 13). *Here's how Slovenia is shaping the new human centric society and pioneering the world in AI.* Forbes. https://www.forbes.com/sites/markminevich/2020/04/13/heres-how-slovenia-is-shaping-the-new-human-centric-society-and-pioneering-the-world-in-ai/?sh=377c28e74860

Miskinis, C. (2019). *The history and creation of the digital twin concept.* Challenge Advisory. https://www.challenge.org/insights/digital-twin-history/

Mylonas, G., Kalogeras, A., Kalogeras, G., Anagnostopoulos, C., Alexakos, C., & Muñoz, L. (2021). Digital twins from smart manufacturing to smart cities: A survey. *IEEE Access, 9*, 143222–143249. https://ieeexplore.ieee.org/document/9576739

Nguyen, H. X., Trestian, R., To, D, & Tatipamula, M. (2021). Digital twin for 5G and beyond. *IEEE Communications Magazine, 59*(2), 10–15. https://doi.org/10.1109/MCOM.001.2000343

NIOO–KNAW. (2023, February 27). *Digital twins predict the future of nature.* https://www.uva.nl/en/shared-content/faculteiten/en/faculteit-der-natuurwetenschappen-wiskunde-en-informatica/news/2023/02/digital-twins-predict-the-future-of-nature.html?cb

Ontotext. (n.d.). What is a knowledge graph? *ontotext.* https://www.ontotext.com/knowledgehub/fundamentals/what-is-a-knowledge-graph/

Peng, C., Xia, F., Naseriparsa, M., & Osborne, F. (2023). Knowledge graphs: Opportunities and challenges. *Artificial Intelligence Review, 56*(11), 13071–13102. https://doi.org/10.1007/s10462-023-10465-9

Piromalis, D., & Kantaros, A. (2022). Digital twins in the automotive industry: The road toward physical-digital convergence. *Applied System Innovation, 5*(4), 65. https://doi.org/10.3390/asi5040065

Protner, J., Pipan, M., Zupan, H., Resman, M., Simic, M., & Herakovic, N. (2021). Edge computing and digital twin based smart manufacturing. *IFAC-PapersOnLine, 54*(1), 831–836. https://doi.org/10.1016/j.ifacol.2021.08.098

Raes, L., Michiels, P., Adolphi, T., Tampere, C., Dalianis, A., McAleer, S., & Kogut, P. (2022). DUET: A framework for building interoperable and trusted digital twins of smart cities. *IEEE Internet Computing, 26*, 43–50. https://doi.org/10.1109/MIC.2021.3060962

Ramírez-Moreno, M. A., Keshtkar, S., Padilla-Reyes, D. A., Ramos-López, E., García-Martínez, M., Hernández-Luna, M. C., et al. (2021). Sensors for sustainable smart cities: A review. *Applied Sciences, 11*(17), 8198. https://doi.org/10.3390/app11178198

Ramu, S. P., Boopalan, P., Pham, Q. V., Maddikunta, P. K. R., Huynh-The, T., Alazab, M., et al. (2022). Federated learning enabled digital twins for smart cities: Concepts, recent advances, and future directions. *Sustainable Cities and Society, 79*, 103663. https://doi.org/10.1016/j.scs.2021.103663

Rasheed, A., San, O., & Kvamsdal, T. (2020). Digital twin: Values, challenges and enablers from a modeling perspective. *IEEE Access, 8*, 21980–22012. https://ieeexplore.ieee.org/iel7/6287639/6514899/08972429.pdf

Rosen, R., Von Wichert, G., Lo, G., & Bettenhausen, K. D. (2015). About the importance of autonomy and digital twins for the future of manufacturing. *Ifac-papersonline, 48*(3), 567–572. https://doi.org/10.1016/j.ifacol.2015.06.141

Sahlab, N., Kamm, S., Müller, T., Jazdi, N., & Weyrich, M. (2021). Knowledge graphs as enhancers of intelligent digital twins. In *2021 4th IEEE international conference on industrial cyber-physical systems (ICPS), Victoria, BC, Canada* (pp. 19–24). https://doi.org/10.1109/ICPS49255.2021.9468219

Sun, T., He, X., & Li, Z. (2023). Digital twin in healthcare: Recent updates and challenges. *DIGITAL HEALTH, 9*, 20552076221149651. https://journals.sagepub.com/doi/pdf/10.1177/20552076221149651

Tao, F., Zhang, H., Liu, A., & Nee, A. Y. (2018). Digital twin in industry: State-of-the-art. *IEEE Transactions on Industrial Informatics, 15*(4), 2405–2415. https://doi.org/10.1109/TII.2018.2873186

Testasecca, T., Lazzaro, M., & Sirchia, A. (2023). Towards digital twins of buildings and smart energy networks: Current and future trends. In *2023 IEEE international workshop on metrology for living environment (MetroLivEnv)* (pp. 96–101). IEEE. https://ieeexplore.ieee.org/abstract/document/10164035

Valverde-Pérez, B., Johnson, B., Wärff, C., Lumley, D., Torfs, E., Nopens, I., & Townley, L. (2021). *Digital water–operational digital twins in the urban water sector: Case studies.* International Water Association. White paper. https://iwa-network.org/wp-content/uploads/2021/03/Digital-Twins.pdf

van Dyck, M., Lüttgens, D., Piller, F. T., & Brenk, S. (2023). Interconnected digital twins and the future of digital manufacturing: Insights from a Delphi study. *Journal of Product Innovation Management, 40*(4), 475–505. https://onlinelibrary.wiley.com/doi/pdf/10.1111/jpim.12685

World Economic Forum. (2022, April 20). *Digital twin cities: Framework and global practices.* https://www.weforum.org/publications/digital-twin-cities-framework-and-global-practices/

UNCRD. (2022). *Training materials for implementing smart cities in Asia and the Pacific for inclusive, resilient, and sustainable societies.* https://uncrd.un.org/sites/uncrd.un.org/files/smart-city-training-material_1_smart-cities.pdf

Wu, Y., Zhang, K., & Zhang, Y. (2021). Digital twin networks: A survey. *IEEE Internet of Things Journal, 8*(18), 13789–13804. https://doi.org/10.1109/JIOT.2021.3079510

Xiong, M., & Wang, H. (2022). Digital twin applications in aviation industry: A review. *International Journal of Advanced Manufacturing Technology, 121*, 5677–5692. https://doi.org/10.1007/s00170-022-09717-9

# Chapter 10
# Force Multiplier: Realising the Benefits of Open and Re-usable Local Digital Twins

**Susie Ruston McAleer and Julia Glidden**

**Contents**



## 10.1 Value Creation for the Public Sector

Digital Twins emerged from the manufacturing industry in 2002 (Grieves, 2006), where they replicated the physical world to provide hard, yes-and-no operational insights. Since this time, the rapid advancement of artificial intelligence and cloud has brought the commercial use of digital twin technology to the public sector. Despite a growing awareness that digital twins can provide numerous benefits, including acting as a force multiplier for urban data, their adoption across the local landscape has been hindered by a lack of clarity surrounding their component technology, precise meaning and ultimate purpose, particularly when juxtaposed against the more data driven world of manufacturing. As a result, new entrants on both the supply and the demand-side have struggled to develop clear and compelling use cases, features, governance and business models (Chap. 1).

Local or urban digital twins are defined as data-based virtual replicas of urban infrastructures. In contrast to more traditional urban models and simulations, digital twins receive real-time updates from the physical world and continually mirror what is happening within a city (Raes et al., 2022). Table 10.1 demonstrates the general

S. R. McAleer (✉)
21C Consultancy Ltd, London, UK
e-mail: susie.mcaleer@21cconsultancy.com

J. Glidden
Pivotl Ltd, London, UK


L. Raes et al. (eds.), *Decide Better*,
https://doi.org/10.1007/978-3-031-81451-8_10

**Table 10.1** General characteristics and differences between a digital model, simulation and LDT

| Features | Model | Simulation | LDT |
|---|---|---|---|
| Character | A simplified representation of a system or process, often mathematical, designed to study specific aspects | An imitation of a system or process over time used to analyse behaviour under various conditions or decisions | A dynamic digital replica of a physical city or region in a localised setting, constantly updated with real-time data to reflect current conditions |
| Data | Static or limited datasets, often based on assumptions or historical data | Input data varies based on scenarios being tested and may use historical or hypothetical data | Continuous real-time data from sensors, IoT devices, and other sources within the local environment |
| Interface | Often 2D, typically accessed via software tools or platforms for analysis | 2D or 3D interactive interfaces based on scenarios being tested to visualise outcomes | Often 3D interfaces with real-time control and analysis capabilities, integrated with local infrastructure |
| Uses | Provide localised information using historical data | Analyse the performance of a specific urban system/ process using different variables | Run simulations to understand the impact of a change across the whole city |
| Scope | Narrow scope, focusing on specific components, data, domains or processes | Broader scope, often focused on one specific scenario but capable of simulating entire systems over time | Comprehensive scope within a localised setting, integrating multiple systems and processes for holistic management |
| Level | Street to city | Part of a city system | City, regional, national |

differences between digital models, simulations and Local Digital Twins (LDTs), though there are exceptions to the rule:

This paper explores, via desktop research, informal interviews with digital twin practitioners and author involvement in several LDT initiatives, the way in which open and reusable LDTs can enhance operational efficiency, decision-making, and innovation and act as force multipliers in urban policy-making, planning, design and implementation.[1]

## *10.1.1 Perceived Benefits of LDTs*

LDTs allow for the integration of data from various city sources, such as traffic, weather and building usage patterns, to create a comprehensive, real-time representation of a city that enables urban planners to simulate and assess diverse scenarios,

[1] Force multiplication, as referred to in this chapter title, refers to the amplification of the effectiveness and impact of a particular force or capability. It involves utilising resources, technologies, or strategies in a way that significantly enhances the outcomes achieved compared to traditional or individual approaches.

test modifications to infrastructure, engage with stakeholders and gauge the impact of novel policies before translating them into the physical realm. In so doing, LDTs have the potential to improve decision-making, streamline planning, enhance sustainability, increase inclusiveness and transparency, and optimise resource allocation. Estimates show that early adopters of LDTs may be able to achieve cost savings of up to $280 billion by 2030 from 'first-time-right designs' (ABI Research, 2021).

Despite these potential benefits, a desktop review of the current state of LDT deployment makes it clear that their full realisation remains hampered by a lack of quantified data on the benefits of LDTs.

Firstly, LDTs are a relatively new and emerging technology. As a result, there has simply not been enough time to conduct the type of comprehensive data collection and analysis at the scale needed to accurately quantify sustained benefits. Whilst the University of Cambridge has noticed an increased focus on socio-technical or benefits-oriented lens factors in more recent research (Nochta et al., 2021), most of the academic work in the field to date has been predominantly technology driven (Lei et al., 2023).

Secondly, LDT projects can vary significantly in scope, scale, and objectives across different cities and regions. Each implementation may have unique factors and context that make it challenging to generalise and provide standardised statistics. Thirdly, data collection and sharing can present challenges surrounding privacy concerns, technical constraints, and limitations in data accessibility that hinder the availability of comprehensive, standardised data. Cities need to assess the feasibility, cost-effectiveness, and potential ROI of an LDT.

Whilst comprehensive, quantitative statistics or data may be lacking, real-life case studies and anecdotal evidence from cities which have started their digital twin transition are beginning to showcase the types of digital dividends investing in an LDT can yield. A desktop review of industry papers and news articles, alongside the author's firsthand experience in the field, show that benefits can be categorised as either agnostic or *action-based*, i.e. an ability to do something new or perform a task more effectively, or *domain-based,* i.e. focused on a defined segment or area (Fig. 10.1).

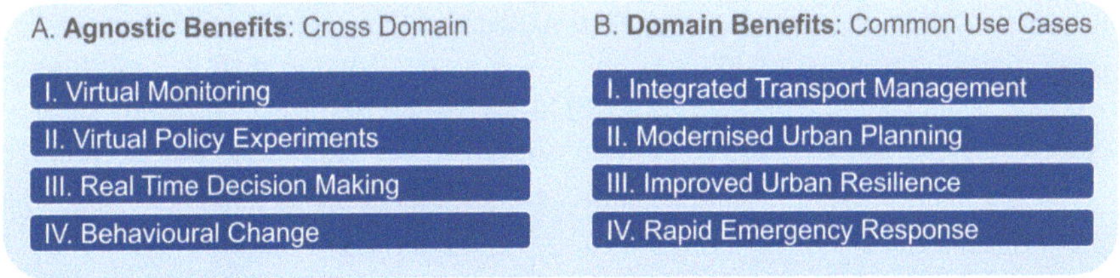


**Fig. 10.1** LDT benefits

## Agnostic Benefits: Cross Domain

Although presented as siloed benefits for the purposes of illustration, as the following examples reveal, agnostic benefits such as virtual monitoring and policy experiments cut across industry fields to provide often overlapping, multidisciplinary dividends.

### Virtual Monitoring

Virtual monitoring consists of 2D and 3D LDT interfaces that provide an easy-to-understand canvas to visualise and understand live urban data, such as traffic status or air quality, in context. Potential outcomes from virtual monitoring include gaining a greater understanding of complex urban processes and the ability to pinpoint potential problems such as traffic congestion, poor air quality, broken infrastructure and a lack of shade in public places.

Although 3D models provide the most visually rich localisation information, LDTs do not need to be in 3D to deliver benefits because their true power lies in unveiling what is underneath the interface. Both 2D and 3D LDTs connect real-time data across disparate systems. In so doing, they provide accurate, real-time mirroring of their real-world counterparts that help cities better understand and monitor how their systems are working. As such, grounding desired use cases and expected outcomes in 2D visualisation represents a valid way to begin an LDT transformation journey.

**Case: City of Pilsen, Czech Republic**
In 2012, Pilsen, a medium-sized city in the Czech Republic, began a gradual route towards creating an LDT in the transportation realm. In partnership with other cities in several European research and innovation projects, Pilsen began by building 2D data models and simulations for historic transport visualisations before moving onto real-time ones (Fig. 10.2).

Since 2021, the city has used lessons learned from its 2D modelling and harmonisation of historical data (Veeckman et al., 2017) to shift its real-time traffic visualisation capabilities to a 3D LDT. Today, the LDT helps city officials manage traffic operations more effectively by simulating and demonstrating the interaction between traffic, air quality and noise pollution.

**Fig. 10.2** 2D visualisation/simulation of Pilsen Roads as a precursor to its 3D LDT (Veeckman et al., 2017)

Real-Time Decision-Making

By combining and utilising data from sensors, simulations, and other sources, LDTs provide a comprehensive, real-time view of a city's environment and processes. In doing so, they empower city officials to go beyond just virtual monitoring, enabling them to react quickly and appropriately to events as they arise, often identifying problems before they occur in the physical world.

**Case: City of Zurich, Switzerland**

For the past ten years, the City of Zurich has been building a 3D spatial model which has evolved into a comprehensive digital twin in which spatial images are consistently enriched by real-world data sources in real-time. Over time, data from this LDT has increasingly been used to enable spatially related actions and decisions in areas ranging from the environment, energy management and urban planning through to location-based cooperation between internal and external partners (Schrotter & Hürzeler, 2020) (Fig. 10.3).

Predictive simulations in Zürich facilitate urban decision-making by deepening understanding of the potential impact of decisions in areas ranging from the deployment of solar panels to the expected benefits from mobile phone coverage across the city and the likelihood of noise propagation from new construction (Stadt Zürich, 2022).

**Fig. 10.3** Zurich Digital Twin (Stadt Zürich, 2022)

Virtual Policy Experimentation

In addition to real-time decision-making, LDT can be used as a ‘playground’ or ‘sandbox’ to test policy ideas or longer-term operational decisions before implementation. Using prediction simulations, LDTs can model the expected impacts of a potential decision across geographies from the whole city down to street level and across multiple domains, including road networks, air quality, shade, noise and mobility. Assessing the impact of potential decisions before they are implemented in real life is critical to promoting a more sustainable and liveable city.

**Case: Flanders Region/Ghent, Belgium**
Ghent is a major city in Flanders with 265,000 inhabitants and a commitment to green mobility. The city has the most extensive car-free city centre in Belgium. It is implementing several mobility plans that will create additional space for cyclists (CoMoUK, 2021) by closing additional city streets to vehicular traffic. In 2022, an LDT created by the innovation project DUET[2] helped to show the effects of different planning options for a new bicycle route in the city centre. LDT visualisations of the different scenarios - ranging from the

(continued)

[2]Digital Urban European Twins (DUET), EU H2020 project, https://cordis.europa.eu/project/id/870697

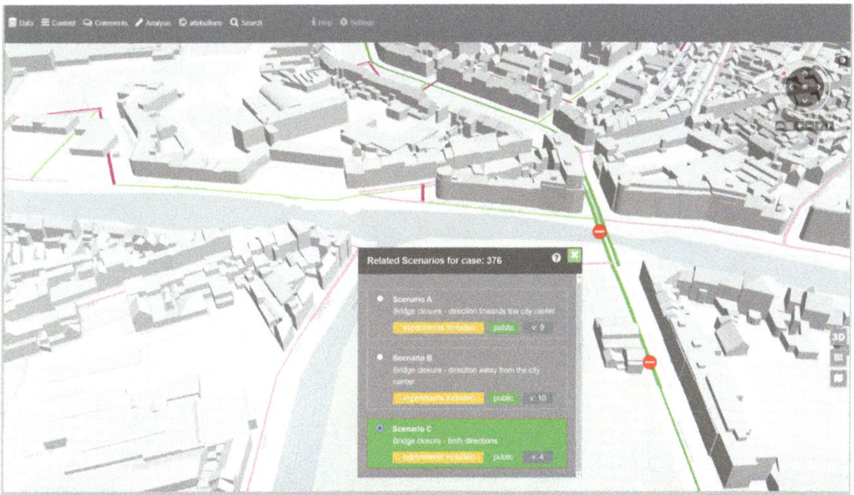


**Fig. 10.4** 3D visualisation/simulation of traffic impact from a full bridge closure in Ghent (DUET & URBANAGE Consortium, n.d.) (Enhanced URBAN planning for AGE-friendly cities through disruptive technologies (URBANAGE), EU H2020 project, https://cordis.europa.eu/project/id/101004590)

complete closure of a significant bridge to cars and trucks through to partial closures in just one direction - enabled both city officials and the public to view proposed scenarios side-by-side and better understand the impact of various options on traffic flows and provide more informed commentary (Fig. 10.4).

The DUET implementation in Ghent won the 'best enabling technology' award at the Smart City Expo and World Conference in 2021, raising awareness of the LDT concept on the global stage.

Behaviour Change

As well as helping city planners better and more quickly understand, improve and communicate the impact of policy decisions, LDTs can also empower policymakers and citizens to act on information, derive their own insights and change their behaviour accordingly. The deployment of easy-to-understand 3D interfaces and data visualisations, for example, can help city managers more clearly communicate with residents, engage citizen scientists to crowdsource data and speed up project delivery times. At the same time, deployment can also help them gain buy-in for proposals by providing city users with immersive and interactive urban experiences that enable them to locate themselves within an urban environment and better understand the impact of things like driving a particular route during school hours.

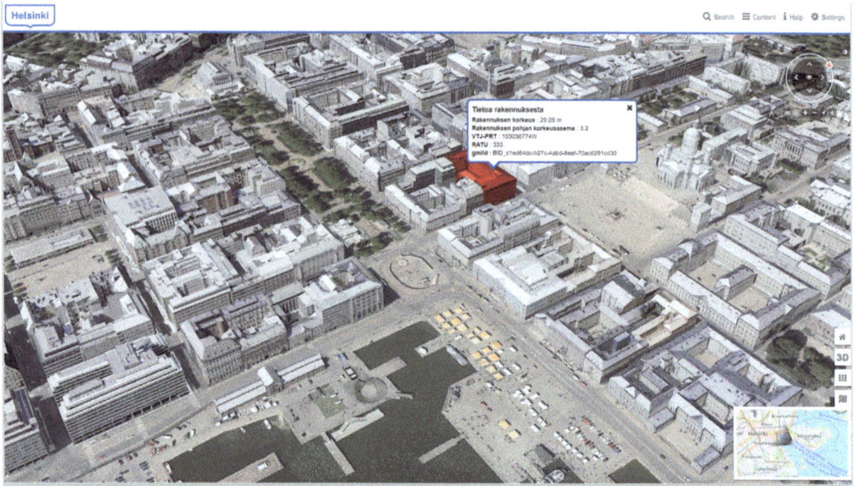


**Fig. 10.5** Helsinki Digital Twin (City of Helsinki, 2024)

**Case: City of Helsinki, Finland**

Forum Virium, the IT agency of Helsinki, developed a digital twin of their Kalasatama district to create a virtual neighbourhood called Smart Kalasatama. The LDT visualised potential new projects and services for city officials and helped them to communicate their potential impact on residents and community organisations before fine-tuning their design and prioritising roll-out. Smart Kalasatam enabled stakeholders from all backgrounds to provide input into developments from their computer and mobile devices and to view the same data used to make official decisions by the city (Fig. 10.5).

Since its roll-out, Smart Kalasatama's open engagement approach to urban planning has become a model for the rest of Helsinki. The Helsinki Success Story is described in the blog "Helsinki Expands Digitalization with Digital Twin" (Bentley Expert, 2020).

## Domain Benefits: Common Use Cases

In contrast to cross-cutting agnostic benefits, domain benefits, as the following case studies reveal, provide new capabilities to transform traditional processes within particular industries.

### Predictive Transport Management

LDTs are beginning to revolutionise transportation management by creating comprehensive and dynamic representations of transportation systems that leverage usually readily available geolocated data sources. Research shows that connected public transport is the number one use case for smart cities, followed by traffic monitoring (Wegner, 2020). By integrating data from diverse sources, such as sensors, traffic cameras, and mobile devices, LDTs enable transport managers to efficiently monitor, analyse, optimise and manage transportation networks in real-time. They also enable them to simulate and visualise scenarios and make more accurate forecasts about the impact of challenges like congestion on the city as a whole. Ultimately, LDTs help to drive more effective, sustainable and customised transportation systems by providing real-time insights into operational parameters such as traffic flows and infrastructure conditions and facilitating pre-deployment testing and evaluation.

**Case: City of Santander, Spain**

As part of a Horizon Europe project called URBANAGE, Santander developed a digital replica of its urban environment to help it create more age-friendly cities where older residents can better live and navigate the city with dignity. This platform combines data from various sources, including sensors, mobile devices, and public transportation systems, to create a dynamic and comprehensive virtual model of the city and its transport services.

The LDT enabled Santander not only to better simulate scenarios to predict impacts to manage its own service operations and support urban planning but also to offer an age-friendly routing solution that optimises results for citizens based on personalised needs, for example, step-free access, closeness of toilets, seating availability, as well as real-time incidents, such as a broken escalator or traffic accident. By offering citizens the ability to visualise and simulate different routing scenarios based on their own needs, users can assess the impact of potential changes in the transportation infrastructure and plan their own journeys accordingly. This data driven approach enables both the city and the citizens to respond proactively to changing conditions and evolving transport demands (Fig. 10.6).

Using LDTs, Santander has been able to prove they improve mobility within the city and offer critical societal benefits, including independence, dignity and choice.

**Fig. 10.6** Santander LDT Route Planner. (From the URBANAGE project, n.d., Licensed under CC-BY 4.0)

Urban Planning Modernisation

Planning systems often lag in transformation efforts due to a reliance on paper-based descriptions and scale models for decision-making. LDTs can help to modernise these efforts by simulating and testing different planning scenarios in a digital environment before implementing them in real life. Specifically, Geospatial Information Systems (GIS) enables the integration of diverse datasets such as land use, infrastructure, and topography, facilitating holistic planning approaches. By overlaying different layers of information within an LDT, planners can better identify spatial relationships, detect patterns, and assess the suitability of proposed interventions.

**Case: Punggol District, Singapore**
Before the physical construction of the Singapore Punggol (JTC, 2022) District began, an LDT was used to simulate and test various urban planning scenarios, including the impact of different building designs and the allocation of public space. During construction, the district used advanced digital

(continued)

**Fig. 10.7** Punggol New Town

technologies, such as sensors and data analytics, to gather real-time insights into the usage patterns of the area (Sagar, 2020), which were ultimately fed back into the Digital Twin to create a continuous cycle of improvement for urban planning and District management (Fig. 10.7).

Deployment of an LDT has enabled the Punggol District to more accurately predict demand and supply for services, adapt power consumption, cleaning and cooling services based on footfall and push innovation by establishing an ambitious 30% energy saving target compared to a standard building (Sagar, 2020).

Improved Urban Resilience

Urban decision-makers are tasked with keeping people safe, ensuring that city spaces work for everyone and offering a high quality of life for all residents. Rapid urbanisation, climate change, population growth and ageing populations, not to mention unforeseen events like the recent pandemic, make their job more challenging than ever. LDTs can help them bolster overall urban resilience by simulating high-risk scenarios and providing real-time situational awareness about critical infrastructure that can be used to identify risk mitigation options before a problem arises, track progress against resilience goals and allocate resources more effectively.

**Fig. 10.8** City of Valencia

**Case: City of Valencia, Spain**

The City of Valencia is an early urban twin pioneer. As far back as 2014, the city's water utility organisation built a water-focused digital twin to leverage more than six billion data points across the city. The twin provided Valencia with a detailed view of pressure and flow across the whole water network, which helped managers control availability and pressure, minimise leaks, improve maintenance planning, and enhance customer experience (Conejos et al., 2019) (Fig. 10.8).

Since 2014, Valencia has increased network efficiency by 40% and saved 4.5 billion litres of water annually (Aquatech, 2019).

Emergency Response

LDTs can play a vital role in improving emergency responses through the integration of infrastructure-level sensors and sensing and scenario simulation into community management processes (Ford & Wolf, 2020). This integration enables emergency response planners to better coordinate systems in advance of catastrophic events while also providing real-time situational awareness throughout a crisis.

**Fig. 10.9** Cauayan, Philippines (Base map from Open Street Map)

**Case: City of Cauayan, Philippines**
The first ever LDT in the Philippines is located in the small city of Cauayan, with a total population of just 160,000 inhabitants. Dominated by farmland, the city suffers disproportionately from natural disasters. With approximately 20 typhoons hitting the area yearly, Cauayan is at constant risk of flooding. Whilst it used to take months to assess the damage after a storm event, the deployment of an Artificial Intelligence (AI)-enabled digital twin that is fuelled by data from official drones has reduced damage assessment to just hours (Fig. 10.9).

Recently, instead of taking months, Cauayan's Digital Twin was able to help the city quickly assess damage of over $12.5 million, identify more than 7000 families in need of urgent help and distribute nearly 37,000 relief packs ("Cauayan City's digital twin helps in disaster response") (Poon, 2021).

## Driving Benefits at Scale

As the previous section underscores, deploying an LDT can provide a diverse array of discrete and often overlapping benefits ranging from smarter policy-making and planning to enhanced operational deployment and efficiency. Scaling, or adjusting the size, scope, or complexity of an LDT representation to match a real-world system, amplifies these benefits by providing increasingly accurate and flexible real-time visualisations and simulations that help decision-makers to better perceive and respond to vast multi-dimensional systems which have heretofore been impossible to intuitively grasp due to their size and complexity (Chuncheng & Tian, 2023).

#### Scaling Sectoral Data Sharing and Collaboration

LDTs provide a central focal point for diverse departments, sectors and stakeholders within a city to share data and collaborate. In so doing, they help to break down traditional divisions between domains such as urban planning, mobility, energy, and the environment by encouraging and empowering teams to work together with a shared digital representation of the city. Cross-sectoral data sharing and collaboration, coupled with replicable simulation models, was an outcome of the SELECT4Cities[3] project, which provided city workers with a more comprehensive and accurate comprehension of urban dynamics, whilst the harmonisation of sectoral-specific insights enabled them to optimise resource allocation and elevate the overall quality of urban life (Dembski et al., 2020). The benefits of a collaborative city-level approach like this one can be further extended at the geographical level to create regional and national digital twin networks (Gov.uk, 2023) that enhance insights and outcomes at scale.

#### Scaling Policy Alignment

LDTs also have the potential to better coordinate objectives and actions across multiple levels of governance by offering a platform for aligning policies—from local to regional, national, and even international levels (Capgemini Research Institute, 2022a)—and enabling stakeholders from various administrative tiers to collaborate, share insights, and coordinate efforts. They can facilitate the harmonisation of policies by providing a common platform for everyone to use for data sharing and analysis, which ultimately helps reduce conflicts and ensure a more integrated and coherent policy landscape.

#### Scaling ICT Infrastructure

The establishment of integrative Information and Communication Technology (ICT) infrastructure is also a pivotal factor in scaling the value of LDTs (Raes, 2022). Replicable simulation models, rooted in standardised data inputs, enable

[3] Standardized, opEn, data-driven, service-oriented user-centric pLatform Enabling large-scale Co-creation, Testing validation of IoE services for Cities (SELECT4Cities), EU H2020 project, https://cordis.europa.eu/project/id/688196

seamless scalability and intercity comparisons (Coenen et al., 2021). Shared ICT infrastructure components, including cloud-based computing and edge analytics, contribute to the efficiency, reliability and security of LDT operations at scale. Meanwhile, the deployment of robust data platforms facilitates the aggregation, sharing, and analysis of data across sectors and policy levels.

## *10.1.2 Building and Scaling an LDT*

Innovation in the LDT domain has expanded rapidly over the past three years as a result of fallout from the pandemic and ongoing market developments. These include the availability of new government initiatives and funding to incentivise early adoption from the World Economic Forum, European Commission and British Government, among others. Analyst firm GlobalData marks the overall value of the digital twin market as $1.75 billion in 2023 and notes that it is expected to grow by 36% CAGR (Compound Annual Growth Rate) by 2030 (GlobalData, 2023). These findings are echoed by Capgemini, which forecasts a 35% increase over the next five years in digital twin usage across all industries, including the public sector (Capgemini Research Institute, 2022b).

Whilst these market conditions have propelled digital twin technology from a niche application into a prominent management best practice for data driven decision-making (Future Digital Twin, 2023), starting and scaling a digital twin journey remains a complex undertaking which requires an intricate combination of planning, technology implementation and collaboration.

#### Models to Support Scalability

Because LDT adoption is still in an early stage, implementation roadmaps and models are relatively new and limited.

Gemini Principles

In 2018, a task force for the Centre for Digital Built Britain provided the first framework of its kind for the built environment, working towards the concept of a national twin. The resulting framework provided the following Gemini Principles or indicators to help drive scalable alignment and better enable LDTs to join together to create federated regional and national digital twins (Table 10.2).

These high-level principles provided the first essential guidepost for urban digital twin practitioners, encouraging a more connected and data-centric future, not only for digital twin adoption but also for the wider smart city sector. Since their creation, the principles have been expanded to create a Digital Twin Toolkit (Hayes, 2012) to help adopters create a business case for their implementations.

**Table 10.2** The Gemini Principles (Centre for Digital Built Britain, 2018)

| Purpose | Security | Federation |
|---|---|---|
| **Principle 1:** *Public good* Must be used to deliver genuine public benefit in perpetuity | **Principle 4:** *Security* Must enable security and be secure itself | **Principle 7:** *Federation* Must be based on a standard connected environment |
| **Principle 2:** *Value creation* Must enable value creation and performance improvement | **Principle 5:** *Openness* Must be as open as possible | **Principle 8:** *Curation* Must have clear ownership, governance and regulation |
| **Principle 3:** *Insight* Must provide determinable insight into the built environment | **Principle 6:** *Quality* Must be built on data of an appropriate quality | **Principle 9:** *Evolution* Must be able to adapt as technology and society evolve |

### ARUP Digital Twin Framework

Three years after the rollout of the Gemini Principles, the prominent engineering firm Arup rolled out a 5-level framework "to evaluate the current state of digital twins across five key levels" and initiate discussions and further understanding around the direction of LDTs, especially within the built environment (ARUP, 2021). Arup defined levels in relation to four indicators - autonomy, intelligence, learning and fidelity. Levels increased in complexity, with 1 being a linked model to the real world without any feedback and 5 being a fully autonomous situation.

### LDT Maturity Model

More recently, the European Commission's first LDT project supplemented the Gemini Principles and Arup Framework with a comprehensive maturity model (Fig. 10.10) to help city officials implement LDTs to improve public sector decision-making. Serving as a high-level diagnostic tool, the roadmap-type model helps decision-makers to assess their city's LDT through the lens of 3 pivotal enablers: people, governance, and technology; across four progressive levels: strategy, exploratory, insightful and future-ready (Kogut, 2022). The roadmap first helps to identify a city's current state ('as is') before facilitating the definition of the desired future state ('to be'). By driving clarity in this manner, this methodology enables city practitioners to forge a clear and compelling roadmap for LDT deployment and scaling.

#### Awareness of Twins: Strategy Phase

The awareness phase is mainly devoted to research and upskilling and is aimed at the novice city. At the start of its journey, the city is asked to identify the urban domains that would benefit the most from digital twin technology and define a test use case that involves at least two domains. It is also asked to identify the necessary data sources, technologies and stakeholders needed to support the use cases, create a plan for running an LDT pilot and secure initial funding.

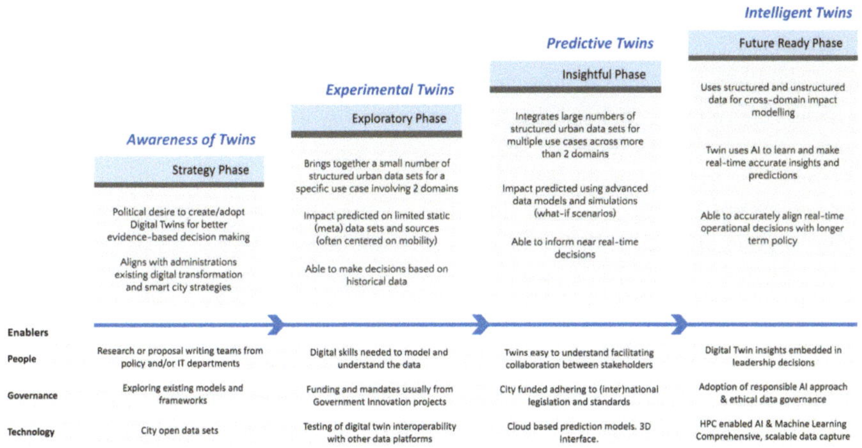


**Fig. 10.10** LDT Maturity Model (Kogut, 2022)

Experimental Twins: Exploratory Phase

In this phase, the city is asked to train city officials and implement the first LDT pilot based on its identified use case. Implementation will involve conducting simple simulations and tests to ensure the LDT accurately represents the use case and can be used to model various scenarios effectively. Based on the first results, the city is then asked to evaluate whether it wishes to launch additional pilot projects in new areas or domains to further validate effectiveness. Cities are cautioned to take care to ensure that data privacy and security measures are in place to comply with relevant regulations, protect sensitive information, and provide a strong evaluation methodology.

Predictive Twins: Insightful Phase

During this phase, a city is asked to conduct an evaluation of the exploratory phase to help establish the objectives for the expansion of the LDT. Goals may include improving the overall efficiency of a whole domain, enhancing citizen services perhaps, or increasing sustainability. The evaluation should assess whether the current technology infrastructure can support scaling as well as performance and capacity requirements. At this stage, simulation models will need to be updated and expanded, and an investment in software, hardware and cloud resources may be required. Governance structures and policies for the scaled twin, including detailed roles and responsibilities, data sharing protocols and access controls, should be established along with monitoring systems and accompanying metrics to track the performance and impact of the scaled twin.

#### Intelligent Twins: Future Ready Phase

In this phase, a city is asked to seamlessly integrate the expanded digital twin into existing city systems, such as GIS and urban planning tools. It is also asked to evaluate the viability and benefits of integrating with digital twins from other cities. The LDT is likely to be AI-enabled to help optimise services and, automatically predict and help mitigate urban issues, and feature a culture of continuous improvement to ensure regular updates as soon as new data, technology, and urban needs emerge. To build trust and support for the new LDT, the city is asked to continually engage with the public and stakeholders.

### Challenges and Blockers to LDT Scalability

Cities that embrace and scale digital twin technology at an early stage can optimise their urban systems, ameliorate pain points, foster collaboration, enhance efficiency, and elevate the overall quality of life for residents and visitors alike. Despite these advantages, initiating an LDT strategy at scale necessitates overcoming an array of challenges - challenges which predominantly centre around the handling of data, and which have been vastly amplified following AI's explosion into day-to-day life, such as the launch of ChatGPT in the winter of 2022.

#### Technical Challenges

Technical challenges range from the integration, management and analysis of diverse data sources through to the establishment of a new technological infrastructure and the safeguarding of sensitive information.

Firstly, the construction of a successful digital twin necessitates the seamless integration and exchange of vast amounts of (often real-time) data from a diverse range of sources. This integration requires the establishment of robust interoperability between systems and platforms through the deployment of standardised data formats, protocols, and interfaces. Ensuring high performance at scale requires the efficient handling of data, involving synchronisation between physical systems and their digital counterparts and sufficient expertise and support for real-time analytics.

Secondly, as recent research argues, concerns about "trust and privacy issues in sharing sensitive data" represent a major obstacle to the take-up and adoption of digital twins (Ramu et al., 2022). Before approving a digital twin, urban residents want to know that their personal data will remain confidential, and that unauthorised access will be prevented. As a result, planners must build comprehensive data protection throughout the lifecycle of a digital twin into a technical infrastructure that is transparent and trusted by all stakeholders.

Thirdly, trust in the validity and verifiability of the data underpinning a digital twin is essential for successful deployment. Simply put, before making high-impact decisions on the back of a digital twin, end-users must be able to prove beyond a shadow of a doubt that the highly complex model accurately represents the behaviour and characteristics of a physical system. Doing so necessitates a delicate balance between detail, computational efficiency, and accuracy.

Whilst not new, the rapid pace of change in the roll-out and adoption of AI-infused systems has further compounded these technical challenges. Concerns about black boxes and hallucinations alongside high-profile failures such as the launch of Google's Gemini (Nolan, 2024), for example, have exponentially increased public awareness about the dangers of data bias distorting reality beyond all recognition. If digital twins are based on data inputs, how do urban planners ensure that this data is factual and unbiased? How, in other words, do they prevent the old adage 'garbage in, garbage out' from not only falsifying reality itself but endangering citizens in the process?

Meanwhile, high-profile lawsuits such as the New York Times suit against OpenAI (Grynbaum & Mac, 2023) have placed increased pressure on organisations to put technical measures in place to ensure not just data integrity but also data provenance. Access to the predictive insights of real-time data empowers decision-makers to respond swiftly to evolving conditions, address policy challenges, and enact targeted interventions to improve operations. Automation of core citizen service processes can reduce costs whilst vastly enhancing the overall quality of service. To realise these benefits, however, city planners must be able to demonstrate that an LDT does not violate copy and intellectual property rights in leveraging data. Failure to do so runs the risk of costly and protracted lawsuits.

### Legal and Regulatory Challenges

The implementation of data driven digital twins that are open and reusable also introduces a range of legal and regulatory challenges that, much like the technical challenges discussed above, begin with data sharing and collaboration and give rise to questions regarding ownership and intellectual property rights.

The introduction of the General Data Protection Regulation (European Parliament & Council, 2016) in Europe in 2016 set a global template for data governance and privacy regulations. To varying degrees, over the past eight years, countries around the world have legislated elements of GDPR's requirements surrounding data consent, protection and anonymisation. As a result, these requirements have heavily influenced the implementation of urban digital twins - challenging cities to balance the benefits of sharing proprietary models, data, or algorithms against the risk of data breaches and IPR violations.

The 27-member EU bloc is once again leading the world on data legislation and regulation with the recent introduction of the AI Act (European Parliament, 2024). This first-of-its-kind regulatory framework aims to introduce a risk-based approach to AI that balances "the safety and fundamental rights of people and businesses" against a drive to "strengthen uptake, investment and innovation in AI." (Environment and Energy Leader, 2024). Like GDPR before it, the EU's 4-tiered approach—which ranges from an outright prohibition on high-risk usages such as social scoring by governments through to low-risk usage such as spam filters—is likely to eventually establish a new global standard in critical areas such as liability and accountability.

Nevertheless, the global legal and regulatory path ahead for LDT adopters is far from clear. The AI Act is already being criticised in European business circles for placing an undue burden on technical innovations that utilise AI, like digital twins (Matthews, 2023). The US and UK are openly challenging the EU's approach by placing greater emphasis on innovation and growth than risk reduction (Larsen, 2022). India has abruptly dropped a requirement for platforms to obtain government approval before launching AI products (Singh, 2024). China is also attempting to rally southern hemisphere countries around an overtly statist approach (Koetse, 2024). Until harmonisation occurs, LDT practitioners will need to balance the risk of getting ahead of regulation against the risk of falling behind on innovation.

### Organisational Challenges

Demonstrating a clear return on investment and articulating the business value associated with digital twins can be challenging, particularly during the initial stages of adoption. Overcoming these hurdles requires a strategic approach that aligns organisational objectives with transformative potential.

To fully harness the advantages offered by LDTs, organisations must cultivate a culture that promotes knowledge sharing and innovation. Doing so involves fostering an environment that encourages collaboration, embraces new ideas, and supports continuous learning. It also requires the development and management of specialist skill sets across multiple disciplines, including domain knowledge, data analytics, modelling, and software development.

Implementing organisational and cultural shifts of this nature can present particular challenges for cities which, like the rest of the wider public sector, have struggled to keep pace with private sector pay and benefits packages. As a result, organisations may encounter difficulties in attracting and retaining talent with the requisite expertise, which can only be overcome through effective talent acquisition and retention strategies. Finally, the implementation of digital twins also requires significant investments in infrastructure, technology, and resources.

### Social Challenges

Although designed to reflect the real world in real-time, historically, LDT deployment models have tended to focus on legal and technical aspects over critical social or non-material areas such as human interactions, competition, cooperation, social norms, laws, regulations, history, politics, democracy and human ethics. As a result, the societal challenges underpinning urban digital twins represent a relatively unexplored area, particularly when it comes to the integration of social and emotional intelligence into the decision-making process (Ruston McAleer et al., 2021).

The emerging concept of 'Societal Twins' is intended to address this deficiency by insisting digital twin practitioners move beyond simply recreating physical objects and instead focus on the way in which a society functions, evolves, and interacts with its environment by integrating social data points such as culture and demographics. In other words, Societal Twin advocates propose enhancing straightforward physical simulations by including the complex social or communal aspects inherent in an urban environment. Challenging as this endeavour is, demand for Societal Twins is likely to grow in the years ahead as AI advances fuel increasing concern about the wider societal implications of a technology that has the potential to displace, if not physically harm, humans at scale.

## 10.2 Implementing Scalability Strategies

Scaling an LDT to represent the entire urban system is essential for maximising their potential to help city planners drive positive social and economic outcomes such as identifying and implementing more effective sustainability strategies, anticipating and avoiding environmental crises, and ultimately, creating more liveable and humane urban environments. Successfully doing so requires a comprehensive approach that is grounded in strong collaboration between stakeholders on both the supply and demand-side.

### *10.2.1 Stakeholder Collaboration*

Cooperation on industry standards, best practices, and regulatory guidelines is essential to help mitigate scaling challenges and successfully deploy LDTs that are open, reusable and scalable.

#### Supply-Side

Policymakers, researchers and technologists comprise the key stakeholders of the LDT. Engaging these stakeholders in a collaborative effort is necessary to derive a holistic view of the environmental as well as the social impact of operations:

- *Policymakers:* Policymakers play a pivotal role in shaping the regulatory framework and guidelines for the scaling of digital twins in the public sector. Their involvement is vital for understanding the potential benefits and risks associated with LDTs and formulating policies that promote their compliant, responsible and effective use. Policymakers are responsible for addressing legal and ethical considerations, data governance, privacy, and security concerns. Through collaboration with other stakeholders, they ensure that the scaling of digital twins aligns with broader policy objectives, such as protecting the environment and societal needs, such as the creation of healthier, more liveable cities;

- *Researchers:* Researchers contribute to the advancement of digital twins through academic studies and innovation. They conduct research to enhance understanding of LDTs, explore their potential applications and identify benefits and challenges. Researchers likewise investigate new algorithms, methodologies and technologies to improve the operational functionality and effectiveness of digital twin systems. Their work helps identify best practices, address limitations, and enhance the overall knowledge base regarding the scaling of digital twins. In doing so, they help to facilitate evidence-based decision-making and foster continuous improvement in digital twin technologies;
- *Technologists:* Technologists are instrumental in designing, developing, and implementing scalable LDT solutions. They leverage AI and cloud technologies to create digital replicas and enable real-time data analysis and visualisation. Technologists select appropriate hardware and software infrastructure, integrate diverse data sources, and ensure data interoperability. Their expertise is vital in optimising the performance and scalability of LDT systems and addressing the technical challenges that may arise during scaling. Through close collaboration with policymakers and researchers, technologists contribute to the deployment of digital twin technologies that are not only safe but also scalable.

### Demand-Side

As users and citizens are ultimate beneficiaries of LDTs; they represent the most important demand-side stakeholders in the scaling of LDTs.

- *Users and citizens:* Users and citizens benefit from the fact that LDTs have the potential to enhance urban operations, improve overall quality of life and increase general knowledge about the lived urban environment. Through LDTs, they gain access to real-time data and insights about a city as well as the ability to quickly and easily provide valuable feedback, participate in collaborative problem-solving and actively shape the development and optimisation of urban planning efforts;
- *Public sector organisations:* Government agencies and municipalities are responsible for providing public services and managing urban operations. By facilitating the real-time visualisation, monitoring and analysis of city operations, LDTs enable them to monitor and analyse data from various sources in real-time, make more informed decisions, optimise resource allocation, streamline their processes, achieve more accurate and collaborative operations management, and ultimately, improve service delivery.

## *10.2.2 Strategies for Effective Governance*

Strong governance across four interconnecting strategies is essential to the responsible and successful deployment of digital twins in the public sector:

### Understanding the Needs and Requirements of Stakeholders

Effective governance begins with an understanding of the needs and requirements across the stakeholder community - policymakers, technologists, researchers, users, citizens, and public sector organisations. Active involvement of key stakeholders throughout the planning and implementation process enables governance strategies to help design digital twin solutions that align with stakeholder expectations, priorities and concerns to engender strong acceptance and engagement.

### Ensuring Collaboration and Coordination Among Stakeholders

Fostering an environment of trust and collaboration is necessary to ensure that an LDT reflects the collective wisdom and support of all relevant stakeholders. Establishing robust governance mechanisms to coordinate regular communication, information sharing, and collaborative decision-making enables stakeholders to pool resources, align objectives, and resolve conflicts effectively. For example, work by OASC and Living-in.eu ("Living-in.eu", n.d.) on data-based collaborative standards (e.g., minimum interoperability mechanisms, or MIMs, that enable the evolution and scalability of critical digital infrastructure) will help drive greater adoption and value extraction (OASC, 2024).

### Developing Appropriate Regulatory Frameworks

Policymakers play a central role in formulating regulations that guide the responsible use of digital twins in the public sector - a role which, as we have argued above, is only going to intensify as AI permeates more and more aspects of urban life. As a result, before embarking on any LDT project, urban planners must take great care to establish a robust regulatory framework that addresses issues such as data governance, privacy protection, and security measures, as well as the ethical considerations surrounding the use of data in LDTs. At the same time, they must take care to balance clarity and accountability in critical areas like data ownership, access rights, and usage restrictions against a need to remain flexible and adaptable to accommodate emerging innovations in digital twin technologies.

**Ensuring Data Privacy and Security**

The paramount importance of ensuring privacy and security in the era of AI makes it imperative that LDT governance strategies include durable measures to ensure the protection of sensitive data that is collected and processed by digital twins. Doing so requires the implementation of strong data security protocols, encryption techniques, access controls, and regular audits. Stakeholders must prioritise data anonymisation and aggregation techniques to protect an individual's privacy in a manner that still enables the extraction of data driven insights. To mitigate distrust, they must likewise ensure transparency in data handling practices, informed consent from users and compliance with relevant data protection regulations and ethical guidelines.

### *10.2.3 A Dedicated LDT Governance Model*

LDTs have the potential to revolutionise urban policy-making by providing previously unattainable real-time insights into urban dynamics. However, as the previous sections have shown, the integration of LDTs into the policy-making process raises important questions related to data ownership, privacy, security, and fairness, not least of all because LDTs are part of the current trend towards data driven policy-making, or the making of policy decisions on the basis of objective empirical and evidence-based evaluation research about the context, need and efficacy of different policy programs rather than subjective intuition (Janssen & Helbeig, 2018; Ruppert et al., 2013).

To avoid the inherent pitfalls and dangers surrounding the use and misuse of data, LDT practitioners need clear, LDT specific guidelines and frameworks that include clear rules and processes for data collection, storage, and access. To ensure compatibility and integration across different systems and platforms, they need technical standards and interoperability that establish guidelines for data formats, communication protocols, and interfaces. To ensure transparency, trust and participation, they need mechanisms or models for sharing information and involving stakeholders that are democratic, accountable and subject to scrutiny - mechanisms which guarantee that the collection and use of personal data adhere to legal and ethical standards, align with privacy protection and reflects consent-based data sharing practices.

In 2021, the EU-funded DUET innovation project took an important initial step in meeting these requirements through the development of the first typology of an LDT governance model. (D'Hauwers et al., 2021). The model, as depicted below, examined data and ecosystem governance in relation to LDT end users and controllers within a digital twin exploitation process (Fig. 10.11):

**Fig. 10.11** Digital Urban Twin governance scenarios. (Adapted from D'Hauwers et al., 2021)

## Government-Controlled LDT

The government-controlled urban digital twin for policy-making is an inside-in model that utilises governmental data resources. It serves as a tool for government decision-making processes regarding policies, specifically focusing on areas like mobility. In this model, the government has full control over the data resource and uses the digital twin to inform policy decisions.

## Citizen-Engaging LDT

The citizen-engaging urban digital twin with government data is an inside-out model that facilitates interaction with the ecosystem while utilising governmental data resources. In this model, the government retains control over the data resources, and the digital twin serves as a platform for citizen participation. By sharing the digital twin outcomes with citizens, the government encourages involvement in decision-making processes.

## Ecosystem Driven LDT

The ecosystem driven urban digital twin is an outside-out model that draws from diverse data sources - including governmental data, company data, IoT data, and transportation data - and is used to drive open innovation. The ecosystem itself controls the data under this model.

### Ecosystem-Controlled LDT

The ecosystem-controlled urban digital twin for policy-making is an outside-in model which utilises data from within the ecosystem and provides opportunities for citizen participation in policy-making processes. Similar to the ecosystem driven model, the ecosystem-controlled model retains control over the data resources.

As the diagram reveals, governance varies across these four scenarios. A 'Gov Owned' LDT, for example, primarily focuses on bringing together useful data and tends to be an internal tool that fails under the government's jurisdiction. It is built using open source software to avoid vendor lock-in. Vienna's digital twin, which aims to enhance policy-making, reduce risks, and improve urban planning by integrating diverse data sources such as GIS, census, socioeconomic, energy consumption, and maintenance data, provides a strong example of this type of LDT (Lehner & Kordasch, 2020). An 'Ecosystem Driven' LDT shares many of the same traits as a 'Gov Owned' LDT but has an additional focus on managing an entire ecosystem.

Unlike both the 'Gov Owned' and 'Ecosystem Driven' LDT, the 'Citizen Engaging' LDT exhibits a higher level of openness as it is intentionally designed to be accessible to a wider community. This model encourages collaboration between the public and private sectors and is designed to promote the creation of new services. The model leverages public investment to build technical infrastructure, gather data and drive innovation. A prime example of this type of LDT is Helsinki's digital twin (City of Helsinki, 2024) which offers the Energy and Climate Atlas as an open web service and is designed to benefit housing companies, property developers, solar panel manufacturers, and citizens.

The 'Ecosystem Driven' LDT is the most decentralised model. Here, costs are shared among participants, and the ecosystem, rather than a city, drives the initiative, implementation, and management. While true examples of an 'Ecosystem LDT' are scarce initiatives like the EU's Data Governance Act (European Parliament and Council, 2022), Gaia-X (2023), and EIF4SCC (European Commission, 2023) represent early harbingers of open, interoperable LDT ecosystems.

Finally, an 'Ecosystem Owned' LDT is by far the most decentralised. The model shares data and infrastructure with the local administration but limits access to policymakers. While these types of LDTs are in the early stages, Örebro's efforts to create a linked data ecosystem demonstrate progress in this direction, particularly in relation to the leveraging of sensor data for urban improvement.

Because LDT models serve distinct purposes, they differ in terms of control and accessibility. 'Gov Owned' and 'Ecosystem Owned' LDTs, for example, primarily serve policy-making within the government. 'Citizen Engaging' and 'Ecosystem Driven' LDTs, on the other hand, are open to wider communities and democratic participation. These models are not exclusive, however. Models can coexist and complement each other, leaving cities to adopt a number of different types of LDTs, each serving a distinct purpose. At the end of the day, the choice of the LDT model depends on local needs, priorities, data requirements, and desired maturity levels.

## 10.3 Conclusion

As we have seen throughout this chapter, research and implementation in the realm of Local Digital Twins (LDTs) in the public sector is at a nascent stage. Insights into major areas like scalability and sustainability remain thin. Empirical data on use-case-based challenges and benefits has yet to reach critical mass. Implementation roadmaps, decision frameworks and governance models have only recently begun to emerge. As a result, despite and, in certain instances, because of the rapid onset of new technologies like Artificial Intelligence (AI), LDT implementation remains a bespoke, resource-intensive and often risky endeavour which demands substantial infrastructure, computing power and multidisciplinary expertise.

Encouragingly, a growing number of innovative use cases from cities around the world have begun to provide the basis for the development of foundational principles and high-level maturity models for LDTs. Nevertheless, the absence of a mature, standardised governance framework for creating and interconnecting LDTs continues to hamper progress and adoption at scale. To fully harness the positive potential of digital twin technology, even stronger collaboration between researchers, civil servants, technologists, and policymakers is urgently needed to better understand the evolving human motivations political and policy drivers underpinning LDTs. Further work is likewise needed to advance the foundational technologies underlying digital twin development, especially when it comes to delivering interoperability, safeguarding data and implementing trusted and transparent governance protocols.

There is no doubt that the path ahead for LDT adoption is challenging and unclear, particularly in the light of the rapid pace of AI driven change. Nevertheless, by working together across bureaucratic and geographic silos and carefully balancing technical innovation against human-centred priorities, today's LDT pioneers have an unparalleled opportunity to ensure that new and emerging digital twin capabilities are harnessed to deliver public sector value at scale.

## References

ABI Research. (2021, July). Urban planning and digital twins (AN-5416). *ABI Research*. https://www.abiresearch.com/market-research/product/7779044-urban-planning-and-digital-twins/

ARUP. (2021, November). Digital twin towards a meaningful framework. *ARUP*. https://www.arup.com/perspectives/publications/research/section/digital-twin-towards-a-meaningful-framework

Aquatech. (2019, December). Valencia: Sun, sea and digital twins. *Aquatech*. https://www.aquatechtrade.com/news/utilities/goaigua-digital-twin-valencia/

Bentley Expert. (2020). Success story | City of Helsinki expands digitalization with city-wide digital twin. *Virtuosity*. https://blog.virtuosity.com/success-story-helsinki-expands-digitalization-with-digital-twin

Capgemini Research Institute. (2022a). Digital twins: Adding intelligence to the real world. *Cap Gemini*. https://www.capgemini.com/gb-en/wp-content/uploads/sites/5/2022/11/DigitalTwins_adding-intelligence-to-the-real-world.pdf

Capgemini Research Institute. (2022b, June). All signs point to a 'growing appetite' for digital twins: Report. *Smart Cities Dive*. https://www.smartcitiesdive.com/news/digital-twin-smart-cities-sustainability-capgemini-report/624980/
Centre for Digital Built Britain. (2018). The Gemini principles. *Centre for Digital Built Britain*. https://www.cdbb.cam.ac.uk/system/files/documents/TheGeminiPrinciples.pdf
Chuncheng, L., & Tian, Y. (2023). Recognition of digital twin city from the perspective of complex system theory: Lessons from Chinese practice. *Journal of Urban Management, 12*(2), 182–192, ISSN 2226-5856. https://doi.org/10.1016/j.jum.2023.04.001
City of Helsinki. (2024). Helsinki 3D. *City of Helsinki*. https://www.hel.fi/en/decision-making/information-on-helsinki/maps-and-geospatial-data/helsinki-3d
Coenen, T., et al. (2021). Open urban digital twins—Insights in the current state of play. In *Sustainability: Smart cities, city dashboards, planning and evaluation of urban performances* (Vol. 12(6)). iMec. https://www.imec.be/sites/default/files/inline-files/Urban%20Digital%20Twins_Paper.pdf
Conejos, P., et al. (2019, September). Development and use of a digital twin for water supply and distribution network of Valencia (Spain). In *International computing & control for the water industry conference* (vol. 17th(1–4)). https://www.researchgate.net/publication/340236600_Development_and_Use_of_a_Digital_Twin_for_the_Water_Supply_and_Distribution_Network_of_Valencia_Spain
CoMoUK. (2021). Shared mobility and a car-free Centre in Ghent—A people focussed approach. *CoMoUK*. https://www.como.org.uk/documents/comouk-mobility-hubs-ghent-case-study
Dembski, F., et al. (2020). Urban digital twins for smart cities and citizens: The case study of Herrenberg, Germany. In *Sustainability: Smart cities, city dashboards, planning and evaluation of urban performances* (Vol. 12(6)). MDPI. https://www.mdpi.com/2071-1050/12/6/2307/htm
D'Hauwers, R., Walravens, N., & Ballon, P. (2021). From an inside-in towards an outside-out urban digital twin: Business models and implementation challenges. *ISPRS Annals of the Photogrammetry, Remote Sensing and Spatial Information Sciences, VIII-4/W1-2021*, 25–32. https://doi.org/10.5194/isprs-annals-VIII-4-W1-2021-25-2021
DUET and URBANAGE Consortium. (n.d.). URBAN DIGITAL TWIN - Change the way you see your city and decide better! *Urban Digital Twin*. https://citytwin.eu/
Environment and Energy Leader. (2024, March). EU parliament approves landmark AI act setting the stage for ethical and sustainable AI innovation. *Environment and Energy Leader*. EU. https://www.environmentenergyleader.com/2024/03/eu-parliament-approves-landmark-ai-act-setting-the-stage-for-ethical-and-sustainable-ai-innovation/
European Commission. (2023, March). EIF4SCC for smart cities & communities—Proposal for a European interoperability framework for smart cities and communities. *Interoperable Europe*. https://joinup.ec.europa.eu/collection/nifo-national-interoperability-framework-observatory/document/proposal-european-interoperability-framework-smart-cities-and-communities-eif4scc
European Parliament. (2024, March). *The EU artificial intelligence act—Up-to-date developments and analyses of the EU AI Act*. https://artificialintelligenceact.eu/
Ford, D. N., & Wolf, C. M.. (2020, April). Smart cities with digital twin systems for disaster management. *Journal of Management in Engineering, 36*. Special Collection on Engineering Smarter Cities with Smart City Digital Twins. ASCE Library. https://ascelibrary.org/doi/full/10.1061/%28ASCE%29ME.1943-5479.0000779
Future Digital Twin. (2023, April). Moving the conversation on digital twin forward. *LinkedIn*. https://www.linkedin.com/pulse/moving-conversation-digital-twin-forward-future-digital-twin/
GlobalData. (2023, January). Digital twin market size, share, trends and analysis by region, product and service (service and software), vertical (manufacturing, construction, defense, medical devices and pharmaceutical, energy, utilities, transportation and logistics, and others … *GlobalData*. https://www.globaldata.com/store/report/digital-twin-market-analysis/
GOV.UK. (2023, November). Research and analysis—RTA: Digital twins. *Gov.uk*. https://www.gov.uk/government/publications/rapid-technology-assessment-digital-twins/rta-digital-twins

Grieves, M. (2006). *Product lifecycle management: Driving the next generation of lean thinking by Michael Grieves*. McGraw-Hill.

Grynbaum, M. M., & Mac, R. (2023, December). The times sues OpenAI and Microsoft over A.I. Use of copyrighted work. *The New York Times*. https://www.nytimes.com/2023/12/27/business/media/new-york-times-open-ai-microsoft-lawsuit.html

Hayes, S. (2012, March). Digital twin toolkit - Public resources - DT hub community. *Digital Twin Hub*. https://digitaltwinhub.co.uk/files/file/62-digital-twin-toolkit/. https://www.digitalurbanttwins.com/post/duet-s-digital-twin-maturity-model-supports-cities-in-their-digital-transformation

JTC. (2022, September). Open digital platform: The digital backbone of Punggol Digital District. *JTC*. https://estates.jtc.gov.sg/pdd/stories/open-digital-platform-the-digital-backbone-of-pdd

Koetse, M. (2024, January). In the race for AI supremacy China and the UA are travelling on different tracks. *The Guardian*. https://www.theguardian.com/world/2024/jan/09/in-the-race-for-ai-supremacy-china-and-the-us-are-travelling-on-entirely-different-tracks

Kogut, P. (2022, November). *DUET's digital twin maturity model supports cities in their digital transformation*. DUET Project. https://www.digitalurbantwins.com/post/duet-s-digital-twin-maturity-model-supports-cities-in-their-digital-transformation

Larsen, B. C. (2022, December). *The geopolitics of AI and the rise of digital sovereignty*. Brookings Institute. https://www.brookings.edu/articles/the-geopolitics-of-ai-and-the-rise-of-digital-sovereignty

Lei, B., et al. (2023). Challenges of urban digital twins: A systematic review and a Delphi expert survey. *Automation in Construction, 147*. Science Direct, 104716. https://doi.org/10.1016/j.autcon.2022.104716

Living-in.eu. (n.d.). The European way of digital transformation in cities and communities. *Living-in.Eu*. https://living-in.eu/

Lehner, H., & Kordasch, S. L. (2020). Digital geoTwin Vienna. *Cultural Heritage and New Technologies*. https://www.chnt.at/wp-content/uploads/Digital-geoTwin-Vienna.pdf

Janssen, M., & Helbeig, N. (2018). Innovating and changing the policy-cycle: Policy-makers be prepared! *Government Information Quarterly, 35*(4), S99–S105. https://doi.org/10.1016/j.giq.2015.11.009

Matthews, D. (2023, December). AI act agreement gets mixed reaction from European tech. *Science Business*. https://sciencebusiness.net/news/ai/ai-act-agreement-gets-mixed-reaction-european-tech

Nochta, T., et al. (2021). A socio-technical perspective on urban analytics: The case of city-scale digital twins. *Journal of Urban Technology, 28*(1–2), 263–287. Routledge Taylor & Francis. https://doi.org/10.1080/10630732.2020.1798177

Nolan, B. (2024). Sergey Brin says Google 'definitely messed up' after its Gemini chatbot caused a firestorm. He has a lot riding on its success — Or failure. *Business Insider*. https://www.businessinsider.com/google-sergey-brin-gemini-definitely-messed-up-images-ai-model-2024-3

OASC. (2024). Minimal interoperability mechanisms—MIMs. *Open Agile Smart Cities*. https://oascities.org/minimal-interoperability-mechanisms/

Poon, Y. X. (2021, May). *How a Philippines city uses digital twins for disaster recovery*. GovInsider. https://govinsider.asia/intl-en/article/cauayan-graffiquo-how-a-philippines-city-uses-digital-twins-for-disaster-recovery

Raes, L. (2022, June). *Additional report on request of the EC*. Project Deliverable. DUET. https://www.digitalurbantwins.com/_files/ugd/a245c2_eedcd4b452124524a59c41ee4683c135.pdf

Raes, L., et al. (2022). Local digital twins: Optimising data, shaping policies, transforming lives. Policy Brief. *Zenodo*. https://zenodo.org/record/7386127#.Y4icpXZBxhE

Ramu, S. P., Boopalan, P., Pham, Q.-V., Maddikunta, P. K. R., Huynh-The, T., Alazab, M., Nguyen, T. T., & Gadekallu, T. R. (2022). Federated learning enabled digital twins for smart cities: Concepts, recent advances, and future directions. *Sustainable Cities and Society, 79*, 103663. https://doi.org/10.1016/j.scs.2021.103663

Regulation (EU) 2016/679 of the European Parliament and of the Council of 27 April 2016 on the Protection of Natural Persons with Regard to the Processing of Personal Data and on the Free Movement of Such Data, and Repealing Directive 95/46/EC (General Data Protection

Regulation) (Text with EEA Relevance), Pub. L. No. EU 2016/679, EUR-Lex (2016). https://eur-lex.europa.eu/eli/reg/2016/679/oj

Regulation (EU) 2022/868 of the European Parliament and of the Council of 30 May 2022 on European Data Governance and Amending Regulation (EU) 2018/1724 (Data Governance Act) (Text with EEA Relevance), Pub. L. No. EU 2022/868, EUR-Lex (2022). http://data.europa.eu/eli/reg/2022/868/oj

Ruppert, T., Bernard, J., & Kohlhammer, J. (2013). Bridging knowledge gaps in policy analysis with information visualization. In *Electronic government and electronic participation—Joint proceedings of ongoing research of IFIP EGOV and IFIP ePart 2022* (pp. 92–103). Gesellschaft für Informatik e.V.

Ruston McAleer, S., McAleer, M., & Kogut, P. (2021, September). Forging the future of responsive cities through local digital twins. *ERCIM News*. https://ercim-news.ercim.eu/en127/special/forging-the-future-of-responsive-cities-through-local-digital-twins

Sagar, M. (2020). Punggol digital district powered by first-of-its-kind open digital platform. *OpenGov Asia*. https://opengovasia.com/punggol-digital-district-powered-by-first-of-its-kind-open-digital-platform/. Accessed 7 February 2023.

Schrotter, G., & Hürzeler, C. (2020). The digital twin of the City of Zurich for urban planning. *PFG—Journal of Photogrammetry, Remote Sensing and Geoinformation Science, 88*, 99–112. Springer. https://doi.org/10.1007/s41064-020-00092-2

Singh, M. (2024, March). India reverses AI stance, requires government approval for model launches. *Tech Crunch*. https://techcrunch.com/2024/03/03/india-reverses-ai-stance-requires-government-approval-for-model-launches/?guccounter=1&guce_referrer=aHR0cHM6Ly93d3cuZ29vZ2xlLmNvbS8&guce_referrer_sig=AQAAANRhnB6yO3jWQ_6GdXvs_ZGQ58TPXrkJzMoYfB0ePj8vFkFRShwH8R1syKxP6M9MEJhwsX3ztdO-jU-JHXlSBF9901uEb5KT_GveNnNtAXxwe_5b5rsePCj7flCK4dfcJLTC1wE-plyGPamBk_QbUNe1bjfO9PheKjk7-eEiklYc

Stadt Zurich. (2022). 3D-Stadtmodell. *Stadt Zürich*. https://www.stadt-zuerich.ch/ted/de/index/geoz/geodaten_u_plaene/3d_stadtmodell.html

URBANAGE consortium. (n.d.). *URBANAGE - Plan Better*. https://www.urbanage.eu/

Veeckman, C., Jedlička, K., De Paepe, D., Kozhukh, D., Kafka, Š., Colpaert, P., & Čerba, O. (2017). Geodata interoperability and harmonization in transport: A case study of open transport net. *Open Geospatial Data, Software and Standards, 2*(1), 3. https://doi.org/10.1186/s40965-017-0015-6

Wegner, P. (2020, September). The top 10 Smart City use cases that are being prioritized now. *IOT Analaytics*. https://iot-analytics.com/top-10-smart-city-use-cases-prioritized-now/#:~:text=IoT%20Analytics%20published%20a%20comprehensive,monitoring%2C%20and%20water%20level%20monitoring

# Chapter 11
# Rights and Responsibilities: Legal and Ethical Considerations in Adopting Local Digital Twin Technology

**Francesco Mureddu, Alessandro Paciaroni, Tomáš Pavelka, Annabel Pemberton, and Luca Alessandro Remotti**

## Contents



## 11.1 Introduction

Studying the consequences of legal, ethical, and transparency frameworks related to digital twins is a new domain expected to gain increasing importance due to the growing complexity and variety of digital twin systems. This focus is especially

---

F. Mureddu (✉) · A. Paciaroni
The Lisbon Council, Brussels, Belgium
e-mail: francesco.mureddu@lisboncouncil.net

T. Pavelka
Dentons, Prague, Czech Republic
e-mail: tomas.pavelka@cantab.net

A. Pemberton
Sparring, Prague, Czech Republic
e-mail: annabel@lawschool2-0.com

L. A. Remotti
DataPower Srl, Cagliari, Italy



L. Raes et al. (eds.), *Decide Better*,
https://doi.org/10.1007/978-3-031-81451-8_11

needed with the rise of fully automated digital twin decision-based processes, as the integration of disruptive technologies like Artificial Intelligence (AI) and Machine Learning (ML) can lead to less predictable and explainable outcomes.

The European Commission (2021) formulated the Local Digital Twin (LDT) concept to emphasise EU values of openness, data ethics, privacy protection, transparency and sustainability. The impact of new technologies like AI, pre-processed data, and complex simulation modelling create new challenges to transparency and privacy protection. Van Der Aalst et al. (2021) stress the importance of human intelligence in Urban Digital Twins (UDTs) to balance the impact of new disruptive technologies like AI and ML. Al-Sehrawy et al. (2023) advocate a societal assessment framework to integrate broader social elements and views into a digital twin. Wang (2021) stresses the need for transparency in creating a smart city to support decision-making, while sensitive non-technical-entrepreneurial thinking related to smart cities and digital twins is needed. Wang and Burdon (2021) propose a framework of trustworthiness based on the ability, integrity, and benevolence to be applied to digital twin (automated) decision-making processes.

Suffia (2023) scrutinises how a proactive law approach based on "keeping humans in the loop" and "precautionary principles" can serve policymakers in their attempts to incorporate respect for rights and solidarity in the smart city. Suffia is especially concerned about the impact of real-time and predictive digital twins. The same author (Suffia, 2022) summarises the current ongoing discussions well by mentioning four critical points: protecting personal data, safeguarding ethical-constitutional elements, using open versus closed software, and following legal frameworks.

The above authors all emphasise the growing importance and interest in digital twins' ethical and legal consequences in the smart city field. This chapter will contribute to the ongoing discussion by sketching legal frameworks, underlining ethical aspects, and facilitating the application of ethics and (new) relevant legislation into practice via the gap analysis methodology. Because data and information management are key elements, alternative ways to manage LDT data and information are presented.

## 11.2 Legal and Ethical Challenges Presented by LDTs

The implementation of LDTs brings forth significant legal and ethical challenges that must be addressed to ensure their responsible use. Key issues include the protection of personal information, the development of robust privacy frameworks, and the ethical implications of data usage and algorithmic decision-making. This subsection explores these challenges, highlighting the need for comprehensive policies and ethical guidelines to govern LDT technologies.

### 11.2.1 LDT Legal Frameworks and Considerations

The regulatory approach to technology can be reduced to a dyad. On the one hand, some argue that there is a gap between existing regulations and a desired state. This group advocates for new regulations, for example, the AI Act in Europe (European Parliament and of the Council, 2021). On the other hand, there are those who lean more towards the laissez-faire approach. This group defends the role played by existing regulations, for instance, arguing that the General Data Protection Regulation (GDPR) (European Parliament and of the Council, 2016) already enforces control on data processors and the use of data in general and that the AI Act is superfluous.

LDTs are no different. The five domains covered in the European Union legal framework suitable for disruptive technologies are data protection, consumer protection, equality, AI, and digital markets (ETAPAS project).[1] The GDPR aims to safeguard citizens against misuse of personal data or breaches of their privacy. To achieve this, it puts into place a system of (i) notifications on the data gathered when accessing platforms online or buying a digital product or service and the purpose, (ii) constraints on the use and duration of storage of such data, (iii) bans on full automation in decision-making and (iv) rights to delete all the data about a person or inquire on its use. Consequently, the GDPR is a solid foundation for safeguarding personal data.

Additionally, consumer protection aims to safeguard consumers from harm caused on the "side" of the product or service. This approach, however, excludes products and services that do not have a physical component, which is one of the reasons why the regulator proposed the AI Act in the first place. This regulation is specific to AI and is challenging policymakers to find a suitable balance between innovation and fundamental rights. It proves how difficult it is to disentangle the complex value chain behind AI products and services, and also points to the importance of safeguarding the European industry, whose backbone is small and medium enterprises. In this aspect, the Digital Market Act (European Parliament and of the Council. Regulation, 2022b) recently entered into force as the European Union's attempt to regulate online markets. Finally, regarding the most delicate and fundamental ethical risks, the European treaties and secondary law safeguard equality in employment and in other spheres.

These regulatory frameworks also define the playing field for LDTs, both for public and private organisations that aim to design and implement them. However, some may argue that this does not fit the specific purpose. A case in point is Barcelona, where stakeholders have begun a collaboration to define the use of personal data in the context of the smart city. The idea proposed so far aims to establish

[1] Ethical Technology Adoption in Public Administration Services (ETAPAS), EU H2020 project, https://cordis.europa.eu/project/id/101004594/es

the so-called data commons, built on the concept of commons,[2] which is well-known to economists. This approach is also echoed in the COMPAIR[3] European project, where open Citizen Science data is used as input for an LDT to fill the gap between sparse high-end measurement data and dense local information with lower reliability. More like creative commons than common goods, data commons would be a framework to set a citizen-centric approach to the use of personal data that revolves around the rights given to data by the owner (Monge et al., 2022). This approach to governing data acknowledges individual's ownership of their data, allowing them to set boundaries on its use and sharing. It is substantially aligned with the GDPR provision on the proportionality of the use of personal data according to the consent given by the data owner. However, data commons take a step back and approach the issue in a more citizen-centric way whereby people are not only asked for consent but consulted beforehand and involved in the decision-making process regarding the use of their data.

**Use of Personal Information**

An LDT consists of creating a digital copy of a living city. Citizens are an integral part of the city, making their data an integral part of a digital twin. Using personal data is a conundrum that policymakers are addressing but not necessarily disentangling. The collection of personal data already puts citizens' privacy at risk. Nonetheless, effective data governance may preserve citizens' privacy. This focus is arguably one of the cornerstones of trusted technology. The collection and use of personal data in a privacy-preserving manner may still cause harm. If data is aggregated to a certain level, such as a neighbourhood, and a minority mainly inhabits this neighbourhood, then aggregate data may also still prompt legitimate questions about the exposure given to a specific group of individuals, and raise issues about inherent bias and representation.

**Privacy Protection Issues**

Even with proper data governance in place, cybersecurity is still an issue. The improper sharing or use of data may result from criminal activity such as cyberattacks. LDTs offer business opportunities next to improved life conditions. These actions open up the system to malicious actors who seek to profit by stealing data or attempting to influence certain activities or spheres of the life of a city by illegal means. Cybersecurity must be a major priority for international organisations like the UN, European Union, NATO, as well as states and companies that handle personal data. Despite the growing awareness and effort, there is still a genuine risk that citizen's data is not always adequately safeguarded. The idea of a digital twin as a

[2] The commons is the cultural and natural resources accessible to all members of a society, including natural materials such as air, water, and a habitable Earth. These resources are held in common even when owned privately or publicly. Commons can also be understood as natural resources that groups of people (communities, user groups) manage for individual and collective benefit, https://commonslibrary.org/practising-commoning/

[3] Community Observation Measurement & Participation in AIR Science (COMPAIR), EU H2020 project, https://cordis.europa.eu/project/id/101036563

complex living environment, supporting private and public actors in collaborating on the design, implementation and operation of the twin, both in the real world and the digital one, makes the factual preservation of privacy extremely cumbersome.

## *11.2.2 LDT Ethical Aspects*

**Personal Services Versus Providing Personal Information**

Tailored services or products require information to be customised. This is a trivial consideration that bears significant implications for the ethics of digital twins (and digital transformation in general). The equation that sees citizens sharing personal data to receive personalised services seems to work in as much as it stays in a vacuum. Personalised services must be proactive. Suppose a personalised service always includes a certain extent of proactiveness on the side of the provider. In that case, it may be suggesting a certain option based on the preferences of the individual or offering a certain provision based on habits or other parameters.

For instance, the so-called proactive service delivery is nothing more than a highly personalised (proactive) delivery of services based on data already stored by a public authority. An LDT can use personal data to provide (proactive) services to groups like older adults, as demonstrated by the URBANAGE project,[4] which proposed innocuous services like finding shelters in their neighbourhood during hot summer days. Another example is a notification service that suggests applying for childcare bonuses or kindergarten places to parents, a service entirely based on the population registry. Whilst there are surely personalised services that one may desire, there are indeed services that elicit further considerations. How far should personalisation go in areas like health, for example? Is it ethical to try to nudge a particular individual into different habits or other choices, such as moving to a neighbourhood with better air quality if the person is at risk for respiratory diseases? Is it ethical to show only certain routes or transport options to a person who prefers a sedentary lifestyle but suffers from medical conditions related to that?

The situation is perhaps even more complex as inequality and fairness also make their way into the consideration of LDTs. It is therefore important to acknowledge that there is a digital divide between age groups, ethnicities, and geographical areas (Cullen, 2001). Despite this being a priority in political agendas, the gap still needs to be closed. Therefore, acknowledging that the picture depicted by the digital twin is a relative representation of reality is of utmost importance for positive societal development.

**Digital Technologies and Supervision**

Arguably, the first risk associated with the use of digital technologies is dehumanisation. This risk covers several aspects, such as the replacement of human

[4] Enhanced URBAN planning for AGE-friendly cities through disruptive technologies (URBANAGE), EU H2020 project, https://cordis.europa.eu/project/id/101004590

supervision in the provision of services and agency and accountability thereof. The root of the problem is that wrongdoing or a simple error may be complex to trace back to the real origin. Somewhere between the lack of accountability and human oversight is another concern. An automated decision based on interpretations that can't be repeated or which are based on a false interpretation of data may lead to the failure to obtain a right or benefit. The absence of humans in service provision is tied to the effect of digitalisation on certain groups. Older adults may be isolated and left behind, putting local governments in the position of having to manage a trade-off between improved services and increased inequality.

The risks associated with the absence of a human in control are projected into risks of accountability. It is vital to underline that this is the origin of some other risks linked to it. Indeed, the lack of accountability for decisions made by machines exacerbates the issue of transparency. At the risk of simplifying a complex matter, administrative procedures and policy-making is often cumbersome. Rarely can a single citizen point the finger at the person who decided what exactly. However, here lies the difference, a technical system will record that someone is eventually responsible for a decision.

The absence of human supervision over the specific decision-making processes and the opaque system of responsibility make risks associated with the misuse or disuse of data more dangerous. The risk of bias is probably the most spoken of. Ethnic and gender biases are also well-known, and people who take an optimistic stance look for them and try to address them. But what about biases that have yet to be found? Additionally, representing a city on a screen is a giant leap from reality, even though it is a digital twin. There is the possibility that hidden agendas or unqualified profiles misinterpret the information or misrepresent certain insights regardless of biases.

**Digital Twin and Artificial Intelligence Legislation**

Digital twins for decision support are increasingly being enhanced with AI. Until today, the most significant contribution of AI in an LDT context has been in digital imaging and image interpretation of aerial photographs and terrain data instead of decision support. The reason is mainly because the use of AI in simulation modelling is in its early phase. Most current relevant smart city models, including air quality, noise, traffic, and flooding models, are algorithm-based without a self-learning dimension. It is expected that future LDTs will be more and more affected by AI components like AI-generated datasets, AI-based simulation models and AI-based decision support systems (Chap. 9).

The OECD defines an AI system as "a machine-based system that, for explicit or implicit objectives, infers, from the input it receives, how to generate outputs such as predictions, content, recommendations, or decisions that can influence physical or virtual environments. Different AI systems vary in their levels of autonomy and adaptiveness after deployment." (Grobelnik et al., 2024).

In the US, the Biden administration launched in 2023 an Executive Order on the Safe, Secure, and Trustworthy Development and Use of Artificial Intelligence (White House, 2023) that wants to ensure that AI systems in government are designed and used in ways that respect human rights and avoid harm.

In 2024, the European Union went further. It was the first to adopt an ambitious AI Act (European Parliament and Council, 2021) through which the EU aims to create a regulatory and ethical framework for the use of AI in the European Union. The first steps towards the AI Act were taken in April 2019, when the EU's own High-Level Expert Group on AI published the Ethics Guidelines for Trustworthy AI, proposing seven essential requirements aligned wit`h fundamental rights. These include human agency and oversight, technical robustness and safety, privacy and data governance, transparency, diversity, non-discrimination and fairness, societal and environmental well-being, and accountability (European Commission, 2019; Arents & Vanderstraete, 2024).

The European AI Act uses a risk-based approach. It represents an innovative attempt to tailor obligations and oversight requirements to potential material harms of AI instead of imposing complete bans on particular AI techniques. In this manner, the EC hopes to continue stimulating positive innovation and competitiveness (Fig. 11.1).

Digital twins, as such, are not mentioned as specific application areas in the AI Act. When looking more closely at potential high-risk application areas, the management and operation of critical infrastructures, including, for example, transport infrastructure, is mentioned. Bi-directional digital twins require specific measures, especially if their AI controls bridges, locks, traffic flows and other urban infrastructure and processes. The AI Act states that providers must implement comprehensive risk management systems and submit for conformity assessments verified by regulators who will ensure that mandatory requirements are fulfilled before approving the CE[5] marking that allows AI-enabled products market access.

[5] CE Mark, https://europa.eu/youreurope/business/product-requirements/labels-markings/ce-marking/

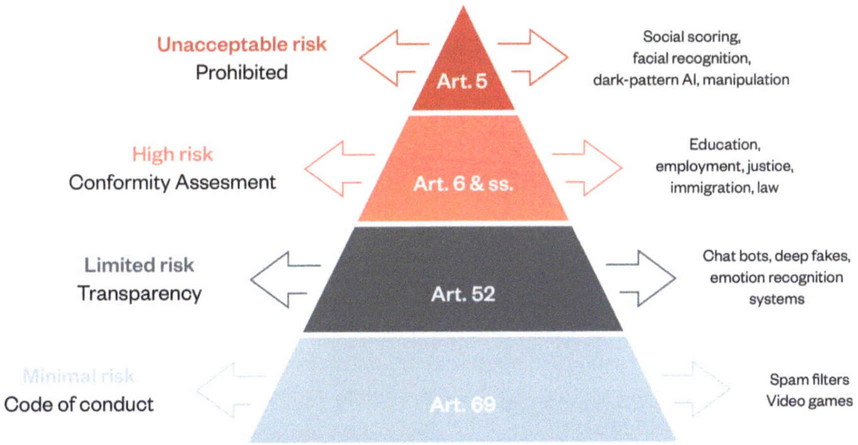


**Fig. 11.1** The Artificial Intelligence Act risk-based approach (Edwards, 2021)

Before launching a high-risk AI system on the EU market or putting it into service, a provider must subject the system to a conformity assessment. This approach will allow the provider to demonstrate that their system complies with the mandatory requirements for trustworthy AI (e.g., data quality, documentation and traceability, transparency, human oversight, accuracy, cybersecurity and robustness). This assessment must be repeated if the system or its purpose is substantially modified. Meeting these mandatory requirements before market access presents a significant challenge for AI system providers.

Digital twins using AI fall under the AI-enabled applications in the minimal risk category. The AI act advises providing transparency, relying on non-binding codes of conduct. Because digital twins are typically government applications, adherence to a code of conduct based on the EU's High-Level AI Expert Group ethics guidelines is strongly advised.

However, the use of AI in decision support can have serious consequences; the risk of automated decision support is only mentioned in its relation to safety and public health (recital 47) and the administration of justice and democratic processes (recital 61). From an ethical and trust perspective, citizens may more readily accept automated decision-making if they are confident that the underlying algorithms are aligned with democratically defined rules, and know they can appeal these automated decisions anytime. The AI Act also mentions the need for AI literacy (recital 20). In the context of an LDT, this is an extension of the needed data literacy. The following section explains how ethical and legal measures can be structurally implemented into smart city applications, including digital twins.

## 11.3 Application of Ethics and Legislation in an LDT Context

The complexity of an LDT reflects its complex interaction with regulation. In particular, the principles on which rules are built, encompassing ethics and the rules forming legislation, create a complex interplay with digital twins used for evidence-informed decision-making based on personal data, complex algorithms and AI-based simulation models.

### *11.3.1 Ethics*

A discussion of regulations applicable to smart cities, including digital twins, would only be complete with reference to ethical requirements and the gap between ethics and the current law. In practice, legal requirements and ethics work together in two ways. The first is that ethics guide individual actors to a "right" outcome, while the law provides a specific course to execute such actions. The second is the legal delegation of ethical decision-making to specific actors (such as healthcare practitioners).[6]

There are at least three concurrent principles that shape that boundary and relationship:

- Ethical principles provide the foundations for the creation of legal requirements;
- No solution can be considered ethical unless it also meets the applicable (minimum) legal requirements.[7] In other words, there are limited grounds to argue that a solution which fails to meet the minimum legal requirements should nevertheless be allowed because it serves a particular ethical purpose;
- Legal requirements set the minimum standard, while ethics can be more aspirational and seek to impose a higher or the maximum standard. In other words, just because a solution is legal does not mean that it is the right thing to do.

A good example and imminent challenge is posed by AI-driven and automated (model-based) decision systems as part of an LDT. These decision systems are often constituents of various data models and policy-ready-data-as-a-service solutions, which are becoming an indispensable part of smart cities' decision-making processes. EU institutions seek to involve stakeholders in creating dedicated codes of ethics for their use. The initiative aims to develop codes of ethics not only for public authorities but also for private companies (which may be far more advanced and experienced in the use of AI systems). LDT adopters should consider the following principles suggested by the private sector.

- AI products should reflect an "invented for life" ethos or a "responsible AI" approach, which combines a quest for innovation with a sense of social responsibility;
- AI decisions that affect people should not be made without a human arbiter. Instead, AI should be a tool for people;
- Develop safe, robust, and explainable AI products which encompass mechanisms to prevent discrimination and ensure transparency;
- Trust is one of the fundamental values. Only trustworthy AI products should be developed and put into use.

These considerations may also apply to software and data models, which, albeit not AI in the strict sense (because they may lack the machine-learning aspect), may nevertheless involve elements of automated decision-making and thus suffer from similar pitfalls such as opacity or the black-box problem, inherent bias, or lack of human oversight.

[6] The Covid-19 pandemic has raised the public awareness of how the ethical principles-based decision making by healthcare service providers works in practice when it comes to patients' selection, prioritisation, or repurposing of medical resources.

[7] This follows from the assumption that at least in the European area, constitutional norms should nowadays guarantee that no laws manifestly in breach of fundamental ethical requirements can be adopted or would survive judicial review. Contrast with historical examples such as the antisemitic and racist Nuremberg Laws of 1935.

AI systems are on the cutting edge of ethical conundrums today, but the ethical requirements permeate the whole range of other issues tackled by smart cities daily, often intertwined with complex legal regulations. Examples include personal data processing (privacy), safety of systems (Internet of Things (IoT) networks and cybersecurity), understanding of the data (issue of data quality, transparency) and sharing the data and making it available for further use in the ever-expanding data economy. Using the privacy-data regulation as an example, this subchapter seeks to illustrate how the interplay between law and ethics works to achieve desirable results and help make policymakers' processes more robust, transparent and accountable. In conclusion, this subchapter explains how the legal-ethical approach to privacy and data governance should integrate into the emerging concept of data spaces as the cornerstone of Europe's digital economy and governance.

### *11.3.2 Regulation*

While ethics set the tone and course of action, the law provides the framework and specifics for the execution. The EU data governance legal landscape encompasses several pieces of legislation, the most important among which are the General Data Protection Regulation (GDPR), the Regulation on the Free Flow of Non-Personal Data (European Parliament and of the Council, 2018) and the ePrivacy Directive (European Parliament and of the Council, 2002) for EU institutions and bodies. This framework is to be complemented by the ePrivacy Regulation, which is currently pending in the legislative process.

### *11.3.3 Personal Data Processing*

Policymakers, system designers, data analysts, and other experts involved in LDT should distinguish between personal and non-personal data to ensure compliance. However, before exploring this section, it is important to note that in most cases, anonymised data is sufficient for smart city use.

For example, ask the upstream data provider, who best understands the data, to anonymise the data before it is supplied. Furthermore, where data is anonymised or pseudonymised, do not proactively take steps to re-identify the data and link the data to individual persons. The following techniques and procedures, for example, should be avoided unless the goal is to re-identify otherwise anonymous or pseudonymised data:

- *Singling out:* This corresponds to the possibility of isolating some or all records which identify an individual in the dataset;
- *Linkability:* This is the ability to link at least two records concerning the same data subject or a group of data subjects (either in the same database or in two

different databases). If an attacker can establish (e.g., by means of correlation analysis) that two records are assigned to the same group of individuals but cannot single out individuals in this group, the technique provides resistance against "singling out" but not against linkability;
- *Inference:* This is the possibility to deduce, with significant probability, the value of an attribute from the values of a set of other attributes.

If the risk of re-identification materialises on a given dataset, take all reasonable steps, seek appropriate expert advice and apply all relevant professional standards to mitigate the risk of a privacy breach and further unlawful personal data processing. LDTs are data-rich applications that potentially combine a multitude of (linked) spatial and personal data. Digital twins bear a risk of re-identification, and it is essential to rule out that the dataset can lead to tracing an individual or family when combined with other data. Data analysts and experts have a big responsibility. A combination of skills from multiple persons (the four-eyes principle) is vital to rule out any problems.

In some circumstances, it is strictly necessary to the task and proportionate to meet the predefined purpose of the activity to use personal data. When the personal data of individuals residing in the EU is implicated in a use case, architects of smart cities must be aware of the GDPR.

The GDPR represents the milestone of EU data protection, which lays down the general principles, rules, and procedures to be followed by any actors involved in personal data processing (thereby including collection, storage, use, re-use, or sharing of personal data) related to individuals residing in the EU. Notably, the principle of free movement of personal data, under which the free flow of personal data within the EU shall neither be restricted nor prohibited, is laid down under Art. 1(3) thereof. In terms of material scope, Art. 2(1) provides that the Regulation applies to the processing of personal data wholly or partly by automated means. It is thus relevant in terms of smart city activities, where big data is at stake. The GDPR clarifies what constitutes personal data, identifies the main actors, and sets out their rights and obligations. It lays down rules and procedures for processing personal data.

In particular, the GDPR lays down six principles about the processing of personal data:

- *Lawfulness, fairness and transparency*: Personal data must be processed lawfully and transparently, ensuring fairness towards the individuals whose personal data is being processed;
- *Purpose limitation*: There must be specific purposes for processing the data, and the company/organisation must indicate those purposes to individuals when collecting their personal data. A company/organisation cannot simply collect personal data for undefined purposes and further use the personal data for other purposes that are not compatible with the original purpose, except for certain narrow circumstances;
- *Data minimisation*: The company/organisation may collect and process only personal data to the extent that is necessary to fulfil that purpose;

- *Accuracy*: The company/organisation must ensure personal data is accurate and up-to-date, having regard to the purposes for which it is processed, and rectify the data where it is not;
- *Storage limitation*: The company/organisation must ensure that personal data is stored for no longer than necessary for the purposes for which it was collected;
- *Integrity and confidentiality*: The company/organisation must install appropriate technical and organisational safeguards that ensure the security of personal data, including protection against unauthorised or unlawful processing and accidental loss, destruction or damage, using appropriate technology. In particular, it is key to ensure data security and use trusted third-party service providers (e.g., approved by the future European Union Cybersecurity Certification Scheme on Cloud Services (EUCS)).

While drafted with the interest of the free flow of data at heart, as described above, data protection legislation has evolved to become more centred around the individual. While granting more protection to individuals, this gives rise to a conflict of interest between organisations and individuals; the former wishing to leverage citizen's data to improve existing systems and the latter looking to safeguard their personal information. However, a balance can be struck. Privacy by design explores the intersection between the law protecting the interests of EU citizens and the practicalities of the systems that cities wish to create. In practice, this means smart city systems must follow the principles set by the GDPR listed above and comply with all legal requirements regarding using, acquiring, processing or storing personal data. Smart city systems, including digital twins, should therefore ensure that they follow the above principles when creating systems that process personal data. Practical guidance to ensure solutions are compliant can be found at the end of this section.

### 11.3.4 Governance of Non-personal Data

Legislation, however, continues into the realm of non-personal data. In November 2018, the European Parliament and the Council adopted the "Free Flow of Non-Personal Data Regulation" to further facilitate the cross-border exchange of data and boost the data economy. This instrument is based on the principle of free flow of non-personal data. Under this principle, Member States are prohibited from imposing requirements on where data should be localised in all cases unless such requirements are proportionate and duly justified by public security. On top of this, Member States have to communicate any data localisation restrictions to the European Commission on a single online information point readily available for users and service providers. In addition, the Regulation also lays down the principle of data availability, rendering competent authorities able to access data for supervisory control wherever it is stored or processed in the EU. Finally, the Regulation enshrines the principle of data portability, which allows users to port data between cloud service providers. This approach encourages cloud service providers and cloud users to jointly develop codes of conduct based on the principles of transparency and openness, making it easier to switch between cloud service providers.

Furthermore, the European Data Act (European Parliament and of the Council, 2023) and the Data Governance Act (European Parliament and of the Council, 2022a) aim to facilitate the use of non-personal data by parties and fully utilise the dataset's potential. The proposal's impact will have two likely effects on data usage by smart cities. The first will be that consumers will be able to access non-personal data generated through the use of their device and request the sharing of this data with third parties that can provide value-added services. In practice, this could mean broadening the right to data portability under the GDPR beyond the scope of personal data, allowing consumers also to access non-personal data generated by products they use. For smart cities, this means allowing citizens residing in the EU open access to non-personal data and personal data. On the flip side, the proposal may benefit smart cities by making datasets for machine learning more accessible, as service providers will have access to more non-personal data from other industries.

The Free Flow of Non-Personal Data Regulation, the Data Governance Act and the Data Act Proposal principles can be extended to LDTs to maximise the re-use and portability of datasets between digital twins and increase the quality of simulations and decision outcomes.

### *11.3.5 Other (Non-data) Regulation*

Smart cities should also be aware of other emerging regulations that can impact the design and development of modelling, such as the Digital Markets Act (DMA) (European Parliament and Council, 2022b). Smart cities are advised to note two main consequences it may have on tackling several persistent issues. First, Article 5 of the DMA prohibits designated gatekeepers from requiring users to subscribe to any core platform services as a precondition for using the gatekeeper's cloud services, which should mitigate the concerns about alleged tying/bundling practices of the leading cloud firms. Second, Article 6 of the DMA provides, among others, an obligation of the gatekeepers to provide end users with effective data portability and real-time access to data provided for or generated in the context of the use of the relevant core platform service (such as cloud service). This approach may further help smart cities maximise value and flexibility in running their systems and services if they are using the services of companies that can be designated as gatekeepers (Amazon Web Services, Google, Microsoft Azure, etc.). The proposed Data Act may have similar implications for switching between cloud services and the promotion of interoperability and data transfers. In the frame of federated LDTs, it is essential that services can run on different cloud providers to ensure freedom of choice for every data, model, visualisation and system component provider.

Secondly, smart cities should closely follow the development of the European AI Act. The European Parliament seeks to protect individuals and entities from the potential harms of AI systems, ensuring clarity for enterprises. The Act proposes to achieve this by following a risk-based approach and banning discriminatory AI applications. Additionally, individuals will gain enhanced protections against the dangers of utilising "high-risk" systems, encompassing AI involved in health, safety, fundamental rights, environmental concerns, political campaign influences, and recommendation algorithms on social media platforms. Nevertheless, this will necessitate added disclosures and documentation for processing sensitive personal data which could fall within the remit of smart cities. Furthermore, smart cities should be aware of additional obligations that may arise when using foundational models or generative AI, such as proposed mandatory labelling. Smart cities that utilise a model developed in-house should also note that registration in the EU database is proposed to be a prerequisite before introducing their models to the EU market.

### *11.3.6 Future Regulation*

The proposed ePrivacy Regulation (European Parliament and of the Council, 2002) is expected to replace the ePrivacy Directive with added relevance for Smart Cities. The proposal is considered politically sensitive, and after the European Commission submitted a draft in early 2017, it has only very slowly progressed through the legislative process. However, in 2022, the Council of the EU, the European Parliament and the European Commission proceeded with trilogue negotiations about the final text of the ePrivacy Regulation after a hiatus. Expected to come into force after 2023, the ePrivacy Regulation aims—inter alia—to close specific application gaps of the ePrivacy Directive as regards the concept of electronic communication services and its inclusion of machine-to-machine communication services (M2M) and "IoT services", and to clarify the rules on use and storage of information on users' terminal equipment, such as mobile phones or connected vehicles, as well as regulate further types of data processing activities, such as use of helpful metadata for wider benefit. These elements are essential features of the IoT and large-scale data analysis and, thus, are likely to be highly relevant for smart cities and digital twins. The proposal is part of the EU's Digital Single Market Strategy (EU4Digital Facility, 2024), the overarching objective of which is to increase trust in and the security of digital services in the internal market.

## 11.4 Gap Analysis

The wide variety of LDT use cases and system components, including data, simulation models and visualisations, comes with ethical questions, dilemmas, and demands for legal compliance checks related to data protection and beyond. A gap analysis is a widely used and suitable tool for compliance checks that are also applicable to digital twins when considering the following two dimensions:

- The first dimension is related to specific vertical policy areas covered by the digital twin, such as urban planning, traffic, social services, education, etc;
- The second dimension is related to vertical and horizontal integration of LDT functions and datasets.

The first vertical dimension can already pose complex ethical and personal data protection problems. Problems linked to a single domain can be further amplified by creating a system integrating horizontal and vertical functions and datasets coordinated in the digital twin. Individual personal data, healthcare data, data on properties and real estate, traffic, and mobility data, including traffic and administrative offences, may be integrated—depending on the design and functions of the digital twins—in a single information system giving powerful disproportionate insights into e.g. a single household situation.

The integration of personal information into an LDT can be significant, with privacy and ethical implications largely dependent on the strategic setup and design of the urban area model. Effective data protection and addressing data-related ethical concerns are closely tied to the design of the digital twin, its functions, and the logical interconnections between the various datasets it uses.

Each LDT, therefore, requires the completion of a gap analysis to evaluate risks and potential threats, as well as the current state of compliance. The gap analysis will also specifically focus on the areas and "business lines" that need a careful assessment to correct organisational and risk management gaps to better serve the fundamental rights and freedoms of natural and legal persons.

### 11.4.1 Defining a GAP Analysis Framework

A well-designed and implemented gap analysis begins with the definition of the comprehensive framework of data capture, data flows, data processing and data combinations and then moves further to define the roadmap for implementing measurable correction measures. The gap analysis needs to design a comprehensive picture of the entire system and the subsystems handling specific areas to which specific services are delivered. The relevant topics include:

- Background and meta-system descriptions: An LDT can be considered a system of specialised subsystems which monitor the functions of the metropolitan area and support its operations;
- The mechanisms of operation, functions (data gathering, sensors, data processing, data storage and data transmission) and processes supported;
- Typologies of data and meta-data, clusters of data, data aggregates;
- Uses of data;
- Data protection and ethical standards to comply with;

- Assessment of human resources and of the organisation running and using the digital twin in the urban area;
- Policies and procedures: allocation of roles and responsibilities;
- Security of processing and risk management;
- Reviewing and updating processing;
- Awareness and training;
- Exercising rights and managing data breaches.

The completed gap analysis will support the definition of the road map to identify and implement the measures to ensure compliance with the set standards as well as continuous monitoring. The plan will define all actions to determine and measure:

- The state of processing mechanism and resilience of operations;
- The state of awareness, skills, training and focus of personnel;
- The level of compliance with personal data processing (including the right to be forgotten).

The gap analysis will also determine the critical point in business and organisational processes and the handling of personal data. Such critical points include:

- The supply chain;
- Data processing and data use authorisations;
- The rules to suppliers in relation to data protection and ethical policies;
- Mapping all the data processing performed;
- Instructing all the organisational units to carry out a "privacy check-up" of each mapped processing operation;
- The legal framework and, at the same time, determine the legal requirements to be complied with;
- Policies and procedures: allocation of roles and responsibilities;
- An action plan consisting of concrete actions to adapt policies and procedures to business objectives and regulatory requirements.

### *11.4.2 Security of Processing and Risk Management*

Once the comprehensive picture has been created, mitigating measures for risks can be defined. The result of the GAP analysis may suggest urgent measures in the context of security processing and avoiding imminent risks. Less urgent measures are best implemented as part of a well-documented roadmap and associated project management and follow-up. Analysis requires the verification and assessment of the security measures in place to protect the data flowing through the business processes of the LDT. The implementation of an appropriate ISMS (i.e., an Information Security Management System) is necessary to meet the requirements of data protection policies and ethical standards levels. These measures need to be implemented in the various areas of the LDT and in the system as a whole. Elements of an LDT oriented ISMS are:

- Anonymisation and pseudonymisation and personal data encryption;
- Confidentiality, integrity, availability and resilience of processing systems and services on a permanent basis;
- Restoration of the availability and access to personal data in the event of a physical or technical incident;
- Regular testing, verification and evaluation of the effectiveness of technical and organisational measures;
- User profiling, identification and authorisation measures;
- Measures for physical security, protection of data transmission, event logging, and system configuration.

Once the gap analysis is completed and the first set of urgent measures is taken, a road map must be drawn to ensure the adoption of technical and organisational measures in the medium term to achieve "structural" compliance with policies and requirements of data protection and ethical standards. The periodic review of the policy is integrated into the design to ensure that processes are aligned with the vision, mission, business objectives and regulatory framework of the LDTs.

## 11.5 Overcoming Ethical and Legal Gaps

While the exploration of the regulations above provides a framework for compliance, for practical purposes, smart cities can consult the following guidance measures when building and designing smart city solutions like LDTs.

**Measure: Understand Where You Are Acting as a Data Controller or Data Processor**

Pursuant to the GDPR, processing of personal data means any operation or set of operations which is performed on personal data or sets of personal data, whether or not by automated means, such as collection, recording, organisation, structuring, storage, adaptation or alteration, retrieval, consultation, use, disclosure by transmission, dissemination or otherwise making available, aligning or combining, restricting, erasing or destroying. Merely storing personal data in the cloud is thus perceived as personal data processing.

Based on data processing, cities, and by extension, government agencies, act as data controllers. This means they determine the purposes and methods of processing personal data, either alone or with others. If EU or EU Member State law specifies the purposes and methods, it may also define the data controller or criteria for its appointment.

A cloud service provider is considered a data processor, a natural or legal person, a public authority, agency or other body which processes personal data on behalf of the controller. All service sub-providers who provide cloud (or other data processing) services to the main cloud service provider are sub-processors, i.e. subjects processing personal data on behalf and under the responsibility of the data processor. Sub-processors are liable to only process data on the controller's instructions as shared through the processor. They may be liable for the failure to follow the instructions and safeguards they state to have in place. However, the data controller should be aware of all such sub processors (and consent to them beforehand, if agreed so with the data processor) at any moment of processing of the personal data, as the data controller is liable for how the personal data is processed.

Cities and government agencies, being data controllers, should be aware that they do not cease to be the data owners because they are using cloud service providers and storing the data on someone else's servers (data storage facilities). Pursuant to the GDPR, if the data processor infringes the GDPR by determining the purposes and means of processing, the processor shall be considered to be a controller in respect of that processing. However, this infringement of the GDPR does not relieve the data controller of their position as the data owner. Therefore, by virtue of storing the data in the cloud, the data processor processes the data owned by other data owners and is liable to that data owner as well as to supervisory authorities for fulfilling its duties for the whole period of processing.

To mitigate risk, smart cities should therefore:

- Use only trusted data processors (cloud service providers) providing sufficient guarantees to implement appropriate technical and organisational measures in such a manner that processing will meet the requirements of the GDPR and ensure the protection of the rights of data subjects, i.e. subjects whose personal data are processed (stored) in the cloud. The European Agency for Cybersecurity (ENISA, n.d.) proposed a single cybersecurity certification scheme for clouds. EUCS (ENISA, 2021) is a helpful step in this direction, which would ideally become law as soon as practicable;
- When possible, test technical and organisational measures. However, it is understood that, in practice, some characteristics may be specific to cloud infrastructures that may raise difficulties when applying the GDPR requirements. For instance, as a rule of principle, the data controller's right to audit or inspect the (cloud) data processor should be generally guaranteed and not limited to the case where the cloud service provider has not been certified by an independent body. The data controller may not always have the right to audit the processor for various reasons. For example, a cloud provider with thousands of clients will not be willing to enable their clients to carry out such audits for practical reasons;
- Carefully assess the cloud provider's Terms & Conditions regarding audits as well, among other requirements.

**Measure: Understand Your Data Origins (Accountability and Data Sovereignty)**

In the cases where data sets are acquired, users should know the origin of the data, its lawful and ethical uses, and any limitations on their sharing or publication. This scenario includes understanding the origin of data when working with private/public data sources, as expressed by the European Union Agency for Cyber Security—ENISA. When selecting and possibly buying data sets, understanding whether a data source is based on private or public data is a key step to ensuring data use does not infringe on the user's rights.

There are several areas of interest smart cities must take into account to ensure compliance when selecting a data source. These include the following concerns:

- How the data was initially collected;
- Purpose limitation and why the data was initially collected and processed, including any usage limitations;
- Whether the data was collected privately or scrapped from a public database;
- Anonymisation methods and mechanisms used;
- Ascertaining the consent of users and usage limits from the previous supplier;
- Data purpose limitation and the danger of function creep.

**Measure: Understand Where Your Data Is Stored (Data Location)**
The application owner(s) and manager(s) should ensure that they have identified where data will be stored, as storage is part of the processing of personal data, and evaluate any potential data protection or ethical implications of this location. In particular, with the interconnected nexus from the use of cloud storage, smart cities handling data of citizens residing in the EU should take several considerations into account to ensure compliance when storing personal data, possibly in third countries:

- Safeguards for individuals residing in the EU include: (i) The maintenance of a European-based data centre; (ii) in the case personal data must be transferred from Europe to a third country, implementing safeguards including Standard Contractual Clauses (SCCs), Corporate Binding Rules (BCRs), and ensuring a sufficient adequacy decision from the European Commission allowing the transfer of personal data to this location;
- Mitigating risks associated with storing data: When working with multiple databases or datasets, data may be indirectly stored in another country. Issues can be raised when personal data is stored in a country where the government maintains a broader discretion in accessing personal company data, such as the US or China. If this event does arise, it is important when processing personal data that smart cities: (i) ensure the above safeguards are in place[8]; (ii) request notification upon the request from government authorities of the disclosure of personal information; (iii) notify users of the smart city in relevant notices and applications of the potential for their personal data to be transferred to another country;
- In the event that no safeguards can be attained, the smart city should seek to use an alternative data source.

If a cloud service is utilised, smart cities should also ask the following questions:

- Does the chosen cloud environment provide any additional services? If so, does the smart city own all the outputs from this service? An example here includes using Cloud-provided AI tools. These tools can be used to improve data manage-

[8] Some jurisdictions have found transfers to the US not compliant with European Data Protection Law, such as France - "CNIL concludes that transfers to the United States are currently not sufficiently regulated", https://www.cnil.fr/en/use-google-analytics-and-data-transfers-united-states-cnil-orders-website-manageroperator-comply

ment, data hygiene, or any part of processing data in the cloud. In the process, Cloud AI tools potentially recognise, ingest, and classify data, therefore giving access to a large quantity of a smart city's data and potentially leveraging the data to create new outputs. If cloud-provided tools have access to personal data, additional clauses should be agreed upon that processing shall only occur on the smart city's instructions and no rights in the outputs shall be transferred to the cloud provider;
- Does the cloud provider/data space have access to data stored? Will the cloud provider use the data to improve their services and products? If cloud-provided tools have access to personal data, additional clauses should be agreed that processing shall only occur on the smart city's instructions and the outputs will only be used by the smart city;
- If data is shared in a data space, who has ownership over the imputed data and takes the role of a controller? Clear delineation of roles and responsibilities should be defined within the data space before the smart city shares data;
- If data is shared in a data space, are there mechanisms to ensure the security and protection of personal data through technical or organisational security measures? Technical and organisational security measures and policies should be shared with the smart city before the smart city shares data.

**Measure: Provide Transparency as to Data Usage and Storage**
In addition to smart city application owners and managers knowing what data is collected and for what purposes, the data subjects (e.g., the citizens) should know what data you collect about them and for what purposes. In practice, this means:

- Being transparent about the scope and source of the data, as well as the limitations of the data;
- Explaining what information the data contains, how (and where) it was collected, whether it is static data, updated regularly, or real-time;
- Whether the data is being processed through automated means or is being processed through AI;
- If the data is publicly available, provide a link to the origin data repository/source URL (Uniform Resource Locator) and ensure that decision-makers are aware of the data's deficiencies/limitations.

**Measure: Understand your Data's Quality**
To ensure the data is the best for your purposes, specific steps should be taken, such as ensuring that the data has sufficient and, ideally, best possible quality:

- As reasonably possible, data is complete, correct, up-to-date and fit for purpose;
- Data has a transparent track record covering their collection methods, storage methods, and has logs of previous processing (including data provenance);
- Data has a clear licence allowing (further) use.

Furthermore, smart cities should take active steps to ensure and maximise the quality, objectivity, usefulness, integrity and security of data, as highlighted in this guidance.

- Understanding if data can be used publicly. If the data is sufficient beyond an internal use (within the city's services), it is typically equally good for making the data publicly accessible (open). If data is published publicly, ensure that you align with the above rules concerning the publication of public data, have cleared the applicable legal requirements, and use open standards and open licences.

**Measure: Ensure the Transparent and Fair Use of AI and Computer Models**
Cities and government agencies should strive to develop officials' ability to understand, interpret, and use automated decision-making systems and "fight the opacity" problem. They should understand at least the basics of the underlying algorithms and the data used. This can be achieved by targeted education and training, for example.

In addition to the notice requirements shared in this chapter, data subjects (citizens) should be informed that automated decisions are being made about them and using their data. Cities and government agencies should strive to ensure that data subjects also understand the underlying algorithms.

Algorithms and automated decisions should be fair and proportional. In practice, this means they should not prejudice the data subjects. Even though some bias may be inherent in data, the algorithms and the data they use (or train on) should not create or perpetuate material biases (racial, ethnical, sexual, political, religious, etc.).

Finally, smart cities and regions should ensure an element of human control over the AI:

- Individuals to whom human oversight is assigned should fully understand the capacities and limitations of the AI system and should be able to duly monitor its operation so that signs of anomalies, dysfunctions and unexpected performance can be detected and addressed as soon as possible;
- Data subjects should be granted the right to appeal regarding data processing and the automated decisions affecting them.

**Measure: Ensure Representative Presentation of Data or Results**
While on the cusp of the law and regulations, maintain ethical standards at all stages of data processing. This adherence includes understanding how data or data-based decisions are presented and avoiding creating or perpetuating bias (e.g., using red and green colour coding for visualisations).

**Measure: Understand Data Ownership, Management and Information**
Data ownership typically goes hand in hand with the responsibility for data management. In particular, application owners and managers should be vigilant in understanding the data flow of suppliers and third parties who also process data. This approach includes third parties contracted out for city data management. When selecting a supplier, smart cities should carry out checks to ensure adequate technical and organisational security measures are in place; a data processing agreement is signed, information on whether the supplier's data is public or private, and the limitations on data usage.

Furthermore, organisational security measures include ensuring relevant training and sufficient data usage information within the team that may be processing personal data. Ensure sufficient information about the application, including how it works and the data the model is sourcing from. If applicable, provide a contact to the application administrator for possible troubleshooting. Finally, everyone involved must understand general ethical and legal principles and seek further legal guidance if necessary.

## 11.6 Alternative Ways of LDT Related Data and Information Management

The responsible use of data and information is one of the critical elements of smart city applications and LDTs. New concepts like data spaces and data altruism provide new methodologies and tools that contribute to legal and ethical ways of dealing with data and information.

**Measure: Make Use of Data Spaces to Organise Data Access and Management in a Structured Way**

As the usage of cloud infrastructures evolves, so do the methods of organising data within these structures. While data platforms pose one location for storing smart city data, data spaces can pose another challenge for data protection through the shared nature of the space. A dataspace is a decentralised infrastructure for trustworthy data sharing and exchange in data ecosystems based on commonly agreed principles (Reach Consortium, n.d.). Using data spaces allows data to be shared in an LDT context across policy domains and industries: health, industrial, agriculture, finance, mobility, environment, energy, public administration, and skills.

While presenting a free flow of data, the movement from cloud infrastructures to data spaces could give rise to data protection implications for individuals—e.g., data being used for purposes and by stakeholders of which the data subject was unaware. While there is no special legal guidance on the use of data spaces, similar precautions should be followed when sharing personal data with other service providers:

- If the utility of the data is not significantly reduced, smart cities should anonymise personal data to allow for a free flow of data within the data space without the risk of harm to data subjects. Once anonymised, there is a lowered risk to data subjects from data mishandling or processing for undisclosed purposes;
- Smart cities may share personal data outside of the data space if an individual agreement is in place which meets the standard of data protection under GDPR;
- Clear sovereignty over data should also be imposed. This measure ensures there is a responsible owner who can respond to data subject requests if the data is not anonymised.

**Measure: Data Altruism**
The concept of "data altruism" under the Data Governance Act (DGA),[9] where data subjects can agree to their data being used for the public good, may provide an alternative for smart cities while respecting data subject rights.

To comply with the DGA, Smart cities should:

- Comply with the requirements of the DGA, Article 15 to qualify for data altruism, including:
  - Be a legal entity meeting general interest objectives;
  - Operating on a not-for-profit basis and being independent from any entity that operates on a for-profit basis;
  - Performing the activities related to data altruism through a legally independent structure, separate from other activities undertaken.
- Follow the data altruism entity requirements under DGA, Article 19 by:
  - Ensuring transparency requirements are met, and appropriate disclosure is made to data subjects, including that data collected will be used for the general interest;
  - Obtaining consent from data subjects for the processing;
  - Ensuring the data is only used for general-interest purposes.

It is evident that current legal frameworks are curated for an infrastructure focused on the cloud rather than data and information-focused data spaces and data sharing. For smart cities to prepare for the future, it will be essential to define data sovereignty principles and clear data ownership to protect personal data while ensuring the free flow of data, such as through data altruism. Furthermore, inspiration should be taken from other data space initiatives for future legal framework evolution.

## 11.7 Conclusion

Due to the early stage of digital twins' diffusion in smart city settings, current knowledge covers a relatively limited number of practical digital twin experiences. The application of digital twins in more smart city research and development would allow for further development and analysis, for example, exploring positive effects on social networks, social inclusion and citizen interaction, which would benefit from a bottom-up urban development approach.

[9] The Data Governance Act defines Data Altruism in Article 2 as "the consent by data subjects to process personal data pertaining to them, or permissions of other data holders to allow the use of their non-personal data without seeking a reward, for purposes of general interest, such as scientific research purposes or improving public services..."

Despite the benefits, there are challenges and risks associated with deploying digital twin technologies, particularly regarding the use of personal data. Any use case related to the use of personal data must undergo scrutiny from the data protection authorities and civil society. For instance, use cases related to welfare benefits and smart housing data, such as energy consumption, solar power production and security need significant oversight. The integration of such data into an LDT (Local Digital Twin) raises ethical considerations regarding fairness and structural biases, as well as the potential misuse of information against residents.

The benefits of using smart housing data include improved energy efficiency, better resource management, enhanced security, and more effective public services. However, these benefits must be balanced against the risks to privacy and fairness to ensure ethical and equitable use of technology.

When data is gathered and used on a larger scale, such as in a neighbourhood or district, the risks increase. Use cases involving transportation and energy consumption in a city can provide valuable insights but also pose privacy risks. Legal and ethical concerns arise not only from the collection of personal data, as defined by the General Data Protection Regulation (GDPR), but also from its use in service delivery, potentially leading to ethical and structural biases.

Furthermore, in the scope of the evolving legal landscape and the development of LDTs, cities should be aware of the intersection of existing and incoming legal frameworks in combination with ethics. Ethical and privacy frameworks are certainly desirable as they provide general principles and rules to safeguard and boost European values. In practice, existing data protection regulations provide a stable foundation for city practitioners to build solutions that collect and process personal data. Nonetheless, they alone pose a noteworthy challenge for public and private organisations seeking to develop and deploy innovative solutions that inevitably transform processes and services, thereby requiring a certain level of propension towards rethinking how things are done. Hence, there is a need to operationalise those frameworks into concrete supportive tools for both private and public organisations, as well as for civil society, to help facilitate the dialogue between stakeholders in developing and deploying truly citizen-centric LDTs collaboratively.

Artificial Intelligence (AI) is a case in point. The recent developments and uptake of AI called for global coordination on its use. International organisations published general principles. Governments worldwide began developing national strategies to set visions, ambitions, and goals as to where and how the use of AI technologies should bring modern society. Only recently have governments, such as the U.S. and the European Union, albeit differently, decided to undertake the legislative process towards regulating the use and application of AI technologies. A European Union-wide initiative appears useful in aligning the internal market and ensuring a common approach across member states.

Nonetheless, only the use of a shared vocabulary and the widespread use of common approaches will eventually ensure the sustainable uptake of AI into smart city applications. As of today, it is likely that public and private organisations will undergo a period of capacity and capability building before deploying AI technologies on a large scale. In the future, however, when using AI to process personal and non-personal data, cities should be prepared to follow responsible AI principles and adopt a legal-ethical approach. In practice, this will mean extending existing data protection guidelines to govern the creation of generative outputs that are based on model-produced assumptions. In that respect it is strongly advised to integrate the ethical AI guidelines for trustworthy AI formulated by the EU High-Level Expert Group on AI into all LDT applications affected by AI, even if they are in the EU AI act minimal risk category. It is also expected that the text of proposed regulations, such as the European AI Act, will transfer into horizontal standards drawn from the language found in International Standardization Organization (ISO) and other commonly followed security certifications and standards.

On a different note, legal requirements may encourage the adoption and diffusion of new technologies or approaches to the use of data. The GDPR and ethical considerations regarding data sharing may boost the adoption of approaches that ensure privacy protection by default, such as homomorphic encryption. Hence it seems fair to say that legal and ethical frameworks exert an influence on the direction of innovation and, thus, on the use of a certain technology.

Overall, these considerations lead to the core aspect of LDTs and digital transformation at large. Whether real innovation will occur or incremental improvements will be applied to certain areas of public services is yet to be seen. Will LDT services consist of citizen-centric services, or will they only bring a simple improvement in efficiency? Whereas a conclusive answer would certainly abound in arrogance, it appears that innovative, citizen-centric public services are already in place and will not be constrained by legal or ethical frameworks. If anything, one may argue that these frameworks will only ensure the sustainability of such innovation as they provide a safeguard against misuse, albeit only their effective implementation and uptake will secure this.

## References

Al-Sehrawy, R., Kumar, B., & Watson, R. (2023). The pluralism of digital twins for urban management: Bridging theory and practice. *Journal of Urban Management, 12*(1), 16–32. https://doi.org/10.1016/j.jum.2023.01.002

Arents, H. C., & Vanderstraete, T. (2024). The European AI act: A regulatory framework to achieve the necessary trust in AI. *European Public Mosaic (EPuM).: Open Journal on Public Service, 22*, 38–51.

Cullen, R. (2001). Addressing the digital divide. *Online Information Review, 25*(5), 311–320.

Edwards, L. (2021). *The EU AI Act: A summary of its significance and scope*. Artificial Intelligence (the EU AI Act), 1.

ENISA. (n.d.). *European agency for cybersecurity—A trusted and cyber secure Europe*. https://www.enisa.europa.eu/news/enisa-news/cloud-certification-scheme

ENISA. (2021, June 9). *EU cloud certification scheme*. https://ec.europa.eu/newsroom/cipr/items/713799/en

EU4Digital Facility. (2024). EU4Digital—EU digital strategy. *EU4Digital*. https://eufordigital.eu/discover-eu/eu-digital-strategy/

European Commission. (2019, April). Ethics guidelines for trustworthy AI. *Shaping Europe's Digital Future*. https://digital-strategy.ec.europa.eu/en/library/ethics-guidelines-trustworthy-ai

European Commission. (2021, March 2). Workshop—Local digital twins technology. Shaping Europe's digital future. *Shaping Europe's Digital Future*. https://digital-strategy.ec.europa.eu/en/events/workshop-local-digital-twins-technology

European Parliament and of the Council. Regulation (EU) 2016/679 on the Protection of Natural Persons with Regard to the Processing of Personal Data and on the Free Movement of Such Data, and Repealing Directive 95/46/EC (General Data Protection Regulation) (Text with EEA Relevance), Pub. L. No. EU 2016/679, EUR-Lex (2016). https://eur-lex.europa.eu/eli/reg/2016/679/oj

European Parliament and of the Council. Directive 2002/58/EC Concerning the Processing of Personal Data and the Protection of Privacy in the Electronic Communications Sector (Directive on Privacy and Electronic Communications) (2002). https://eur-lex.europa.eu/legal-content/EN/ALL/?uri=celex%3A32002L0058

European Parliament and of the Council. Regulation (EU) 2022/868 on European Data Governance and Amending Regulation (EU) 2018/1724 (Data Governance Act) (2022a). https://eur-lex.europa.eu/eli/reg/2022/868/oj

European Parliament and of the Council. Regulation (EU) 2022/1925 on Contestable and Fair Markets in the Digital Sector and Amending Directives (EU) 2019/1937 and (EU) 2020/1828 (Digital Markets Act) (2022b). https://eur-lex.europa.eu/legal-content/EN/TXT/?uri=celex%3A32022R1925

European Parliament and of the Council. Regulation (EU) 2023/2854 on Harmonised Rules on Fair Access to and Use of Data and Amending Regulation (EU) 2017/2394 and Directive (EU) 2020/1828 (EU Data Act) (2023). https://eur-lex.europa.eu/eli/reg/2023/2854

European Parliament and of the Council. Proposal for a REGULATION OF THE EUROPEAN PARLIAMENT AND OF THE COUNCIL LAYING DOWN HARMONISED RULES ON ARTIFICIAL INTELLIGENCE (ARTIFICIAL INTELLIGENCE ACT) AND AMENDING CERTAIN UNION LEGISLATIVE ACTS, 21/4/2021. https://eur-lex.europa.eu/legal-content/EN/TXT/?uri=CELEX:52021PC0206

Grobelnik, M., Perset, K., & Russell, S. (2024, March). What is AI? Can you make a clear distinction between AI and non-AI systems? *OECD AI Policy Observatory*. https://oecd.ai/en/wonk/definition

Monge, F., Barns, S., Kattel, R., & Bria, F.. (2022). A new data deal: The case of Barcelona. *UCL Institute for Innovation and Public Purpose*.

Reach Consortium. (n.d.). Introduction to European data spaces. *Reach*. Retrieved 3 July 2024. https://www.reach-incubator.eu/what-are-data-spaces/

Regulation (EU) 2018/1807 of the European Parliament and of the Council of 14 November 2018 on a Framework for the Free Flow of Non-Personal Data in the European Union (Text with EEA Relevance.), Pub. L. No. EU 2018/1807, EUR-Lex (2018). https://eur-lex.europa.eu/eli/reg/2018/1807/oj

Suffia, G. (2022). Legal issues of the digital twin cities in the current and upcoming European legislation: Can digital twin cities be used to respond to urbanisation problems? In *Proceedings of the 15th International Conference on Theory and Practice of Electronic Governance* (pp. 534–537). https://doi.org/10.1145/3560107.3560188

Suffia, G. (2023). How to regulate a digital twin city? Insights from a proactive law approach: How "human in the Loop" and "precautionary Principles" can serve policymakers in their attempt to incorporate respect of rights and solidarity in the smart city. In *Proceedings of the 24th Annual International Conference on Digital Government Research* (pp. 122–128). https://doi.org/10.1145/3598469.3598482

Van Der Aalst, W. M. P., Hinz, O., & Weinhardt, C. (2021). Resilient digital twins: Organizations need to prepare for the unexpected. *Business & Information Systems Engineering, 63*(6), 615–619. https://doi.org/10.1007/s12599-021-00721-z

Wang, B. (2021). The seductive smart city and the benevolent role of transparency. *Interaction Design and Architecture(s), 48*, 100–121. Scopus.

Wang, B. T., & Burdon, M. (2021). Automating trustworthiness in digital twins. In *Advances in twenty-first century human settlements* (pp. 345–365). Scopus. https://doi.org/10.1007/978-981-15-8670-5_14

White House. (2023, October 30). *Executive order on the safe, secure, and trustworthy development and use of artificial intelligence.* https://www.whitehouse.gov/briefing-room/presidential-actions/2023/10/30/executive-order-on-the-safe-secure-and-trustworthy-development-and-use-of-artificial-intelligence/

# Chapter 12
# Pioneering Practitioners: Key Lessons Learned from Local Digital Twin Implementations

**Lieven Raes, Jurgen Silence, and Karl-Filip Coenegrachts**

**Contents**



## 12.1 Towards Key Lessons

The field of urban digital twins came into the spotlight about a decade ago, and interest has been exponentially growing for five years. The insights in this book are based on the experiences of a broad group of multi-domain experts who have a shared vision of Local Digital Twins (LDTs) as a promising instrument for data supported decision-making. This chapter provides an overview of their shared insights gathered from each contributor's field of research and expertise via interviews, surveys, discussions and research publications, along with specific insights within this book. This chapter structures this myriad of insights along the three phases of an LDT implementation. Based on the common understanding and experience of the authors, a set of recommendations has been formulated as a guideline for tailored implementations of LDTs based on local needs and expectations. The first recommendations are related to considerations when planning an LDT. The second set of

L. Raes (✉) · J. Silence
Digital Flanders, Brussels, Belgium
e-mail: lieven.raes@vlaanderen.be; jurgen.silence@vlaanderen.be

K.-F. Coenegrachts
Open Agile Smart Cities, Brussels, Belgium
e-mail: karl-filip.coenegrachts@vub.be



L. Raes et al. (eds.), *Decide Better*,
https://doi.org/10.1007/978-3-031-81451-8_12

recommendations is oriented to the implementation itself, while the third set is about maximising the impact of LDTs.

## 12.2 Experiencing LDTs

Urban digital twins, even on a local (district) scale, are rare, and LDTs are rarer still. A recent overview lists that there have been 27 worldwide initiatives of district-scale urban digital twins (Alva et al., 2022). Most of these initiatives are still in the proof-of-concept phase. However, the vast majority, 24 of the initiatives, take into account at least one of the three LDT distinguishing elements: (I) policy development, (II) participatory planning, and (III) policy scenario modelling. Only eight initiatives cover two of these three LDT distinguishing elements. Other recent urban digital twin initiatives containing LDT elements occurred in Aarhus, Athens, Flanders (cities of Ghent and Bruges), Helsinki, Porto, Pilsen, Rotterdam and Santander. These experiences are reflected throughout this book and form the basis of the research in this chapter.

### *12.2.1 The Early Adopters' Approach and Experience*

The digital twin concept is one of the most recent technologies dominating the smart city hype cycle (Hemetsberger, 2020). While the technology has already been around for decades in engineering, thanks to recent ideas about data governance in cities, more advanced data and (geospatial) information processing tools, more powerful processing and cloud storage, it has now entered the realm of city planning and development. Looking more closely, there are several drivers for why early adopters have embraced LDTs.

#### An LDT as the Next Step in a GIS Digitisation Strategy

Implementing an LDT solution may be a logical step in extending the current investments in Geospatial Information systems (GIS). This approach often means implementing a 3D visualisation of buildings and public domain infrastructure using advanced imaging techniques like LIDARs. Combined with metadata and specified attributes, it can be an important step towards a semantic model of the city, which eventually can lead to a Building Information Model (BIM) of an urban area, city, or beyond. The initial view of extending the current GIS system fits well into further developing a closed tool for government use (see the business model typology in Chap. 9). Applying semantic 3D models proved to be an essential step toward more open and reusable BIM solutions.

#### An LDT as a Part of an Overarching Data Strategy Enabling Strategic Cooperation

Today, governments face new societal challenges that one department alone cannot solve. Strategic cooperation in setting, measuring and reaching policy goals must be based on various input data and parameters. Dealing with these new challenges creates the need for new strategies for data management, information management and evidence-based policy support. An LDT solution combines data driven business intelligence dashboards with advanced geospatial representations. The strategic cooperation approach is more organisational and service delivery-oriented than the GIS digitisation strategy-oriented approach. Overall, the outcome is still mainly government-oriented but less centralised and IT-driven.

#### An LDT as an Emancipatory City Management Vision

Another small group of early adopters started their LDT journey from a solid societal and even ideological vision. The vision begins from realising that the government cannot meet all needs alone, necessitating an emancipatory approach towards society, including the private sector and research partners. Espoo City Council in Finland translated this vision by delivering an ICT business model for offering the public information technology and software. It acknowledges that a city cannot meet every need of its citizens based on the work done by city officials. Instead, services are provided by the entire city community, not just the official city organisation. This approach was part of a broader "city as a service (CAAS)" vision (Lehtola & Markkula, 2022).

### *12.2.2 The Innovation Perspective*

An ICT-based solution like an LDT often suggests an innovation focus on new technology concepts. This is partially the case in how LDTs bring existing solutions and technologies together in a System-of-Systems (SoS) approach, especially when a federated and distributed approach is used. LDTs also stimulate innovations like High-Performance Computing (HPC) and Artificial Intelligence (AI)-based self-learning simulation modelling. In addition, LDTs have a less explored social innovation dimension in their ability to add societal elements to the data driven policy-making focus of urban digital twins.

#### The System-of-Systems Perspective of an LDT

Innovation in modern engineering is mainly driven by digitalisation. An LDT uses complex software engineering that is often combined with the results of technical hardware engineering, e.g. data collected by Internet of Things (IoT) sensors and devices. LDT software engineering must be integrated into at least one, but often multiple, product development processes to integrate existing, often independent, software products, e.g. visualisation tools, simulation models and IoT Advanced Programming Interfaces (APIs) or alternative open interfaces. On the one hand, the resulting products evolve into advanced systems with greater functionality and quality. On the other hand, the challenges of increasing interdisciplinarity, interoperability and overall complexity must be managed. Therefore, development cannot be achieved from the perspective of a single discipline. Successful development must focus on the overall multidisciplinary system in all activities (Anacker et al., 2022). An SoS can fulfil this role.

There is no exact definition of an SoS; according to Sage and Cuppan (2001), an SoS in system and software engineering can be seen as a collection of trans-domain networks of heterogeneous systems that are likely to exhibit operational and managerial independence, geographical distribution, and emergent and evolutionary behaviours that would not be apparent if the systems and their interactions are modelled separately.

The value of SoS in an LDT context lies in its ability to combine innovative components like the latest 3D viewer technology, including Augmented Reality (AR) and Virtual Reality (VR) (HPC-based) simulation modelling techniques, AI-based simulation models, new remote sensing techniques and sensor technologies and standards. The added value of an LDT also lies in its ability to combine existing and new domain-specific and cross-domain techniques to provide additional (more advanced and better tailored) insights and better-substantiated decisions. The technical innovations aim to improve policy implementation.

## The Social Dimension of LDT Innovations (for and by the People)

By analogy, with the possibilities for new technical integrations, an LDT offers similar opportunities to initiate social innovation by integrating the human factor. New evolutions to make decision-making more democratic by supporting citizen involvement using ICT align well with LDT in several ways. The first way an LDT can support is by providing policy data and insights. A more active way in the policy-making and decision process is the use of co-creation and even co-decision. A specific and largely unexplored terrain is integrating citizen science (CS) data from sensors operated by citizens and the scientific community.

I. Insights into Policy Data and the Decision Process

Using LDTs as an instrument for providing insights to citizens, community groups, and local businesses is rare. One example in operation today is the city of Helsinki, which offers a 3D map of the city, providing insights into the building's energy-saving potential for public and private properties (City of Helsinki, 2022a). The Helsinki example allows the public to view and explore concrete data to make decisions regarding renovations of public and privately owned buildings (Fig. 12.1).

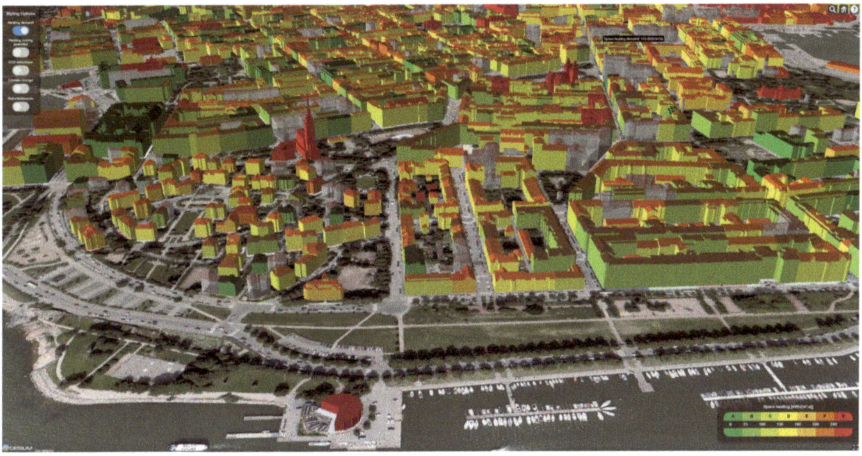

**Fig. 12.1** Helsinki digital twin 3D Energy and Climate Atlas. (City of Helsinki, 2022b)

Additional examples, such as the Energy and Climate Atlas,[1] offer insights to citizens and contribute to society's data literacy. As part of education programmes and government data visualisation tools, data literacy investments allow people to communicate and discuss with policymakers and decision-makers more equally.

II. Co-creation and Co-decision

Carrying out co-creation activities is a critical tool in developing solutions for citizenship. Getting citizens and civil servants together is an effective way of gaining valuable insights to help develop a user-centric LDT.

While co-creation techniques in, e.g. Athens, Flanders, Pilsen (Walravens, 2020; Walravens et al., 2020) and Santander (Molina et al., 2022) were used to define the LDT solution itself, co-decision is linked to the decision as an outcome of the policy cycle. Examples of using LDTs during the entire co-decision trajectory are sparse. A user-centric LDT solution fits well in the quadruple helix smart city approach, where government, academia, industry, and civil society are all involved in creating new innovative societal solutions.

III. Integrating Citizen Science

LDTs have a constant need for local qualitative data. Rolling out sensor networks with a sufficiently high density is often troublesome in terms of effort and cost. Combining different sensor types and measurements is another point of concern. CS

[1] The Helsinki Energy and Climate Atlas is a data model-based tool that contains a wide variety of information related to energy, which can be freely used by property owners, city planners and companies providing energy-saving services, among others. The Helsinki Energy and Climate Atlas supports the energy efficiency of the building stock, the use of renewable energy and, in the future, adaptation to climate change in a visual and informative form

can bring an additional source of high-density information into an LDT, even though the accuracy may often be lower. LDTs can bring various sources of information together and deliver a higher density by combining different sensor networks measuring the same environment, as well as sensors measuring different data (e.g. air quality and traffic volumes). The EU innovation project, COMPAIR,[2] is developing calibration mechanisms to further develop air quality sensor calibration algorithms based on combining low-cost and reference-grade sensor data located at a distance from the low-cost sensors. This approach, developed and validated in testbeds in Belgium and The Netherlands, is deployed as a cloud-based calibration service that improves the accuracy of sensor data in real-time and makes the calibrated data available for integration into decision support systems like LDTs (Hofman et al., 2022). Integrating qualitative 'scientifically monitored data collected by citizens' can provide local coverage that is very helpful in supporting local policy-making initiatives. The practical use of CS data for policy-making also offers essential incentives for citizens to continue participation in a measurement campaign and can deliver a valuable source of information for an LDT.

## 12.3 Experiencing the Incomplete LDT

LDTs and, by extension, any evidence-based and informed decision support system has a starting point representing an incomplete view and often a partial presentation and interpretation of the physical reality. An example of such an interpretation is a colour scale representing a value like energy consumption, air quality or traffic volume. It is important to be constantly aware of the information and interpretations that lie at the basis of an LDT supported decision. Elements of this incompleteness or data interpretation are not neutral and can be a result of (1) the lack of sufficient and available data, (2) the lack of assessment instruments, e.g. simulation models, (3) the use of data evaluation schemes,[3] (4) the assessment of the data that is needed, (5) an incomplete knowledge of the available data and tools, (6) a lack of integration that hinders the evaluation and simulation process. Cultural differences can also impact the perception of 'neutrality,' which is important to keep in mind in diverse societies.

The absence of human agents as part of the evidence-based discourse is easily seen as a positive element of neutrality. On the other hand, the absence of human agents in the digital twin conceptualisations focuses our attention on the instrumentality of the technique while steering us away from its social implications (Korenhof

[2] Community Observation Measurement & Participation in AIR Science (COMPAIR), EU H2020 project, https://cordis.europa.eu/project/id/101036563

[3] A good example is AQI (Air Quality Index systems that differ from each other). The use of another indexing system and the related data visualisation can influence the interpretation of LDT results and outcomes

et al., 2021). LDTs can also drive away the qualitative value elements that are more difficult to integrate, like the contribution of a decision to empower well-being or overall satisfaction.

The representation of the results influences the LDT‘s completeness. The representation itself and the amount of detail influence what results are emphasised, and which results should be more or less accentuated or left out. The reality of an LDT as a biased and influenced result is an element to keep in mind as part of the recommendations. An LDT does not stand independently but is, like a GIS system or a Business Intelligence tool, always part of a broader reference framework.

## 12.4 Recommendations for Starting and Implementing LDTs

Starting, implementing or further expanding an LDT is a complex process in terms of determining objectives, requirements, data collection, implementation and management. Learning from previous experiences can save much time, lead to more mature and better-tailored solutions from the start, and help avoid wrong strategic decisions impacting the future development of digital twins. The recommendations include practical implementation advice and tips to start and gradually extend your LDT solution. The first set of recommendations is related to evidence-informed policy-making and involvement. The second set of recommendations is about implementing LDTs, while the third set is about extending the impact of LDTs. Each recommendation is explained through the actual experiences of LDT early adopters.

### *12.4.1 Recommendations Related to Evidence-Informed Policy-Making and Involvement*

LDTs can scientifically support policy decisions. Often associated with evidence-based decision-making, LDTs play a crucial role. However, in exponentially evolving fields like mobility, environment, or spatial planning, relying solely on the best available information can be unrealistic. Instead, evidence-informed policy advice and management practices are often more practical for public sector managers than strictly evidence-based policies (Head, 2013). As Head explains, an evidence-informed approach is effective when time is limited, data is incomplete, or when decisions are non-strategic and reversible. Additionally, LDTs can enhance the detection of social needs through their capacity to involve citizens in the decision-making process.

### Recommendation 01: Implement an LDT as an Instrument for Evidence-Informed Decision-Making

**Lesson** Implementing decision support features can vary from reasonably simple features to advanced solutions influencing each other, leading to more complex and less predictable insights. An LDT as a representation of the city in 2D or 3D, including a BIM, can support evidence-informed decisions in, for example, an urban planning context. Adding geo-time series data, e.g. delivered by IoT sensors, can also help to recognise trends and provide more in-depth insights. More intelligence can be obtained by adding simulation models. These models vary in complexity from almost standard 3D GIS functionalities like a shadow model simulating the sun's position to more complex sector-specific simulation models like traffic models, air quality models and noise models that allow predictive insights of the effects of simulated measures. From a smart city and policy prediction perspective, the most complex and interesting combination lies in multi-domain and multi-layered simulation models combining multiple thematic models (e.g. combining the output of a traffic model as the input for an air quality model). Another beneficial combination is using a fast-calculation model that provides a simplified synchronised result (e.g. by calculating differences in yearly averages) and an asynchronous model providing detailed information during a typical day at a specific moment. The power of an LDT can be strongly increased by realising the combination and interplay of multi-model capabilities in a digital twin and the underlying semantically aligned datasets using common ontology elements. It is recommended that the capabilities of multiple simulation models, datasets, and dataset semantics should be studied to scrutinise the combinations that allow for the generation of relevant results to support evidence-based decisions. Bringing model and data experts together to cover the involved policy domains is the best way to formulate requirements linked to LDT use cases and their related decision processes.

**Case: Athens's goal was a pilot implementation to assess the LDT's effectiveness in supporting green routing policies by providing insights for better evidence-informed decisions.** The pilot required combining diverse data such as traffic flows, road capacity, transportation, and GIS information on the existing green spaces in the city. LDT visualisation tools appeared to be convenient for integrating the above data sources and support an efficient decision-making process for green urban planning (DAEM & I. Christantoni, personal communication, 2022).

The main *obstacles and challenges* when implementing advanced simulation models lie in integrating domain-specific simulation models outside the chosen visualisation or GIS solution. Openness in terms of data access and integration, as well as simulation model integration, demands willingness and integration expertise on the side of the urban digital twin solution provider and the simulation model provider. The more models that need to be integrated, the more challenging this will be.

Open software, standards and architecture-based LDTs deliver the best *opportunities and solutions* by allowing the linking of multiple data sources, simulation models and federated software and hardware. The approach can also lead to new forms of cooperation inside an organisation (new collaborations between departments), organisations and solution providers, and the scientific world, which is often responsible for the logic behind the simulation models.

### Recommendation 02: Design and Implement an LDT with a Focus on Contributing to Community (Users) Needs

**Lesson** An LDT is successful when it can contribute to solving the societal needs of people, ideally contributing to local needs (so that progress can be seen) and more universal goals like the UN Sustainable Development Goals (SDG) or the European Green Deal. User-centric design (UCD) principles and tools like co-design workshops, interviews, data jams and hackathons are well-proven UCD tools that fit well. UCD itself is a process in which end-users influence how a design takes shape as a philosophy and a variety of methods (Abras et al., 2004). Identifying key stakeholders that affect data driven policy-making on a Policy Network Canvas from the early start is one of the UCD techniques that are highly effective. An important lesson is that the variety of expertise from different stakeholders leads to a wide range of scenario specifications translated into user requirements during workshops. It even provides insights into business model requirements.

**Advice: When deploying solutions, well-planned validation processes must be carried out, involving end-users** from the beginning and, in the following steps, maintaining a balance between the demanded effort and the results obtained. To summarise, stay within close range of the end user (J. Echevarria & Santander, personal communication, 2022).

**Case: Mobilising community participation in Aarhus.** One of the most important benefits of having a digital twin of Aarhus is the way this urban representation can be intuitively visualised to facilitate a trusted environment for inclusive dialogue about city development with citizens and politicians, who typically do not have the technical expertise to use other smart city systems, such as GIS (Jørgensen, personal communication, 2022).

The added value of UCD goes hand in hand with expectation management. It is *challenging* to translate the various inputs from a diverse group of stakeholders into coherent prioritised use cases and communicate with the stakeholders about the outcome. It is expected that the level of knowledge about LDTs is unequally distributed amongst stakeholders and that additional workshops will be needed to get a more unbiased view of a) the social needs and b) the solution an LDT can deliver. Expert data science and domain-specific knowledge are needed to check whether the available data and simulation models can support the desired outcomes. A successful *solution* is to share the UCD results accompanied with contextual information like scenario specifications with the stakeholders and clarify the feasibility of a specified scenario regarding data, modelling and stakeholder engagement.

**Advice: Use cases often arise from socio-technical understanding.** While the discussion around the digital twins often becomes very data- and technology-centric, the processes behind the data are not purely technical and contain many social, society-oriented elements. Citizen perception is as important as hard sensor facts in a smart city. For example, urban maintenance processes, participatory planning, and handling of citizen feedback involve multiple stakeholders, responsibilities, and parties. Representing these different roles and processes in the digital twin supports the creation of new applications which work towards a well-functioning city in a more human-centric way. When advancing towards increasingly detailed demographic data, it is also expected that the urban digital twin and 'personal digital twin' formed by citizens' data begin to interact with each other (Forum Virium Helsinki et al., personal communication, 2022).

**Case: The Athens LDT implementations revealed citizens' high interest in participating in initiatives that improve the quality of life in the neighbourhoods of the city.** The opportunity for citizens to express their opinions, as implemented by the DUET[4] LDT, provides a ground for active participation in the process after having insight into the proposed decisions. Applied gamification during workshops allowed citizens to play the role of solution proposers, strategy testers, and providers of local insights that went beyond the evidence-related data of the LDT (DAEM & I. Christantoni, personal communication, 2022).

### Recommendation 03: Use Your LDT to Visualise and Communicate Insights in an Understandable Way

**Lesson** The combination of new insights, made possible thanks to data driven knowledge creation, offers a wide range of innovative visualisation opportunities for an LDT. For effective impact, ensure that insights are visualised and communi-

[4] Digital Urban European Twins (DUET), EU H2020 project, https://cordis.europa.eu/project/id/870697

cated neutrally and recognisably. Be aware that visualisation subjects will vary in terms of sensitivity.

For example, an informative map showcasing the degree of insulation of city buildings, ranging from high heat loss to well-insulated, will not be highly sensitive, as it provides free services without direct consequences. Whereas showing the effects of a local mobility plan and the changes in mobility combined with visualising the change in expected road use related to (new) road capacities can lead to more discussions among citizens and the government. With new digital twins, it can be a good idea to begin by visualising more neutral themes and test how the information can/will be interpreted by those (not) involved.

However, LDTs can become complex and difficult to interpret. It is especially challenging to communicate complex outcomes clearly and neutrally. In many cases, guidance will be needed; for example, if a pollutant is shown, it is advised to communicate using authoritative colour scales from the UN or EC. A good approach is to empathise with the user or to ask a limited number of uninvolved people how they interpret the information to be sure it can be understood correctly. This approach allows for the elimination of pitfalls and obstacles.

Suppose multiple data sources must be interpreted simultaneously (e.g. speed and traffic accidents or traffic volumes and air quality). In that case, additional guidance is needed to interpret the data and draw valid conclusions. A combination of the LDT visualisation with introduction pages can provide insights into the data and models and explain what they clarify and what they do not. Using interactive dashboards or more passive storytelling offers opportunities to combine visualisations (data views), interpreted insights and reference frameworks. Implementing additional tools helps give this extra background to a non-specialist audience and can be part of local community engagements, e.g. through a local website (see Recommendation 12).

We recommend creating an LDT with multiple output channels, such as a simplified 3D map for navigation, a dashboard for providing deeper insights, and user-oriented landing pages for step-by-step guidance to explore the LDT cases and for contextual storytelling.

**Advice: The user interface is crucial when interacting with citizens and is, when implemented well, one of the main LDT benefits.** This advice is particularly important when addressing problems for lower Social-Economic-Status, or SES, groups or older adults, as there is a wide variety of skills amongst these groups regarding involvement and (data) literacy. An approachable and appealing way of communicating based on data is even more important with these groups. Collaboration between policymakers and experienced communications specialists is crucial (J. Echevarria & Santander, personal communication, 2022).

## 12.4.2 Recommendations Regarding Implementing LDTs

A decision on how to implement an LDT is not an evident foregone conclusion, because of the complexity involved. However, it is becoming a necessity to support and even drive sustainable urban development. Questions arise about the different parts of an LDT solution, how an LDT can fit with the existing legacy systems, and how to avoid vendor lock-in. An obvious answer is to be aligned with open standards, semantics and existing LDT solutions. All of these are valid questions impacting decisions that every party who wants to make an investment has to consider regarding what to build and buy. The recommendations below offer a thinking framework that must be tailored to the local situation, desired use cases, and business models.

### Recommendation 04: If Starting Your LDT from a 3D City Visualisation Model or a Limited Use Case, Remember to Have Future Extensions in Mind

**Lesson** There are multiple ways of implementing an LDT solution. The first digital twins of cities and regions started by implementing a 3D model, varying from a city district in Helsinki up to the entire area of Singapore. The 3D model was the basis for thinking about its potential use. The 3D model was seen as an indispensable base layer, analogous to digital orthophoto plans in the late nineties as part of a 2D GIS environment. Many departments saw the 3D model and the orthophoto plans as essential commodities, allowing investment. Choosing an open licence and standards-based 3D city model, e.g. using the cityGML (Kolbe et al., 2021) standard, allows reuse and future extension. An essential decision to make early on is whether to use a 3D city mesh with limited metadata and capabilities, or a 3D visualisation based on a detailed semantic model such as the cityGML, CityJSON or Industry Foundation Classes (IFC). The *challenge* is to elaborate on what the 3D visualisation model of the city can add to the specific challenges a city faces today.

A case driven approach offers an *alternative recommended way* of starting your LDT journey. This approach begins from societal challenges translated into policy questions that need better insights and solutions. By selecting a minimal set of preferably open components you need, you can start building your first LDT in a feasible way by integrating the data layers, simulation models and visualisation components you need. For many policy-related use cases, investing significantly in a highly detailed 3D model (LOD 2 or higher) is unnecessary since such detailed models do not significantly improve the quality of decision-making. Another advantage of a case driven approach is its better feasibility in data management and governance, especially when data governance processes need to be optimised by data providers.

**Advice: Integration with city processes is essential for both maintenance/updating and utilisation of the digital twin.** As the city digital twin is composed via data integration from a number of registries and surveying processes, it cannot be realised without considering these underlying supporting processes. Process integration ensures that data remains well-maintained and up-to-date. Similarly, applying new LDT use cases requires involving the stakeholders in these processes. Without the process integration, the digital twin easily becomes a 'one-off' execution that expires soon (Forum Virium Helsinki et al., personal communication, 2022).

A combination of a data-centred approach supported by an open system supporting extension with data and simulation models from multiple sources/suppliers, combined with a use case driven approach providing direction to the LDT endeavours, offers a *solution and opportunity* to create a feasible and extensible system. It can be expected that LDTs will converge from an open data approach and a use case driven and policy-related approach using an open LDT solution.

**Advice: Manage expectations.** Be very cautious with what you promise and when. An LDT in itself is not an outcome. Be clear that it is, in the first place, a tool for supporting outcomes and benefits for the citizens. Focus in the first place on the benefits for end users realistically and feasibly and stress that LDTs are part of a transformation process (J. Echevarria & Santander, personal communication, 2022).

### Recommendation 05: Be Future-Proof by Using Minimal Interoperability Mechanisms (MIMs) and Open Standards

**Lesson** LDTs, as an SoS ICT solution, are part of the digital transformation process in the way they contribute to using digital technologies to transform existing traditional non- or partial digital business processes (including decision processes) and services into new digital ones. From a technological system design perspective, there is a high need for standardisation. The Espresso project[5] *learned* that interoperability in a broader smart city context could avoid entry barriers or vendor lock-in by promoting common meta-data structures and interoperable open interfaces instead of proprietary ones (Fabisch & Henninger, 2018).

Minimal Interoperability Mechanisms (MIMs) offer a way to look beyond individual ICT standards by providing practical capabilities based on open technical

[5] Systemic standardisation approach to empower smart cities and communities (ESPRESSO), EU H2020 project, https://cordis.europa.eu/project/id/691720

specifications that allow cities and communities to replicate and scale solutions globally. MIMs provide technical foundations for procuring and deploying urban data platforms and end-to-end solutions in cities and communities worldwide (OASC, 2022). Implementing MIMs helps avoid obstacles and describes the overarching elements like context information management, minimal common data models, contracts for ecosystem transaction management and future MIMs regarding trust, transparency and security. The MIMs offer a thinking framework combined with practical skills. Translating MIMs into an LDT specification is a *challenge* that needs to be integrated into an overarching LDT solution design.

**Case: Geometric depiction is only a part of the Helsinki digital twin.** The 3D city model becomes interesting when city statistics, IoT sensor data feeds, and other relevant object structures are consistent, standardised and integrated into the Helsinki 3D city model. The approach allows integrating, e.g. buildings with their energy consumption data feed into semantic models containing energy information next to data about geometry and appearance (Forum Virium Helsinki et al., personal communication, 2022).

Robalo-Correia et al. (2023) designed a component driven LDT Toolbox, providing insights into the relationship between LDT building blocks, standards and potential software stacks based on the current state of play in the ICT landscape. Aside from the use of MIMs, the Pivotal Points of Interoperability (PPI) (NIST, 2021) concept helps to define areas where interoperability has the highest priority and impact and can help to choose the most relevant domains to ensure feasibility and the necessary degree of interoperability. It is impossible for a complex system like an LDT to be fully comprehensive regarding standards. Focus on interface standardisation between the LDT software layers, including the data service layer (1), the catalogue and metadata layer (2), the interaction layer (3) and the visualisation layer (4).

**Case: Fostering innovation with the 'open approach' in Porto.** For the city, it is important to have open source and open API components that enable the development and integration of other tools or add-ons. Also, a digital twin should help to maximise the reuse of existing data models and standards as much as possible to reduce inefficiencies (Bastos, personal communication, 2022).

### Recommendation 06: Use a Combination of Domain-Agnostic and Domain-Specific Standards

Realising an open digital twin requires applying domain-agnostic standards to realise the LDT basic architecture. It might also be necessary to apply domain-specific standards to support related use cases. In an SoS approach where data, models and software applications are connected from multiple policy domains, each domain-specific business application is expected to have its standards at the level of semantics, syntax, business rules, and visualisation conventions and standards. The semantic web allows web ontologies (such as W3C Web Ontology Language—OWL) to ensure that semantic relationships between domains can be realised. It is essential to consider these domain-specific standards in developing LDT use cases and elaborate on how they can contribute to the realisation of sustainable cross-domain LDT use case implementations. Domain-specific standards can also be applied to various visualisations, such as displaying traffic volumes and road capacity or colour schemes and scales for expressing air quality.

Examples:

- CityGML or CityJSON are domain-agnostic standards used for the 3D visualisation of infrastructure objects such as buildings, which can be used to calculate air quality or noise impacts in the city;
- The OpenLR is a domain-agnostic standard developed by a mobility sector player (TomTom company) for system-agnostic dynamic location referencing. It allows domain-specific simulation models to use the same understanding of a road segment when calculating and communicating model results;
- The systematic use of recognised and accepted colour codexes to represent model results, such as recognised and Air Quality Indexes, is an example of a non-ICT domain-specific standard.

Combining domain-agnostic and domain-specific standards in an LDT is still largely unexplored and challenging. To make a thoughtful choice, ICT and domain-specific knowledge must be brought together during the analysis phase of each specific LDT use case. From an ICT perspective, it is important to check whether well-supported domain-specific ICT standards are available in addition to generic standards.

### Recommendation 07: Implement Privacy and Ethics by Design

**Lesson** At first glance, protecting personal data and privacy (GDPR-related) is not always considered an issue in current LDT implementations. Data privacy is often solved at the source level (e.g. using anonymised and aggregated datasets like floating car data or aggregated census data in a traffic simulation model). The lack of use cases and provision of personal services based on sensitive (personal) data does not bring privacy and ethical considerations to the forefront. Personal data is expected to play a more prominent role in the future when LDTs are enriched with local data (e.g. information about the interior layout of buildings or behavioural data of citizens) or when personal data is used as a source to get personal services and advice. Growing niches, including data management, (cyber)security, big data and HPC large-scale data processing, AI, and cloud computing are new elements that need attention from a privacy, ethical and legal perspective. They are addressed in various legislative initiatives, such as the EU AI Act (European Commission, 2023).

Ethical considerations regarding data selection and simulation models and their relation to decision- and policy-making processes appear to be the most critical elements of predictive LDTs. The Cities Guides to Legal Compliance (including ethics) for data driven decision-making from the DUET project were the basis for a gap analysis framework, as presented in Chap. 10. The framework integrates legal compliance checks with ethically aware process flows (Pavelka et al., 2022; Pavelka & Piantoni, 2021).

Implementing privacy and ethics by design assessment methodologies like the PIA (Privacy Impact Analysis) (Kirvan & Cole, 2023) and the SATORI[6] Ethics Assessment Framework (Satori project editors, 2017) provides methods to avoid difficult-to-solve issues such as the lack of trust which can lead to a loss of credibility. Privacy and ethics assessment tools are especially relevant in the complex LDT environment where a lot of data collected and owned by different quadruple helix stakeholders contributes to society and its digital representation.

Another challenge related to using data and simulation models (algorithm and AI-based) is explaining the level of uncertainty related to the simulation and measurement outcomes. Handling data according to the limits of a simulation model, and communicating the interpreted outcomes and limitations without bias, is necessary to create and maintain trust.

Ethical elements related to evidence supported decision-making will play an even more significant role in the future when new use cases, such as (semi)automated decision support of individual files like building and environmental permits, depend on the outcome of an LDT.

**Case: Each LDT type of user, like the system manager, policymaker, provider (investor), or (registered) citizen, uses the LDT differently. The role and use of the LDT also translate into different ethical considerations and legal requirements.** For example, in the case of the joint digital twin developed in Athens, Flanders, and Pilsen, a citizen user of a publicly available version of the LDT solution will typically not have legal or factual access to sensitive or confidential data, but, on the other hand, may use the data and models made available for any possible legitimate purpose. Conversely, a DUET system manager or a city policymaker with direct access to the DUET system will have access to various restricted data types. Still, it will be constrained by the purposes for which they may use them. The ethical considerations of an investor will be about the data quality and modelling results quality offered and how the services can be re-used concerning IP protection. The ethical considerations of a citizen are linked to how the data is processed, to what purpose data will be used, and if the data is used with respect to people's privacy. An involved and concerned citizen will also know about the automated processes used in decision-making and how trust and transparency are guaranteed (Noti et al., 2021).

---

[6] Stakeholders Acting Together On the ethical impact assessment of Research and Innovation (SATORI), EU FP7 project, https://cordis.europa.eu/project/id/612231

### Recommendation 08: Implement a Scalable and Federated LDT Solution

**Lesson** Implementing an LDT in an organisation implies a make-or-buy decision at a particular moment. Looking at current LDT projects, a buy-decision based on the current GIS system tradition follows a similar integrated system approach based on a single vendor offering an integrated (centralised) data-management and visualisation approach often relying on Extraction, Transformation and Load (ETL) data integration in a centralised data solution. A federated system approach provides new *solutions and opportunities* and combines several advantages compared to out-of-the-box (GIS-based) LDT solutions. A federated architecture typically follows a more event-driven approach, often including microservices. Components are connected with external systems like (IoT) data sources and simulation models and integrated into a data catalogue and one or more visualisation clients through a set of access components. These access components control the incoming and outgoing data flows to a central data and message broker (API gateway). A management model handles user management, including access rights, and allows models and data access to create a managed user community. The federated approach allows linking external services (e.g. noise and air quality models or vast data sources like satellite data stored in a data space) without losing components' independence. Existing open components can be integrated as a new component for delivering output as a microservice, for example. New services, provided by different independent vendors, can be added to offer new functionalities and support new policy simulations when the principles outlined in Recommendations 04 to 07 are applied.

**Advice: API access is essential for supporting application development in the private sector.** Officials alone cannot answer all potential development needs, especially concerning technical platforms and the development of application-specific tools. To support the private sector's involvement in innovation, the data forming the city's digital twin has to be available via APIs. This benefits not only private companies but also the city. In the ideal situation, tools for using the digital twin become modular and interchangeable (Forum Virium Helsinki et al., personal communication, 2022).

Potential *obstacles* are the higher complexity, implementation time and initial cost. The learning curve will be steeper, and the implementation will demand more collaboration than out-of-the-box solutions.

### Recommendation 09: Gradually Accelerate Your LDT

**Lesson** Accelerating the use of an LDT can be achieved by intensifying the solution's use to support the decision-making process (promoting the LDT as is) and by extending the LDT functionalities into new domains by adding new services (e.g. data, modelling and visualisation services) (Fig. 12.2).

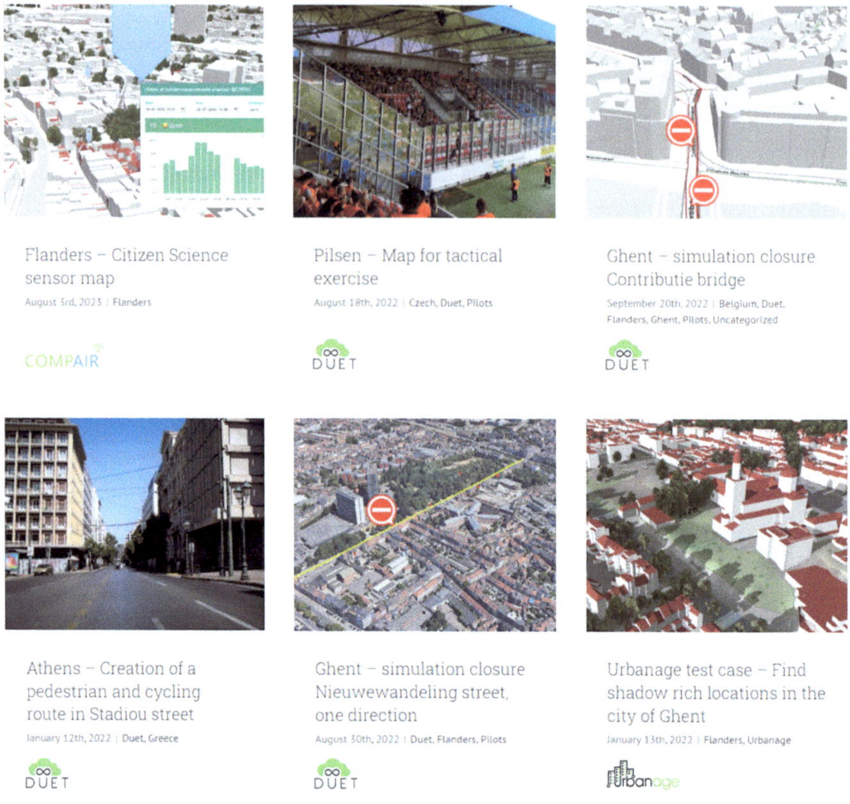


**Fig. 12.2** LDT policy cases overview. (DUET, 2023)

Both approaches will reinforce each other and are ideally use case and community driven. Using solution accelerators can speed up the implementation of LDT solutions like open LDT core components or core component connectors (e.g. connecting data spaces and data lakes with a data catalogue and central message broker) and solutions supporting specific LDT use cases. Neebal Technologies (2024) defines a solution accelerator as pre-built tools, frameworks, or components designed to expedite and simplify the development of specific software solutions or applications. Microsoft positions solution accelerators as the starting points for your own IoT solutions. They are designed to be scalable, modular, understandable, extensible, and secure (Stackowiak, 2019). They also help speed up the development process and go hand in hand with the scalable microservices approach described in Recommendation 08.

A continuous *challenge* is keeping societal values in mind while extending and promoting the system. An LDT has much to offer regarding communication and delivering insights into the rationale behind decisions. Next to developing new use cases and expanding the LDT system, is the communication of new insights and outcomes, providing concrete contributions to policy support, and developing potential new use cases and user stories. A combination of well-chosen visuals and a description of the challenge, approach, outcomes, data and simulation models can provide the much-needed insight and show the added value an LDT offers to communities.

**Advice: Answering all potential use cases with a single model may not be possible.** Process-driven LDT cases like participatory urban planning and model-based approvals of building permits come with different requirements for the digital twin compared to visualisations of energy-related cases like estimating the photovoltaic power production visualisation. Depending on the situation, some existing registries are more likely to be integrated within the digital twin (and used directly as input), while other data sources can be better maintained as separate entities (Forum Virium Helsinki et al., personal communication, 2022).

**Advice: A digital twin is as accurate as the underlying models.** There is still great ambiguity about the term. Digital twins are models and models are abstractions from reality. Models need to be very closely tested against the system they are twinned with, and they also need to share information between themselves and the system they are simulating (Batty, personal communication, 2022).

Gradually accelerating the solution also creates new *opportunities* such as new community approaches. By connecting different suppliers and researchers around a specific theme, new innovative communities of practice can emerge. A good example is the cooperation between simulation model experts active in different policy domains.

### *12.4.3 Recommendations to Maximise Your LDT Impact*

The first step towards maximising the impact of your LDT is to support as many relevant issues-based[7] policy cases as possible by providing domain-specific evidence. Addressing policy issues in smart city fields, such as land-use planning,

[7] Public policy issues have a prevailing contested socio political nature that amplifies the complexity of evidence creation processes: decision processes in public policy-making is not a standard, not a rational decision exercise; it is more a "struggle over ideas and values" (Russell et al., 2008, quoted by Parkhurst, 2017)

mobility, environment, or energy, is just one of the actions an LDT can support. An LDT offers many opportunities as a cooperation tool for supporting cross-sector and cross-border decisions. A new, almost entirely unexplored terrain is using an LDT as a tool for providing tailored advice to individual citizens, businesses and community groups.

### Recommendation 10: Tailor Governance and Business Models and Strategies

**Lesson** Formulating a vision explaining the broader context of an LDT as part of a long-term smart city strategy within the overall city vision can provide the necessary context for the current and future governance and business models. The governance and business model must align with a city's existing digital and organisational maturity level and the expected evolution.

The vision can include elements such as supporting each quadruple helix actor, long-term data management and knowledge creation, or the ICT department's role in the management structure. The above elements can be part of an LDT governance model typology (see Chap. 9). The governance model typology can evolve from a centralised government-oriented approach to a decentralised network-oriented model. Digital Maturity Assessment (DMA) tools allow for measuring the current level of digitalisation within an organisation, and some tools also provide a structured pathway to digital transformation and maturity. A good example of an open DMA tool is the LORDIMAS self-assessment tool (European Union, 2023).

The chosen LDT implementation approach (see Recommendations 04–09) will determine the necessary efforts to switch from one scenario to another. It is expected that an integrated system approach (see Recommendation 06) will be a greater *obstacle* that makes it at least more *challenging* to shift towards a decentralised and ecosystem-oriented approach. Elaborating the governance and business model from the beginning, including tuning it with long-term and broader societal goals (see Recommendation 02), will also impact the organisational structure, such as the need for domain-overarching information managers and data analysts. An LDT will probably influence the focus, place, and role of supporting departments, such as the ICT and organisation development departments.

**Case: Pilsen started building new technologies and communities of practice using its LDT.** The Pilsen LDT was one of the starting points for discovering new practices where new players use the LDT. An example is the security field where Pilsen modelled crisis events around the football stadium. The LDT was used to design countermeasures and evaluate the effectiveness of rescue actions. The security test also included combining LDT insights with drone technology. The LDT was crucial for testing new governance models and cooperation strategies and for fast communication and cooperation among different partners. Pilsen also used the LDT as part of private-sector cooperation to define a test and development zone for autonomous driving with Skoda. Both projects are good examples of how an LDT can support new cooperation models and strategies to create an ecosystem based on shared use cases, joint education initiatives, and urban labs (L. Santora & City of Pilsen, personal communication, 2022).

### Recommendation 11: Use an LDT to Break Down Policy Silos and Promote Cohesion

**Lesson** Implementing an LDT has significant potential to break down policy silos and foster cooperation between different policy domains and organisations. An LDT aligns well with a domain-overarching smart city strategy by promoting inter-organisational collaboration and integration. To ensure the success of an LDT in dismantling policy silos and adding value across policy domains, it is crucial to:

- *Provide valuable instruments:* Develop and offer tools and instruments within the LDT that are beneficial and appealing to each involved policy domain;
- *Enhance trust in data and models:* Focus on enhancing trust in data and simulation model outcomes by explaining the modelling potential, integrating qualitative data, providing comprehensive metadata (also explaining quality), ensuring reliable data provenance, and by providing robust data and model services;
- *Foster a sharing culture:* By using the LDT to support an organisational culture that prioritises data and information sharing across different sectors and stakeholders.

By addressing these key elements, an LDT can effectively contribute to a cohesive and integrated smart city initiative, driving innovation and collaboration across various policy and organisational boundaries.

**Advice: Data at the municipality is spread across different levels of technology maturity** and is often held by different departments that do not necessarily share their information at all or in a harmonised way. Breaking this silo approach is complex, and each specific data request needs a good rationale (J. Echevarria & Santander, personal communication, 2022).

**Advice: Requirements for mainstream adoption.** More advanced LDTs with a high degree of maturity could be achieved within the next ten years, but only with economic stimuli through investment in these technologies and a commitment to standards and protocols. Creating a culture of information sharing and awareness of cultural transformation and governance towards cross-border cooperation between public administrations is crucial (Molina, personal communication, 2022).

Nevertheless, it is *challenging* for an LDT to compete with existing domain-specific specialised systems that departmental policymakers are used to working with. Especially at the early start, when an LDT solution has to prove itself, and only a few domain-overarching results are available, it can be hard to sell the investment in time, cost and effort. Based on the experience in Athens, Flanders and Pilsen, the most prominent promoters of an LDT are on the management level, where an overview of the overall impact of policy measures is seen as an added value. Trust in others' data and simulation models—and the perceived reliability of the outcomes—is especially seen by domain experts as the main implementation barrier and *obstacle*.

Offering additional values connected to a digital twin's basic functionalities can help overcome these barriers. An LDT can, for example, create added value for city management and city departments by providing easier access to data sources (by adding a more comprehensive data catalogue), integrating existing working tools into the LDT (e.g. existing simulation models), and adding new functionalities (e.g. additional views on the terrain) or new communication instruments.

Also, parallel efforts in data management and information culture will prevent the LDT from being seen as an opportunistic tool, leading to inferior results compared with existing domain-specific tools.

#### Recommendation 12: Leverage Your LDT as a Tool for Cooperation and Community Support

**Lesson** As in so many smart city-related initiatives affecting citizens and local businesses' daily routines, effective dissemination and communication is essential to successfully implement impactful smart city measures. A component-based LDT, as described in Chaps. 4 and 5, offers the opportunity to open an LDT solution to citizens and the wider community for co-creation, including co-design and co-decision.

Co-creation is about creating new value together with external experts and stakeholders. An LDT can bring together the necessary information, insights and knowledge for co-designing policies and can support specialist techniques like design thinking, problem definition support, ideation support and prototype simulation testing. It can also be used as a gamification tool during participative workshops.

Using CS data and other local knowledge can add new levels of involvement. However, such data can be difficult to integrate into an LDT.

Co-decision and decision participation are part of a co-creation process and have a focus on the final decision itself or decision preparation.

An approach well-known for architectural competitions is the comparison between different designs.

LDTs can be used in a similar way to compare and discuss the outcomes of policy scenarios.

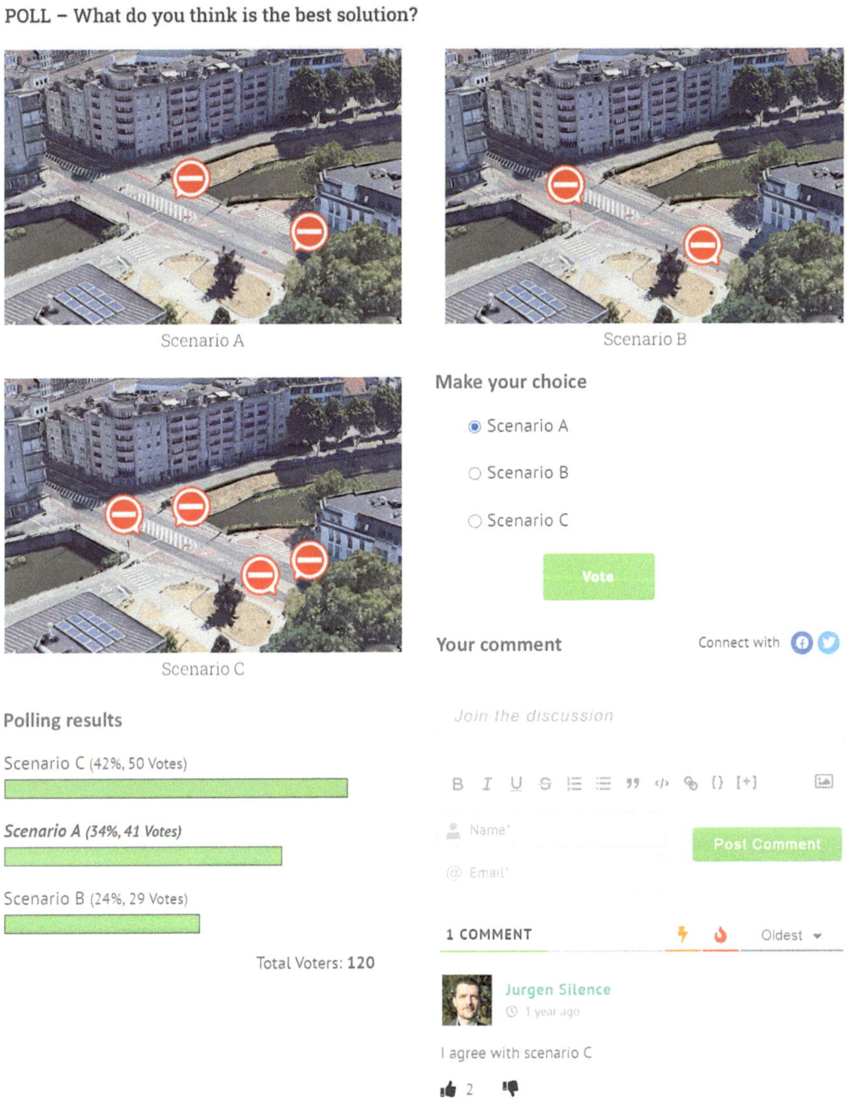


**Fig. 12.3** LDT policy scenarios overview as part of a co-decision approach. (DUET, 2023)

As an example, Fig. 12.3 describes an easy-to-compare effect of a bridge closure and allows citizens to vote and share their opinions on the different options. The user can visualise each scenario in the digital twin and navigate the map to evaluate the overall impact.

**Advice: Use LDT Scenarios.** Presenting potential scenarios is pivotal for enhancing citizens' understanding of planned spatial interventions in the city. Through detailed exploration using LDTs, citizens gain insights into how their neighbourhoods will be affected. When coupled with feedback tools like polling and commenting, this provides local civil servants valuable insights into citizens' support for proposed urban updates. Introducing scenarios early in decision-making allows citizen feedback to shape co-creation and participation efforts, promoting transparency and engagement. With more advanced LDTs, as tested in the DUET project, citizens can even create their own alternative scenarios, fostering collaboration between the public and municipalities and leading to more inclusive and effective outcomes (Digital Flanders & J. Silence, personal communication, 2023).

**Case: LDT optimisation by co-creation**. The Green Comfort Index tool of the H2020 URBANAGE[8] project is an inspiring example of co-creative fine-tuning of use cases. The project created a widely supported and broadly applicable solution through intensive consecutive co-creation workshops with all relevant stakeholders. The concept of comfort was assigned a specific definition tailored to the target groups, including aged citizens, and the relevant comfort parameters were identified and incorporated into the tool. This will result in an LDT tool that can accurately quantify the comfort of older people in the city's public areas (Digital Flanders & J. Silence, personal communication, 2023).

The use and implementation of different participation techniques are just getting started. New techniques, such as sentiment analysis, do not need a formal organisation but can contribute to insights that cannot be revealed by 'hard' data and model driven evidence.

A well-known and sensitive *obstacle* with these citizen-oriented approaches is the potential risk of biased conversations, where particular groups monopolise media channels to push their opinions. Combining quantitative and qualitative interpretations of the outcomes of the public consultation can balance the discussion and even lead to new solution designs (e.g. the creation of new alternative scenarios).

[8] Enhanced URBAN planning for AGE-friendly cities through disruptive technologies (URBANAGE), EU H2020 project, https://cordis.europa.eu/project/id/101004590

## 12.5 Conclusions

The field of digital twins for smart cities, focusing on predictive digital twins, has gained increasing interest in recent years. A growing group of digital twin experts considers it a promising area. Early adopters of Local Digital Twins (LDT) have embraced LDT principles, as stated in the LDT definition, for various reasons.

Some see it as a logical extension of their current investments in 3D Geospatial Information Systems (GIS) systems, while others view it as part of an overarching strategy from data management to evidence-informed decision-making. There is also a group of early adopters who see LDTs as an important element in an emancipatory city management vision, where services are provided by the entire city community, not just the official city organisation.

They also have a social dimension, supporting citizen involvement through co-creation, co-decision, and integration of Citizen Science (CS) data. However, it is essential to recognise the incompleteness and biases of LDTs caused by the lack of data availability, issues with data quality, limitations of simulation models, and the problematic integration of urban cognitive intelligence all influence LDT outcomes. This is why an LDT can best be considered an evidence-informed solution where outcomes are combined with other evaluation techniques instead of an evidence-based solution, suggesting that the result must be taken for granted. LDTs offer technical innovations through the System-of-Systems (SoS) perspective, integrating different software products and technologies.

The recommendations in this chapter relate to each of the following LDT development phases: the LDT planning and starting phase, the LDT implementation phase, and the impact maximisation phase. Recommendations related to the planning phase highlight potential, largely use case-agnostic goals and focus on a planned LDT solution. Recommendations regarding the LDT implementation focus on realising a future-proof, extendable, and scalable LDT that covers security, privacy, and ethics. The final group of recommendations includes governance, business models, cross-sector cooperation, and communication and community opportunities. The recommendations reflect the wide range of possibilities and endeavours discovered by the pioneering practitioners in the LDT field.

The current state of the art on LDTs also comes with knowledge-related challenges that need further action. Integrating cognitive urban intelligence into an LDT to avoid techno-deterministic outcomes is one element that needs to be further scrutinised. The use of LDTs as an instrument for citizen engagement, co-creation, co-design and decision scenario evaluation using state-of-the-art 3D and Extended Reality (XR) visualisation techniques is another largely unexplored domain. On a technical, standardisation and integration level, research into the interplay between LDTs and Pivotal Points of Interoperability (PPI) (see Chap. 5) forms a continuous research domain in a world of developing standards. In this regard, progress should continue with due consideration of the large unchartered territory of simulation model interactions. Also, at a governance level, there is a need for good LDT implementation practices related to new innovative business models and strategies to maximise the LDT impact and enhance the liveability of our cities and (public) living environment.

## References


Abras, C., Maloney-Krichmar, D., Preece, J., et al. (2004). User-centered design. In W. Bainbridge (Ed.), *Encyclopedia of human-computer interaction* (Vol. 37(4), pp. 445–456). Sage Publications.

Alva, P., Biljecki, F., & Stouffs, R. (2022). *Use cases for district-scale urban digital twins* (pp. 5–12). The International Archives of the Photogrammetry, Remote Sensing and Spatial Information Sciences, XLVIII-4/W4-2022. https://doi.org/10.5194/isprs-archives-xlviii-4-w4-2022-5-2022

Anacker, H., Gunther, M., Wyrwich, F., & Dumitrescu, R. (2022, June 7). Pattern based engineering of system of systems—A systematic literature review. *2022 17th Annual System of Systems Engineering Conference (SOSE)*. https://doi.org/10.1109/sose55472.2022.9812697

City of Helsinki. (2022a, March 17). *Helsinki 3D view the models*. Helsingin Kaupunki. https://hri.fi/data/en_GB/dataset/helsingin-3d-kaupunkimalli

City of Helsinki. (2022b, October 10). *Helsinki's Energy and Climate Atlas provides information about the building stock and the emissions reduction potential in heating*. City of Helsinki. https://www.hel.fi/en/news/helsinkis-energy-and-climate-atlas-provides-information-about-the-building-stock-and-the-emissions

DUET. (2023, January). *Digital Urban Twin Cases overview*. CityTwin.EU; DUET Consortium. https://citytwin.eu/

European Commission. (2023, January 26). *A European approach to artificial intelligence*. Shaping Europe's Digital Future. https://digital-strategy.ec.europa.eu/en/policies/european-approach-artificial-intelligence

European Union. (2023, November 24). *LORDIMAS: A digital maturity assessment tool for regions and cities*. European Data. https://data.europa.eu/en/news-events/news/lordimas-digital-maturity-assessment-tool-regions-and-cities

Fabisch, M., & Henninger, S. (2018). ESPRESSO—systEmic Standardisation apPRoach to Empower Smart citieS and cOmmunities, best practices and case studies. *Smart Cities in Smart Regions, 2018*, 115–126.

Head, B. W. (2013). Chapter 9: Evidence-based policy-making for innovation. In *Handbook of innovation in public services* (pp. 143–156). Elgaronline.

Hemetsberger, L. (2020, May 26). *Cities & digital twins: From hype to reality*. Open & Agile Smart Cities; OASC. https://oascities.org/three-key-challenges-towards-digital-twin-adoption-at-scale/

Hofman, J., Nikolaou, M., Shantharam, S. P., Stroobants, C., Weijs, S., & La Manna, V. P. (2022). Distant calibration of low-cost PM and NO2 sensors; evidence from multiple sensor testbeds. *Atmospheric Pollution Research, 13*(1), 101246. https://doi.org/10.1016/j.apr.2021.101246

Kirvan, P., & Cole, B. (2023, October 30). Privacy impact assessment (PIA). *TechTarget*. https://www.techtarget.com/searchsecurity/definition/privacy-impact-assessment-PIA

Kolbe, T. H., Kutzner, T., Smyth, C. S., Nagel, C., Roensdorf, C., & Heazel, C. (2021). *OGC City Geography Markup Language (CityGML) Part 1: Conceptual Model Standard*. Open Geospatial Consortium. https://docs.ogc.org/is/20-010/20-010.html

Korenhof, P., Blok, V., & Kloppenburg, S. (2021). Steering representations—Towards a critical understanding of digital twins. *Philosophy & Technology, 34*(4), 1751–1773. https://doi.org/10.1007/s13347-021-00484-1

Lehtola, V., & Markkula, M. (2022, December 21). *Can digital twin techniques serve city needs?* GIM International. https://www.gim-international.com/content/article/can-digital-twin-techniques-serve-city-needs

Molina, P., Urra Uriarte, S., De Lancker, S., Devis, J., & Vicari, C. (2022). Deliverable D2.3 challenges, user requirements and solutions co-creation. In *EU Cordis*. URBANAGE Consortium. https://cordis.europa.eu/project/id/101004590/results

Neebal Technologies. (2024). *The role of solution accelerators in streamlining solution development*. Neebal. https://www.neebal.com/blog/the-role-of-solution-accelerators-in-streamlining-solution-development

NIST. (2021). *NIST's Pivotal Points of Interoperability Enable Smart City Standardization*. https://www.nist.gov/news-events/news/2021/11/nists-pivotal-points-interoperability-enable-smart-city-standardization

Noti, K., Pavelka, T., & Raes, L. (2021). *D1.5 ethical principles for using data driven decision in the cloud*. DUET Consortium. https://cordis.europa.eu/project/id/870697/results

Open & Agile Smart Cities vzw (OASC). (2022, June). MIMs. Open & Agile Smart Cities; Open & Agile Smart Cities vzw. https://oascities.org/minimal-interoperability-mechanisms/.

Parkhurst, J. (2017). *The politics of evidence: From evidence-based policy to the good governance of evidence*. Routledge.

Pavelka, T., & Piantoni, M. (2021). *D1.3 cities guide to legal compliance for data driven decision making*. DUET Consortium, https://cordis.europa.eu/project/id/870697/results

Pavelka, T., Pemberton, A., & Lauro, M. (2022). *D1.4 cities guide to legal compliance for data driven decision making*. DUET Consortium, https://cordis.europa.eu/project/id/870697/results

Robalo-Correia, A., Sousa, M., Santos, F., Barroca, J., Niepceron, D., Mulquin, M., Campolargo, M., Pour, M., Rasmussen, M., Branco, M., Ebrahimy, R., Ali, K., & Banaei, M. (2023). *D02.02 mapping EU-based LDT providers and users* (p. 95). European Commission—DG CNECT. https://data.europa.eu/doi/10.2759/547098

Sage, A. P., & Cuppan, C. D. (2001). On the systems engineering and management of systems of systems and federations of systems. *Information Knowledge Systems Management, 2*(4), 325–345.

Stackowiak, R. (2019). IoT central and solution accelerators. In *Azure internet of things revealed* (pp. 119–143). Apress. https://doi.org/10.1007/978-1-4842-5470-7_6

Walravens, N. (2020). D2.2 scenario specifications of the DUET solution. In *EU Cordis*. DUET Consortium. https://cordis.europa.eu/project/id/870697/results

Walravens, N., Silence, J., Malik, Z., & Tsakanika, D. (2020). D2.3 final list of user requirements for the DUET solution. In *EU Cordis*. DUET Consortium. https://cordis.europa.eu/project/id/870697/results

# Index




L. Raes et al. (eds.), *Decide Better*,
https://doi.org/10.1007/978-3-031-81451-8

## L



## M



## P



## S



## U

MIX
Papier aus verantwortungsvollen Quellen
Paper from responsible sources
FSC® C105338

If you have any concerns about our products,
you can contact us on
**ProductSafety@springernature.com**

In case Publisher is established outside the EU,
the EU authorized representative is:
**Springer Nature Customer Service Center GmbH**
**Europaplatz 3, 69115 Heidelberg, Germany**

Printed by Libri Plureos GmbH
in Hamburg, Germany